Save Yourself the Time and Trouble of Manual File Entry . . . Order *The New BASICs* Programs on Disk

All the programs in this book are also available on disk (MS-DOS format), with full source code.

To order, return this postage-paid self-mailer with your payment of $25 plus sales tax if you are a California resident, to: M&T Publishing, 501 Galveston Drive, Redwood City, CA 94063. Or, call toll-free 800-533-4372 (In CA 800-356-2002). Ask for Item #44-5.

Yes! Please send me **The New BASICs** software on disk for $25 _____

CA residents add applicable sales tax __%__

TOTAL _____

☐ Check enclosed. Make payable to M&T Publishing.
Charge my ☐VISA ☐MasterCard ☐American Express

Card # _____ Exp. Date _____

Name _____
Address _____
City _____ State ____ Zip _____

4028

NO POSTAGE
NECESSARY
IF MAILED
IN THE
UNITED STATES

BUSINESS REPLY MAIL
FIRST CLASS PERMIT 871 REDWOOD CITY, CA

POSTAGE WILL BE PAID BY ADDRESSEE

M&T Books
501 Galveston Dr.
Redwood City, CA 94063

The New BASICs

M&T BOOKS

The New BASICs

Programming Techniques and Library Development

Namir Clement Shammas

M&T Publishing, Inc.
Redwood City, California

M&T Books
A Division of M&T Publishing, Inc.
501 Galveston Drive
Redwood City, CA 94063

M&T Books
General Manager, Ellen Ablow
Project Manager, Michelle Hudun
Editor, Mike Padilla
Software Coordinator, Sally J. Brenton
Cover Design, Michael Hollister
Production, Sahnta Pannutti

Copyright © 1987 by M&T Publishing, Inc.

Printed in the United States of America
First Edition published 1987

All rights reserved. No part of this book may be reproduced or transmitted in any form or by any means, electronic or mechanical, including photocopying, recording, or by any information storage and retrieval system, without prior written permission from the Publisher. Contact the Publisher for information on foreign rights.

Library of Congress Cataloging-in-Publication Data

Shammas, Namir Clement, 1954–
  The new BASICs programming techniques and library development.

  Includes index.
  1. Basic (Computer program language) I. Title.
QA76.73.B3S44 1987   005.13'3   87-22661
ISBN 0-934375-37-2 (book)
ISBN 0-934375-43-7 (book/disk)
ISBN 0-934375-44-5 (disk)

91 90 89 88 87   4 3 2 1

UNIX is a trade mark of AT&T Bell Laboratories.
MS-DOS is a trademark of Microsoft Corporation.

To

My Parents Clement and Daisy

Limits of Liability and Disclaimer of Warranty

The Author and Publisher of this book have used their best efforts in preparing the book and programs contained in it. These efforts include the development, research, and testing of the theories and programs to determine their effectiveness.

The Author and Publisher make no warranty of any kind, expressed or implied, with regard to these programs or the documentation contained in this book. The Author and Publisher shall not be liable in any event for incidental or consequential damages in connection with, or arising out of, the furnishing, performance, or use of these programs.

How to Order the Accompanying Disk

All the software listings in this book are available on disk. The disk price is $25.00. California residents must add the appropriate sales tax.

Order by sending a check, or credit card number and expiration date, to:

The New BASICs Disk
M&T Books
501 Galveston Drive
Redwood City, CA 94063

Or, you may order by calling our toll-free number between 8:00 A.M. and 5:00 P.M. PST: 800/533-4372 (800/356-2002 in California).

Contents

Introduction 9

1: The New BASICs and their Environments 11
QuickBASIC Environment 11
Turbo BASIC Environment 17
True BASIC Environment 21

2: The New Programming Framework 27
BASIC Option 27
Branching and Line Numbers 30
BASIC Data Types 32
Strings 36
Arrays 38
Decision Making: Where Do We Go From Here? 46
Loops: Recycled Code 52
EXIT: The Great Escape 59
Error Handling 62
File Handling 68
User Defined Functions 70
BASIC Subroutines: Borrowing from FORTRAN? 74
Library Development: The Big Picture 84

3: BASIC Libraries 99

Library Module TOOLBOX0 100

Library Module TOOLBOX1 140

Library Module NUMANAL 177

Library Module BASTAT 223

Library Module LINREG 236

Library Module SORT 250

Library Module LISTS 275

Library Module SETS 296

Library Module BINTREE 343

Library Module DOSFILE 368

Index 415

Introduction

The Good News About New Wave BASICs

Programming languages have proliferated over the last twenty years. Programmers have pushed the computer and its languages to unexpected limits. We have become a generation of more sophisticated programmers, seeking efficient and powerful implementations. In 1964, Dr. John Kemeny and Dr. Thomas Kurtz of Dartmouth College invented BASIC. Their goal was to create an interactive, general-purpose interpreted language that would serve as a tool for teaching progamming languages. A decade later, BASIC found its way into the microcomputer. It appeared to be the ideal language.

Microsoft provided MS-BASIC, GW-BASIC, and, later, Advanced BASIC (BASICA) for the IBM PC as the defacto standards for microcomputer BASIC. These versions were bundled with most of the micros, and more and more people began to use them. This trend was expected to last practically forever, until French math professor Philippe Kahn gave us Turbo Pascal. Things haven't been the same since. We tried Pascal and we liked it! Most of us looked back at BASIC and said "Why can't BASIC be more like Pascal?".

Fortunately, many implementors, including Kemeny, Kurtz, Microsoft, and that same French math professor, heard us and created the new BASICs to be more like Pascal and FORTRAN. This book shares the good news about these 'New Wave' BASICs. It looks at programming with QuickBASIC 3.0, Turbo Basic 1.0, and True BASIC 2.0. The first two represent the latest and fastest BASIC compilers implemented by two of the top five software companies. True BASIC comes from the creators of BASIC and supports advanced software engineering concepts.

Trying to cover every programming aspect of three feature-loaded BASICs in one book is like trying to collect the Pacific Ocean in a bucket. This book concentrates on the new aspects of BASIC programming and on the creation of BASIC libraries. I have chosen not to cover low level asembly language calls and high resolution graphics. Nor will this book compare all aspects of the three BASIC implementations that were available in BASICA and MS-BASIC. QuickBASIC and Turbo BASIC are upward compatible with the very popular BASICA. Since True BASIC uses a different syntax, I recommend that you obtain a book on True BASIC to become more familiar with it.

The first chapter in this book discusses the various BASIC environments. The second covers the new aspects of BASIC programming used to create better BASIC programs. Chapter 3 presents libraries for general utilities, string handling, numerical analysis, statistics, data structures, and file manipulatuion. For each library, one or more application programs illustrate its use.

I hope the BASIC libraries in this book become part of your programming toolbox.

Happy programming!

Namir Clement Shammas

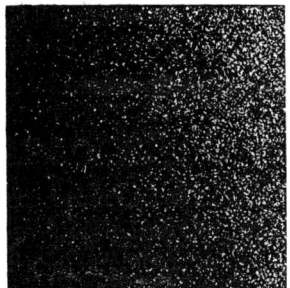

1
The New BASICs and their Environments

The new BASICs offer more sophisticated user-interface than MS-BASIC and BASICA. In this chapter I will lead you through a relatively brief tour of each of the three BASIC implementations. Throughout the book, I will be discussing the features of QuickBASIC 3.0, Turbo BASIC 1.0, and True BASIC 2.0.

QuickBASIC Environment

Microsoft provides the QuickBASIC programmer with a good user-interface that includes an editor, compiler, and debugger. The top line of the QuickBASIC window contains pull-down menus for file operations, editing, viewing text, search operations, and running/compiling a program. The on-line help is available on a full screen. Figure 1.1 (p. 12) shows the QuickBASIC environment displaying its on-line help screen for using the keyboard commands.

Using a mouse with QuickBASIC greatly enhances your ability to edit text and select options, and it is therefore highly recommended.

Figure 1.2 (p. 12) shows the normal QuickBASIC window while the option for FILE operations is invoked. You may select an item either by using the cursor keys, by typing the first letter of the option, or by using the mouse. This is also true for all other pull-down menus. The FILE operations include creating a new QuickBASIC file, loading, saving, and autosaving a program. Other options are listing the file to a printer, invoking the MS-DOS shell, and exiting.

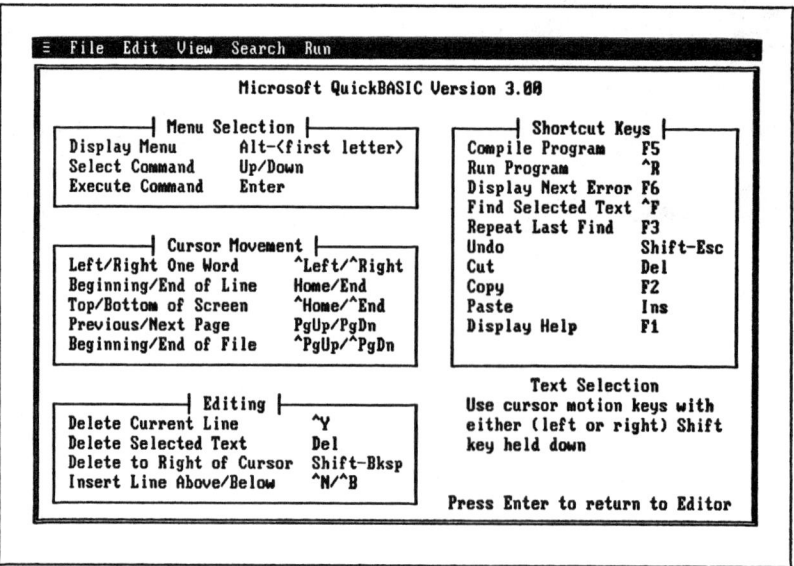

Figure 1.1 *QuickBASIC on-line help screen*

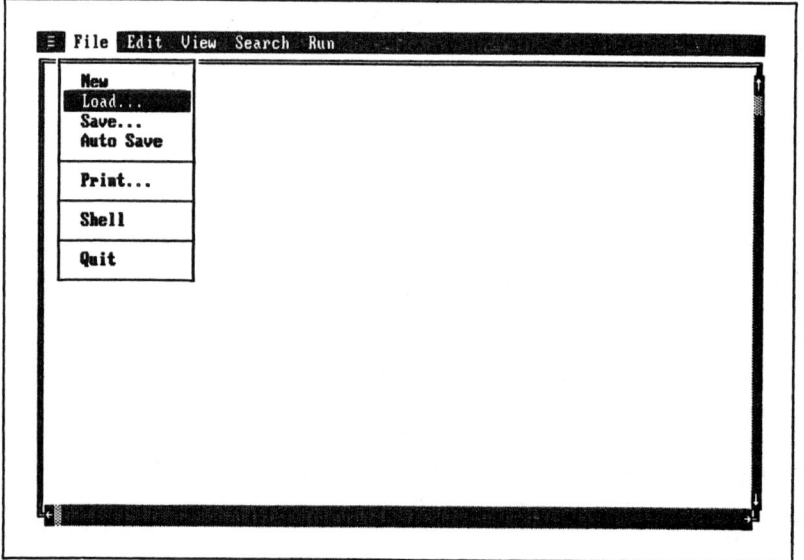

Figure 1.2 *QuickBASIC FILE options pull-down menu*

QuickBASIC also supports a number of keystroke combinations known as *short cut keys*.

When the FILE LOAD option is selected, QuickBASIC displays the name of the current directory, current path and file extension (default is *.BAS*), and the file names with BAS extension. You may select another directory by typing the new path name and file extensions. The second step is to actually select a file. This is carried out by using the tab key to jump into the list of files. The selected file is highlighted in reverse video and the selection is changed using the cursor keys. Pressing the [ENTER] key confirms the current selection. Figure 1.3 shows a screen image for the above process. A mouse enables you to navigate more smoothly through the file selections.

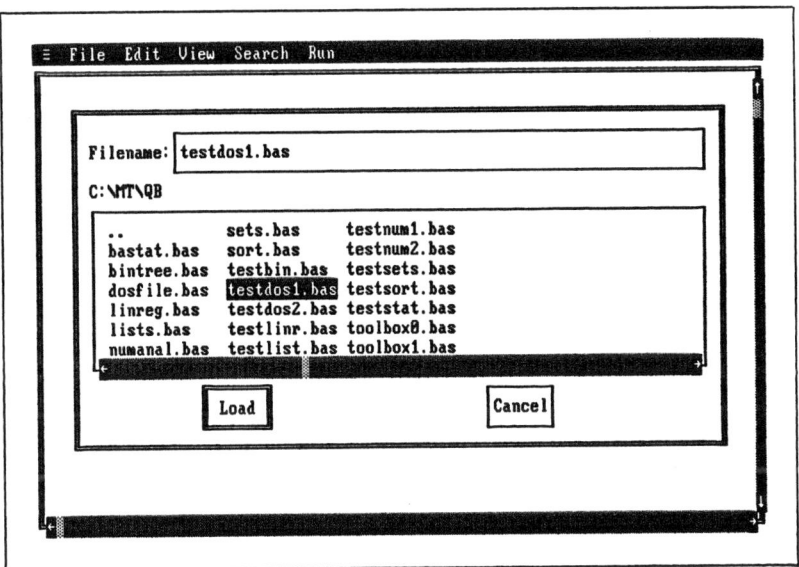

Figure 1.3 *QuickBASIC screen image for file selection*

The EDIT options include options to cut, paste, copy, and undo. Using a mouse greatly enhances the cut and paste operations: you can mark and manipulate a block of lines. To move a line of text you must first delete it using [CTRL][Y]. Then position the cursor at the destination location and press the [INS] key. This copies the deleted line from the buffer into the new location. To copy a line of text, follow the same procedure but insert it twice: once at its original location and once at its destination. Deleted text lines are placed into a buffer. Pressing the [INS] reinserts them into the text at the current cursor location as many times as is needed.

The VIEW options enable you to view (or review) compiler errors, if any. Another VIEW option enables you to set up the foreground and background colors and the tab stops, and to customize the QuickBASIC window display.

The SEARCH options allow you to find or translate (that is, find and replace) string text in your program. Figure 1.4 shows the screen image for translating text. You can move on from one item to another by using the tab key or the mouse. The translation includes options for whole words, case sensitivity, and operating with or without query. In the query mode you have the option of carrying out the change, skipping the current string, and stopping the translating.

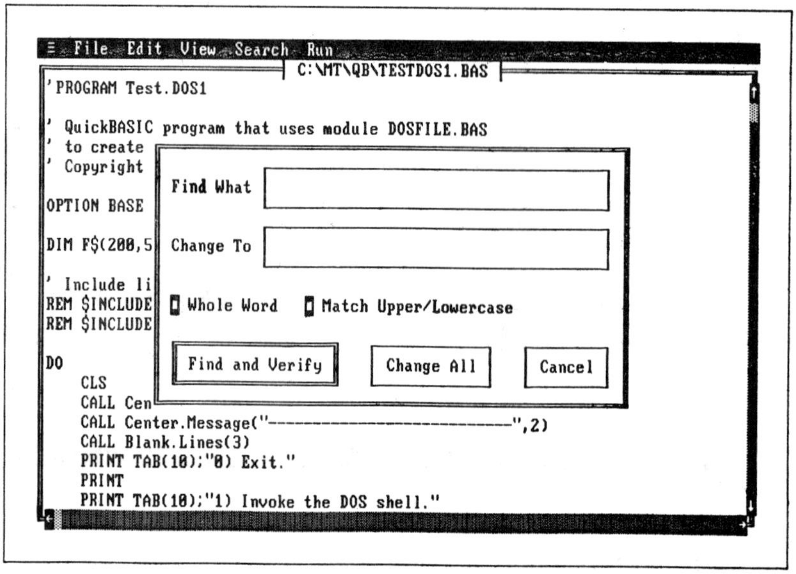

Figure 1.4 *SEARCH/REPLACE option window*

The RUN options permit you to compile a program, run it, and change compile options. The [F5] function key is the short cut key for compiling a program. The [CTRL][R] keys are used as the short cut keys for compiling (if needed) and running a program compiled in memory. The compile options are shown in Figure 1.5 (p. 15). They consist of three groups of switches:

1. Compiler options: provide the switches to fine-tune the compiler operation. These options relate to debugging, error handling, event trapping, minimizing string data, and storing arrays in row order (as opposed to column order).

2. Output options: determine the type of generated output file. You may compile a QuickBASIC program in memory, create EXE files, or emit OBJ files to build compiled libraries or link with other files. Compiling into memory or generating EXE files automatically invokes the linker.

3. Optimization options: reduce either the compiled run-time or EXE file size of a QuickBASIC program.

The compiler goes through your program accumulating any errors it finds. The number of lines compiled and errors found are displayed. If errors are found, the compiler invokes the editor and you may view your errors and make the required corrections. The errors are stored as a circular list. Pressing the [F6] function key displays the next error. If the error is located in an included file, the main program is quickly swapped with the included file. Pressing the [F6] function key enables you to inspect the errors in the included file. Once you have finished, pressing [F6] one more time takes you back to the main file. QuickBASIC tracks any altered files and prompts you to store them.

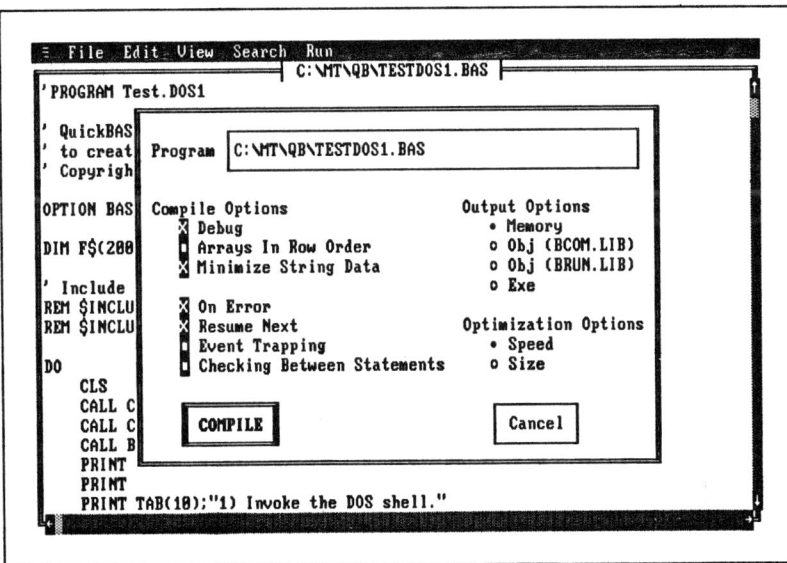

Figure 1.5 *QuickBASIC compiler options window*

The QuickBASIC environment includes a powerful debugger. Among the debugging features are the following:

1. watching the contents of variables
2. tracing program execution
3. setting, clearing, and finding breakpoints
4. stepping into a program
5. viewing or editing a QuickBASIC source code
6 resuming execution at full speed

The QuickBASIC compiler may be invoked from the MS-DOS level. You may specify the BASIC file to be compiled and the accompanying compiled library (*see* Chapter 2). Compiler switches may also be set from MS-DOS (Table 1.1).

Table 1.1 *QuickBASIC Compiler Options*

MS-DOS Switch	Action
/b	use with monochrome screen and graphics card
/c	specify buffer size.
/cmd	pass string to BASIC COMMAND$ function.
/d	debug option.
/e	use with ON ERROR GOTO.
/g	use color graphics.
/l	specify alternate compiled library.
/mbf	use to compile programs of older versions; converts Microsoft Binary Format numbers to IEEE format.

Table 1.1 *(continued)*

MS-DOS Switch	Action
/o	produce OBJ code.
/q	increase program execution speed at the cost of size.
/r	store arrays by contiguous rows.
/s	minimize string data.
/v	check between statements.
/w	trap events.
/x	use with RESUME NEXT.

Turbo BASIC Environment

The Turbo BASIC compiler operates solely from the Turbo environment. The environment is very flexible and can be easily customized. The default environment displays five rectangular windows: a one-line main menu, edit, message, run, and trace. The main menu contains the following options:

1. file and directory manipulation

2. invoking the text editor

3. compiling a Turbo BASIC program

4. compiling and running a Turbo BASIC program

5. compiler options

6. setup options

7. window options

8. debug options

The FILE option invokes a pull-down menu that enables you to manage files and directories, invoke the MS-DOS shell, and quit. Options are selected by using the cursor keys or by pressing the highlighted letters that correspond to the menu choices. The LOAD option is used to select your workfile. The two-step process begins by displaying a window with the default path name and file names (default is *.BAS). Pressing the [RETURN] key confirms your selection of the above defaults. You may type a new path name and/or file wild cards. The second step is the display of the files in the specified path name that match the wild cards. Figure 1.6 displays the Turbo BASIC environment listing the available files.

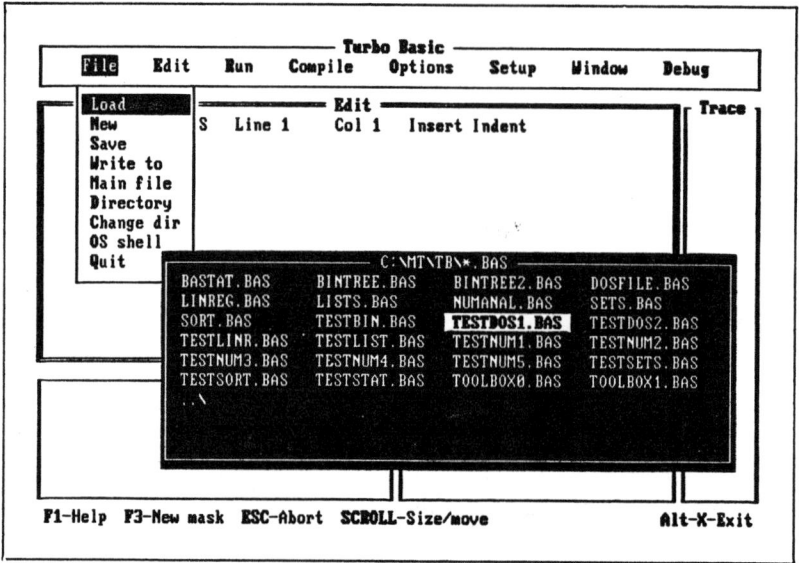

Figure 1.6 *Turbo BASIC file load option*

The NEW option is used to inform the Turbo BASIC editor that you will start typing a file from scratch. The default NONAME.BAS is used. The SAVE option allows you to save your current workfile and backup the previous copy. The WRITE TO option permits you to save the current workfile under another name. The MAIN FILE option is involved in compiling large programs or relatively small programs that include libraries of routines. In either case, the entire code resides in two or more files. Thus, you specify the main file to enable the environment to handle recompiling after locating errors in an include file. The mechanism works like this: the included library is loaded and the editor points to the offending text. You perform any required corrections and ask to recompile. Since you have specified the main workfile, the compiler checks whether or not the current file is the main one. If it is not, you are prompted to save the current file and the main program is reloaded for another compiler run.

The EDIT option in the main menu invokes a WordStar-like editor. Pressing the [F5] function key enables you to zoom in on the text and display it using the entire screen. Since many programmers are familiar with WordStar and/or the editor of Turbo Pascal, using this editor does not involve much of a learning curve.

The COMPILE option compiles the current workfile and displays statistics in the MESSAGE window. The Turbo BASIC compiler will stop at the first error, display an error message, invoke the editor, and point out the offending text. The RUN option compiles the workfile, if needed, and runs it. A run-time error also invokes the editor and the error-causing statement is indicated with a diagnostic message. Figure 1.7 shows the Turbo BASIC environment after invoking the RUN option.

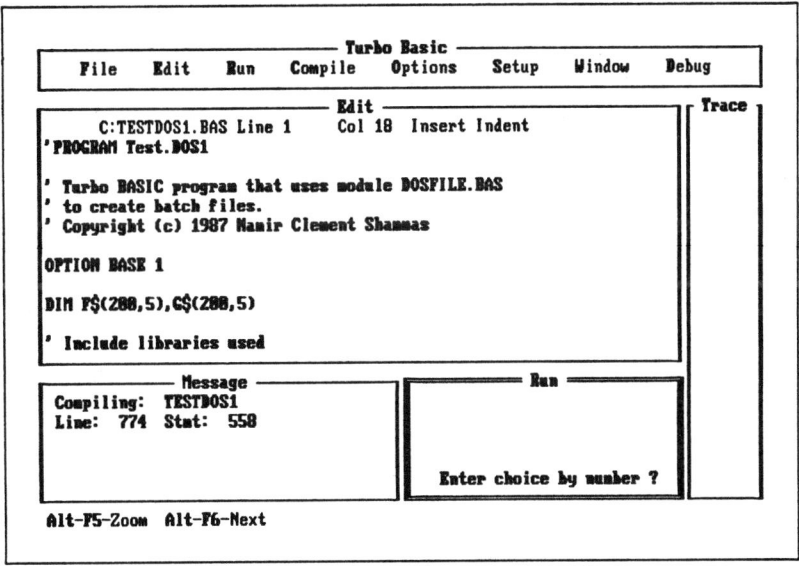

Figure 1.7 *Using Turbo BASIC's Run option*

Selecting OPTIONS from the main menu gives you access to a pull-down menu for the compiler switches. The first option is whether to compile to memory, create EXE files, or create chained files. In addition, the following switches may be toggled:

1. 8087 required: determines whether or not an 8087 must be used. Turbo BASIC programs compiled with this switch on will not run if the 8087 is not available. The default value (off) permits compiled programs to run on all machines making use of 8087 when detected or using the emulator in the absence of the 8087. If you know that all of the machines running your compiled Turbo BASIC code have 8087, turn the switch on. This reduces the size of the EXE file, since the code for the 8087 emulator is not included.

2. Keyboard break: enables or disables the use of the [CTRL][BREAK] keys to interrupt a Turbo BASIC program while running.

3. Bounds: checks the indexes of an array. The default state of this switch is off.

4. Overflow: detects a mathematical overflow and signals a run-time error when the switch is on. The default state is off, making math overflow operations yield bad results.

5. Stack test: protects your stack from stack collisions when loading a routine.

Turning the above switches on makes your programs run more safely. The size of EXE files emitted by the compiler increases when this switch is turned on.

Turbo BASIC also permits you to enter a string that simulates command-line arguments. Normally, the predefined COMMAND$ function returns the string in question. This option enables you to type it in from within Turbo BASIC. Another option allows you to alter a number of metastatements, namely, the stack, music buffer, and communication port buffer. Figure 1.8 (p. 21) illustrates the OPTIONS pull-down menu.

Customizing the Turbo BASIC interface is achieved by using the SETUP and WINDOW options. The results are stored in a special configuration file. The customization aspect covers the color and size of the windows and the load/save directories.

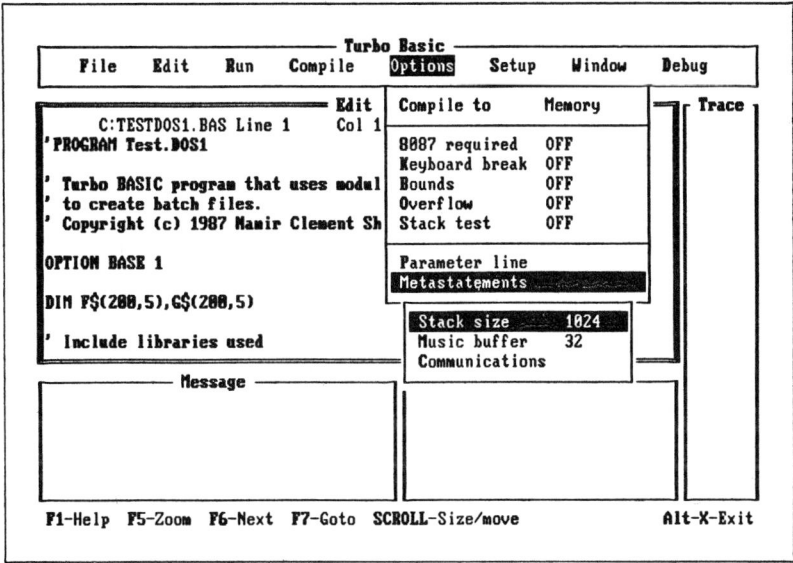

Figure 1.8 *Turbo BASIC's 'Options'*

The DEUBUG option in the main menu offers two choices: trace or run-time error. The TRACE option enables you to trace the execution of a program by displaying the names of labels, functions, and subroutines encountered by the program pointer. The RUN-TIME ERROR option enables you to detect run-time errors in EXE of TBC files.

True BASIC Environment

True BASIC offers an environment that is visually simpler than those of QuickBASIC and Turbo BASIC. You are able to run BASIC programs from MS-DOS or from the True BASIC environment. To run a program from MS-DOS, type:

```
HELLO <program_name>
```

The default extension name for True BASIC programs is TRU. When the True BASIC compiler is invoked from MS-DOS without specifying a True BASIC program file name, you enter the environment. The screen is split into two regions: the upper portion contains any text and the bottom portion contains the command section. The [F1] function key places the cursor into the edited text window, while the [F2] key returns you to the command mode. True BASIC prompts you with "Ok." Typing "SPLIT" from the command mode displays a one-line help that maps the function keys with their commands. Figure 1.9 shows a typical True BASIC environment screen. The figure contains a True BASIC program in the editor's window and the on-line help for the function keys.

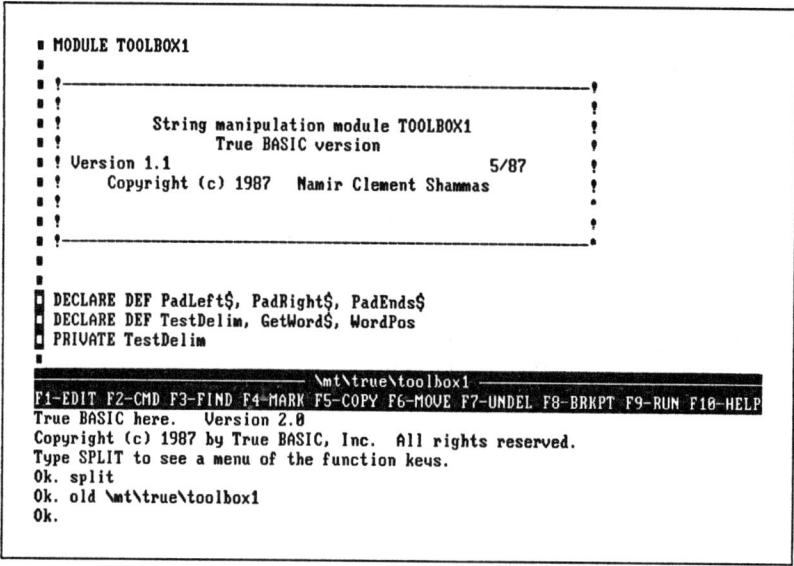

Figure 1.9 *Typical True BASIC environment screen*

On-line help is available from the command mode. You are able to ask for help on a certain topic. The command window retains the history of the commands issued (up to a certain level, of course). You may inspect the history by scrolling up and down. The [F6] function key is employed in copying an old command to the current command line. This has proven to save some typing effort. Loading, saving, replacing, and renaming files, as well as running programs, is carried out from the command prompt.

As with any new editor, you will need to develop your reflexes with True BASIC. Copying and moving is carried out on entire lines. Use the [F4] function key to mark the first and last lines. Then use the [F6] or [F5] keys to copy or move lines, respectively. The [F3] function key is used to locate text, as shown in Figure 1.10. Pressing the [F3] key results in a "FIND :" prompt appearing in the command window. You enter the string you are looking for or just press [ENTER] to look-up a string you had specified earlier. Text translation (find/replace) is carried out by typing "CHANGE <old string>,<new string>" from the command mode. Strings with punctuation characters, commas, and spaces should be quoted.

```
! SUB RemoveCharRange(S$, FC$, LC$)
! ! Remove all characters that meet the following criterion:
! !
! !     ASCII(FC$) <= ASCII(char) <= ASCII(LC$)
!
! LET ASCII_LC = ORD(LC$)
! LET ASCII_FC = ORD(FC$)
!
! LET L = LEN(S$)
! LET J = 0
! FOR I = 1 TO L
!     LET J = J + 1
!     LET A = ORD(S$[J:J])
!     IF (ASCII_FC <= A) AND (A <= ASCII_LC) THEN
!         IF J = 1 THEN
!             LET S$ = S$[2:MAXNUM]
!         ELSEIF J = LEN(S$) THEN
———————————————————— \mt\true\toolbox1 ————————————————————
F1-EDIT F2-CMD F3-FIND F4-MARK F5-COPY F6-MOVE F7-UNDEL F8-BRKPT F9-RUN F10-HELP
Find: ASCII_LC
Find:
Ok.
```

Figure 1.10 *Searching for text with True BASIC*

Typing RUN will cause the True BASIC compiler to examine your entire program and report any errors. Typical errors are reported using a line reference, error diagnosis message, and a display of the offending code segment. The error messages are clear and very adequate.

The True BASIC environment supports extending the language. This is carried out by typing "LOAD <library name>". The library of modules (more on this to be covered in Chapter 2) is loaded into memory and becomes part of the language. No additional reference to loaded libraries/modules is needed. This is also beneficial in light of the fact that compiling programs is faster when the modules they use are loaded into memory. To unload all libraries and modules, type

"FORGET" from the command mode prompt. This also clears the command history.

Another powerful feature of the True BASIC environment is the ability to invoke other programs or external subroutines. Invoking another True BASIC program may be useful if it contains interactive instructions or on-line documentation for the task at hand. Invoking external subroutines is used to process the text in the memory (*see* Chapter 2). You may invoke an external subroutine to convert your program to upper-case or lower-case text, format your program, trace execution, etc.

The True BASIC environment enables you to echo the screen output to a text file or the line printer. Typing an ECHO command echoes the output to the printer. Typing "ECHO <file name>" echoes to a text file. The ECHO OFF command turns the echoing off. You may limit the echoed output with RUN, FILES and DO commands by appending ">> <file name>". The omission of the file name invokes the line printer as the echo device.

True BASIC has implemented its own version of batch file processing and script files. Typing "SCRIPT <file name>" invokes the script processor that uses the lines in the specified file as True BASIC commands. If you include a RUN command in the script, True BASIC permits you to provide input for prompts. Input lines begin with a question mark. Consider the following script file:

```
old editfile
run
? infile.txt
? outfile.txt
? oldstr
? newst
```

This script file may be used to invoke a fictitious True BASIC program EDITFILE.TRU. Looking at the input lines, you may guess that the program requires the names of the input file, output file, old string, and new string.

True BASIC has implemented the parallel of AUTOEXEC.BAT, called STARTUP.TRU. When the True BASIC compiler is loaded, it looks for the STARTUP.TRU script file and executes it, if found. Script files may be supplied with arguments, similar to MS-DOS batch variables. Consider the following script file that loads a file and alters a string:

```
old <1>
CHANGE <2>,<3>
```

Assuming the script file name is MYSCR.TRU, to invoke it to alter all the "S$" strings in file "MYPROG.TRU" with "Str$". you must type the following command:

```
SCRIPT MYSCR MYPROG, S$, Str$
```

From the above dicussions, it becomes clear that the enviroments of the new BASICs have a friendlier user-interface. They are also more geared toward large software development.

The New Programming Framework

The first level of the new BASICs involves the fundamental components of a BASIC program: data types, looping, decision making, etc. I will discuss the new and altered constructs of each implementation.

BASIC Option

BASIC dialects have traditionally supported the OPTION BASE statement to enable the programmer to select the lower bound of arrays. The choice was limited to either zero or one. QuickBASIC and True BASIC still enforce these limits for the OPTION BASE. Turbo BASIC has extended the language, allowing you to use any valid integer that suits your purpose. Since Turbo BASIC also provides a syntax to explicitly declare lower array bounds, using OPTION BASE beyond one may be limited to fewer applications.

The default OPTION BASE in QuickBASIC and Turbo BASIC is zero. True BASIC assigns a default lower limit of one.

True BASIC offers other BASIC OPTION statements.

1. The OPTION ANGLE DEGREES and OPTION ANGLE RADIANS make the arguments of trigonometric functions as degrees and radians, respectively. Using the degrees angular mode, it is possible to write BASIC code with angle values that are easier to understand:

```
OPTION ANGLE DEGREES
FOR I = 0 TO 90 STEP 5
    PRINT USING "Sin(##) = #.#####": I,SIN(I)
NEXT I
```

2. The OPTION NOLET enables you to write programs that need not include the LET keyword with every assignment statement.

3. The OPTION TYPO protects you against misspelled variable names. All of your variables must be listed in a LOCAL statement. The following short True BASIC program calculates the first ten factorials. It also demonstrates the use of OPTION TYPO and OPTION NOLET:

```
! True BASIC Program to calculate first ten factorials
OPTION TYPO
OPTION NOLET

LOCAL I, J, Factorial
FOR I = 1 TO 10
    Factorial = 1
    FOR J = 1 TO I
        Factorial = Factorial * J
    NEXT J
    PRINT "The factorial of ";I;" = ";Factorial
NEXT I
END
```

QuickBASIC and Turbo BASIC support another option construct, namely, metacommands that are embedded into the BASIC source code. Turbo BASIC offers more metacommands than QuickBASIC does. The two implementations differ in the metacommand syntax used. QuickBASIC requires you to place the metacommands into the source code as a REMark, as in:

```
REM $<metacommand1>   $<metacommand2>
```

or

```
REM $<metacommand>: <optional argument>
```

or

```
REM $<metacommand1>: <optional argument> $<metacommand2>
```

Turbo BASIC does not require the use of REMed metacommands. Instead, they may be placed directly at the beginning of a line and are followed by any number of arguments required.

The following three metacommands are available in both QuickBASIC and Turbo BASIC:

1. $STATIC: declares that all arrays dimensioned following the metacommand have their spaces allocated at compile time.

2. $DYNAMIC: declares that all arrays dimensioned following the metacommand have their spaces allocated at run time.

3. $INCLUDE: enables you to include additional BASIC source code stored in a separate file. For the current version of Turbo BASIC, the $INCLUDE metacommand provides an important vehicle for using libraries.

You may inquire about the differences in using declaring arrays as static or dynamic. The following differences exist between static arrays and dynamic arrays:

1. Static arrays occupy slightly less memory space than dynamic arrays.

2. Static arrays are accessed faster.

3. Dynamic arrays can be redimensioned using REDIM, while static arrays are only dimensioned once.

4. The ERASE statement resets all of the elements of a static array to zeros or nulls, but does not remove the array. By contrast, dynamic arrays are deallocated from memory by the ERASE statement.

Turbo BASIC offers the following additional metacommands:

1. $COM <*size*> allocates memory space for the serial port input buffer.

2. $EVENT {ON|OFF} controls the generation of event-trapping.

3. $IF/$ELSE/$ENDIF offers powerful C-like conditional compilation. The syntax used is:

```
$IF <constant>
    statements
[$ELSE
  statements]
$ENDIF
```

Conditional compilation is used to compile certain code line and skip others.

4. $INLINE [byte list | code source file] enables you to insert inline machine code. You may either insert the list of bytes in your BASIC source or read them from a separate file.

5. $SEGMENT enables you to break the 64K barrier. The compiled BASIC code that follows a $SEGMENT metacommand is placed in a separate code segment. Up to 16 code segments may exist in a Turbo BASIC program. This metacommand must not be placed in the middle of structured blocks, such as FOR-NEXT and DO-LOOP loops, or within IF and SELECT CASE statements.

6. $SOUND <*Buffer size*> allocates the size of the background music buffer.

7. $STACK <*size*> allocates a run time stack size that ranges between 1024 bytes (the default minimum) and 32K. This metacommand ensures that highly nested or recursive programs are able to internally specify adequate stack size. This spares you from having to explicitly alter the stack size in the Turbo BASIC environment.

Branching and Line Numbers

Line numbering is one of the "ground level" features of the BASIC language. Over time, many have criticized it because it encouraged zig zag flowing code, or "spaghetti code." Many felt that line numbers in BASIC have become a liability rather than an asset for the language. The new wave BASICs have dealt with that problem very effectively. The BASIC implementations included in this book offer the following alternatives:

1. In QuickBASIC, line numbers are not only optional, but you are encouraged to use alphanumeric labels with GOTO and GOSUB statements. The following listings show two QuickBASIC versions to solve a root of a nonlinear function. The first uses the traditional line numbers:

```
1000 ' QuickBASIC program to solve the root
1010 ' of a function using line numbers.
1020 '
1040 DEFDBL A-Z
1050 INPUT "Enter guess ";X
1060 Accr = 1.0E-8
1070 H = 0.01
1080 IF ABS(X) > 1 THEN H = H * X
1090 XX = X + H : GOSUB 2000 : FH = F
1100 XX = X     : GOSUB 2000
1110 Diff = H * F/(FH - F)
1120 X = X - Diff
1130 IF ABS(Diff) > Accr THEN GOTO 1070
1140 PRINT "Root = ";X
1150 END
2000 'Subroutine to evaluate the nonlinear function
2010 F = EXP(XX) - XX
2020 RETURN
```

The second QuickBASIC program uses the more readable labels:

```
' QuickBASIC program to solve the root
' of a function using labels.
'
DEFDBL A-Z
INPUT "Enter guess ";X
Accr = 1.0E-8
START.LOOP:
    H = 0.01
    IF ABS(X) > 1 THEN H = H * X
    XX = X + H : GOSUB GET.FUNCTION : FH = F
    XX = X     : GOSUB GET.FUNCTION
    Diff = H * F/(FH - F)
    X = X - Diff
IF ABS(Diff) > Accr THEN GOTO START.LOOP
PRINT "Root = ";X
END
'Subroutine to evaluate the nonliear function
GET.FUNCTION:
F = EXP (XX) - XX
RETURN
```

The second program contains two labels, namely, *START.LOOP* and *GET.FUNCTION*. These labels are more meaningful than line numbers. When you read the program and encounter the GOTO or GOSUB statements, you can easily identify the jump destination.

2. Turbo BASIC offers optional line numbers and labels just like in QuickBASIC. However, in Turbo BASIC the numbers may be put in any order, as long as they are not duplicated. This resembles CBASIC and FORTRAN where line numbers are nothing but labels.

3. True BASIC supports optional line numbers, but not labels. To use a GOTO or GOSUB you must use line numbers with the entire program. Otherwise, no line numbers are needed! The True BASIC version of the root-solving program that uses line numbers is very similar to the first QuickBASIC program. To write a True BASIC version without line numbers, more extensive editing is needed. First, you must to resort to a genuine function definition (you cannot simulate functions with GOSUB-type subroutines and avoid line numbers simultaneously). Second, the simulated REPEAT-UNTIL loop is replaced with a DO-LOOP UNTIL (more about this later). The logical expression in the UNTIL clause has its test reversed. The program becomes:

```
! True BASIC program to solve the root
! of a function using no line numbers.
OPTION NOLET
DEF FF(X) = EXP(X) - X
INPUT PROMPT "Enter guess ":X
Accr = 1.0E-8
DO
    H = 0.01
    IF ABS(X) > 1 THEN H = H * X
    FH = FF(X+H)
    F  = FF(X)
    Diff = H * F / (FH - F)
    X = X - Diff
LOOP UNTIL ABS(Diff) <= Accr
PRINT "Root = ";X
END
```

BASIC Data Types

Following in the footsteps of MS-BASIC and BASICA, QuickBASIC supports data types such as integers, single precision reals, double precision reals, and strings. Characters are considered single-element strings and are therefore compatible with strings of all sizes. Turbo BASIC supports a superset of the above data types by adding the long integer type. True BASIC takes a different approach and reduces the explicit number of data types. It supports strings and numbers. Numeric types are stored internally using either an integer format or a floating point format. The True BASIC compiler examines a numeric value before storing it at the variable's address. If the number has no significant fractional part, it is stored as an integer. Otherwise, it is stored as a real. Table 2.1 compares the data types supported by the BASIC implementations. The table includes the type size in bytes, the range of value, and the characters used to explicitly declare the data type of a BASIC variable.

Implementation	Data Type	Type Size	Lower Limit	Upper Limit	Symbol
Quick-BASIC	integer	2	-32768	32767	%
	single real	4	2.9E-39	1.7E+38	!
	double real	8			#
	IEEE single real	4	8.43E-37	3.37E+38	!
	IEEE double real	8	4.19E-307	1.67E+308	#
	string	variable			$
Turbo BASIC	integer	2	-32768	32767	%
	long integer	4	-2 billion	2 billion	&
	single real	4	1E-38	1E+38	!
	IEEE double real	8	1E-308	1E+308	#
	string	variable			$
True BASIC	numeric				none
	(IEEE format: no 8087)	8	1.125E-308	3.6E+308	
	(IEEE format: with 8087)	8	2.225E-308	1.8E+308	
	string	variable			$

Table 2.1 *BASIC data types.*

The three BASIC implementations support the eight-byte IEEE floating point format. For QuickBASIC and Turbo BASIC, this means that they provide functions to pack/unpack reals into strings using (1) the IEEE format and (2) Microsoft Binary Format (MBF).

Variables are assigned data types in two ways: implicitly and explicitly. The explicit typing method appends a data-type symbol to the variable's name. This enables you to override any implicit data type declarations. The latter are implemented in QuickBASIC and Turbo BASIC by using DEFINT, DEFDBL, DEFSNG, and DEFSTR (I will refer to the entire set as DEFxxx) that are familiar to the BASICA and MS-BASIC programmer. Turbo BASIC adds DEFLNG for implicit typing that involves long integers. True BASIC does not support the DEFxxx syntax: identifiers that end with a dollar sign contain strings, otherwise they store numbers. Using Turbo BASIC's long integers, you can write a short program to calculate the factorial using long integers instead of floating points.

```
' Turbo BASIC program that calculates
' long integer factorials
DEFINT I-O
DEFLNG F

CLS
INPUT "Enter number ";N : PRINT
FOR I = 1 TO N
    Factorial = Factorial * I
NEXT I
PRINT N;"! = ";Factorial
END
```

Turbo BASIC and QuickBASIC also implement constants. Until now, this formal data type was available only in languages like Pascal, Ada, and Modula-2. QuickBASIC supports constants that may be strings, integers, or single and double precision reals. The CONST keyword is used to declare a list of constants. The type-indicator characters are used to define the data type of the constant. These symbols are not part of the constant's name and may be omitted when using the constant. Moreover, the DEFxxx declaration does not affect the name of the constant. The following QuickBASIC code segment declares three constants: the arrays' upper limits, the numeric code for missing data, and default initial values:

```
OPTION BASE 1
' Declare constants
CONST MAX.LIMIT% = 100
CONST MISSING.DATA# = -1.0E-30 : DEFAULT.VAL# = 1

DIM X#(MAX.LIMIT), Y#(MAX.LIMIT)

FOR I% = 1 TO MAX.LIMIT
```

```
    X#(I%) = MISSING.DATA
    Y#(I%) = DEFAULT.VAL
NEXT I%
```

Notice that when the constants were used the data-type symbols were dropped.

Turbo BASIC currently supports only integer-typed constants. The constant name must begin with a '%' character. Named constants may be used instead of numeric constants, enabling you to make changes in your program without creating new bugs due to forgetting about a few old constant values. Another attractive area is the dimensioning of arrays, as in the following code fragment:

```
OPTION BASE 1
%Option.Base = 1
%FirstYear = 1980
%LastYear  = 1990
%UpperLimit = 7

DIM Year$(%FirstYear:%LastYear)
DIM Days.Of.Our.Lives(%UpperLimit)
```

The above defines an array of strings, *Year$()*, as having an index value of 1980 to 1990. The second array, *Days.Of.Our.Lives()*, has seven elements. The array limits assigned by named constants may be further used in the BASIC program. For example, they may be passed as arguments to CALLable subroutines or used to define FOR-NEXT loop limits.

While Turbo BASIC's constants are limited to integers, their notation makes BASIC constants easier to locate. Using all uppercase names for constants is another way to spot them.

In general, a named constant may be simulated by a parameterless function that simply returns a value. Since functions may be of any supported data types, so may the constants they simulate. Hence, it is possible to declare simulated named constants, such as:

```
' Simulated named constants in QuickBASIC
DEF FNMax.Limit% = 100
DEF FNActor$ = "Don Johnson"
DEF FNInterest.Rate! = 0.18


' Simulated named constants in Turbo BASIC
```

```
DEF FNMax.Limit& = 40000   ' long integer type
DEF FNActor$ = "John Wayne"
DEF FNMissing.Number.Code# = -1E+20


! Simulated named constants in True BASIC
DEF Actor$ = "Tom Selleck"
DEF Max_Limit = 1000
DEF Missing_Code = -1E+20
```

Functions can also implement more sophisticated types of constants. Simulating arrays of constants is one instance where functions can be put to work. Consider the following:

```
DEF FNWorking.Hours%(Day.Num%)

    FNWorking.Hours% = 0    'default value
    IF (Day.Num% = 1) OR  (Day.Num% = 7) THEN
        FNWorking.Hours% = 5
    IF (Day.Num% > 1) AND (Day.Num% < 7) THEN
        FNWorking.Hours% = 8

END DEF
```

The function *FNWorking.Hours%()* returns a constant value (or parameter, if you like) depending on its argument. This is really the border line between constants and variables.

Strings

The three BASIC implementations support strings that exceed 255 characters. QuickBASIC and Turbo BASIC allow strings to be up to 32K and 64K for string arrays. True BASIC allows a string to be up to 64K and permits string arrays to be as large as the available memory space. String manipulation in QuickBASIC and Turbo BASIC follows the same syntax and uses the same built-in functions of MS-BASIC and BASICA. Turbo BASIC uses a slightly different string access notation, similar to Hewlett-Packard HP-BASIC for the series 70, 80 computers. In True BASIC strings, constants, variables, functions, and expression are concatenated using the ampersand symbol &, as in:

```
OPTION NOLET

Actor$ = "Don Johnson"
Series$ = "Miami Vice"
PRINT "I like watching " & Actor$ & " on " & Series$

END
```

The above short program concatenates the string variables and constants to reveal one of my favorite actors and TV shows.

Indexing strings in True BASIC uses the following notation:

```
<string>[<first character>:<last character>]
```

Thus, in the following assignments:

```
Actor$ = "Don Johnson"
First_Name$ = Actor$[1:3] ! assigns "Don" to new string
Last_Name1$ = Actor$[5:LEN(Actor$)]
Last_Name2$ = Actor$[5:MAXNUM]
Actor$[1:3] = "Tom" ! replaces "Don" with "Tom"
PRINT Actor$ ! displays Tom Johnson
```

the string *First_Name$* receives the first, second, and third characters from string *Actor$*. Accessing the last portions of a string may be done in a variety of ways. The first uses the *LEN()* function to indicate the last character. If a value larger than the actual string length is used, True BASIC resorts to the actual string length. Thus, one can use the predefined True BASIC constant *MAXNUM* instead of the string length function. The bracket notation may be used in re-assigning portions of a string, much like *MID$()* in the other BASIC implementations.

The following True BASIC functions may be used to mimic the frequently used built-in string functions in the other BASICs:

```
DEF LEFT$(A$, Count) = A$[1:Count]
DEF RIGHT$(A$, Count) = A$[(LEN(A$)-Count+1):MAXNUM]
DEF MID$(A$,Index, Count) = A$[Index:(Index+Count-1)]
```

Arrays

A number of new features in array declaration and management are introduced by the three BASIC implementations.

Turbo BASIC and True BASIC enable you to explicitly declare the lower and upper array bounds. In Turbo BASIC the lower and upper bounds are separated by a colon, while in True BASIC the keyword *to* is used, as shown in the programs below:

```
' Turbo BASIC example for declaring
' upper and lower array bounds
OPTION BASE 1
DEFDBL A-Z
DIM Year(1950:1959,2), Balance(1950:1959)
Sum.Import = 0 : Sum.Export = 0
FOR J% = 1950 TO 1959
    PRINT "For the year ";I%
    INPUT "Enter $ for US export ";Year(J%,1)
    Sum.Export = Sum.Export + Year(J%,1)
    INPUT "Enter $ for US import ";Year(J%,2)
    Sum.Import = Sum.Import + Year(J%,2)
    Balance(J%) = Year(J%,1) - Year(J%,2)
    PRINT
NEXT J%

PRINT "Between 1950 and 1959"
PRINT "Total $ for import = ";Sum.Import
PRINT "Total $ for export = ";Sum.Export


FOR I% = 1950 TO 1959
    PRINT "Balance for ";I%;" = ";Balance(I%)
NEXT I%

END
```

The True BASIC version is:

```
! True BASIC example for declaring
! upper and lower array bounds
OPTION BASE 1
OPTION NOLET
DIM Year(1950 to 1959,2), Balance(1950 to 1959)
Sum_Import, Sum_Export = 0
```

```
FOR J = 1950 TO 1959
    PRINT "For the year ";I
    INPUT PROMPT "Enter $ for US export ":Year(J,1)
    Sum_Export = Sum_Export + Year(J,1)
    INPUT PROMPT "Enter $ for US import ":Year(J,2)
    Sum_Import = Sum_Import + Year(J,2)
    Balance(J) = Year(J,1) - Year(J,2)
    PRINT
NEXT J

PRINT "Between 1950 and 1959"
PRINT "Total $ for import = ";Sum_Import
PRINT "Total $ for export = ";Sum_Export

FOR I = 1950 TO 1959
    PRINT "Balance for ";I;" = ";Balance(I)
NEXT I

END
```

The three BASIC implementations provide two predefined functions that return the lower and upper array bounds. The *LBOUND()* and *UBOUND()* functions work with single and multi-dimensional arrays. QuickBASIC and True BASIC implement these functions identically (following the new ANSI BASIC). For one-dimensional arrays, only the array name is needed. With multi-dimensional arrays, a second argument is needed to select the dimension number. Using the array bound function with the last example, we have the following QuickBASIC version:

```
' QuickBASIC example for declaring
' upper and lower array bounds
OPTION BASE 1
DEFDBL A-Z
DIM Year(10,2), Balance(10)
Sum.Import = 0 : Sum.Export = 0
First.Year% = LBound(Year,1) ' or = LBound(Balance)
Last.Year%  = Ubound(Year,1) ' or = UBound(Balance)
FOR J% = First.Year% TO Last.Year%
    PRINT "For the year ";(1949+I%)
    INPUT "Enter $ for US export ";Year(J%,1)
    Sum.Export = Sum.Export + Year(J%,1)
    INPUT "Enter $ for US import ";Year(J%,2)
    Sum.Import = Sum.Import + Year(J%,2)
    Balance(J%) = Year(J%,1) - Year(J%,2)
    PRINT
NEXT J%
```

```
    PRINT "Between "(1949+First.Year%);
    PRINT " and ";(1949+Last.Year%)
    PRINT "Total $ for import = ";Sum.Import
    PRINT "Total $ for export = ";Sum.Export

    FOR I% = First.Year% TO Last.Year%
        PRINT "Balance for ";I%;" = ";Balance(I%)
    NEXT I%

    END
```

Notice that in the above version of the program we have assigned the range of years to two integer-type variables. The program shows how the *LBOUND()* and *UBOUND()* functions may be used with either type of array.

Turbo BASIC employs a slightly different syntax for *LBOUND()* and *UBOUND()*. Both functions take one argument: the name of the array with the dimension number enclosed in parentheses. The above QuickBASIC version may be rewritten for Turbo BASIC.

```
' Turbo BASIC example for declaring
' upper and lower array bounds
OPTION BASE 1
DEFDBL A-Z
DIM Year(1950:1959,2), Balance(1950:1959)
Sum.Import = 0 : Sum.Export = 0
First.Year% = LBound(Year(1))  ' or = LBound(Balance(1))
Last.Year%  = Ubound(Year(1))  ' or = UBound(Balance(1))
FOR J% = First.Year% TO Last.Year%
    PRINT "For the year ";I%
    INPUT "Enter $ for US export ";Year(J%,1)
    Sum.Export = Sum.Export + Year(J%,1)
    INPUT "Enter $ for US import ";Year(J%,2)
    Sum.Import = Sum.Import + Year(J%,2)
    Balance(J%) = Year(J%,1) - Year(J%,2)
    PRINT
NEXT J%

PRINT "Between "First.Year%);" and ";Last.Year%
PRINT "Total $ for import = ";Sum.Import
PRINT "Total $ for export = ";Sum.Export

FOR I% = First.Year% TO Last.Year%
    PRINT "Balance for ";I%;" = ";Balance(I%)
NEXT I%

END
```

The array bound functions provide a very powerful tool for building general-purpose array manipulating functions and subroutines. For example, you can write general libraries of subroutines that sort arrays, search in arrays, and solve simultaneous equations. This topic is discussed in a later section.

Redimensioning an array at run-time is required by many applications that tackle arrays exhibiting a wide variation in size. One way of handling such an application is to declare the arrays with sufficient space that satisfies most cases. Redimensioning routines are used in the few rare cases where a larger array size is needed.

As mentioned earlier, QuickBASIC and Turbo BASIC support static and dynamic arrays. The latter type can be redimensioned with the REDIM statement. This enables you to change the size and the number of dimensions (if needed). The REDIM statement has the same effect of calling the ERASE statement to deallocate the array, followed by a DIM declaration. This means that to retain data in redimensioned arrays they must first be copied. This strategy works well until the available memory space is insufficient to store the copy of the original array and the redimensioned array.

The following program performs basic descriptive statistics on an array of data. The source of the data is a fictitious BASIC file *DATAFILE.DAT* that contains nothing but DATA statements. The QuickBASIC program keeps reading the items in the DATA statement until a negative value is encountered (assume that it is always the last element). First, I will present the program:

```
' QuickBASIC program
OPTION BASE 1
' declare arrays to be dynamic.
REM $DYNAMIC
DIM X(100)

' Include file with DATA statements containing positive data
' Note: assume that last READ item is negative
REM $INCLUDE: 'DATAFILE.DAT'

Count% = 0
Array.Size% = Ubound(X)
Size.Increment% = 25 ' increase by 25 elements

READ Item ' read first piece of information

WHILE Item > 0
    Count% = Count% + 1
    IF Count% > Array.Size% THEN
```

```
        ' create the temporary array
        REDIM Xcopy(Array.Size%)
        FOR I% = 1 TO Array.Size%
            XCopy(I%) = X(I%)
        NEXT I%
        New.Array.Size% = Array.Size% + Size.Increment%
        REDIM X(New.Array.Size%)
        FOR I% = 1 TO Array.Size%
            X(I%) = XCopy(I%)
        NEXT I%
        ERASE XCopy ' deallocate temporary array
        Array.Size% = New.Array.Size% ' update array size
    END IF

    X(Count%) = Item

    READ Item

WEND


SumX = 0 : SumXX = 0
Sum = Array.Size%

FOR I% = 1 TO Array.Size%

    SumX  = SumX  + X(I%)
    SumXX = SumXX + X(I%)^2

NEXT I%

PRINT "Mean = ";SumX / Sum
PRINT "Sdev = ";SQR((SumXX - SumX^2 / Sum) / (Sum-1))

END
```

QuickBASIC initially dimensions the principal array, *X()*, to 100 elements. As DATA statements are read the program keeps count of the number of items read. If more space is needed, the program carries out the following:

1. Creates the copy array, *XCopy()*, to have a size equal to the current size of array *X()*.

2. Copies the values of array *X()* onto *XCopy()*.

3. Redimensions array *X()*.

4. Restores the original values of *X()* from *XCopy()*.

5. Erases the temporary array *XCopy()*.

6. Updates the array size counter.

Out of memory error may occur at either REDIM statement, depending on the available memory space and the size of the arrays.

True BASIC uses different constructs and offers two routes for array redimensioning. The first method follows the same general idea discussed for QuickBASIC and Turbo BASIC. True BASIC uses some of its matrix MAT commands to resize arrays. The MAT commands are not new to BASIC, as they are available in many mainframe implementations of BASIC as well as microcomputer BASIC dialects, such as HP-BASIC. The matrix commands work on arrays with any number of dimensions, and not just two-dimensional matrices, as the command names might suggest. Concerning array redimensioning, the matrix equality and the matrix *ZER()* function are used to resize and zero a matrix. The True BASIC version is shown below:

```
! True BASIC program that demonstrates array resizing
OPTION BASE 1
OPTION NOLET
! declare temporary arrays to have one element
DIM X(10), XCopy(1)

DATA 1,2,3,4,5,6,7,8,9,10,22,33,44,556,121,12,
DATA 312,212,747,736
DATA 3,2,5,67,2,1,99,33,2,65,123,432,45,678,987,6554,332,32
DATA 4773,32,123,455,666,928,3762,7373,192,384,
DATA 183,8475,384,9
DATA -1 ! End-Of-Data

Count = 0
Array_Size = Ubound(X)
Size_Increment = 25 ! increase by 25 elements

READ Item ! read first piece of information

DO WHILE Item > 0
   Count = Count + 1
   IF Count > Array_Size THEN
      ! create the temporary array and copy values
      ! from array X()
      MAT XCopy = X
      New_Array_Size = Array_Size + Size_Increment
      MAT X = ZER(New_Array_Size)
      FOR I = 1 TO Array_Size
         X(I) = XCopy(I)
```

```
    NEXT I
    ! re-minimize size of temporary array
    MAT XCopy = ZER(1)
    Array_Size = New_Array_Size ! update array size
  END IF

  X(Count) = Item

  READ Item

LOOP


SumX, SumXX = 0 ! multiple assignment statement
Sum = Array_Size

FOR I = 1 TO Array_Size

   SumX  = SumX  + X(I)
   SumXX = SumXX + X(I)^2

NEXT I

PRINT "Mean = ";SumX / Sum
PRINT "Sdev = ";SQR((SumXX - SumX^2 / Sum) / (Sum-1))

END
```

In addition to replacing the $INCLUDE metacommand with an actual set of DATA statements, the following lists the differences between the QuickBASIC and True BASIC versions:

1. The temporary array *XCopy()* is declared in the True BASIC DIM statement.

2. The statement *MAT XCopy = X* performs two tasks. First, it makes the size of array *XCopy()* equal to that of array *X()*. Secondly, it copies all of the values from array *X()* to *XCopy()*.

3. The temporary array is not deallocated, as in the QuickBASIC version. Instead, its size is shrunk to one member by using the *ZER(1)* function. This comes close to deallocating the entire array, but keeps one element for possible future use of *XCopy()*. This is similar to withdrawing most of your money from a bank account, but leaving just enough there to maintain it.

True BASIC offers a second method for array redimensioning. Its greatest advantage is that an array can be enlarged while it maintains its data. However, this fast operation has one drawback: it works on the first dimension. For simple arrays this imposes no restrictions, but for multidimensional arrays its does. The effect on a two-dimensional matrix is that you can increase the number of rows but not the number of columns. To alter both dimensions you have to use the first method. Using the True BASIC MAT REDIM, the last program version is rewritten as:

```
! True BASIC program that demonstrates array resizing
OPTION BASE 1
OPTION NOLET
! No temporary array is needed
DIM X(10)

DATA 1,2,3,4,5,6,7,8,9,10,22,33,44,556,121,12, 312,212,747,736
DATA 3,2,5,67,2,1,99,33,2,65,123,432,45,678,987,6554,332,32
DATA 4773,32,123,455,666,928,3762,7373,192,384,183,8475,384,9
DATA -1 ! End-Of-Data

Count = 0

READ Item ! read first piece of information

DO WHILE Item > 0

    Count = Count + 1

    IF Count > UBound(X) THEN MAT REDIM X(Count)

    X(Count) = Item

    READ Item

LOOP

Array_Size = UBound(X)
SumX, SumXX = 0 ! multiple assignment statement
Sum = Array_Size

FOR I = 1 TO Array_Size

    SumX  = SumX  + X(I)
    SumXX = SumXX + X(I)^2

NEXT I

PRINT "Mean = ";SumX / Sum
```

```
PRINT "Sdev = ";SQR((SumXX - SumX^2 / Sum) / (Sum-1))

END
```

Notice that the IF statement contains only the MAT REDIM statement and is considerably shorter than in the previous True BASIC version. In addition, the program does not use the temporary array and the identifier *Size_Increment*.

Increasing the size of multidimensional arrays requires the use of temporary arrays to copy the current values of the current array.

Decision Making: Where Do We Go From Here?

Decision-making constructs offer powerful programming tools. The number and types of decision-making constructs affect program readability and ease of coding. Most of the BASIC dialects for microcomputers have suffered in this area from poor and limited decision-making constructs. The good news is that the new BASICs have addressed this area. They have not only extended the IF construct, but have also added the SELECT-CASE multi-way switch.

The three BASIC implementations have extended the IF statement so that the THEN and ELSE clauses may span over many lines. The general syntax of the new extended IF-THEN construct is:

```
IF <logical expression> THEN

    <sequence of statements>

END IF
```

and that for the extended IF-THEN-ELSE construct is:

```
IF <logical expression> THEN

    <sequence of statements>

ELSE

    <sequence of statements>

END IF
```

The third extension includes one or more ELSEIF-THEN clauses:

```
IF <logical expression #1> THEN

    <sequence of statements>

ELSEIF <logical expression #2> THEN

    <sequence of statements>

<other ELSEIF-THEN clauses>

ELSE

    <sequence of statements>

END IF
```

An example of using the new IF statement is seen in the following short program that solves for the roots of a quadratic equation:

```
' QuickBASIC program to solve the
' roots of quadratic equations.

DEFDBL A-Z
PRINT "Solving A X^2 + B X + C = 0"
PRINT
' Enter coefficients
INPUT "Enter A ";A : PRINT
INPUT "Enter B ";B : PRINT
INPUT "Enter C ";C : PRINT
' Calculate discriminant
DISCRIM = B * B - 4 * A * C
IF DISCRIM = 0 THEN

    PRINT "The two identical real roots are ";
    PRINT (-B) / (2*A)

ELSEIF DISCRIM > 0 THEN

    ROOT1 = ((-B) + SQR(DISCRIM) ) / (2 * A)
    ROOT2 = ((-B) - SQR(DISCRIM) ) / (2 * A)
    PRINT "The real roots are ";
    PRINT ROOT1," and ",ROOT2

ELSE ' DISCRIM < 0
```

```
        DISCRIM = ABS(DISCRIM)
        ROOT1 = (-B) / (2 * A)
        ROOT2 = SQR(DISCRIM)   / (2 * A)
        PRINT "The imaginary roots are ";
        PRINT ROOT1;" +/- i ";ROOT2

END IF

END
```

The three BASICs have implemented the SELECT CASE statement. The general syntax of the CASE construct is:

```
SELECT CASE <expression>

    CASE <list #1 of test values>

        <statement block #1>

    CASE <list #2 of test values>

        <statement block #2>

    CASE ELSE

        <statement block #3>

END SELECT
```

The power of the BASIC CASE construct exceeds that of the CASE statements in other languages such as Pascal, Modula-2, and Ada. This is due to the fact that each tested value in every CASE clause may be one of the following:

1. Single items.

2. Range of items using the "*<first>* to *<last>*" syntax.

3. Partial logical expression.

Turbo BASIC implements the SELECT CASE statement slightly differently from QuickBASIC and True BASIC. These differences are:

1. Turbo BASIC allows the CASE clauses to be expressions. QuickBASIC and True BASIC permit constants only, following the new BASIC ANSI.

2. Turbo BASIC does not support the IS keyword when using a partial logical expression.

I will demonstrate the use of the case statement with a few examples. The first example is a rewrite of the quadratic solution program listed earlier. I have replaced the IF statement with SELECT CASE:

```
' QuickBASIC program to solve the
' roots of quadratic equations.

DEFDBL A-Z
PRINT "Solving A X^2 + B X + C = 0"
PRINT
' Enter coefficients
INPUT "Enter A ";A : PRINT
INPUT "Enter B ";B : PRINT
INPUT "Enter C ";C : PRINT
' Calculate the discriminant value
DISCRIM = B * B - 4 * A * C

SELECT CASE DISCRIM

    CASE 0

        PRINT "The two identical real roots are ";
        PRINT (-B) / (2*A)

    CASE IS 0 <

        ROOT1 = ((-B) + SQR(DISCRIM) ) / (2 * A)
        ROOT2 = ((-B) - SQR(DISCRIM) ) / (2 * A)
        PRINT "The real roots are ";
        PRINT ROOT1," and ",ROOT2

    CASE ELSE

        DISCRIM = ABS(DISCRIM)
        ROOT1 = (-B) / (2 * A)
        ROOT2 = SQR(DISCRIM)  / (2 * A)
        PRINT "The imaginary roots are ";
        PRINT ROOT1;" +/- i ";ROOT2

END SELECT

END
```

The Turbo BASIC version is similar except that *CASE IS < 0* is replaced with *CASE < 0*.

The second CASE program prompts you to press a key and displays the category of the key you pressed according to its ASCII code:

```
' Turbo BASIC program that illustrates the SELECT CASE
PRINT "Press a key "
A$ = INPUT$(1)  ' get on character
PRINT A$ : PRINT
PRINT "The key you pressed is ";

SELECT CASE ASC(A$)

    CASE < 32
        PRINT "a control character"
    CASE 33 to 47, 58 to 64, 91 to 96, 123 to 127
        PRINT "a punctuation character"
    CASE ASC("0") to ASC("9")
        PRINT "a digit"
    CASE ASC("A") to ASC("Z")
        PRINT "an uppercase letter"
    CASE ASC("a") to ASC("z")
        PRINT "a lowercase letter"
    CASE > 128
        PRINT "an extended ASCII code"
    CASE ELSE
        PRINT "unrecognizable!"
        PRINT "Call you computer serviceman...and hurry!"
END SELECT

END
```

To convert the above Turbo BASIC program into either a QuickBASIC or True BASIC version, the predefined ASC() functions must be replaced by integer constants that represent the ASCII codes.

One of the benefits of structured IF and CASE statements is that you can use them in a nested fashion while still maintaining good readability. Consider the above Turbo BASIC program that classifies a typed character. I will make two modifications to the program. First, the uppercase and lowercase characters are put in the same CASE clause. The second modification inserts a nested SELECTED CASE to identify whether or not the character is a vowel:

```
' Turbo BASIC program that illustrates the SELECT CASE
PRINT "Press a key "
A$ = INPUT$(1) ' get on character
PRINT A$ : PRINT
PRINT "The key you pressed is ";

SELECT CASE ASC(A$)

    CASE < 32
        PRINT "a control character"
    CASE 33 to 47, 58 to 64, 91 to 96, 123 to 127
        PRINT "a punctuation character"
    CASE ASC("0") to ASC("9")
        PRINT "a digit"
    CASE ASC("A") to ASC("Z"), ASC("a") to ASC("z")

        ' Start nested SELECT CASE
        SELECT CASE ASC(A$)
            CASE "I","O","E","U","A","i","o","e","u","a"
                PRINT "a vowel"
            CASE ELSE
                PRINT "a non-vowel letter"
        END SELECT

    CASE > 128
        PRINT "an extended ASCII code"
    CASE ELSE
        PRINT "unrecognizable!"
        PRINT "Call you computer serviceman...and hurry!"
END SELECT

END
```

Turbo BASIC supports versions of the EXIT statement that enable you to exit an IF or CASE block. Their use relieves the programmer from writing code blocks that are telescoped. They make readability easier, especially since the EXIT IF and EXIT CASE replace GOTOs.

QuickBASIC and Turbo BASIC support slightly modified ON/GOTO and ON/GOSUB decision-making constructs. The line numbers found in the MS-BASIC and BASICA versions are now replaced with labels. Other than that, their use is the same as in the interpreter BASIC versions. The CASE SELECT construct has outdone the ON/GOTO and ON/GOSUB. They are supported by the compiler to maintain code portability with older interpreter BASIC programs.

Loops: Recycled Code

The three BASICs have introduced new sophisticated loops. QuickBASIC only supports the FOR-NEXT and WHILE-WEND loops inherited from BASICA and MS-BASIC. Table 2.2 shows the comparison of looping and decision-making constructs. I will concentrate on the new DO-LOOP and its variants.

	Quick-BASIC	Turbo BASIC	True BASIC
multiline IF-THEN-ELSE	Yes	Yes	Yes
ELSEIF	Yes	Yes	Yes
SELECT CASE	Yes	Yes	Yes
FOR-NEXT	Yes	Yes	Yes
WHILE-WEND	Yes	Yes	No
WHILE MORE DATA	No	No	Yes
WHILE MORE <file buffer>	No	No	Yes
DO-LOOP	Yes	Yes	Yes
DO [WHILE]-LOOP [UNTIL]	Yes	Yes	Yes
EXIT FOR	Yes	Yes	Yes
EXIT LOOP or EXIT DO	Yes	Yes	Yes
EXIT WHILE	No	Yes	N/A

Table 2.2 *Decision-making and looping constructs comparison table.*

The DO-LOOP is, in essence, an open loop that can iterate forever. An EXIT statement supplies the escape route that saves your program from being trapped (loop EXIT is discussed at the end of this section). The general syntax of the DO-LOOP is:

An example of the DO WHILE-LOOP is the following code fragment that removes leading spaces in a string variable:

```
' Variable A$ contains a number of characters and
' possible leading spaces.
DO WHILE (LEFT$(A$,1) = " ") AND (LEN(A$) > 1)
    A$ = MID$(A$,2)
LOOP
```

Consider the second example, below, for using the DO WHILE-LOOP. The program prompts for a major credit card purchase and the regular payments you would make. It prints the monthly finance charges and their total:

```
' Turbo BASIC program to calculate credit card
' finance charges.
DEFDBL A-Z
CLS
INPUT "Enter credit card purchase $";Purchase : PRINT
INPUT "Enter amount of regular monthly payments $";Payment
Interest = 0.18 / 12 ' 18% annual interest rate
' Initialize balance, sum of charges and month number
Balance = Purchase
Sum.Charges = 0
Month% = 1

DO WHILE Payment < Balance

    Balance = Balance - Payment
    Charges = Interest * Balance
    Sum.Charges = Sum.Charges + Charges
    Month% = Month% + 1
    PRINT "In month # ";Month%;" ';
    PRINT USING "Finance charges = #####.##";Charges

LOOP

PRINT "Last payment is made in month # ";Month%
PRINT
PRINT USING "Total finance charges = ####.##";Sum.Charges

END
```

To build a REPEAT loop, the following general syntax is available:

```
DO

    <sequence of statements>

LOOP UNTIL <logical expression>
```

An example for the DO-LOOP UNTIL is the following short program that calculates the square root of a number using Newton's method:

```
! True BASIC program
OPTION NOLET

DO ! Loop to obtain a positive number

    INPUT PROMPT "Enter number ":SQUARE

LOOP UNTIL SQUARE > 0

PRINT
ROOT = SQUARE / 2

! Start the iteration loop
DO

    ! Update square root guess
    ROOT = (SQUARE / ROOT + ROOT) / 2

LOOP UNTIL ABS(ROOT * ROOT - SQUARE) < 1E-08

PRINT "SQRT(";SQUARE;") = ";ROOT

END
```

Notice that the above program uses two DO-LOOP UNTIL loops. The first ensures that a positive value for the square is entered. Entering a zero or negative value causes the loop to reiterate. The second loop refines the guess for the square root until a preset accuracy is attained.

It is interesting to point out that you may build a loop that uses the WHILE and UNTIL constructs simultaneously, as in:

```
DO WHILE <logical expression #1>

    <sequence of statements>

LOOP UNTIL <logical expression #2>
```

As strange as the above double-test loop may seem, I have used it on a few applications. Using the WHILE and UNTIL tests makes the logic of the loop easier to understand. To demonstrate the last point, I will rewrite the last program to include an iteration counter:

```
! True BASIC program
OPTION NOLET

DO ! Loop to obtain a positive number

    INPUT PROMPT "Enter number ":SQUARE

LOOP UNTIL SQUARE > 0

PRINT
ROOT = SQUARE / 2
MAXITER = 50 ! maximum number of iterations
ITER = 0

! Start the iteration loop
DO WHILE ITER <= MAXITER

    ! Update square root guess
    ROOT = (SQUARE / ROOT + ROOT) / 2
    ITER = ITER + 1

LOOP UNTIL ABS(ROOT * ROOT - SQUARE) < 1E-08

PRINT "SQRT(";SQUARE;") = ";ROOT

END
```

In the above program, the logical expression after WHILE is used to monitor divergence and prevents the program from being trapped in the loop. The two logical expressions can be placed after the WHILE keyword. This change dictates that logical operators used for the accuracy test be reversed. The program is rewritten as:

```
! True BASIC program
OPTION NOLET

DO ! Loop to obtain a positive number

   INPUT PROMPT "Enter number ":SQUARE

LOOP UNTIL SQUARE > 0

PRINT
ROOT = SQUARE / 2
MAXITER = 50 ! maximum number of iterations
ITER = 0

! Start the iteration loop
DO WHILE (ABS(ROOT * ROOT - SQUARE) >= 1E-08) AND (ITER <= MAXITER)

   ! Update square root guess
   ROOT = (SQUARE / ROOT + ROOT) / 2
   ITER = ITER + 1

LOOP

PRINT "SQRT(";SQUARE;") = ";ROOT

END
```

True BASIC supports a special version of the DO WHILE loop that automatically tests for available information in DATA statements. The DO WHILE MORE DATA is used to read all of the DATA statements. The following program reads the names of capitals from the DATA statements, sorts them, and displays the ordered array. Notice that the DIM reserves only one space for the string array *Capital$()*. The array is expanded using the MAT REDIM, located inside the DO WHILE MORE DATA loop.

```
! True BASIC program that demonstrates the use of the
! DO WHILE MORE DATA loop construct.
OPTION BASE 1
OPTION NOLET

DIM Capital$(1)

DATA Paris, London, Washington, Moscow, Rome
DATA Madrid, Lisbon, Bern, Bonn, Tokyo, LAST

Num_Items = 0 ! Reset data counter
```

```
DO WHILE MORE DATA

    READ Item$
    Num_Items = Num_Items + 1
    ! Adjust array size
    MAT REDIM Capitals$(Num_Items)
    Capital$(Num_Items) = Item$
LOOP

! Sort string array using the bubble algorithm
FOR I = 1 TO Num_Items - 1

    FOR J = I+1 TO Num_Items

        IF Capital$(I) > Capital$(J) THEN
           Item$ = Capital$(I)
           Capital$(I) = Capital$(J)
           Capital$(J) = Item$
        END IF

    NEXT J

NEXT I

! Display sorted list
FOR I = 1 TO Num_Items
    PRINT Capital$(I)
NEXT I

END
```

EXIT: The Great Escape

Exiting loops without the explicit use of GOTOs is normally associated with high-level structured languages. The fact that the new wave BASICs support loop exit is a sign of healthy development of BASIC.

The three BASIC implementations support the EXIT FOR statement to exit FOR-NEXT loops. To escape a DO-LOOP, Turbo BASIC uses EXIT LOOP, while QuickBASIC and True BASIC use EXIT DO. These EXIT statements direct the program flow control to the statement after the NEXT or LOOP keywords (that is, the end of the loop). In addition, Turbo BASIC has the EXIT WHILE to similarly tackle WHILE-WEND loops.

The following simple program illustrates the use of EXIT FOR. The program reads strings from DATA statements until it either fills the array or encounters the word *LAST*. When the latter occurs, the FOR loop is exited to refrain from attempting to read more DATA statements. The program goes on to sort the array and display it. The EXIT FOR is used a second time with the bubble sort loops. Should the array be partially ordered, the *Swap.Flag%* variable is used to indicate that no further looping is needed.

```
' Turbo BASIC program that demonstrates a simple EXIT LOOP

OPTION BASE 1
%UpperLimit = 100
DIM Capital$(%UpperLimit)

DATA Paris, London, Washington, Moscow, Rome
DATA Madrid, Lisbon, Bern, Bonn, Tokyo, LAST

Last% = %UpperLimit

FOR I% = 1 TO %UpperLimit
   READ Capital$(I%)
   IF Capital$(I%) = "LAST" THEN
      Last% = I% - 1
      EXIT FOR ' program resumes
   END IF              '         |
NEXT I%   '                      |
' here <--------------------+


' Sort string array using the bubble algorithm

FOR I% = 1 TO Last% - 1

   Swap.Flag% = 0 ' Initialize swap flag

   FOR J% = I%+1 TO Last%

      IF Capital$(I%) > Capital$(J%) THEN
         Swap Capital$(I%), Capital$(J%)
         Swap.Flag% = 1
      END IF

   NEXT J%

   ' Is array ordered?
   IF Swap.Flag% = 0 THEN EXIT FOR

NEXT I%
```

```
' List string array
FOR I% = 1 TO Last%
    PRINT Capital$(I%)
NEXT I%

END
```

A second example of using the EXIT statement is shown below. The following QuickBASIC program prompts the user for a search string, a stop-searching string, and a text file name. The program scans the text file for the search string and prints every line that contains it. This is repeated until the end-of-file or the "stop-searching" string is encountered. The EXIT is also used to control the main program loop:

```
' QuickBASIC program for demonstration EXIT

' Outer open DO-LOOP
DO

    CLS
    INPUT "Enter file name ? (press return to quit) ";F$

    ' use EXIT to quit the open DO-LOOP in the program
    IF F$ = "" THEN EXIT DO

    PRINT
    INPUT "Enter search string ? ";SrchStr$ : PRINT
    INPUT "Enter 'stop-searching' string ? ";StopStr$ : PRINT

    OPEN 1,"I",F$

    LPRINT "Searching for ";SrchStr$;" in file ";F$
    LPRINT : LPRINT

    ' Inner DO UNTIL-LOOP
    DO UNTIL EOF(1)  ' or DO WHILE NOT EOF(1)
        LINE INPUT #1; L$

        ' EXIT if stop string is found
        IF INSTR(L$,StopStr$) > 0 THEN EXIT DO

        IF INSTR(L$,SrchStr$) > 0 THEN LPRINT L$ : LPRINT

    LOOP

    LPRINT CHR$(140)  ' form feed
```

```
        LOOP

    END
```

The above program contains two DO loops:

1. The outer DO-LOOP is an open loop and is exited only when the variable *F$* contains a null string.

2. The inner DO-LOOP uses an UNTIL clause to test for the end-of-file. The first IF statement tests for the presence of the search abort string. An affirmative test causes the EXIT statement to terminate the looping.

Error Handling

QuickBASIC uses an error handling scheme that is derived from BASICA and MS-BASIC. The ON ERROR GOTO is employed to install or remove an error handler. As in interpreted BASIC, an *ON ERROR GOTO 0* removes the error handler. Errors occurring when no error-handlers are installed cause the program to halt. The program will also come to a stop when an error turns up in the error-handling code itself. To install an error-handler, use:

```
ON ERROR GOTO <line number> or <alphanumeric label>
```

The execution of the program is transferred to the code segment where the line number/label is located. The RESUME keyword is employed to continue program execution after the necessary action is taken. A RESUME or RESUME 0 enables you to resume at the error-causing statement. This is useful in situations that handle bad values assigned to variables (such as supplying a bad file name while trying to OPEN it). Alternatively, the RESUME NEXT permits you to resume at the line immediately following the error-causing one. The third alternative is to use RESUME with a line number or label to redirect program flow.

QuickBASIC supports a number of functions that return error-related information. The ERR and ERL provide the error code and line number, respectively. The ERDEV and ERDEV$ return the number and name of a device that declared an error. You may raise your own error by using *ERROR <integer expression>* to simulate an error by number.

QuickBASIC does not support local error-handlers in functions and subroutines. The error handlers must be at the highest program level. This prevents routines from having their own *black-box* error-handlers. However, you can use RESUME from the main program to continue executing a subroutine.

QuickBASIC supports better error-handling within FOR-NEXT loops. Previously, the loop control variable was reset or altered: smooth resumption was a problem. Using WHILE-WEND loops was the recommended replacement for the FOR-NEXT loops. Now, you can easily handle errors that generate inside FOR-NEXT loops. Consider the following simple QuickBASIC program:

```
' QuickBASIC program to demonstrate
' error-handling in a FOR-NEXT loop

ON ERROR GOTO Zero.Div.Err

FOR I = -10 TO 10

    PRINT 1/I

NEXT I

END

' Error handler
Zero.Div.Err:
    PRINT "Infinity"
    RESUME NEXT
```

The above program displays the reciprocals for the numbers 10 to 10. When the loop control variable is zero, a division-by-zero error occurs and the error-handler displays 'infinity'. Program execution is resumed and the negative reciprocals are calculated and displayed.

Turbo BASIC implements error-handling in a manner very similar to QuickBASIC. However, Turbo BASIC permits routines to have their own error-handlers.

The following is a program for an RPN calculator program. The input may be any of the four basic operations, or a number. Press the [ENTER] key to exit. The error handler is used to trap the division-by-zero run-time error. In this example, a warning message is displayed, and the division is not performed When you compile this program with QuickBASIC, make sure that you flag the compiler for using error-handling. If you invoke the compiler directly from

DOS, include the /e switch. If RESUME NEXT is also included in your program, add the /x switch. From the QuickBASIC environment you can use a mouse or the tab keys to set these compiler options. The program listing is shown:

```
' PROGRAM RPN_Calculator
' QuickBASIC program to demonstrate error-handling

OPTION BASE 1

DEFDBL A-Z

DIM Stack(4), S$(4)

DATA "T : ","Z : ","Y : ","X : "

FOR I% = 4 TO 1 STEP -1
   READ S$(I%)
NEXT I%

' Install Error-Handler
ON ERROR GOTO Disp.Error

DO
    CLS
    PRINT "Stack is now"
    PRINT
    FOR I% = 4 TO 1 STEP -1
        PRINT S$(I%),Stack(I%)
    NEXT I%
    PRINT

    INPUT "Enter command/number [press [Enter] to quit] "; A$
    IF (A$ = "") THEN EXIT DO

    IF (LEN(A$) = 1) AND (INSTR("+-*/",LEFT$(A$,1)) > 0) THEN

        SELECT CASE A$

            CASE "+"
                Stack(1) = Stack(2) + Stack(1)
                Stack(2) = Stack(3)
                STack(3) = Stack(4)

            CASE "-"
                Stack(1) = Stack(2) - Stack(1)
                Stack(2) = Stack(3)
                STack(3) = Stack(4)
```

```
            CASE "*"
                Stack(1) = Stack(2) * Stack(1)
                Stack(2) = Stack(3)
                STack(3) = Stack(4)

            CASE "/"
                Stack(1) = Stack(2) / Stack(1)
                Stack(2) = Stack(3)
                STack(3) = Stack(4)
        END SELECT


    ELSE
        FOR I% = 4 TO 2 STEP -1
            Stack(I%) = Stack(I%-1)
        NEXT I%
        Stack(1) = VAL(A$)
    END IF

Resume.Here:
' Recovery from errors continues here

    PRINT
    PRINT "Stack has become"
    PRINT
    FOR I% = 4 TO 1 STEP -1
        PRINT S$(I%),Stack(I%)
    NEXT I%
    PRINT

    PRINT "Press any key ";
    A.KEY$ = INPUT$(1)

LOOP

PRINT
PRINT "End of program"

END

' Error-Handler routine
Disp.Error:
PRINT
PRINT "Cannot divide by zero"
RESUME Resume.Here
```

True BASIC uses a more structured approach for error handling. The WHEN ERROR IN structure is used in the following general manner:

```
WHEN ERROR IN

    <sequence of statements protected by error handler>

USE

    <sequence of statement for the error handler>

END WHEN
```

The sequence of statements that are most likely to cause a run-time error is placed in the WHEN ERROR IN clause. The remedy for the error generated is placed in the USE clause. While the WHEN ERROR IN handler may be placed inside a function or subroutine, the error handling code may not define a function or a subroutine. True BASIC error handlers may be nested. Normally, the error handler tackles errors generated by statements, functions, and subroutines in the WHEN clause. If a function or subroutine in a WHEN clause generates run-time error and possesses its own *local* error handlers, the local handlers will override the global one. Local handlers may use EXIT HANDLER to pass up an error to a higher level handler.

True BASIC supports the predefined functions *Extype*, *Extext$*, and *Exline$* to yield the error number, error message, and the error-generating line associated with the last occurring error. If *Extype* returns zero, no error has yet occurred. Error numbers 1 to 999 are available for the user, and those numbered 1000 and up are reserved for True BASIC. User-defined errors may be raised by using the *CAUSE ERROR <error number>* statement. You may supply your own error message by using:

```
CAUSE ERROR <error-number>, <string message>
```

The following is the True BASIC version for the RPN calculator program. The input may be the letter *Q* to quit, any of the four basic operations, or a number. The error handler is used to trap the division-by-zero run-time error. In this example, a warning message is displayed and the division is not carried out.

```
PROGRAM RPN_Calculator
! True BASIC program to demonstrate error-handling

OPTION BASE 1

DIM Stack(4), S$(4)
```

```
MAT Stack = ZER ! Initialize values

DATA "T : ","Z : ","Y : ","X : "

FOR I = 4 TO 1 STEP -1
    READ S$(I)
NEXT I

DO

    CLEAR
    PRINT "Stack is now"
    PRINT
    FOR I = 4 TO 1 STEP -1
        PRINT S$(I),Stack(I)
    NEXT I
    PRINT

    INPUT PROMPT "Enter command/number ['Q' to quit] ? ": A$
    IF UCASE$(A$[1:1]) = "Q" THEN EXIT DO
    IF (LEN(A$) = 1) AND (POS("+-*/",A$[1:1]) > 0) THEN

        WHEN ERROR IN

            SELECT CASE A$[1:1]

                CASE "+"
                    LET Stack(1) = Stack(2) + Stack(1)
                    LET Stack(2) = Stack(3)
                    LET STack(3) = Stack(4)

                CASE "-"
                    LET Stack(1) = Stack(2) - Stack(1)
                    LET Stack(2) = Stack(3)
                    LET STack(3) = Stack(4)

                CASE "*"
                    LET Stack(1) = Stack(2) * Stack(1)
                    LET Stack(2) = Stack(3)
                    LET STack(3) = Stack(4)

                CASE "/"
                    LET Stack(1) = Stack(2) / Stack(1)
                    LET Stack(2) = Stack(3)
                    LET STack(3) = Stack(4)
            END SELECT

        USE

            PRINT
            PRINT "Cannot divide by zero"

        END WHEN
```

```
        ELSE
            FOR I = 4 TO 2 STEP -1
                LET Stack(I) = Stack(I-1)
            NEXT I
            LET Stack(1) = VAL(A$)
        END IF

        PRINT
        PRINT "Stack has become"
        PRINT
        FOR I = 4 TO 1 STEP -1
            PRINT S$(I),Stack(I)
        NEXT I
        PRINT

        PRINT "Press any key ";
        GET KEY A_KEY

LOOP

PRINT
PRINT "End of program"

END
```

File Handling

In general, file I/O has enjoyed less enhancement than loops, decision making, and other BASIC programming aspects. QuickBASIC and Turbo BASIC have essentially followed the file I/O tradition of BASICA, while True BASIC brought out a new syntax.

File handling in QuickBASIC follows that of BASICA 3.2 where four I/O modes are supported: random access I/O (one mode), sequential input, sequential output, and append. QuickBASIC maintains the same syntax familiar to BASICA and MS-BASIC programmers.

Turbo BASIC more or less follows the BASICA 3.2 syntax and has added one mode for sequential output: nondelimited sequential files.

True BASIC has come out with a different syntax to perform the same file I/O operations available in QuickBASIC. The new syntax includes the ability to query file information using the powerful ASK *<attribute>* statement. The general form for opening a file is:

```
OPEN #<expr> : NAME <str_expr$>, ACCESS <access_mode$>,
                                 CREATE <create_mode$>,
                                 ORGANIZATION <org_mode$>,
                                 RECSIZE <recsize>
```

Table 2.3 lists the file attributes associated with opening a True BASIC file.

Attribute	**String**	**Information**
ACCESS	INPUT	Read-only.
	OUTPUT	Write-only.
	OUTIN	Read and/or write (default state).
CREATE	NEW	Create a new file.
	OLD	File must be existing (default).
	NEWOLD	Use existing or create new one.
ORGANIZATION	TEXT	Sequential text file.
	RECORD	Random access file.
	BYTE	Byte file.

Table 2.3 True BASIC file OPEN attributes.

It is important to note that True BASIC does not support an LPRINT statement. Instead, you must open a communication buffer to your printer using:

```
OPEN #<number>: PRINTER
```

In addition, printing to buffer number zero sends the output to the screen. The above information hints at the fact that you can send an output to the screen, the printer, or a textfile by selecting a buffer (channel) number. As we will see later,

True BASIC subroutines permit buffer numbers to be passed as arguments. This creates a powerful tool for easy output redirection.

User-defined Functions

User-defined functions are not new to BASIC. The early versions of BASIC on the mircocomputers supported one-line functions. If you needed a multi-line function you had to use GOSUBs, which made things a bit cumbersome. Hewlett-Packard BASIC implementations for the micros have supported multi-line functions in the past. The good news is that things have changed for the better. The three BASICs now support multi-line functions that enable them to use loops and decision-making constructs. Today's BASIC provides versatile functions. The three BASICs do not implement functions in exactly the same way, but do have the following features in common:

1. All the parameters of a function are passed by value. As a result, a function cannot alter the value of its arguments outside its own scope.

2. Functions return one result assigned to the function's name.

3. The EXIT DEF statement may be used to exit a function from anywhere in its definition.

The general syntax for multi-line functions is:

```
DEF <function name>
    <sequence of statements>
    <function name> = <result>
END DEF
```

and for single-line functions:

```
DEF <function name> = <expression>
```

Functions are called by name, followed by a list of arguments that must correspond in number and data type with the list of declared parameters. This is known as positional association.

QuickBASIC has built on the function structure available in BASICA and MS-BASIC. This includes the following features:

1. The function name must begin with the letters FN.

2. The function may have an optional data-type symbol to declare its type explicitly. Otherwise, the data type follows any default or DEFxxx declarations.

3. Functions cannot be used before they are declared in a program.

4. The parameters of functions must be scalar variables. No arrays are permitted.

5. Functions may not be recursive.

Turbo BASIC implements functions in a manner similar to QuickBASIC. However, functions in Turbo BASIC may be declared anywhere in the program and they may be recursive.

The following function illustrates a multi-line function that trims the leading spaces of a string:

```
DEF FNLTRIM$(S$)
' Trim left leading blanks in a string S$

DO WHILE (LEFT$(S$,1) = " ") AND (S$ <> "")

   S$ = MID$(S$,2) ' trim string

LOOP

FNLTRIM$ = S$

END DEF
```

The next function illustrates a recursive implementation of a factorial function:

```
' Turbo BASIC recursive functions to calculate factorials
DEF FNFact#(N%)
' Recursive factorial function
IF N% > 1 THEN
   FNFact# = N% * FNFact#(N%-1)
ELSE
   FNFact# = 1.0#
```

```
END IF

END DEF
```

True BASIC implements functions differently:

1. Function names need not begin with the letters FN. The price of lifting this requirement is that your True BASIC program must inform the compiler of the functions' names by using a DECLARE DEF statement.

2. Functions return strings if their names end with a dollar sign. Otherwise, they return a numeric (integer or real) result.

3. Functions may be used before they are declared.

4. Functions may have arrays as parameters. The arrays are passed by value.

5. Functions may be recursive.

6. True BASIC makes a distinction between internal and external functions. Internal functions are those defined BEFORE the unique END statement in a True BASIC program. External functions are those defined either AFTER the END statement or in an external library file. Internal functions are able to share variables with the main program and thus access data from the program in two ways. External functions have a more strict data interface, since they rely on their parameters to obtain data.

The following short True BASIC program illustrates an internal and external function. The program scans for the spaces in a string using a function to return the position of the spaces. The program has two versions of the same function: *IntNextSpace* is the internal version and *ExtNextSpace* is the external one. Notice that the internal function has one parameter, namely, the position to start scanning for a space character. The name of the string is not needed, because the function is processing a specific string. The external version requires that the string being scanned also be supplied as an argument.

```
! True BASIC programs to demo functions
! Functions return the location of the next space character
! in a string, or zero if not found.
```

THE NEW PROGRAMMING FRAMEWORK

```
DECLARE DEF IntNextSpace, ExtNextSpace

DEF IntNextSpace(Start)

   IF Start < 0 THEN LET Start = 1

   LET Found = 0

   DO WHILE Start <= LEN(L$)
      IF L$[Start:Start] <> " " THEN
         LET Found = 1
         EXIT DO
      END IF
      LET Start = Start + 1
   LOOP

   ! returns zero if not
   LET IntNextSPace = Start * Found

END DEF

INPUT PROMPT "Enter a string with many spaces ";L$
PRINT
PRINT "USING INTERNAL FUNCTION"

LET First = IntNextSpace(1)

DO WHILE First > 0

   PRINT "Space at character ";First
   LET First = IntNextSpace(First+1)

LOOP

PRINT
PRINT "USING EXTERNAL FUNCTION"
PRINT

LET First  ExtNextSpace(L$,1)

DO WHILE First > 0

   PRINT "Space at character ";First
   LET First = ExtNextSpace(L$,First+1)

LOOP

END


DEF ExtNextSpace(S$, Start)

   IF Start < 0 THEN LET Start = 1
```

```
         LET Found = 0

         DO WHILE Start <= LEN(S$)
            IF S$[Start:Start] <> " " THEN
               LET Found = 1
               EXIT DO
            END IF
            LET Start = Start + 1
         LOOP

         ! returns zero if not
         LET ExtNextSPace = Start * Found

END DEF
```

BASIC Subroutines: Borrowing from FORTRAN?

Multi-line functions represent an important vehicle for structured code. Their benefits are complemented by CALLable subroutines (named subroutines) that resemble those in FORTRAN. These new subroutines have a name and a parameter list, like functions. Subroutine parameters are passed either by value or by reference. If an argument is an expression, it is passed by value, otherwise it is passed by reference (that is, its address is passed). This enables subroutines to alter the values of parameters passed by reference. Subroutine parameters may be scalar variables or arrays. As a result, named subroutines make very attractive pseudo-functions when more than one result is returned or when the parameter is an array (this is true for QuickBASIC and Turbo BASIC only).

The general syntax for defining named subroutines is:

```
SUB <name>(<optional list of parameters>) [STATIC]

    <sequence of statements>

END SUB
```

Subroutines may not be nested (except for external True BASIC subroutines, which will be discussed later). The three BASICs support the EXIT SUB statement to enable you to exit and return to the caller. The EXIT SUB is very useful in exiting subroutines when parameters with invalid values are passed.

Subroutines are called by name, followed by a list of arguments that must correspond in number and data type with the list of declared parameters. This aspect is identical to function calls. Only Turbo and True BASIC support recursive subroutines.

The subroutine declarations in QuickBASIC must end with the keyword STATIC. This is also a reminder that QuickBASIC does not support recursion. QuickBASIC subroutines exchange data with other program units in two ways: parameters and SHARED variables. Data communication via parameters is the safer and more obvious way. This is because parameter names and argument names are mapped onto each other when you CALL a subroutine, as in the following subroutine:

```
SUB Get.Sqrt(Square#, Root#, ErrorFlag%) STATIC

IF Square# >= 0 THEN
   ErrorFlag% = 0
   Root# = SQR(Square#)
ELSE
   ErrorFlag% = 1
   Root# = -1
END IF

END SUB
```

which may be called using the following statement:

```
CALL Get.Sqrt(N#, S#, Flag%)
```

causing the compiler to map argument *N#* with parameter *Square#*, *S#* with *Root#*, and *Flag%* with *ErrorFlag%*. No name conflict or side effect exists.

The second method for sharing information is using SHARED variables. Unlike parameters, SHARED variables do not undergo any name mapping. They may be scalars and/or arrays. Arrays are indicated by placing empty parentheses after their names. I will rewrite the last QuickBASIC subroutine to illustrate SHARED variables:

```
SUB Get.Sqrt(Square#, Root#) STATIC
' Second version with a SHARED variable
SHARED ErrorFlag%
```

```
    IF Square# >= 0 THEN
        ErrorFlag% = 0
        Root# = SQR(Square#)
    ELSE
        ErrorFlag% = 1
        Root# = -1
    END IF

END SUB
```

Notice that there are now two parameters and not three. The variable *ErrorFLag%* is accessible to the caller, as in:

```
QuickBASIC program to demonstrate SHARED variables

DO

    INPUT "Enter a positive number [0 to quit] ";N#

    IF INT(N#) = 0 THEN EXIT DO

    CALL Get.Sqrt(N#, X#)

    IF ErrorFlag% = 0 THEN
        PRINT "Square root = ";X#
    ELSE
        PRINT "Sorry! No negative numbers"
    END IF
    PRINT

LOOP

PRINT "Program ends"

END
```

In the above QuickBASIC program, the subroutine *Get.Sqrt* has *exported* the variable *ErrorFlag%* to the main program.

SHARED variables have their advantages and disadvantages. They are well suited to the following conditions:

1. Shortening the subroutine parameter list. How do you choose to put a variable in the SHARED or parameter lists? If the same information is communicated to the subroutine using a consistently named variable, then you may place it in the SHARED list.

2. Exporting variables to the main program and, more importantly, to other subroutines (more on this later).

The side effect of SHARED variables is that it perpetuates the "old" BASIC global variables syndrome. It takes as little as two subroutines sharing the same variable for different purposes to put the gremlins to work on your code! In addition to having two subroutines deliberately sharing the same variables, there is another similar problem. Consider the case of a subroutine using a variable that has been declared global as local! Fortunately, QuickBASIC has solved this problem by providing the STATIC declaration. Thus, to isolate a local variable from its *global twin*, place it in the list of STATIC variables. As the name implies, STATIC variables maintain the data between subroutine calls, as shown by the following program:

```
' QuickBASIC program to demonstrate STATIC variables

X = 0 ' Initialize global variable

FOR I = 1 TO 5
   X = X + 2
   PRINT X

   CALL Doo

NEXT I


SUB Doo STATIC

STATIC X

X = X + 1

PRINT "STATIC X = ";X

END SUB
```

When the above program runs, the following is displayed:

```
2
STATIC X = 1
4
STATIC X = 2
6
STATIC X = 3
```

```
STATIC X = 4
10
STATIC X = 5
```

Notice that we are able to maintain two separate variables with the name X, each at a different memory location.

STATIC variables may be arrays. They must be dimensioned immediately after the STATIC declarations AND must be erased before the subroutine ends. An unerased STATIC array generates a run-time error when the subroutine is called for the second time. The following program demonstrates this:

```
' QuickBASIC program to demonstrate STATIC arrays
DIM X(3)

FOR J = 1 TO 2
    FOR I = 1 TO 3
        X(I) = I
        PRINT X(I)
    NEXT I
    PRINT
    CALL Doo
NEXT J

SUB Doo STATIC
' make array X() and loop counter I static
STATIC I, X(1)
DIM X(3)

FOR I = 1 TO 3
    X(I) = I * 1000
    PRINT X(I)
NEXT I
PRINT
```

```
ERASE X ' remove the local array

END SUB
```

If the ERASE statement is removed, the above program will have a run-time error when subroutine *Doo* is called the second time. Notice that I have also declared the subroutine loop counter as STATIC. This illustrates an important practice of making your loop counters local. Most programmers use variables like *I, J, K*, and so forth, repeatedly. Making them STATIC ensures that two loops with the same control variables that are "connected" by a subroutine call do not interrupt (and corrupt) each other!

Turbo BASIC implements subroutines in a fashion similar to QuickBASIC but with the following differences:

1. Subroutines are recursive. If a subroutine is NOT declared STATIC, it may call itself.

2. Local subroutine variables may be declared LOCAL or STATIC. Turbo BASIC makes the explicit distinction between both types. If you want a local variable to maintain its values between subroutine calls, then you must use the STATIC declaration. By contrast, the LOCAL declaration simply isolates your local subroutine variable from its *global twin*. Values for LOCAL variables are placed on the stack and discarded once the subroutine returns to the caller. LOCAL and STATIC arrays in a subroutine must be erased before the subroutine returns.

The following example is a Turbo BASIC subroutine containing SHARED and LOCAL variables:

```
SUB Search.Array(X#(1), XSrch#, Index%) STATIC
' Search through an ordered array X() for XSrch#
SHARED Missing.Data#
LOCAL NData%, I%, Low%, Hi%

Index% = 0 ' pessimistic default value

Low% = LBound(X#(1))
Hi% = UBound(X#(1))

IF X#(Hi%) <= Missing.Data# THEN

   FOR I% = Low% TO Hi%
      IF X#(I%) <= Missing.Data# THEN EXIT FOR
   NEXT I%
```

```
      NData% = I% - Low%

   ELSE
      NData% = Hi% - Low% + 1
   END IF

   'no sense in searching an empty array
   IF NData% = 0 THEN EXIT SUB

   ' call recursive subroutine to perform binary search
   CALL Search(X#(), Low%, NData%, XSrch#, Index%)

   END SUB


   SUB Search(X#(1), First%, Count%, Srch#, Index%)
   ' recursive subroutine to search
   LOCAL Median%

   SELECT CASE Count%

      CASE <= 1
         IF X#(First%) = Srch# THEN Index% = First%

      CASE > 1
         Median% = First% + (Count% - 1) \ 2

         IF X#(Median%) = Srch# THEN
            Index% = Median%
         ELSEIF X#(Median%) < Srch# THEN
            Count% = Count% \ 2
            First% = First% + Count%
            CALL Search(X#(), First%, Count%, Srch#, Index%)
         ELSE
            Count% = Count% \ 2
            CALL Search(X#(), First%, Count%, Srch#, Index%)
         END IF

   END SELECT

   END SUB
```

In the first subroutine, *Search.Array*, the SHARED variable *Missing.Data#* is importing a global variable containing the numeric code for missing data. Notice that the parameter list of *Search.Array* does not contain an explicit count of the number of elements with meaningful data in array *X#()*. In most cases, arrays are NOT used to their fullest extent, since we overestimate their sizes to be safe. This creates a logical partition of the array: the first segment contains our data and the other segment contains garbage. To handle the garbage, I am assuming that the following technique is used: assign and update the 'unused' array elements with a single large negative number as a numeric code to indicate a vacant status. I am also assuming that the SHARED variable *Missing.Data#* imported from the main program contains that numeric code, and that all arrays used with subroutine *Search.Array* have been preconditioned with *Missing.Data#*. The *Search.Array* subroutine contains LOCAL variables to tackle the array size, FOR-NEXT loop, and the array bounds.

Subroutine *Search* is a recursive subroutine that essentially performs the search. Only one LOCAL variable is used to calculate the median index of a sub-array.

Looking at the two subroutines, you can carry out the following changes:

1. The Variables *Srch#* and *Index%* may be accessed as global variables instead of parameters. This is done by removing them from the parameter and argument lists and placing them in a SHARED declaration (one in each subroutine). While this may relieve the stack requirement for recursion, it makes the SHARED variable names the unique gateway for the data they communicate.

2. The array *X#()* may also be transformed into a SHARED variable. This, of course, makes the subroutines work exclusively with array *X#()*.

Both QuickBASIC and Turbo BASIC support the GOSUB, using a label to direct program flow. I have discussed the named subroutines first in order to illustrate their power, versatility, reusability, and superiority to GOSUB's. I recommend that the use of GOSUB's be restricted to very specific tasks involving many global variables.

In True BASIC the parameters of a subroutine may be any combination of scalar variables, arrays, and file channels. True BASIC supports internal and external subroutines, just as with functions. Internal subroutines share the variables of the main program and may be written without any parameters. By contrast, external subroutines rely on their parameters for a two-way data communication. The designers of True BASIC consider internal subroutines to be part of the same programming unit (a member of the family, if you will). By the same rule, external subroutines belong to another program unit, hence the stricter data interface to minimize side effects. Internal subroutines may be written with a full parameter list, just like external ones. However, the reverse is not true. Internal subroutines with full parameter lists can be used to test and prototype external subroutines.

The following True BASIC program contains the following subroutines:

1. *Get_Average1* is an internal subroutine with no parameters. It relies completely on data sharing to access data from the array *X()* and the scalar *Count*. The result is returned as the global variable *Average*.

2. *Get_Average2* is another internal subroutine that uses both data sharing and parameter passing to access data and returned results. I have written it so that the computed average is returned as a parameter.

3. *Get_Average3* is an external subroutine that relies on the parameter list to communicate information to and from the main program. Its arguments include a numeric array, the number of data points, and the returned average.

All three subroutines yield the same result for the average value. The program listing is shown below:

```
! True BASIC program to demonstrate internal and external
! subroutine and show the various levels of data interface

OPTION BASE 1
OPTION NOLET

DIM X(1)

DATA 2,3,4,7,9,3,4,5,2,8,5,1,2,3

Count = 0 ! initialize counter

DO WHILE MORE DATA

   INC Count
   MAT REDIM X(Count)
   READ X(Count)

LOOP


PRINT "CALLING SUBROUTINE Get_Average1"
CALL Get_Average1
PRINT "Mean = ";Average
PRINT

PRINT "CALLING SUBROUTINE Get_Average2"
CALL Get_Average2(Average)
PRINT "Mean = ";Average
```

```
        PRINT

        PRINT "CALLING SUBROUTINE Get_Average3"
        CALL Get_Average3(X(), Count, Average)
        PRINT "Mean = ";Average
        PRINT

        SUB INC_Count
        ! Increment Count by one

           Count = Count + 1

        END SUB


        SUB Get_Average1
        ! Internal subroutine with no explicit data interface
        ! Relies completely on data sharing.

           SumX = 0

           FOR I = LBound(X) TO UBound(X)
              SumX = SumX + X(I)
           NEXT I

           Average = SumX / Count

        END SUB

        SUB Get_Average2(Avrg)
        ! Internal subroutine with a data interface
        ! Relies partially on sharing X() and Count.

           SumX = 0

           FOR I = LBound(X) TO UBound(X)
              SumX = SumX + X(I)
           NEXT I

           Avrg = SumX / Count

        END SUB

        END

        SUB Get_Average3(X(), Count, Avrg)
        ! External subroutine that relies completely on
        ! parameters.

           SumX = 0

           FOR I = LBound(X) TO UBound(X)
              SumX = SumX + X(I)
```

```
    NEXT I
    Avrg = SumX / Count
END SUB
```

Library Development: The Big Picture

The ability to create libraries of BASIC routines is regarded as the most significant enhancement brought by the new wave BASICs. Functions and subroutines form the backbone of library development.

Each of the three BASICs supports BASIC libraries in a very different way. Unfortunately, while there is much in common among the library building blocks, the implemented mechanism for the new libraries is not compatible! Thus, I will discuss the libraries in each implementation separately.

QuickBASIC offers two new forms for BASIC library development: as a compiled user-library and as an included source code.

QuickBASIC supports compiled libraries that are produced as follows:

1. Create a QuickBASIC source code library containing subroutines only.

2. Compile into OBJ form.

3. Use the BUILDLIB.EXE utility by the following DOS command:

```
BUILDLIB <list of OBJ files>,<library name>
```

The list of OBJ files contains one or more files delimited by spaces. The library name is optional, with USERLIB.EXE as the default name. Thus, to create a SORTLIB.EXE from three files SORT.BAS, SEARCH.BAS, and TABLES.BAS, you execute the following steps:

1. Instruct the QuickBASIC compiler to generate SORT.OBJ, SEARCH.OBJ, and TABLES.OBJ from the source code.

2. Invoke BUILDLIB using the following command:

```
BUILDLIB SORT.OBJ SEARCH.OBJ TABLES.OBJ,SORTLIB.EXE
```

The compiled library is automatically used by the QuickBASIC compiler and incorporated into a BASIC program. The default library is USERLIB.EXE. To specify an alternate library, use the /l directive, followed by the library file name while invoking the QuickBASIC compiler from DOS. For example, to use the compiled library SORTLIB.EXE, you type the following from DOS:

```
QB TESTSORT.BAS /l SORTLIB.EXE
```

Compiled QuickBASIC libraries have the following advantages:

1. Software developers are able to distribute them in unreadable EXE forms.

2. They save on compiling time.

However, QuickBASIC libraries have the following limitations:

1. Only one compiled library can be used at a time. To overcome this limitation, always store the OBJ files that form the building blocks of your compiled library. This enables you to re-assemble your library and incorporate any sub-library you want. This means that USERLIB.EXE, the default library, is frequently customized to your needs.

2. They are limited to subroutines If your library contains functions or any other global variables, you must instead include the source code in your BASIC program.

3. QuickBASIC does not enforce any declaration regarding the compiled library used. It is a good practice to include comments that list the OBJ sub-libraries used.

The second type of BASIC library uses the $INCLUDE metacommand in QuickBASIC. Included files enable you to incorporate subroutines, functions, required declarations, and initializations. This is the kind of BASIC library that I will be using in the next chapter. While included library files reveal the source code, you may create special optimized versions. A copy of the original library file is edited to purge unused routines, yielding a custom-optimized included file.

Recall that functions must be declared before they are used in QuickBASIC. Included libraries with functions will most likely need to be placed at the beginning of the QuickBASIC application program.

In discussing QuickBASIC subroutines, I mentioned that subroutines may declare variables to be SHARED with the result of the program. QuickBASIC supports two additional types of variable sharing. The first uses a SHARED declaration in the main program to declare a variable to be global and accessible to lower level routines. In this case, SHARED variables are 'handed down' as opposed to being 'passed upward' by the subroutines. The second mechanism of global sharing uses the COMMON and SHARED declaration in the following manner:

```
COMMON SHARED /<blockname>/<list of variables>
```

If you have programmed in FORTRAN 77, the above should be very familiar. This declaration enables you to easily share long lists of variables and carry out selective sharing.

Turbo BASIC does not support separately compiled libraries. The only method for building BASIC libraries is to include their source code in a Turbo BASIC application program. You may access assembly language coded programs, but this is not part of building libraries strictly using BASIC.

The following program solves for the root of a single nonlinear equation using Newton's method. The heart of the root solver is the following NEWTON.BAS library:

```
' Turbo BASIC Library NEWTON.BAS
' Root solver Using Newton's method
SUB Newton(Guess#, Accuracy#, Max.Iter%, Diverge%) STATIC

LOCAL Diff#, H#, F1#, F2#, Iter%

Iter% = 0  ' Initialize iteration counter
Diverge% = 0  ' Initialize divergence flag

DO
    IF ABS(Guess#) > 1.0 THEN H# = 0.01 * Guess# ELSE H# = 0.01
    F1# = FNF#(Guess#)
    F2# = FNF#(Guess# + H#)
    Diff# = H# * F1# / (F2# - F1#)
    Guess# = Guess# - Diff#
    Iter% = Iter% + 1
    IF Iter% > Max.Iter% THEN Diverge% = 1
```

```
        LOOP UNTIL (ABS(Diff#) < Accuracy#) OR (Diverge% = 1)

    END SUB
```

The application program is listed below:

```
    ' Turbo BASIC program to use library NEWTON.BAS
    DEFDBL A-Z

    CLS

    ' define nonlinear function
    DEF FNF#(X#) = EXP(X#) - 3.0 * X#^2

    ' Include library used
    $INCLUDE "NEWTON.BAS"

    INPUT "Enter guess for root ";Guess : PRINT

    DO
        INPUT "Enter accuracy desired ";Accuracy : PRINT
    LOOP UNTIL (Accuracy < 1) AND (Accuracy > 1.0E-10)

    DO
        INPUT "Enter maximum iterations ";Max.Iter% : PRINT
        Max.Iter% = ABS(Max.Iter%)
    LOOP UNTIL Max.Iter% < 100

    ' call the library routine
    CALL Newton(Guess, Accuracy, Max.Iter%, Diverge%)

    IF Diverge% = 0 THEN
        PRINT "Root = ";Guess
    ELSE
        PRINT "Solution diverges at ";Guess;
        PRINT " after ";Max.Iter%;" iterations"
    END IF

    END
```

True BASIC supports two types of libraries. The first version of True BASIC implemented separate libraries only, while the second version introduced the more sophisticated modules. It is worth pointing out that True BASIC does not support an INCLUDE statement that you insert in a program. This is due to the fact that True BASIC libraries and modules make very adequate alternatives to included files.

True BASIC libraries are separate files that contain functions and subroutines. The library file must begin with the keyword EXTERNAL. The following features are available to True BASIC libraries:

1. Functions and subroutines may contain their own local functions and subroutines. No more than one level of nesting is allowed.

2. All the functions and subroutines in a library are accessible to the application programs using the library. The exception to this rule is the local nested routine.

3. A strict data interface is imposed, making parameter lists the only means of data communications.

4. There is no mechanism that enables library routines to share data hidden from the application program.

The following is the True BASIC library version of routine Newton·

```
EXTERNAL

SUB Newton(Guess, Accuracy, Max_Iter, Diverge)

' Include user-defined library of functions
LIBRARY "USERFUNC.TRU"
' select function F
DECLARE DEF F

LET Iter = 0
LET Diverge = 0

DO
    IF ABS(Guess) > 1 THEN
        LET H = 0.01 * Guess
    ELSE
        LET H = 0.01
    END IF

    LET F1 = F(Guess)
    LET F2 = F(Guess + H)
    LET Diff = H * F1 / (F2 - F1)
    LET Guess = Guess - Diff
    LET Iter = Iter + 1
    IF Iter > Max_Iter THEN LET Diverge = 1
```

```
LOOP UNTIL (ABS(Diff) < Accuracy) OR (Diverge = 1)

END SUB
```

Notice that in the above True BASIC library, subroutine *Newton* declares another library, USERFUNC.TRU, where all the user-defined functions are located. The USERFUNC.TRU may look like:

```
EXTERNAL

DEF F(X) = EXP(X) - 3 * X^2
```

The corresponding True BASIC application program is:

```
! Turbo BASIC program to use library NEWTON.BAS

CLEAR

! Declare used library
LIBRARY "NEWTON.TRU"

INPUT PROMPT "Enter guess for root ":Guess
PRINT

DO
    INPUT PROMPT "Enter accuracy desired ":Accuracy
    PRINT
LOOP UNTIL (Accuracy < 1) AND (Accuracy > 1.0E-10)

DO
    INPUT PROMPT "Enter maximum iterations ":Max_Iter
    PRINT
    Max_Iter = ABS(Max_Iter)
LOOP UNTIL Max_Iter < 100

! call the library routine
CALL Newton(Guess, Accuracy, Max_Iter, Diverge)

IF Diverge = 0 THEN
    PRINT "Root = ";Guess
ELSE
    PRINT "Solution diverges at ";Guess;
    PRINT " after ";Max_Iter;" iterations"
END IF

END
```

True BASIC modules offer a more sophisticated software engineering tool. The general structure of modules is:

```
MODULE <name>

PUBLIC   <list of variables declared global>
SHARE    <list of variable shared among module routines only>
PRIVATE  <list of routine not accessible outside the module>
DECLARE DEF <list of functions in the module>

<optional code for module initialization>

<code for functions and subroutines>

END MODULE
```

The PUBLIC declaration is used to list the names of scalar variables and arrays that are exported to client programs. This makes public variables global and accessible to all parts of the module as well as to the program that calls the module.

The PRIVATE declaration lists the functions and procedures that are local to the module. Compared to Modula-2, this is the reverse of the EXPORT list. All routines that are not listed as private may be called by client programs.

The DECLARE DEF statement indicates the names of all the functions defined inside the module.

The SHARE declaration lists the scalar variables and arrays that are accessible to all the module routines, but not to the client programs. They need not and should not appear in the routines' argument lists. The additional advantages of shared variables are as follows:

1. The support of data abstraction by permitting the access of data structures while hiding the details.

2. Shared variables are static: they retain their values between calls to routines in the module.

3. There is no conflict resulting from using the same variable names in a client program or shared variables in other routines.

Module initialization is carried out automatically before the program starts running. This implies that any PUBLIC variable involved in the initialization step must be assigned an initial value from within the module itself. This makes the initialization step independent of the client programs.

True BASIC libraries and modules differ in the following ways:

	Libraries	Modules
Support local routines	No	Yes
Communicate data using:		
Parameter lists	Yes	Yes
PUBLIC variables	No	Yes
SHARE variables	No	Yes
Initialization available	No	Yes

The following example involves sorting and indexing an array of strings. Certain choices were made in writing the program to demonstrate a number of features in the True BASIC modules. The PUBLIC statement indicates that the module declares the array *Item$()* and the array counter, *NData*, as globally accessible to the client programs. The SHARE declaration lists two arrays: the first is an array of pointers, the second is an index table. These arrays are shared within the routines of the module. The module initialization consists of assigning values to shared variables.

The *Sort* module consists of three exported routines. The first one ensures the adequate size of public array *Item$()* and the shared pointer array. The MAT REDIM statement is used to expand the arrays as needed. The size of the index table is independent of the size of array *Item$()*. It maps indices for the characters *A* through *Z* in upper case only.

Subroutine *Sort_and_Index* performs two tasks: it sorts the array *Item$()* using pointers and then sets up an index table. It calls the local subroutine *ShellSort* to perform a pointer-based Shell sort on array *Item$()*. The second local subroutine *Set_Index* is called to setup array *Table()*. The first entry encountered, starting with the letter *A*, is stored in location one of array *Table()*, that of *B* in location two, and so on. The table index is initialized with zeros.

Function *Search_Index* is used to search for a specific occurrence of a string and returns the index of array *Item$()*, or zero if not found. By using the index table, this function is able to zoom in on a feasible search range, thus enabling it to know where to start and stop.

```
MODULE Sort

PUBLIC Item$(100), NData ! Global array and variable

PRIVATE Set_Up, ShellSort ! Routines local to the module

DECLARE DEF Search_Index

SHARE Ptr(100), Table(26), FALSE, TRUE, HI_CHAR, MAX_DATA

!----------------- Module initialization ----------
let TRUE = 1
let FALSE = 0
let HI_CHAR = 26
let MAX_DATA = 100


!---------------- Routines definition ---------------

sub Set_Up
! Make sure that the arrays have enough space
IF NData > MAX_DATA THEN ! adjust array sizes if needed
   MAT REDIM Item$(NData)
   MAT REDIM Ptr(NData)
END IF

end sub

!----------------------------------------------------

sub Set_Index
! Build index table

MAT Table = ZER ! Initialize array

FOR Char_Index = 1 TO HI_CHAR
   let C$ = CHR$(64 + Char_Index) ! --> 'A' to 'Z'
   IF Char_Index = 1 THEN ! Start searching at the beginning
      let Index = 1
   ELSE
      ! Search backwards
      let Index = 1 ! assume worst case as default
      let J = Char_Index ! use J as copy of index I
      DO WHILE J > 1
         IF Table(J-1) > 0 THEN ! found good 'last index'
            let Index = Table(J-1)
            let J = 0 ! zero to exit loop
         ELSE
            let J = J - 1 ! one step backward
         END IF
      LOOP
   END IF
```

```
        let Found = FALSE

    DO WHILE (Index <= NData) AND (Found = FALSE)
        let J = Ptr(Index)
        let S$ = Item$(J)[1:1]
        IF S$ = C$ THEN ! Match found
            let Found = TRUE
            let Table(Char_Index) = Index ! store entry index
        ELSE
            let Index = Index + 1 ! increment index for more search
        END IF
    LOOP
NEXT Char_Index

end sub

!----------------------------------------------------

sub ShellSort
! Sort the pointers and keep Item$() unchanged

! Initialize pointers
FOR I = 1 TO NData
    let Ptr(I) = I
NEXT I

! Start the Shell sort
let Offset = NData
DO WHILE OFFSET > 1
    let Offset = INT(Offset / 2)
    DO
        let InOrder = TRUE
        FOR J = 1 TO (NData - Offset)
            let I = J + Offset
            IF Item$(Ptr(I)) < Item$(Ptr(J)) THEN
                let Tempo = Ptr(I)
                let Ptr(I) = Ptr(J)
                let Ptr(J) = Tempo
                let InOrder = FALSE
            END IF
        NEXT J
    LOOP UNTIL InOrder = TRUE
LOOP

end sub

!----------------------------------------------------

sub Sort_and_Index

CALL Set_Index
CALL ShellSort
```

```
end sub

!-----------------------------------------------------

def Search_Index(Datum$, Occur)
! Search for the n th Occur(ance) of Datum$ in array Item$()
! Use index table for faster search

let S$ = UCASE$(Datum$[1:1]) ! pick first character in Datum$
let Index = Ord(S$) - 64 ! Get index for search table
let Table_Index = Table(Index) ! get index entry
let Occurrence = ABS(INT(Occur)) ! assign Occur to local copy

IF Table_Index > 0 THEN ! Yes there is an entry!
   let Found = FALSE
   let More_Loop = TRUE

   DO WHILE (Table_Index <= NData) AND (Found = FALSE) AND (More_Loop = TRUE)
      let J = Ptr(Table_Index) ! store pointer in J
      IF Datum$ = Item$(J) THEN ! found a match
         let Occurrence = Occurrence - 1 ! Decrement occurrence count
         IF Occurrence < 1 THEN ! Yes, this the one we want!
            let Found = TRUE
            let Search_Index = Ptr(Table_Index)
         ELSE ! No! keep searching!
            let Table_Index = Table_Index + 1
         END IF
      ELSE ! Should we keep searching?
         IF S$ = Item$(J)[1:1] THEN   ! Yes
            let Table_Index = Table_Index + 1
         ELSE ! No, we are have gone too far and not found a match
            let More_Loop = FALSE ! stop looping
            let Search_Index = 0 ! search has failed
         END IF
      END IF
   LOOP

ELSE
   let Search_Index = 0
END IF

end def

END MODULE
```

The application program listing shows a client program that uses module *Sort*. It contains DATA statements that supply the array *Item$()* with some keywords from the Pascal language. The DO-WHILE loop is used to count the number of items in the DATA statements. A dummy string is used instead of the *Item$()*

array in the READ statement to avoid a possible array-bound-error. The RESTORE statement resets the DATA statement pointer. The program calls subroutine *Set_UP* in module *Sort*. This ensures that the public array *Item$()* and the pointer array (local to the module) have adequate space. The RESTORE statement is followed by a FOR-NEXT loop to READ the DATA statements into array *Item$()*. Module subroutine *Sort_and_Index* is invoked to prepare the index table. I included a DO-UNTIL loop to enable you to type in the Pascal keywords and find their location in array *Item$()*.

```
! PROGRAM Sort_and_Search

Library "Sort.mdl"
DECLARE DEF Search_Index
DECLARE PUBLIC Item$(), NData

CLEAR

let NData = 0
! Count items in DATA statements
DO WHILE MORE DATA
    let NData = NData + 1
    READ Dummy$ ! use dummy variable
LOOP

RESTORE ! DATA counter
CALL Set_Up ! Adjust Item$() if needed

! Read DATA into Item$(), now that we have enough space
FOR I = 1 TO NData
    READ Item$(I)
NEXT I

CALL Sort_and_Index ! Sort and prepare index table

let Occur = 1 ! Search for first occurrence
DO
    INPUT PROMPT "Enter sought keyword or [Q] to exit ? " : Search$
    let Search$ = UCASE$(Search$)
    IF Search$[1:1] <> "Q" THEN
z       PRINT Search$;" is item number ";Search_Index(Search$, Occur)
        PRINT
    ELSE
        PRINT
        PRINT "PRESS ANY KEY TO EXIT "
    END IF
LOOP UNTIL Search$[1:1] = "Q"
```

```
! DATA statements contain a list of Pascal keywords
DATA WRITE, READ, ASSIGN, SEEK, HI, LO, SQRT
DATA SQR, TAN, SIN, COS
DATA IFF, THEN, ELSE, WHILE, REPEAT, BEGIN
DATA FUNCTION, VAR, TYPE
DATA RECORD, SET, FOR, PROCEDURE, PROGRAM

END
```

The above example illustrates data hiding by using static shared arrays within the *Sort* module. The array of pointers and index table remain invisible to the client program. The limitation of the shared variables is that there can only be one instance of each variable. To use them as arguments, the module must include routines to store, recall, and manage the shared arrays to simulate and handle multiple instances.

The new version of True BASIC has implemented a powerful LOAD command. This enables you to load libraries and modules to extend the True BASIC language. Simply type LOAD (from the command mode), followed by the file name containing the library or module. For example, loading a library that implements hyperbolic functions enables you to type (in the command mode) PRINT SINH(2.4) and get a result. The loaded libraries and modules cut down on the time required to link programs with external libraries and modules.

True BASIC also support DO commands with the following general syntax:

```
DO <file name>,<argument>
```

You can invoke another program or execute an external subroutine. The DO command may be used to edit the text currently in the editor. This is performed by executing an external subroutine that has two parameters. The first is an array of strings, the second a scalar string parameter. For example, the following external library subroutine will convert the case of the text in the editor's window to upper-case or lower-case. If you look at the DATA statements, you may realize that I wrote the subroutine to handle QuickBASIC listings!

```
EXTERNAL

SUB AlterCase(Line$(),Arg$)

DATA LINE,INPUT,PRINT,USING,READ,RESTORE,STOP,END
DATA FOR,NEXT,WHILE,WEND,IF,THEN,ELSE,END IF,CASE, SELECT
DATA CALL,SUB,OPEN,CLS,INSTR(,CHR$(,ASC(,"DATA",STATIC
```

```
DATA OPTION,BASE,DEFINT,DEFDBL,DEFSNG,DIM,INT
DATA SIN,COS,LOG,SQR,TAN

DIM KWORD$(1)
CLEAR
RESTORE
LET NK = 1
DO WHILE MORE DATA
   READ KWORD$(NK)
   LET NK = NK + 1
   MAT REDIM KWORD$(NK)
LOOP

LET NK = NK - 1

LET CharSet$ = " .()[]:;#$%!^&*-+\/'"


FOR L = LBOUND(Line$) TO UBOUND(Line$)

   LET Ptr1 = 1
   CALL FirstChar(Line$(L),CharSet$,Ptr1,Ptr2)
   IF Ptr2 = 0 THEN ! Whole line is a series of continuous characters
      LET Found = 0
      FOR I = 1 TO NK
         IF POS(Line$(L),KWORD$(I)) > 0 THEN
            LET FOUND = 1
            EXIT FOR
         END IF
      NEXT I
      IF Found = 0 THEN
         LET Line$(L) = Line$(L)[1:1] & LCASE$(Line$(L)[2:MAXNUM])
      END IF
   ELSE
      DO WHILE (Ptr2 > 0) AND (Ptr2 > (Ptr1+1))
         LET A$ = Line$(L)[Ptr1:Ptr2-1]
         LET Found = 0
         FOR I = 1 TO NK
            IF POS(A$,KWORD$(I)) > 0 THEN
               LET FOUND = 1
               EXIT FOR
            END IF
         NEXT I
         IF Found = 0 THEN
            LET Line$(L)[Ptr1:Ptr2-1] = A$[1:1] & LCASE$(A$[2:MAXNUM])
         END IF

         LET Long = LEN(Line$(L))
         LET Ptr1 = Ptr2 + 1
         DO WHILE (POS(CharSet$,Line$(L)[Ptr1:Ptr1]) > 0) AND (Ptr1 <= Long)
            LET Ptr1 = Ptr1 + 1
         LOOP
         IF Ptr1 >= Long THEN EXIT DO
```

```
            CALL FirstChar(Line$(L),CharSet$,Ptr1,Ptr2)
      LOOP
   END IF
   PRINT Line$(L)
NEXT L


SUB FirstChar(L$,C$,Start,Index)
! local subroutine
LET Index = 0
FOR K = 1 TO LEN(C$)
   LET J = POS(L$,C$[K:K],Start)
   IF (Index < J) THEN LET Index = J
NEXT K

END SUB
```

3
BASIC Libraries

This chapter presents a set of libraries for the three BASIC implementations, along with sample or application programs. The libraries are:

1. TOOLBOX0: a general-purpose toolbox containing frequently used routines

2. TOOLBOX1: a library that extends the string manipulation capabilities of the BASICs

3. NUMANAL: a mini-library for numerical analysis; its routines perform numerical integration, differentiation, interpolation, solution of linear equations, and solving for the roots of polynomials

4. BASTAT: presents routines for basic descriptive statistics

5 LINREG: contains routines to perform simple linear regression with mathematical transformations

6. SORT: offers routines to perform the Shell sort and QuickSort methods; other library routines enable you to perform searches of sorted and unsorted arrays

7. SETS: implements a collection of routines to provide Pascal-like set manipulation functions and operations

8. LISTS: presents routines to implement ordered singly-linked lists

9. DOSFILE: contains routines that scan and filter files from a user-specified directory; other routines create batch files or perform multi-file editing

The BASIC application programs are written to consistently INCLUDE QuickBASIC and Turbo BASIC libraries. In QuickBASIC, you may compile libraries containing subroutines only into EXE form, as discussed in Chapter 2.

Library Module TOOLBOX0

PURPOSE: to provide a collection of general-purpose functions and subroutines that may be used in any application program. There are a few constants (in True BASIC they are implemented as functions with no parameters) to enable you make alterations more efficiently and more quickly. In True BASIC you may replace these functions with PUBLIC variables.

Due to some differences between True BASIC and the other two implementations, I have developed two versions of TOOLBOX0. While many of the routines are found in both, a number of routines are present in one version but not another. Thus, I will present two sets of routine documentations for the convenience of the readers.

Listings 3.1, 3.2, and 3.3 contain the source code for the QuickBASIC, Turbo BASIC, and True BASIC versions, respectively.

ROUTINES FOR QUICKBASIC AND TURBO BASIC

MAX.SCRN.COL% = 80 ' QuickBASIC
%MAX.SCRN.COL% = 80 ' Turbo BASIC

This constant defines the number of video screen columns for the IBM PC.

MAX.SCRN.ROW% = 25 ' QuickBASIC
%MAX.SCRN.ROW = 25 ' Turbo BASIC

This constant defines the number of video screen rows for the IBM PC.

TRUE% = -1 ' QuickBASIC
%TRUE = -1 ' Turbo BASIC

This constant defines the numeric code assigned to the logical TRUE.

FALSE% = 0 ' QuickBASIC
%FALSE = 0 ' Turbo BASIC

This constant defines the numberic code assigned to the logical FALSE.

Missing.Data! = -1.0E+300 ' QuickBASIC
DEF FNMISSING.DATA! ' Turbo BASIC

The QuickBASIC constant defines a numeric code for missing data. Since Turbo BASIC 1.0 does not support non-integer constants, a function is used.

DEF FNCharFromTo$(A$, First%, Last%)

This function enables QuickBASIC and Turbo BASIC to access substrings in a manner similar to the convention used by True BASIC.

The function parameter list is:

A$	string to be extracted from
First%	position of first character
Last%	position of last character

EXAMPLE:

```
FNCharFromTo$("San Francisco",5,8) returns "Fran"
```

DEF FNCharAt$(A$,I%)

Returns the character indicated by index *I%* from string *A$*. This function is equivalent to *MID$(A$,I%,1)*.

EXAMPLE:

```
FNCharAt$("BASIC",2) returns "A"
```

DEF FNUCASE$(A$)

This function is supplied for QuickBASIC versions that do not have a built-in function to convert a string into uppercase.

EXAMPLE:

```
FNUCASE$("London") returns LONDON
```

SUB INC(I%) STATIC

This subroutine increases its numeric argument by one.

EXAMPLE:

```
I% = 1
PRINT I%  ' prints 1
CALL INC(I%)
PRINT I%  ' prints 2
```

SUB DEC(I%) STATIC

This subroutine decreases its numeric argument by one.

EXAMPLE:

```
LET I% = 1
PRINT I%  ' prints 1
CALL DEC(I%)
PRINT I%  ' prints 0
```

SUB SINC(I%, J%) STATIC

Increases its argument *I%* by *J%*.

EXAMPLE:

```
LET I% = 1
LET J% = 5
PRINT I% ' prints 1
CALL SINC(I%,J%)
PRINT I% ' prints 6
```

SUB SDEC(I%, J%) STATIC

Decreases its argument *I%* by *J%*

EXAMPLE:

```
LET I% = 10
LET J% = 5
PRINT I% ' prints 10
CALL SDEC(I%,J%)
PRINT I% ' prints 5
```

SUB AppendStr1(S$, A1$) STATIC

This subroutine is used to append string *A1$* to *S$*.

EXAMPLE:

```
FIRST$ = "BOBBI "
LAST$  = "SHAMMAS"
NAME$ = ""
CALL AppendStr1(NAME$, FIRST$)
CALL AppendStr1(NAME$, LAST$)
PRINT NAME$ ' prints BOBBI SHAMMAS
```

SUB AppendStr2(S$, A1$, A2$) STATIC
SUB AppendStr3(S$, A1$, A2$, A3$) STATIC

These two subroutines are similar to *AppendStr1*, but they append more strings per call.

EXAMPLE:

```
FIRST$ = "NAMIR "
LAST$  = "SHAMMAS"
NAME$ = ""
CALL AppendStr2(NAME$, FIRST$, LAST$)
PRINT NAME$ ' prints NAMIR SHAMMAS
```

SUB Blank.Lines(M%) STATIC

This subroutine prints *M%* blank lines on the screen.

EXAMPLE:

```
INPUT "Enter number ";X
CALL Blank.Lines(3)
PRINT "X = ";X;"   X^2 = ";X^2
CALL Blank.Lines(4)
```

DEF FNSayTF$(N)

This function returns the string "TRUE" if its numeric argument is positive; otherwise, it returns the string "FALSE".

EXAMPLE:

```
Inventory% = Ordered% - Sold%
PRINT "Need to restock : ";FNSayTF$(Inventory%)
```

SUB Fill.Char.Lines(M%,C$) STATIC

This subroutine fills *M%* screen lines with the character *C$*. The character filling starts at the current screen row.

EXAMPLE:

```
CALL Fill.Char.Lines(2,"*") ! fills two lines with "*"
```

SUB   Fill.Pattern.Lines(Num.Lines%,M%,C$(1),Rpt%(1))   STATIC

This subroutine is similar to the previous one. It handles more complex screen-filling patterns.

Num.Lines%	number of lines to be filled with character patterns
M%	number of patterns per line
C$()	array containing the different character patterns
Rpt%()	array indicating the frequency of a corresponding character pattern

EXAMPLE:

```
DIM C$(10),Rpt%(10)
LET Num.Lines% = 2 ' fill patterns in two lines
LET M% = 3
LET C$(1) = " "
LET C$(2) = "-"
LET C$(3) = "|"
LET Rpt%(1) = 1
LET Rpt%(2) = 2
LET Rpt%(3) = 1
CALL Fill.Pattern.Lines(Num.Lines%,M%,C$(),Rpt%())
```

The above call prints two lines with the following pattern:

.--|.--|.--|.--|.--|.--|.--|.--|.--|. --|.--|.--|.--|.--|.--|

DEF   FNYesNo$(Msg$)

This function is used to prompt the user with a message assigned to parameter *Msg$*, and returns either "Y" or "N". This function is useful in more error-proof queries. Should you key in characters other than "Y" or "N" and press return, the function erases the input and reprompts you.

EXAMPLE:

```
Msg$ = "More calculations"
DO
    INPUT "Enter number ";X
    PRINT X;"^2 = ";X^2
LOOP UNTIL FNYesNo$(Msg$) = "N"
END
```

DEF FNNum.In.Range!(Msg$,Low!,Hi!)

This function prompts you for a numeric input that lies within the *(Low!,Hi!)* range. The limits are not displayed, unless they are part of the prompting message.

The following short program prompts you to enter a number between 1 and 1000. Any number outside the above range is rejected and you are prompted again. Your valid input is squared and the result displayed. This is followed by a prompt from the *YesNo$* function asking whether or not you want to perform more calculations.

EXAMPLE:

```
Msg1$ = "More calculations"
Msg2$ = "Enter number between 1 and 1000"
Low! = 1
Hi! = 1000
DO
    X! = FNNum.In.Range!(Msg2$, Low!, Hi!)
    PRINT X!;"^2 = ";X!^2
LOOP UNTIL FNYesNo$(Msg1$) = "N"
END
```

DEF FNInteger.In.Range%(Msg$,Low%,Hi%)

This function is very similar to the previous one, except that it returns an integer.

DEF FNNum.Outside.Range!(Msg$,Low!,Hi!)

This function prompts you for a numeric input that lies outside the (*Low!,Hi!*) range. The limits are not displayed, unless they are part of the prompting message.

The following short program prompts you to enter a number between 1 and 1000. Any number inside the above range is rejected and you are prompted again. Your valid input is squared and the result displayed. This is followed by a prompt from the *YesNo$* function asking whether or not you want to perform more calculations.

EXAMPLE:

```
Msg1$ = "More calculations"
Msg2$ = "Enter number (< 1 or > 1000)"
Low! = 1
Hi! = 1000
DO
    X! = FNNum.Outside.Range!(Msg2$, Low!, Hi!)
    PRINT X!;"^2 = ";X!^2
LOOP UNTIL FNYesNo$(Msg1$) = "N"
END
```

DEF FNInteger.Outside.Range%(Msg$,Low%,Hi%)

This function is similar to the above one, except that it returns an integer.

DEF FNOne.Line.Menu$(Menu.Message$,Options$,Line.Num%)

This function is useful in displaying a one-line menu and returning a valid choice. User entries that do not match valid selections will cause the function to reprompt for a correct entry.

Menu.Message$	string containing menu message and displaying the characters for valid choices
Option$	string containing the characters for valid choices
Line.Num%	row number on which the menu appears

EXAMPLE:

```
Menu$ = "A)dd  C)hange  D)elete  Q)uit"
Option$ = "ACDQ"
Line.Num% = 22
Answer$ = FNOne.Line.Menu$(Menu$,Options$,Line.Num%)
```

The above call displays the following message on row 22:

```
A)dd  C)hange  D)elete  Q)uit ?
```

Typing the letters A, C, D, or Q returns a valid choice.

SUB Center.Message(Msg$, Line.Num%) STATIC

This subroutine is among the most frequently used. As its name suggests, it centers the string *Msg$* on screen row *Line.Num%*.

EXAMPLE:

```
' Center the greeting string on the first screen row
CALL Center.Message("H  E  L  L  O",1)
CALL Center.Message("-------------",2)
```

DEF FNGet.String$(Msg$, Num.Char%, InUpperCase%, TruncateChars%)

This function is used to prompt for a string with a number of input-specifiers. These include:

1. restricting the maximum number of characters

2. whether or not to truncate the string if the number of characters exceeds the maximum specified

3. converting the input into upper case

The parameter list is:

 Msg$ string containing the prompt message

 Num.Char%   maximum number of input characters

 InUpperCase%   flag for uppercase conversion:
           if TRUE, input string is converted,
           else string is not converted

 TruncateChars%   flag for character truncation:
           if TRUE, input string is truncated if needed,
           else you are reprompted if string is too long

The following code fragment prompts you to enter your name. You are allowed to type a maximum of 30 characters. Exceeding this limit will cause the function to reprompt you for your name and will erase your previous input. Your name is not converted to upper case.

EXAMPLE:

```
Msg$ = "Enter your name"
Num% = 30
InUpperCase% = FALSE%
TruncateChars% = FALSE%
NAME$ = FNGet.String$(Msg$,Num%,InUpperCase%,TruncateChars%)
```

DEF FNGetXY.String$(X%, Y%, Msg$, Num.Char%, InUpperCase%, TruncateChars%)

This function is a variant of the last one. The additional parameters specify the row and column location where the input prompt appears.

SUB Put.String(X%,Y%,LeString$,Num.Char%, InUpperCase%,UseCR%)STATIC

This subroutine is used to display a string with the following capabilities and options:

1. specifying the screen row and column position where the string is displayed
2. displaying up to a maximum number of characters
3. displaying the string in upper case
4. terminating the string with a carriage return

The parameter list of the subroutine is:

X%	screen column position where the string is displayed.
Y%	screen row position where the string is displayed.
LeString$	displayed string.
Num.Char%	maximum number of characters allowed.
InUpperCase%	flag to indicate whether or not the string is displayed in upper case
UseCR%	flag used to signal whether or not to terminate the string with a carriage return

EXAMPLE:

```
NAME$ = "Don Johnson"
X% = 10
Y% = 5
N% = LEN(NAME$)
UseUpper% = TRUE
UseCR% = TRUE
CLS
' Displays DON JOHNSON at row 5 and column 10
CALL Put.String(X%,Y%,NAME$,N%,UseUpper%,UseCR%)
PRINT "Miami's Nice" ' appear on row 6
```

SUB PAUSE(Period) STATIC

This subroutine will cause a program to wait for *Period* seconds.

SUB Blink(A$, Speed) STATIC

This subroutine is used to blink the string *A$* for *Speed* seconds and then display the string in normal video.

EXAMPLE:

```
CALL Blink("Hello There",5) ! blink "Hello There" for 5 sec
```

ROUTINES FOR TRUE BASIC

DEF MAX_SCRN_COL = 80

This function defines a pseudo-constant that returns the number of video screen columns for the IBM PC.

DEF MAX_SCRN_ROW = 25

This function defines a pseudo-constant that returns the number of video screen rows for the IBM PC.

DEF TRUE = 1

This function defines a pseudo-constant that returns the numeric code assigned to the logical TRUE.

DEF FALSE = 0

This function defines a pseudo-constant that returns the numeric code assigned to the logical FALSE.

DEF Missing_Data = -1.0E+300

This function defines a pseudo-constant that returns the numeric code for missing data.

DEF MID$(A$,Index,Count)

This function mimics the *MID$()* function that is implemented in QuickBASIC and Turbo BASIC. The function must be used on the right-hand side of the assignment operator. The function examines the values of the index and count parameter and adjusts their values, if necessary.

EXAMPLE:

```
MID$("Washington",4,2) returns "hi"
MID$("BASIC",0,3) returns "BAS"
MID$("BASIC",100,3) returns "BAS"
MID$("PASCAL",100,0) returns "P"
```

DEF LEFT$(A$,Count)

This function mimics the *LEFT$()* function that is implemented in QuickBASIC and Turbo BASIC. The function examines the value of the count parameter and adjusts its value, if necessary.

EXAMPLE:

```
LEFT$("BASIC",3) returns "BAS"
LEFT$("PARIS",0) returns "P"
LEFT$("THE WHOLE THING",100) returns "THE WHOLE THING"
```

DEF RIGHT$(A$,Count)

This function mimics the *RIGHT$()* function that is implemented in QuickBASIC and Turbo BASIC. The function examines the value of the count parameter and adjusts its value, if necessary.

EXAMPLE:

```
RIGHT$("BASIC",3) returns "SIC"
RIGHT$("PARIS",0) returns "S"
RIGHT$("THE WHOLE THING",100) returns "THE WHOLE THING"
```

DEF CharAt$(A$,I)

Returns the character indicated by index *I* from string A$. This function is equivalent to *MID$(A$,I,1)* in QuickBASIC.

EXAMPLE:

```
CharAt$("BASIC",2) returns "A"
```

SUB INC(I)

This subroutine increases its numeric argument by one.

EXAMPLE:

```
LET I = 1
PRINT I ! prints 1
CALL INC(I)
PRINT I ! prints 2
```

SUB DEC(I)

This subroutine decreases its numeric argument by one.

EXAMPLE:

```
LET I = 1
PRINT I ! prints 1
CALL DEC(I)
PRINT I ! prints 0
```

SUB SINC(I, J)

Increases its argument *I* by *J*.

EXAMPLE:

```
LET I = 1
LET J = 5
PRINT I ! prints 1
```

```
CALL SINC(I,J)
PRINT I ! prints 6
```

SUB SDEC(I, J)

Decreases its argument *I* by *J*.

EXAMPLE:

```
LET I = 10
LET J = 5
PRINT I ! prints 10
CALL SDEC(I,J)
PRINT I ! prints 5
```

SUB AppendStr1(S$, A1$)

This subroutine is used to append string *A1$* to *S$*.

EXAMPLE:

```
LET FIRST$ = "NAMIR "
LET LAST$  = "SHAMMAS"
LET NAME$ = ""
CALL AppendStr1(NAME$, FIRST$)
CALL AppendStr1(NAME$, LAST$)
PRINT NAME$ ! prints NAMIR SHAMMAS
```

SUB AppendStr2(S$, A1$, A2$)
SUB AppendStr3(S$, A1$, A2$, A3$)

These two subroutines are similar to *AppendStr1*. They simply append more strings per call.

EXAMPLE:

```
LET FIRST$ = "NAMIR "
LET LAST$  = "SHAMMAS"
LET NAME$ = ""
CALL AppendStr2(NAME$, FIRST$, LAST$)
PRINT NAME$ ! prints NAMIR SHAMMAS
```

SUB Blank_Lines(M)

This subroutine prints *M* blank lines on the screen.

EXAMPLE:

```
INPUT PROMPT "Enter number ":X
CALL Blank_Lines(3)
PRINT "X = ";X;"   X^2 = ";X^2
CALL Blank_Lines(4)
END
```

DEF SayTF$(N)

This function returns the string "TRUE" if its numeric argument is positive; otherwise, it returns the string "FALSE".

EXAMPLE:

```
LET Balance = Income - Expenses
PRINT "In the black : ";SayTF$(Balance)
```

SUB Fill_Char_Lines(M,C$)

This subroutine fills *M* screen lines with the character *C$*. The character filling starts at the current screen row.

EXAMPLE:

```
CALL  Fill_Char_Lines(2,"*") ! fills two lines with "*"
```

SUB Fill_Pattern_Lines(Num_Lines,M,C$(),Rpt())

This subroutine is similar to the previous one, but handles more complex screen filling patterns.

Num_Lines   number of lines to be filled with character patterns

M	number of patterns per line
C$()	array containing the different character patterns
Rpt()	array indicating the frequency of a corresponding character pattern.

EXAMPLE:

```
DIM C$(10),Rpt(10)
LET Num_Lines = 2 ! fill patterns in two lines
LET M = 3
LET C$(1) = "_"
LET C$(2) = "-"
LET C$(3) = "|"
LET Rpt(1) = 1
LET Rpt(2) = 2
LET Rpt(3) = 1
CALL Fill_Pattern_Lines(Num_Lines,M,C$(),Rpt())
```

The above call prints two lines with the following pattern:

_--|_--|_--|_--|_--|_--|_--|_--|_--|_--|_--|_--|_--|_--|_--|

DEF YesNo$(Msg$)

This function is used to prompt the user with a message assigned to parameter *Msg$*, and returns either "Y" or "N". This function is useful in more error-proof queries. If you key in characters other than "Y" or "N" and press return, the function erases the input and reprompts you.

EXAMPLE:

```
LET Msg$ = "More calculations"
DO
    INPUT PROMPT "Enter number ":X
    PRINT X;"^2 = ";X^2
LOOP UNTIL YesNo$(Msg$) = "N"
END
```

DEF Num_In_Range(Msg$,Low,Hi)

This function prompts you for a numeric input that lies within the (*Low,Hi*) range. The limits are not displayed, unless they are part of the prompting message.

The following short program prompts you to enter a number between 1 and 1000. Any number outside the above range is rejected and you are prompted again. Your valid input is squared and the result displayed. This is followed by a prompt from the *YesNo$* function asking whether or not you want to perform more calculations:

EXAMPLE:

```
LET Msg1$ = "More calculations"
LET Msg2$ = "Enter number between 1 and 1000"
LET Low = 1
LET Hi = 1000
DO
    X = Num_In_Range(Msg2$, Low, Hi)
    PRINT X;"^2 = ";X^2
LOOP UNTIL YesNo$(Msg1$) = "N"
END
```

DEF Integer_In_Range(Msg$,Low,Hi)

This function is very similar to the previous one, except that it returns an integer.

DEF Num_Outside_Range(Msg$,Low,Hi)

This function prompts you for a numeric input that lies outside the (*Low,Hi*) range. The limits are not displayed, unless they are part of the prompting message.

The following short program prompts you to enter a number less than 1 and greater than 1000. Any number outside this range is rejected and you are prompted again. Your valid input is squared and the result displayed. This is followed by a prompt from the *YesNo$* function asking whether or not you want to perform more calculations:

EXAMPLE:

```
LET Msg1$ = "More calculations"
LET Msg2$ = "Enter number (< 1 or > 1000)"
LET Low = 1
LET Hi = 1000
DO
    X = Num_Outside_Range(Msg2$, Low, Hi)
    PRINT X;"^2 = ";X^2
LOOP UNTIL YesNo$(Msg1$) = "N"
END
```

DEF Integer_Outside_Range(Msg$,Low,Hi)

This function is similar to the above one, except that it returns an integer.

DEF One_Line_Menu$(Menu_Message$,Options$,Line_Num)

This function is useful in displaying a one-line menu and returning a valid choice. User entries that do not match valid selections will cause the function to reprompt for a correct entry.

Menu_Message$	string containing menu message and displaying the characters for valid choices
Option$	string containing the characters for valid choices
Line_Num	row number on which the menu appears

EXAMPLE:

```
LET Menu$ = "A)dd  C)hange  D)elete  Q)uit"
LET Option$ = "ACDQ"
LET Line_Num = 22
CALL One_Line_Menu$(Menu$,Options$,Line_Num)
```

The above call displays the following message on row 22:

```
A)dd  C)hange  D)elete  Q)uit ?
```

Typing the letters A, C, D, or Q returns a valid choice.

SUB Center_Message(Msg$, Line_Num)

This subroutine is among the most frequently used. It centers the string *Msg$* on screen row *Line_Num*.

EXAMPLE:

```
! Center the greeting string on the first screen row
CALL Center_Message("H  E  L  L  O",1)
CALL Center_Message("-------------",2)
```

DEF Get_String$(Msg$, Num_Char, InUpperCase, TruncateChars)

This function is used to prompt for a string with a number of input-specifiers. These include:

1. restricting the maximum number of characters

2. truncating the string if the number of characters exceeds the maximum specified

3. converting the input into upper case

The parameter list is:

Msg$	string containing the prompt message
Num_Char	maximum number of input characters

InUpperCase	flag for upper case conversion:
	    if TRUE, input string is converted,
	    else string is not converted

TruncateChars	flag for character truncation:
	    if TRUE, input string is truncated if needed,
	    else you are reprompted if string is too long

The following code fragment prompts you to enter your name. You are allowed to type a maximum of 30 characters. Exceeding this limit will cause the function to reprompt you for your name and will erase your previous input. Your name is not converted to upper case:

EXAMPLE:

```
LET Msg$ = "Enter your name"
LET Num = 30
LET InUpperCase = FALSE
LET TruncateChars = FALSE
LET NAME$ =
Get_String$(Msg$,Num,InUpperCase,TruncateChars)
```

DEF GetXY_String$(X, Y, Msg$, Num_Char, InUpperCase, TruncateChars)

This function is a variant of the last one. The additional parameters specify the row and column location where the input prompt appears.

SUB Put_String(X,Y,LeString$,Num_Char,InUpperCase,UseCR)

This subroutine is used to display a string with the following capabilities and options:

1. specifying the screen row and column position where the string is displayed

2. displaying up to a maximum number of characters

3. displaying the string in upper case

4. terminating the string with a carriage return

The parameter list of the subroutine is:

X	screen column position where the string is displayed
Y	screen row position where the string is displayed
LeString$	displayed string

BASIC LIBRARIES

Num_Char   maximum number of characters allowed

InUpperCase   flag to indicate whether or not the string is displayed in upper case

UseCR   flag used to signal whether or not to terminate the string with a carriage return

EXAMPLE:

```
LET NAME$ = "Don Johnson"
LET X = 10
LET Y = 5
N = LEN(NAME$)
UseUpper = TRUE
UseCR = TRUE
CLEAR ! Clear screen
! Displays DON JOHNSON at row 5 and column 10
CALL Put_String(X,Y,NAME$,N,UseUpper,UseCR)
PRINT "Miami's Nice" ! appear on row 6
```

SUB Blink(A$, Speed)

This subroutine is used to blink the string *A$* for *Speed* seconds and then display the string in normal video.

EXAMPLE:

```
CALL Blink("Hello There",5) ! blink "Hello There" for 5 sec
```

Listing 3.1 *QuickBASIC source code for library TOOLBOX0.BAS.*

```
'----------------------------------------------------------'
'                                                          '
'          General purpose module TOOLBOX0                 '
'              QuickBASIC version                          '
'                                                          '
' Version 1.1                                    2/87      '
' Copyright (c) 1987   Namir Clement Shammas              '
```

```
'                                                            '
'------------------------------------------------------------'
'-------------- local function ---------------
' Background character for the IBM PC
DEF FNBACKCHAR$ = CHR$(219)

'------------------------------------------------------------------
CONST MAX.SCRN.COL% = 80, MAX.SCRN.ROW% = 25
CONST TRUE% = -1, FALSE% = 0, Missing = -1.0E+30

'-------------------------
DEF FNCharFromTo$(A$, First%, Last%) = MID$(A$, First%, (Last% -
First% +1))

'-------------------------
DEF FNCharAt$(A$,I%) = MID$(A$,I%,1)

'-------------------------
DEF FNUCASE$(A$)
   F% = ASC("a")
   L% = ASC("z")
   Offset% = F% - ASC("A")
   FOR I% = 1 TO LEN(A$)
     B% = ASC(MID$(A$,I%,1))
     IF ((B% >= F%) AND (B% <= L%)) THEN MID$(A$,I%,1) = CHR$(B% - Offset%)
   NEXT I%
   FNUCASE$ = A$
END DEF

'-------------------------
SUB INC(I%) STATIC
    I% = I% + 1
END SUB

'-------------------------
SUB DEC(I%) STATIC
    I% = I% - 1
END SUB

'-------------------------
SUB SINC(I%, J%) STATIC
    I% = I% + J%
END SUB

'-------------------------
SUB SDEC(I%, J%) STATIC
    I% = I% - J%
END SUB

'-------------------------
SUB AppendStr1(S$, A1$) STATIC
    S$ = S$ + A1$
END SUB

'-------------------------
```

BASIC LIBRARIES

```
SUB AppendStr2(S$, A1$, A2$) STATIC
    S$ = S$ + A1$ + A2$
END SUB

'-------------------------
SUB AppendStr3(S$, A1$, A2$, A3$) STATIC
    S$ = S$ + A1$ + A2$ + A3$
END SUB

'-------------------------
SUB Blank.Lines(M%) STATIC
    ' print M% blank lines
    N% = M%                 ' assign to local value
    WHILE N% > 0
       PRINT
       N% = N% - 1
    WEND
END SUB

'-------------------------
DEF FNSayTF$(N%)
    ' SayTF$ = "TRUE" if N% > 0, otherwise SayTF$ = "FALSE"
    IF SGN(N%) > 0 THEN FNSayTF$ = "TRUE" ELSE FNSayTF$ = "FALSE"
END DEF

'-------------------------
SUB Fill.Char.Lines(M%,C$) STATIC
    ' Fill M% lines with character C$
    N% = M%                 ' assign to local value
    WhereY% = CSRLIN
    WhereX% = POS(0)
    LOCATE WhereY%,1
    WHILE N% > 0
       PRINT STRING$(MAX.SCRN.COL%,C$);
       N% = N% - 1
    WEND
END SUB

'-------------------------
SUB Fill.Pattern.Lines(Num.Lines%,M%,C$(1),Rpt%(1)) STATIC
    IF Num.Lines% < 1 THEN EXIT SUB
    N% = M%                 ' assign to local value
    WhereY% = CSRLIN
    WhereX% = POS(0)
    LOCATE WhereY%,1
    Low% = LBound(Rpt%)
    Hi%  = UBound(Rpt%)
    IF (Low% + M% - 1) < Hi% THEN Hi% = Low% + M% - 1
    FOR J% = 1 TO Num.Lines%
        FOR I% = Low% TO Hi%
            IF Rpt%(I%) > 0 THEN PRINT STRING$(Rpt%(I%),C$(I%));
        NEXT I%
        PRINT                   ' start a new line
    NEXT J%
END SUB
```

```
'-------------------------
DEF FNYesNo$(Msg$)
' return "Y" or "N"
    WhereY% = CSRLIN
    WhereX% = POS(0)
    A$ = " "
    WHILE (INSTR("YyNn",A$) = 0)
       LOCATE WhereY%, WhereX%
       PRINT STRING$((MAX.SCRN.COL%-WhereX%)," ");
       LOCATE WhereY%, WhereX%
       PRINT Msg$;
       INPUT  " (Y/N) "; A$
       IF LEN(A$) > 0 THEN A$ = LEFT$(A$,1)
    WEND

    IF A$ = "y" THEN A$ = "Y"
    IF A$ = "n" THEN A$ = "N"

    FNYesNo$ = A$

END DEF

'-------------------------
DEF FNNum.In.Range!(Msg$,Low!,Hi!)
    WhereY% = CSRLIN
    WhereX% = POS(0)
    A! = Low! - 1
    WHILE NOT ((A! >= Low!) AND (A! <= Hi!))
       LOCATE WhereY%, WhereX%
       PRINT STRING$((MAX.SCRN.COL%-WhereX%)," ");
       LOCATE WhereY%, WhereX%
       PRINT Msg$;
       INPUT  " "; A!
    WEND
     FNNum.In.Range! = A!
END DEF

'-------------------------
DEF FNInteger.In.Range%(Msg$,Low%,Hi%)
    WhereY% = CSRLIN
    WhereX% = POS(0)
    A% = Low% - 1
    WHILE NOT ((A% >= Low%) AND (A% <= Hi%))
       LOCATE WhereY%, WhereX%
       PRINT STRING$((MAX.SCRN.COL%-WhereX%)," ");
       LOCATE WhereY%, WhereX%
       PRINT Msg$;
       INPUT  " "; A%
    WEND
     FNInteger.In.Range% = A%
END DEF

'-------------------------
DEF FNNum.Outside.Range!(Msg$,Low!,Hi!)
    WhereY% = CSRLIN
    WhereX% = POS(0)
```

```
        A! = Low! + 1
        WHILE NOT ((A! < Low!) OR (A! > Hi!))
            LOCATE WhereY%, WhereX%
            PRINT STRING$((MAX.SCRN.COL%-WhereX%)," ");
            LOCATE WhereY%, WhereX%
            PRINT Msg$;
            INPUT  " "; A!
        WEND
         FNNum.Outside.Range! = A!
    END DEF

    '--------------------------
    DEF FNInteger.Outside.Range%(Msg$,Low%,Hi%)
        WhereY% = CSRLIN
        WhereX% = POS(0)
        A% = Low% + 1
        WHILE NOT ((A% < Low%) OR (A% > Hi% ))
            LOCATE WhereY%, WhereX%
            PRINT STRING$((MAX.SCRN.COL%-WhereX%)," ");
            LOCATE WhereY%, WhereX%
            PRINT Msg$;
            INPUT  " "; A%
        WEND
         FNInteger.Outside.Range% = A%
    END DEF

    '--------------------------
    DEF FNOne.Line.Menu$(Menu.Message$,Options$,Line.Num%)
        LOCATE Line.Num%,1
        A$ = " "
        WHILE INSTR(Options$,A$) = 0
            LOCATE Line.Num%,1
            PRINT STRING$(MAX.SCRN.COL%," ");
            LOCATE Line.Num%,1
            PRINT Menu.Message$;
            INPUT  " "; A$
            IF LEN(A$) > 0 THEN A$ = LEFT$(A$,1)
        WEND
         FNOne.Line.Menu$ = A$
    END DEF

    '--------------------------
    SUB Center.Message(Msg$, Line.Num%) STATIC
        LOCATE Line.Num%,1
        PRINT STRING$(MAX.SCRN.COL%," ");
        LOCATE Line.Num%, INT((MAX.SCRN.COL% - LEN(Msg$))/2)
        PRINT Msg$;
    END SUB

    '--------------------------
    DEF FNGet.String$(Msg$, Num.Char%, InUpperCase%, TruncateChars%)
        WhereY% = CSRLIN
        WhereX% = POS(0)
        L% = LEN(Msg$) + 2
        OK% = FALSE%
        WHILE OK% = FALSE%
```

```
            LOCATE WhereY%, WhereX%
            PRINT STRING$((MAX.SCRN.COL% - WhereX%)," ");
            LOCATE WhereY%, WhereX%
            PRINT Msg$ + STRING$(Num.Char%,FNBACKCHAR$);
            LOCATE WhereY%, WhereX% + L%
            INPUT   " ";LeString$
            OK% = TRUE%
            IF LEN(LeString$) > Num.Char% THEN
                        IF TruncateChars% = FALSE% THEN
                            OK% = FALSE%
                ElSE
                    LeString$ = LEFT$(LeString$,Num.Char%)
                END IF
            END IF
            IF (OK% = TRUE%) AND (InUpperCase% = TRUE%) THEN
                LeString$ = FNUCASE$(LeString$)
            END IF
        WEND
        FNGet.String$ = LeString$
    END DEF

    '--------------------------
    DEF FNGetXY.String$(X%,Y%,Msg$,Num.Char%,InUpperCase%,TruncateChars%)
        LOCATE Y%, X%
        L% = LEN(Msg$) + 2
        OK% = FALSE%
        WHILE OK% = FALSE%
            LOCATE Y%, X%
            PRINT STRING$((MAX.SCRN.COL% - X%)," ");
            LOCATE Y%, X%
            PRINT Msg$ + STRING$(Num.Char%,FNBACKCHAR$);
            LOCATE Y%, X% + L%
            INPUT   " ";LeString$
            OK% = TRUE%
            IF LEN(LeString$) > Num.Char% THEN
                        IF TruncateChars% = FALSE% THEN
                            OK% = FALSE%
                    ELSE
                        LeString$ = LEFT$(LeString$,Num.Char%)
                    END IF
            END IF
            IF (OK% = TRUE%) AND (InUpperCase% = TRUE%) THEN
                LeString$ = FNUCASE$(LeString$)
            END IF
        WEND
        FNGetXY.String$ = LeString$
    END DEF

    '---------------------------------------
    SUB Put.String(X%,Y%,LeString$,Num.Char%,InUpperCase%,UseCR%) STATIC
        L% = LEN(LeString$)
        IF Num.Char% < 1 THEN Num.Char% = L%
        IF Num.Char% < L% THEN LeString$ = LEFT$(LeString$,Num.Char%)
        IF InUpperCase% = TRUE% THEN LeString$ = FNUCASE$(LeString$)
        LOCATE Y%, X%
        PRINT LeString$;
```

```
        IF UseCR% = TRUE% THEN PRINT
END SUB

'----------------------------------------
SUB PAUSE(Period) STATIC
    Start = TIMER
    Finish = TIMER
    WHILE (Finish - Start) < Period
        Finish = TIMER
    WEND
END SUB

'----------------------------------------
SUB Blink(A$, Speed) STATIC
' blink string A$ at current cursor position
    X% = CSRLIN
    Y% = POS(0)
    FOR I% = 1 TO 10
        LOCATE X%,Y%
        PRINT A$;
        CALL PAUSE(Speed)
        LOCATE X%,Y%
        PRINT STRING$(LEN(A$)," ");
        CALL PAUSE(Speed)
    NEXT I%
    LOCATE X%,Y%
    PRINT A$
END SUB
```

Listing 3.2 *Turbo BASIC source code for library TOOLBOX0.BAS.*

```
'-----------------------------------------------------------'
'                                                           '
'            General purpose module TOOLBOX0                '
'                  Turbo BASIC version                      '
' Version 1.1                              2/87             '
' Copyright (c) 1987           Namir Clement Shammas        '
'                                                           '
'                                                           '
'-----------------------------------------------------------'

'-------------- local functions --------------
DEF FNBackChar$ = CHR$(219)      ' Background character for the IBM PC

'-----------------------------------------------------------
' Constants and pseudo-constants
%MAX.SCRN.COL = 80          ' for the IBM-PC
%MAX.SCRN.ROW = 25          ' for the IBM-PC
%TRUE = -1
%FALSE = 0
```

```
DEF FNMissing! = -1.0E+30

'--------------------------
DEF FNCharFromTo$(A$, First%, Last%) = MID$(A$, First%, (Last% - First% +1))

'--------------------------
DEF FNCharAt$(A$,I%) = MID$(A$,I%,1)

'--------------------------
SUB INC(I%) STATIC
    I% = I% + 1
END SUB

'--------------------------
SUB DEC(I%) STATIC
    I% = I% - 1
END SUB

'--------------------------
SUB SINC(I%, J%) STATIC
    I% = I% + J%
END SUB

'--------------------------
SUB SDEC(I%, J%) STATIC
    I% = I% - J%
END SUB

'--------------------------
SUB AppendStr1(S$, A1$) STATIC
    S$ = S$ + A1$
END SUB

'--------------------------
SUB AppendStr2(S$, A1$, A2$) STATIC
    S$ = S$ + A1$ + A2$
END SUB

'--------------------------
SUB AppendStr3(S$, A1$, A2$, A3$) STATIC
    S$ = S$ + A1$ + A2$ + A3$
END SUB

'--------------------------
SUB Blank.Lines(M%) STATIC
    ' print M% blank lines
    N% = M%                  ' assign to local value
    WHILE N% > 0
        PRINT
        N% = N% - 1
    WEND
END SUB

'--------------------------
DEF FNSayTF$(N%)
    ' SayTF$ = "TRUE" if N% > 0, otherwise SayTF$ = "FALSE"
```

BASIC LIBRARIES

```
            IF SGN(N%) > 0 THEN FNSayTF$ = "TRUE" ELSE FNSayTF$ = "FALSE"
END DEF

'-------------------------
SUB Fill.Char.Lines(M%,C$) STATIC
    ' Fill M% lines with character C$
    N% = M%                     ' assign to local value
    WhereY% = CSRLIN
    WhereX% = POS(0)
    LOCATE WhereY%,1
    WHILE N% > 0
       PRINT STRING$(%MAX.SCRN.COL,C$);
       N% = N% - 1
    WEND
END SUB

'-------------------------
SUB Fill.Pattern.Lines(Num.Lines%,M%,C$(1),Rpt%(1)) STATIC
     IF Num.Lines% < 1 THEN EXIT SUB
    N% = M%                     ' assign to local value
    WhereY% = CSRLIN
    WhereX% = POS(0)
    LOCATE WhereY%,1
    Low% = LowBound(Rpt%)
    Hi%  = UpBound(Rpt%)
    IF (Low% + M% - 1) < Hi% THEN Hi% = Low% + M% - 1
    FOR J% = 1 TO Num.Lines%
        FOR I% = Low% TO Hi%
            IF Rpt%(I%) > 0 THEN PRINT STRING$(Rpt%(I%),C$(I%));
        NEXT I%
        PRINT                   ' start a new line
    NEXT J%
END SUB

'-------------------------
DEF FNYesNo$(Msg$)
    ' return "Y" or "N"
    WhereY% = CSRLIN
    WhereX% = POS(0)
    DO
       LOCATE WhereY%, WhereX%
       PRINT STRING$((%MAX.SCRN.COL-WhereX%)," ");
       LOCATE WhereY%, WhereX%
       PRINT Msg$;
       INPUT  " (Y/N) "; A$
       IF LEN(A$) > 0 THEN A$ = UCASE$(LEFT$(A$,1).
    LOOP UNTIL (A$ = "N") OR (A$ = "Y")
     FNYesNo$ = A$
 END DEF

'-------------------------
DEF FNNum.In.Range!(Msg$,Low!,Hi!)
    WhereY% = CSRLIN
    WhereX% = POS(0)
     DO
        LOCATE WhereY%, WhereX%
```

```
         PRINT STRING$((%MAX.SCRN.COL-WhereX%)," ");
         LOCATE WhereY%, WhereX%
         PRINT Msg$;
         INPUT   " "; A!
    LOOP UNTIL (A! >= Low!) AND (A! <= Hi!)
    FNNum.In.Range! = A!

END DEF

'-------------------------
DEF FNInteger.In.Range%(Msg$,Low%,Hi%)

    WhereY% = CSRLIN
    WhereX% = POS(0)

    DO
         LOCATE WhereY%, WhereX%
         PRINT STRING$((%MAX.SCRN.COL-WhereX%)," ");
         LOCATE WhereY%, WhereX%
         PRINT Msg$;
         INPUT   " "; A%
    LOOP UNTIL (A% >= Low%) AND (A% <= Hi% )

    FNInteger.In.Range% = A%

END DEF

'-------------------------
DEF FNNum.Outside.Range!(Msg$,Low!,Hi!)

    WhereY% = CSRLIN
    WhereX% = POS(0)

    DO
         LOCATE WhereY%, WhereX%
         PRINT STRING$((%MAX.SCRN.COL-WhereX%)," ");
         LOCATE WhereY%, WhereX%
         PRINT Msg$;
         INPUT   " "; A!
    LOOP UNTIL (A! < Low!) OR (A! > Hi!)

    FNNum.Outside.Range! = A!

END DEF

'-------------------------
DEF FNInteger.Outside.Range%(Msg$,Low%,Hi%)

    WhereY% = CSRLIN
    WhereX% = POS(0)

    DO
         LOCATE WhereY%, WhereX%
         PRINT STRING$((%MAX.SCRN.COL-WhereX%)," ");
         LOCATE WhereY%, WhereX%
         PRINT Msg$;
```

BASIC LIBRARIES

```
            INPUT   " "; A%
        LOOP UNTIL (A% < Low%) OR (A% > Hi% )

        FNInteger.Outside.Range% = A%

    END DEF
    '-------------------------
    DEF FNOne.Line.Menu$(Menu.Message$,Options$,Line.Num%)

        LOCATE Line.Num%,1

        DO
           LOCATE Line.Num%,1
           PRINT STRING$(%MAX.SCRN.COL," ");
           LOCATE Line.Num%,1
           PRINT Menu.Message$;
           INPUT   " "; A$
           IF LEN(A$) > 0 THEN A$ = LEFT$(A$,1)
        LOOP UNTIL INSTR(Options$,A$) > 0

        FNOne.Line.Menu$ = A$

    END DEF
    '-------------------------
    SUB Center.Message(Msg$, Line.Num%) STATIC

        LOCATE Line.Num%,1
        PRINT STRING$(%MAX.SCRN.COL," ");
        LOCATE Line.Num%,INT((%MAX.SCRN.COL - LEN(Msg$))/2)
        PRINT Msg$;

    END SUB
    '-------------------------
    DEF FNGet.String$(Msg$, Num.Char%, InUpperCase, TruncateChars%)

        WhereY% = CSRLIN
        WhereX% = POS(0)
        L% = LEN(Msg$) + 2
        DO
           LOCATE WhereY%, WhereX%
           PRINT STRING$((%MAX.SCRN.COL - WhereX%)," ");
           LOCATE WhereY%, WhereX%
           PRINT Msg$ + STRING$(Num.Char%,FNBackChar$);
           LOCATE WhereY%, WhereX% + L%
           INPUT   " ";LeString$
           OK% = %TRUE
           IF LEN(LeString$) > Num.Char% THEN
              IF TruncateChars% = %FALSE THEN
                 OK% = %FALSE
              ELSE
                 LeString$ = LEFT$(LeString$,Num.Char%)
              END IF
           END IF
```

```
            IF (OK% = %TRUE) AND (InUpperCase% = %TRUE) THEN
               LeString$ = UCASE$(LeString$)
            END IF
      LOOP UNTIL OK = %TRUE
      FNGet.String$ = LeString$
END DEF

'----------------------------
DEF FNGetXY.String$(X%,Y%,Msg$,Num.Char%,InUpperCase%,TruncateChars%)

      LOCATE Y%, X%
      L% = LEN(Msg$) + 2
      DO
         LOCATE Y%, X%
         PRINT STRING$((%MAX.SCRN.COL - X%)," ");
         LOCATE Y%, X%
         PRINT Msg$ + STRING$(Num.Char%,FNBackChar$);
         LOCATE Y%, X% + L%
         INPUT   " ";LeString$
         OK% = %TRUE
         IF LEN(LeString$) > Num.Char% THEN
            IF TruncateChars% = %FALSE THEN
               OK% = %FALSE
            ELSE
               LeString$ = LEFT$(LeString$,Num.Char%)
            END IF
         END IF
         IF (OK% = %TRUE) AND (InUpperCase% = %TRUE) THEN
            LeString$ = UCASE$(LeString$)
         END IF
      LOOP UNTIL OK% = %TRUE
      FNGetXY.String$ = LeString$
END DEF

'-----------------------------------------
SUB Put.String(X%,Y%,LeString$,Num.Char%,InUpperCase%,UseCR%) STATIC

      L% = LEN(LeString$)
      IF Num.Char% < 1 THEN Num.Char% = L%
      IF Num.Char% < L% THEN LeString$ = LEFT$(LeString$,Num.Char%)
      IF InUpperCase% = %TRUE THEN LeString$ = UCASE$(LeString$)
      LOCATE Y%, X%
      PRINT LeString$;
      IF UseCR% = %TRUE THEN PRINT
END SUB
'-----------------------------------------
SUB PAUSE(Period) STATIC
      Start = TIMER
      Finish = TIMER
      WHILE (Finish - Start) < Period
         Finish = TIMER
      WEND
END SUB

'-----------------------------------------
SUB Blink(A$, Speed) STATIC
```

```
' blink string A$ at current cursor position
    X% = CSRLIN
    Y% = POS(0)
    FOR I% = 1 TO 10
        LOCATE X%,Y%
        PRINT A$;
        CALL PAUSE(Speed)
        LOCATE X%,Y%
        PRINT STRING$(LEN(A$)," ");
        CALL PAUSE(Speed)
    NEXT I%
    LOCATE X%,Y%
    PRINT A$
END SUB
```

Listing 3.3 *True BASIC source code for module TOOLBOX0.TRU*

```
MODULE TOOLBOX0

!--------------------------------------------------------------!
!                                                              !
!           General purpose module TOOLBOX0                    !
!                 True BASIC version                           !
! Version 1.1                                      2/87        !
! Copyright (c) 1987    Namir Clement Shammas                  !
!                                                              !
!                                                              !
!--------------------------------------------------------------!

DECLARE DEF TRUE, FALSE, YesNo$, Num_In_Range, Num_Outside_Range
DECLARE DEF One_Line_Menu$, Integer_In_Range, Integer_Outside_Range
DECLARE DEF MAX_SCRN_COL, MAX_SCRN_ROW, Missing_Data, SayTF$
DECLARE DEF BackChar$, CharAt$
DECLARE DEF Get_String$, GetXY_String$
DECLARE DEF MID$, LEFT$, RIGHT$

PRIVATE BackChar$

!-------------- local functions --------------
DEF BackChar$ = CHR$(219)     ! Background character for the IBM PC

!--------------------------------------------------------------
DEF MAX_SCRN_COL = 80        ! for the IBM-PC
DEF MAX_SCRN_ROW = 25        ! for the IBM-PC
DEF TRUE = 1
DEF FALSE = 0
DEF Missing_Data = -1.0E+300
```

```
!------------------------
DEF MID$(A$,Index,Count)
! similar to BASICA MID$() function

LET L = LEN(A$)
IF (Index < 1) OR (Index > L) THEN LET Index = 1
IF Count < 1 THEN LET Count = 1
IF (Index + Count - 1) > L THEN LET Count = L - Index + 1
LET MID$ = A$[Index:(Index+Count-1)]
END DEF

!------------------------
DEF LEFT$(A$,Count)
! similar to BASICA LEFT$() function

LET L = LEN(A$)
IF Count < 1 THEN LET Count = 1
IF Count > L THEN LET Count = L
LET LEFT$ = A$[1:Count]

END DEF

!------------------------
DEF RIGHT$(A$,Count)
! similar to BASICA RIGHT$() function
LET L = LEN(A$)
IF Count < 1 THEN LET Count = 1
IF Count > L THEN LET Count = L
LET RIGHT$ = A$[(L-Count+1):L]

END DEF

!------------------------
DEF CharAt$(A$,I)
LET CharAt$ = A$[I:I]
END DEF

!------------------------
SUB INC(I)
LET I = I + 1
END SUB

!------------------------
SUB DEC(I)
LET I = I - 1
END SUB

!------------------------
SUB SINC(I, J)
LET I = I + J
END SUB

!------------------------
SUB SDEC(I, J)
LET I = I - J
END SUB
```

```
!------------------------
SUB AppendStr1(S$, A1$)
LET S$ = S$ & A1$
END SUB

!------------------------
SUB AppendStr2(S$, A1$, A2$)
LET S$ = S$ & A1$ & A2$
END SUB

!------------------------
SUB AppendStr3(S$, A1$, A2$, A3$)
LET S$ = S$ & A1$ & A2$ & A3$
END SUB

!------------------------
SUB Blank_Lines(M)
! print M blank lines

LET N = M                  ! assign to local value

DO WHILE N > 0
   PRINT
   LET N = N - 1
LOOP

END SUB

!------------------------
DEF SayTF$(N)
! SayTF$ = "TRUE" if N > 0, otherwise SayTF$ = "FALSE"
IF SGN(N) > 0 THEN LET SayTF$ = "TRUE" ELSE LET SayTF$ = "FALSE"
END DEF

!------------------------
SUB Fill_Char_Lines(M,C$)
! Fill M lines with character C$

LET N = M                  ! assign to local value
ASK CURSOR WhereY, WhereX
SET CURSOR WhereY,1

DO WHILE N > 0
   PRINT REPEAT$(C$,MAX_SCRN_COL);
   LET N = N - 1
LOOP

END SUB

!------------------------
SUB Fill_Pattern_Lines(Num_Lines,M,C$(),Rpt())

IF Num_Lines < 1 THEN EXIT SUB
LET N = M                  ! assign to local value
ASK CURSOR WhereY, WhereX
```

```
    SET CURSOR WhereY,1
    LET Low = Lbound(Rpt)
    LET Hi = UBound(Rpt)
    IF (Low + M - 1) < Hi THEN LET Hi = Low + M - 1

    FOR J = 1 TO Num_Lines
        FOR I = Low TO Hi
            IF Rpt(I) > 0 THEN PRINT REPEAT$(C$(I),Rpt(I));
        NEXT I
        PRINT                  ! start a new line
    NEXT J

END SUB

!------------------------
DEF YesNo$(Msg$)
! return "Y" or "N"

ASK CURSOR WhereY, WhereX

DO
   SET CURSOR WhereY, WhereX
   PRINT REPEAT$(" ",(MAX_SCRN_COL-WhereX));
   SET CURSOR WhereY, WhereX
   PRINT Msg$;
   INPUT PROMPT " (Y/N) ? ": A$
   LET A$ = UCASE$(A$[1:1])
LOOP UNTIL (A$ = "N") OR (A$ = "Y")

LET YesNo$ = A$

END DEF

!--------------------------
DEF Num_In_Range(Msg$,Low,Hi)

ASK CURSOR WhereY, WhereX

DO
   SET CURSOR WhereY, WhereX
   PRINT REPEAT$(" ",(MAX_SCRN_COL-WhereX));
   SET CURSOR WhereY, WhereX
   PRINT Msg$;
   INPUT PROMPT " : ": A
LOOP UNTIL (A >= Low) AND (A <= Hi )

LET Num_In_Range = A

END DEF

!------------------------
DEF Integer_In_Range(Msg$,Low,Hi)

ASK CURSOR WhereY, WhereX

DO
```

BASIC LIBRARIES

```
         SET CURSOR WhereY, WhereX
         PRINT REPEAT$(" ",(MAX_SCRN_COL-WhereX));
         SET CURSOR WhereY, WhereX
         PRINT Msg$;
         INPUT PROMPT " : ": A
         LET A = INT(A)
   LOOP UNTIL (A >= Low) AND (A <= Hi )

   LET Integer_In_Range = A

   END DEF

   !--------------------------
   DEF Num_Outside_Range(Msg$,Low,Hi)

   ASK CURSOR WhereY, WhereX

   DO
         SET CURSOR WhereY, WhereX
         PRINT REPEAT$(" ",(MAX_SCRN_COL-WhereX));
         SET CURSOR WhereY, WhereX.
         PRINT Msg$;
         INPUT PROMPT " : ": A
   LOOP UNTIL (A < Low) OR (A > Hi )

   LET Num_Outside_Range = A

   END DEF

   !--------------------------
   DEF Integer_Outside_Range(Msg$,Low,Hi)

   ASK CURSOR WhereY, WhereX

   DO
         SET CURSOR WhereY, WhereX
         PRINT REPEAT$(" ",(MAX_SCRN_COL-WhereX));
         SET CURSOR WhereY, WhereX
         PRINT Msg$;
         INPUT PROMPT " : ": A
         LET A = INT(A)
   LOOP UNTIL (A < Low) OR (A > Hi )

   LET Integer_Outside_Range = A

   END DEF

   !--------------------------
   DEF One_Line_Menu$(Menu_Message$,Options$,Line_Num)

   SET CURSOR Line_Num,1

   DO
         SET CURSOR Line_Num,1
         PRINT REPEAT$(" ",(MAX_SCRN_COL));
         SET CURSOR Line_Num,1
```

```
      PRINT Menu_Message$;
      INPUT PROMPT " ? ": A$
      LET A$ = UCASE$(A$[1:1])
LOOP UNTIL POS(Options$,A$) > 0

LET One_Line_Menu$ = A$

END DEF

!--------------------------
SUB Center_Message(Msg$, Line_Num)

SET CURSOR Line_Num,1
PRINT REPEAT$(" ",MAX_SCRN_COL);
SET CURSOR Line_Num,INT((MAX_SCRN_COL - LEN(Msg$))/2)
PRINT Msg$;

END SUB

!--------------------------
DEF Get_String$(Msg$, Num_Char, InUpperCase, TruncateChars)

ASK CURSOR WhereY, WhereX
LET Msg$ = Msg$ & " ? "
LET L = LEN(Msg$)

DO
   SET CURSOR WhereY, WhereX
   PRINT REPEAT$(" ",(MAX_SCRN_COL - WhereX));
   SET CURSOR WhereY, WhereX
   PRINT Msg$ & REPEAT$(BackChar$,Num_Char);
   SET CURSOR WhereY, WhereX + L
   INPUT PROMPT "":LeString$
   LET OK = TRUE
   IF LEN(LeString$) > Num_Char THEN
      IF TruncateChars = FALSE THEN
         LET OK = FALSE
      ELSE
         LET LeString$ = LeString$[1:Num_Char]
      END IF
   END IF
   IF (OK = TRUE) AND (InUpperCase = TRUE) THEN
      LET LeString$ = UCASE$(LeString$)
   END IF
LOOP UNTIL OK = TRUE

LET Get_String$ = LeString$

END DEF

!--------------------------
DEF GetXY_String$(X, Y, Msg$, Num_Char, InUpperCase, TruncateChars)

SET CURSOR Y, X
LET Msg$ = Msg$ & " ? "
LET L = LEN(Msg$)
```

```
    DO
       SET CURSOR Y, X
       PRINT REPEAT$(" ",(MAX_SCRN_COL - X));
       SET CURSOR Y, X
       PRINT Msg$ & REPEAT$(BackChar$,Num_Char);
       SET CURSOR Y, X + L
       INPUT PROMPT "":LeString$
       LET OK = TRUE
       IF LEN(LeString$) > Num_Char THEN
          IF TruncateChars = FALSE THEN
             LET OK = FALSE
          ELSE
             LET LeString$ = LeString$[1:Num_Char]
          END IF
       END IF
       IF (OK = TRUE) AND (InUpperCase = TRUE) THEN
          LET LeString$ = UCASE$(LeString$)
       END IF
    LOOP UNTIL OK = TRUE

    LET GetXY_String$ = LeString$

END DEF

!----------------------------------------
SUB Put_String(X,Y,LeString$,Num_Char,InUpperCase,UseCR)

LET L = LEN(LeString$)
IF Num_Char < 1 THEN LET Num_Char = L
IF Num_Char < L THEN LET LeString$ = LeString$[1:Num_Char]
IF InUpperCase = TRUE THEN LET LeString$ = UCASE$(LeString$)
SET CURSOR Y, X
PRINT LeString$;
IF UseCR = TRUE THEN PRINT

END SUB

!----------------------------------------
SUB Blink(A$, Speed)
! blink string A$ at current cursor position
ASK CURSOR X,Y

FOR I = 1 TO 10
   SET CURSOR X,Y
   PRINT A$;
   CALL Wait(Speed)
   SET CURSOR X,Y
   PRINT REPEAT$(" ",LEN(A$));
   CALL Wait(Speed)
NEXT I

SET CURSOR X,Y
PRINT A$

END SUB
```

END MODULE

Library Module TOOLBOX1

PURPOSE: to provide a collection of routines for string manipulation. The library contains two sets of routines. The first offers string/character manipulation tools that extend the built-in routines found in the BASIC implementations. The second set attempts to emulate a number of special string functions found in the REXX language. These routines are *word* oriented and enable you to pick, insert, delete, and find words in a string of words.

Listings 3.4, 3.5, and 3.6 contain the source code for the QuickBASIC, Turbo BASIC, and True BASIC versions, respectively.

ROUTINES

The following is a list of headings for function and subroutine definitions borrowed from the QuickBASIC listing. They are identical to those of Turbo BASIC. However, they contain minor syntactical differences compared to those of True BASIC, including:

1. function names in True BASIC do not have to begin with the letters *FN*

2. subroutines in True BASIC need no STATIC declarations

DEF FNPadLeft$(S$, C$, L%)
DEF   PadLeft$(S$, C$, L) ! True BASIC

This function returns a string *S$* with *L* number of *C$* characters padded to its left. If *C$* is a multi-character string, only the first character is used for padding.

EXAMPLE:

```
FNPadLeft$("Hello there","-",5) returns "-----Hello there"
FNPadLeft$("DDJ","+",0) returns "+DDJ"
FNPadLeft$("London","<>",2) returns "<<London"
```

DEF FNPadRight$(S$, C$, L%)
DEF   PadRight$(S$, C$, L) ! True BASIC

This function returns a string *S$* with *L* number of *C$* characters padded to its right. If *C$* is a multi-character string, only the first character is used for padding.

EXAMPLE:

```
FNPadRightt$("Hello there","-",5) returns "Hello there-----"
FNPadRight$("DDJ","+",0) returns "DDJ+"
FNPadRight$("London","<>",2) returns "London<<"
```

DEF FNPadCenter$(S$, C$, L%, Index%)
DEF   PadCenter$(S$, C$, L, Index) ! True BASIC

This function returns a string that is padded in the middle. The parameter *Index* specifies the starting location where *L* numbers of *C$* characters are padded. If *C$* is a multi-character string, only the first character is used for padding. If the *Index* parameter contains a value equal or greater than the length of string *S$*, a blank string is returned. If the *Index* parameter contains a value less than one, the function adjusts its value to two.

EXAMPLE:

```
FNPadCenter$("Hi there",".",2,3) returns "Hi .. there"
FNPadCenter$("Hi there",".",2,2) returns "H..i there"
FNPadCenter$("Hi there",".",2,0) returns "H..i there"
FNPadCenter$("Hi there",".",2,100) returns ""
```

DEF FNPadEnds$(S$, C$, L%)
DEF   PadEnds$(S$, C$, L) ! True BASIC

This function returns a string composed of *S$* padded at both ends. At each end, *L* number of *C$* characters are padded. If *C$* is a multi-character string, only the first character is used for padding.

EXAMPLE:

```
FNPadEnds$("Hello","-",3) returns "---Hello---"
FNPadEnds$("Hello","<-|",3) returns "<<<Hello<<<"
FNPadEnds$("Hello","-",0) returns "-Hello-"
```

SUB DelLeft(S$, C$, KillC%) STATIC
SUB DelLeft(S$, C$, KillC) ! True BASIC

This subroutine scans string *S$* from left to right, seeking the first occurrence of character *C$*. If a match with *C$* is found, all characters to the left of *C$* are deleted. As for the fate of the character *C$* located in the string *S$*, a numeric *flag KillC* is used to decide whether or not it is deleted. If *KillC* is NOT zero, *C$* is deleted. If *C$* is a multi-character string, it is truncated to one character.

EXAMPLE:

```
S1$ = "------->Hello there"
S2$ = S1$ : C$ = ">"
CALL DelLeft(S$1, C$, 1)
PRINT S1$ ' displays "Hello there"
CALL DelLeft(S$2, C$, 0)
PRINT S2$ ' displays ">Hello there"
```

SUB DelRight(S$, C$, KillC%) STATIC
SUB DelRight(S$, C$, KillC) ! True BASIC

This subroutine scans string *S$* from right to left, seeking the first occurrence of character *C$*. If a match with *C$* is found, all characters to the right of *C$* are deleted. As for the fate of the character *C$* located in string *S$*, a numeric flag *KillC* is used to decide whether or not it is deleted. If *KillC* is NOT zero, *C$* is deleted. If *C$* is a multi-character string, it is truncated to one character.

EXAMPLE:

```
S1$ = "Enter Number>--------"
S2$ = S1$ : C$ = ">"
CALL DelLeft(S$1, C$, 1)
PRINT S1$ ' displays "Enter Number"
CALL DelLeft(S$2, C$, 0)
PRINT S2$ ' displays "Enter Number>"
```

SUB LeftTrim(S$) STATIC
SUB LeftTrim(S$) ! True BASIC

This subroutine trims the leftmost spaces from string *S$*. True BASIC has a built-in *LTRIM$()* function for the same purpose. For the sake of library compatibility, a True BASIC version of the subroutine is still implemented using the *RTRIM$()* function.

EXAMPLE:

```
S$ = "          Trencer Spacy"
CALL LeftTrim(S$)
PRINT S$  ' displays "Trencer Spacy"
```

SUB RightTrim(S$) STATIC
SUB RightTrim(S$) ! True BASIC

This subroutine trims the rightmost spaces from string *S$*. True BASIC has a built-in *RTRIM$()* function for the same purpose. For the sake of library compatibility, a True BASIC version of the subroutine is still implemented using the *LTRIM$()* function.

EXAMPLE:

```
S$ = "Trencer Spacy          "
CALL RightTrim(S$)
PRINT S$  ' displays "Trencer Spacy"
```

SUB RemoveStr(S$, SubStr$) STATIC
SUB RemoveStr(S$, SubStr$) ! True BASIC

This subroutine removes all occurrences of subtring *SubStr$* from string *S$*.

EXAMPLE:

```
S$ = "1234hi5123hi45123hi4512345"
SubStr$ = "hi"
CALL RemoveStr(S$, SubStr$)
PRINT S$  ' displays "12345123451234512345"
```

SUB RemoveCharRange(S$, FC$, LC$) STATIC
SUB RemoveCharRange(S$, FC$, LC$) ! True BASIC

This subroutine removes all the characters in string *S$* whose ASCII code number lies within the range of the codes for characters *FC$* and *LC$*.

EXAMPLE:

```
' Remove digits from a strings
FC$ = "0" : LC$ = "9"
S$ = "hhh123jjj456nnn7890ppp"
CALL RemoveCharRange(S$, FC$, LC$)
PRINT S$ ' displays "hhhjjjnnnppp"

' Remove lower case letters
FC$ = "a" : LC$ = "z"
S$ = "SUNday MONday TUEsday"
CALL RemoveCharRange(S$, FC$, LC$)
PRINT S$ ' displays "SUN MON TUE"

' Remove a few uppercase letters
S$ = "HELLO THERE"
CALL RemoveCharRange(S$, "I", "O")
PRINT S$ ' displays "HE THERE"
```

SUB TypeOverStr(S$, SubStr$, Index%) STATIC
SUB TypeOverStr(S$, SubStr$, Index) ! True BASIC

This subroutine overwrites the contents of string *S$* with the smaller substring, *SubStr$*, starting at character *Index*. The substring is truncated, if necessary, to prevent *S$* from increasing in length. The subroutine is exited without any action taken on *S$* if:

1. the character index lies outside the length of string *S$*

2. the substring is a null string

3. the substring *SubStr$* is larger than the string *S$*

EXAMPLE:

```
S$ = "Hello John Doe"
SS$ = "Carl"
I% = INSTR(S$," ") + 1
```

```
CALL TypeOverStr(S$, SS$, I%)
PRINT S$ ' displays "Hello Carl Doe"
```

SUB ReplaceStr(S$, SubStr$, Index%, C$) STATIC
SUB ReplaceStr(S$, SubStr$, Index, C$) ! True BASIC

This subroutine replaces all occurrences of character *C$* in string *S$* with the substring *SubStr$*. The action of the subroutine starts at the character count *Index*. The substring *SubStr$* is not limited to one character. If *C$* is a multi-character string, it is truncated to one character. The subroutine is exited and no action is taken if the value passed by *Index* is greater than the length of string *S$*.

EXAMPLE:

```
' add spaces around the four basic math operators
S$ = "(X+Y*Z)*X+Y/(Z-X)"
CALL ReplaceStr(S$," + ",1,"+")
CALL ReplaceStr(S$," - ",1,"-")
CALL ReplaceStr(S$," * ",1,"*")
CALL ReplaceStr(S$," / ",1,"/")
PRINT S$ ' displays "(X + Y * Z) * X + Y / (Z - X)"
```

SUB ReplaceChar(S$, OldChar$, NewChar$, Start%) STATIC
SUB ReplaceChar(S$, OldChar$, NewChar$, Start) ! True BASIC

This subroutine scans string *S$*, replacing every occurrence of character *OldChar$* with *NewChar$*. The string processing begins at character *Start*. The subroutine is exited without processing string *S$* if:

1. either *OldChar$* or *NewChar$* is a null string

2. parameter *Start* is greater than the length of string *S$*

If either *OldChar$* or *NewChar$* contain more than one character, they are truncated to a single character string.

EXAMPLE:

```
S$ = "1234567890.1234567890."
CALL ReplaceChar(S$, ".", "|", 1)
PRINT S$ ' displays "1234567890|1234567890|"
```

```
CALL ReplaceChar(S$, "|->", ".", 1)
PRINT S$ ' displays "1234567890.1234567890."

' the following call does not alter S$ because 100 > LEN(S$)
CALL ReplaceChar(S$, ".", "|", 100)
PRINT S$ ' displays "1234567890.1234567890."
```

SUB ReplaceCharRange(S$, FirstChar$, LastChar$, NewChar$, Start%) STATIC

SUB ReplaceCharRange(S$, FirstChar$, LastChar$, NewChar$, Start)

This subroutine is similar to *ReplaceChar*, except that the character replacement is carried out if the ASCII code of the scanned character lies within the range of codes for *FirstChar$* and *LastChar$*. Each character that satisfies the above criteria is replaced with the character *NewChar$*.

The string processing begins at character *Start*. The subroutine is exited without processing string *S$* if:

1. Either *NewChar$*, *FirstChar$*, or *LastChar$* is a null string.

2. Parameter *Start* is greater than the length of string *S$*.

EXAMPLE:

```
' remove lower-case letter from the following string
S$ = "1234absc5674hfgd99585"
CALL ReplaceCharRange(S$, "a", "z", ".", 1)
PRINT S$ ' displays "1234....5674....99585"

' remove numerals from the following string
S$ = "1234absc5674hfgd99585"
CALL ReplaceCharRange(S$, "0", "9", ".", 1)
PRINT S$ ' displays "....absc....hfgd....."
```

The following set of routines was inspired by the REXX language. REXX is a language that roughly combines BASIC with a bit of ICON (a strong string-processing language). REXX has built-in routines that perform character manipulation, much like those in BASIC. However, REXX has an additional set of built-in *word* manipulating routines. REXX uses the space character as a word delimiter. Thus, you may handle a string in REXX, such as "Hello there

BASIC LIBRARIES 147

everyone", to extract the second word, delete the third word, and so on. With such REXX functions you talk of words and word positions, as opposed to characters and their positions.

You are also able to expand the set of delimiters used between words. Included in each routine parameter list is the string *Delim$* that contains the set of delimiters. Passing a null string with *Delim$* is interpreted by the routines as a space character.

The word-manipulating functions are written with the following assumptions:

1. a contiguous sequence of delimiters is regarded as a single delimiter
2. there may be leading delimiters in a processed string

DEF FNGetWord$(S$, Delim$, GetNum%)
DEF   GettWord$(S$, Delim$, GetNum)

This function returns word number *GetNum* from string *S$*. If the value of *GetNum* is too high, a null string is returned.

EXAMPLE:

```
'Return the 2nd variable in the expression
S$ = "ROOT= ( NUMBER / ROOT + ROOT ) / 2"
' Note that '=' is not in the set of delimiters
Delim$ = "()+-*/ "
PRINT FNGetWord$(S$, Delim$, 2) ' displays "NUMBER"

' get 1st, 3rd and 4th words
PRINT FNGetWord$(S$, Delim$, 1) ' displays "ROOT="
PRINT FNGetWord$(S$, Delim$, 3) ' displays "ROOT"
PRINT FNGetWord$(S$, Delim$, 4) ' displays "ROOT"
```


DEF FNWordPos(S$, Delim$, Search$, Index%)
DEF   WordPos(S$, Delim$, Search$, Index) ! True BASIC

This function returns the *word position* of substring *Search$* in string *S$*. The search begins with word number *Index*.

EXAMPLE:

```
S$ = "The water is boiling"
Delim$ = " "
PRINT FNWordPos(S$, Delim$, "water", 1) ' displays 2
PRINT FNWordPos(S$, Delim$, "is", 1) ' displays 3
```

SUB DelWord(S$, Delim$, Start%, Count%) STATIC
SUB DelWord(S$, Delim$, Start, Count) ! True BASIC

Deletes *Count* words beginning with word number *Start*. If the value of parameter *Start* is too high, string *S$* is unchanged. If the value of the *Count* parameter is larger than the number of words available for deletion, the difference is ignored.

EXAMPLE:

```
S$ = "Mary had a little white lamb"
CALL DelWord(S$, " ", 4, 2)
PRINT S$ ' displays "Mary had a lamb"
```

SUB InsertWord(S$, Delim$, NewWord$, Index%) STATIC
SUB InsertWord(S$, Delim$, NewWord$, Index) ! True BASIC

This subroutine inserts substring *NewWord$* into *S$* after word number *Index*. The delimiter between word number *Index* and *Index+1* is used to delimit the inserted word and word number *Index+1*.

EXAMPLE:

```
S$ = "Mary Moore"
NewWord$ = "Tyler"
CALL InsertWord(S$, " ", NewWord$, 1)
PRINT S$ ' displays "Mary Tyler Moore"
```

SUB ParseToArray(S$, Delim$, PS$(1), Count%) STATIC
SUB ParseToArray(S$, Delim$, PS$(), Count) ! True BASIC

This subroutine scans string *S$* and returns an array of smaller strings, *PS$()*, that contains the words in *S$*. The parameter *Count* returns the number of extracted words.

EXAMPLE:

```
DIM PS$(20)  ' make sure dimension is adequate
S$ = "X1+X2*X3-X4"
D$ = "+-*/"
CALL ParseToArray(S$, D$, PS$(), N%)
'
' The FOR loop displays the following results
'       X1
'       X2
'       X3
'       X4
'
'       ^
'       |
'       ----------- array PS$()
'
FOR I% = 1 TO N%
    PRINT PS$(I%)
NEXT I%
```

Listing 3.4. *QuickBASIC source code for TOOLBOX1.BAS*

```
'------------------------------------------------------'
'                                                      '
'         String manipulation module TOOLBOX1          '
'               QuickBASIC version                     '
' Version 1.1                               5/87       '
'       Copyright (c) 1987   Namir Clement Shammas     '
'                                                      '
'                                                      '
'------------------------------------------------------'


DEF FNPadLeft$(S$, C$, L%)
' Return a string that is padded to the left with L% numbers of C$ characters
```

```
    IF L% < 1 THEN L% = 1
    IF LEN(C$) > 1 THEN C$ = LEFT$(C$,1)
    FNPadLeft$ = STRING$(L%,C$) + S$

END DEF

DEF FNPadRight$(S$, C$, L%)
'Return a string that is padded to the right with L% numbers of C$ characters

    IF L% < 1 THEN L% = 1
    IF LEN(C$) > 1 THEN C$ = LEFT$(C$,1)
    FNPadRight$ = S$ + STRING$(L%,C$)

END DEF

DEF FNPadCenter$(S$, C$, L%, Index%)
' Return a string that is padded in the center with C$ characters

    IF L% < 1 THEN L% = 1
    IF Index% < 1 THEN Index% = 2

    IF Index% < LEN(S$) THEN
       IF LEN(C$) > 1 THEN C$ = LEFT$(C$,1)
       FNPadCenter$ = LEFT$(S$,Index%-1) + STRING$(L%,C$) +
MID$(S$,Index%)
      ELSE
       FNPadCenter$ = "" ' Bad Index% value
    END IF

END DEF

DEF FNPadEnds$(S$, C$, L%)
' Return a string that is padded at both ends with C$ characters

STATIC T$

    IF L% < 1 THEN L% = 1
    T$ = STRING$(L%,C$)
    FNPadEnds$ = T$ + S$ + T$

END DEF

SUB DelLeft(S$, C$, KillC%) STATIC
' Scan string S$ and delete all characters from the left end and up
' to the first occurence of C$.
' The first occurence is also deleted if  KillC% is not zero.

STATIC L%

    IF LEN(C$) > 1 THEN C$ = LEFT$(C$,1)
    L% = INSTR(S$,C$)
    IF L% = 0 THEN EXIT SUB ' Boundary character not found
    IF (KillC% = 0) THEN L% = L% - 1
    S$ = MID$(S$,L%+1)
```

BASIC LIBRARIES   151

```
END SUB

SUB DelRight(S$, C$, KillC%) STATIC
' Scan string S$ and delete all characters from the right end and up
' to the first occurence of C$.
' The first occurence is also deleted if  KillC% is not zero.

STATIC L%

IF LEN(C$) > 1 THEN C$ = LEFT$(C$,1)

L% = LEN(S$)
WHILE (MID$(S$,L%,1) <> C$) AND (L% > 0)
    L% = L% - 1
WEND

IF L% = 0 THEN EXIT SUB ' Boundary character not found
IF (KillC% <> 0) THEN L% = L% - 1
S$ = LEFT$(S$,L%)

END SUB

SUB LeftTrim(S$) STATIC
' Remove leading spaces from string S$

STATIC L%, I%

LET L% = LEN(S$)
LET I% = 1

WHILE (MID$(S$,I%,1) = " ") AND (I% <= L%)
   I% = I% + 1
WEND

IF I% = L% THEN S$ = "" ' The entire string is full of blanks
IF I% > 1 THEN S$ = RIGHT$(S$,L%-I%+1)

END SUB

SUB RightTrim(S$) STATIC
' Remove trailing spaces from string S$

STATIC L%, I%

LET L% = LEN(S$)
LET I% = L%

WHILE (MID$(S$,I%,1) = " ") AND (I% > 0)
    I% = I% - 1
WEND

IF I% = 0 THEN S$ = "" ' The entire string is full of blanks
IF I% < L% THEN S$ = LEFT$(S$,I%)

END SUB
```

```
SUB RemoveStr(S$, SubStr$) STATIC
' Remove all occureneces of SubStr$ from string S$.

STATIC L%, K%

K% = LEN(SubStr$)
L% = INSTR(S$, SubStr$)

WHILE L% > 0
    IF L% = 1 THEN
        S$ = MID$(S$,(L%+K%))
    ELSE
        S$ = MID$(S$,1,(L%-1)) + MID$(S$,(L%+K%))
    END IF
    L% = INSTR(S$, SubStr$)
WEND

END SUB


SUB RemoveCharRange(S$, FC$, LC$) STATIC
' Remove all characters that meet the following criterion:
'
'     ASCII(FC$) <=  ASCII(char)   <= ASCII(LC$)

STATIC ASCII.LC%, ASCII.FC%, A%, L%, I%, J%

ASCII.LC% = ASC(LC$)
ASCII.FC% = ASC(FC$)

L% = LEN(S$)
J% = 0

FOR I% = 1 TO L%
    J% = J% + 1
    A% = ASC(MID$(S$,J%,1))
    IF (ASCII.FC% <= A%) AND (A% <= ASCII.LC%) THEN
        IF J% = 1 THEN
            S$ = MID$(S$,2)
        ELSEIF J% = LEN(S$) THEN
            S$ = LEFT$(S$,J%-1)
        ELSE
            S$ = LEFT$(S$,J%-1) + MID$(S$,J%+1)
        END IF
        J% = J% - 1
    END IF
NEXT I%

END SUB


SUB TypeOverStr(S$, SubStr$, Index%) STATIC
' The substring SubStr$ overwrites portions of S$ starting at Index%
' The substring may be trunctaed if it causes S$ to expand
' The subroutine is EXITed if
```

BASIC LIBRARIES

```
'       1) The Index% > length of string S$
'       2) The Substring is a null string.
'       3) The subtring SubStr$ itself is larger than the string S$
STATIC J%, L%

L% = LEN(S$)
J% = LEN(SubStr$)

IF Index% < 1 THEN Index% = 1
IF (Index% > L%) OR (J% = 0) OR (J% > L%) THEN EXIT SUB
IF (Index% + J%) > L% THEN SubStr$ = LEFT$(SubStr$,(L% - Index%))

IF Index% = 1 THEN
    S$ = SubStr$ + MID$(S$,J%+1)
ELSEIF (Index% + J%) = L% THEN
    S$ = LEFT$(S$,Index%-1) + SubStr$
ELSE
    S$ = LEFT$(S$,Index%-1) + SubStr$ + MID$(S$,Index%+K%)
END IF

END SUB


SUB ReplaceStr(S$, SubStr$, Index%, C$) STATIC
' Replaces portions of S$ with SubStr$ where character C$ is found.
' Action starts at Index% position of string S$.
' The Substring is not scanned for C$ after it is inserted

STATIC J%, L%

J% = LEN(SubStr$)
IF Index% < 1 THEN Index% = 1
IF Index% > LEN(S$) THEN EXIT SUB
IF LEN(C$) > 1 THEN C$ = LEFT$(C$,1)

L% = INSTR(Index%, S$, C$)
WHILE L% > 0

    Index% = L% + J%

    IF L% = 1 THEN
        S$ = SubStr$ + MID$(S$,2)
    ELSEIF L% = LEN(S$) THEN
        S$ = LEFT$(S$,L%-1) + SubStr$
    ELSE
        S$ = LEFT$(S$,L%-1) + SubStr$ + MID$(S$,L%+1)
    END IF

    L% = INSTR(Index%, S$, C$)
WEND

END SUB


SUB ReplaceChar(S$, OldChar$, NewChar$, Start%) STATIC
```

```
' Replaces all the occurences of OldChar$ with NewChar$

STATIC I%

IF (OldChar$ = "") OR (NewChar$ = "") THEN EXIT SUB
IF Start% < 1 THEN Start% = 1
IF Start% > LEN(S$) THEN EXIT SUB

IF LEN(OldChar$) > 1 THEN OldChar$ = LEFT$(OldChar$,1)
IF LEN(NewChar$) > 1 THEN NewChar$ = LEFT$(NewChar$,1)

FOR I% = Start% TO LEN(S$)
    IF MID$(S$,I%,1) = OldChar$ THEN MID$(S$,I%,1) = NewChar$
NEXT I%

END SUB


SUB ReplaceCharRange(S$, FirstChar$, LastChar$, NewChar$, Start%) STATIC
' Replaces any character between FirstChar$ and LastChar$ with NewChar$

STATIC ASCII.LC%, ASCII.FC%, A%, L%, I%, J%

IF (FirstChar$ = "") OR (LastChar$ = "") OR (NewChar$ = "") THEN EXIT SUB
IF LEN(NewChar$)  > 1 THEN NewChar$ = LEFT$(NewChar$,1)

IF Start% < 1 THEN Start% = 1
IF Start% > LEN(S$) THEN EXIT SUB

ASCII.FC% = ASC(FirstChar$)
ASCII.LC% = ASC(LastChar$)

FOR I% = Start% TO LEN(S$)
    A% = ASC(MID$(S$,I%,1))
    IF (ASCII.FC% <= A%) AND (A% <= ASCII.LC%) THEN
        MID$(S$,I%,1) = NewChar$
    END IF
NEXT I%

END SUB

'-----------------------------------------------------------
' The following routines are inspired by the REXX language
'-----------------------------------------------------------

DEF FNTestDelim%(S$,D$,I%)
' Local function used to test delimiter characters
IF (INSTR(D$,MID$(S$,I%-1,1)) = 0) AND (INSTR(D$,MID$(S$,I%,1)) > 0) THEN
    FNTestDelim% = 1
ELSE
    FNTestDelim% = 0
END IF

ENL DEF
```

BASIC LIBRARIES

```
DEF FNGetWord$(S$, Delim$, GetNum%)
' Scans string S$ and obtain the 'GetNum%' word.
' String Delim$ provides the set of delimiter characters

STATIC I%, N%, L%, Ptr1%

IF GetNum% < 1 THEN GetNum% = 1
IF Delim$ = "" THEN Delim$ = " "

N% = GetNum% - 1
I% = 1
L% = LEN(S$)

' Loop until you find a non-Delim$ char or the end-of-string
WHILE (I% < L%) AND (INSTR(Delim$,MID$(S$,I%,1)) > 0)
    I% = I% + 1
WEND

IF I% > L% THEN
    FNGetWord$ = ""
    EXIT DEF
END IF

IF N% > 0 THEN I% = I% + 1

WHILE (I% <= L%) AND (N% > 0)
    IF (FNTestDelim%(S$, Delim$, I%) = 1) THEN N% = N% - 1
    I% = I% + 1
WEND

IF (N% > 0) THEN
    FNGetWord$ = ""
ELSE

    ' Loop until you find a non-Delim$ char or the end-of-string
    WHILE (I% < L%) AND (INSTR(Delim$,MID$(S$,I%,1)) > 0)
        I% = I% + 1
    WEND

    Ptr1% = I%
    N% = 1
    WHILE (I% <= L%) AND (N% > 0)
        IF (FNTestDelim%(S$, Delim$, I%) = 1) THEN N% = N% - 1
        I% = I% + 1
    WEND
    FNGetWord$ = MID$(S$,Ptr1%,I%-Ptr1%)
END IF

END DEF

DEF FNWordPos(S$, Delim$, Search$, Index%)
' Returns the "word" Count% of Search$ in S$, starting at the Index%'th word

STATIC I%, N%, L%, Ptr%
```

```
    IF (INSTR(S$,Search$) = 0) THEN ' sought word is not is string
        FNWordPos = 0
        EXIT DEF
    END IF

    IF Delim$ = "" THEN Delim$ = " "

    ' Search for the Index%'th word
    L% = LEN(S$)
    N% = Index% - 1
    I% = 1

    ' Loop until you find a non-Delim$ char or the end-of-string
    WHILE (I% < L%) AND (INSTR(Delim$,MID$(S$,I%,1)) > 0)
        I% = I% + 1
    WEND

    IF I% > L% THEN
        FNWordPos = 0
        EXIT DEF
    END IF

    IF N% > 0 THEN I% = I% + 1

    WHILE (I% <= L%) AND (N% > 0)
        IF (FNTestDelim%(S$, Delim$, I%) = 1) THEN N% = N% - 1
        I% = I% + 1
    WEND

    IF N% > 0 THEN
        FNWordPos = 0
    ELSE
        IF I% > 1 THEN I% = I% - 1
        Ptr% = INSTR(I%, S$, Search$)
        Count% = 1
        WHILE (I% < Ptr%)
            IF (FNTestDelim%(S$, Delim$, I%) = 1) THEN Count% = Count% + 1
            I% = I% + 1
        WEND
        FNWordPos = Count% + Index% - 1
    END IF

END DEF


SUB DelWord(S$, Delim$, Start%, Count%) STATIC
' Delete 'Count%' words starting from the Start%'th word.
' If more words are specified there are to delete, the extra number
' is ignored.

STATIC I%, L%, N%, Ptr1%

IF Delim$ = "" THEN Delim$ = " "

' Search for the Start%'th word
```

BASIC LIBRARIES 157

```
    L% = LEN(S$)
    N% = Start% - 1
    I% = 1

    ' Loop until you find a non-Delim$ char or the end-of-string
    WHILE (I% < L%) AND (INSTR(Delim$,MID$(S$,I%,1)) > 0)
        I% = I% + 1
    WEND

    IF N% > 0 THEN I% = I% + 1

    WHILE (I% <= L%) AND (N% > 0)
        IF (FNTestDelim%(S$, Delim$, I%) = 1) THEN N% = N% - 1
        I% = I% + 1
    WEND

    IF (N% = 0) THEN ' found the Start%'th word

        ' Loop until you find a non-Delim$ char or the end-of-string
        WHILE (I% < L%) AND (INSTR(Delim$,MID$(S$,I%,1)) > 0)
           I% = I% + 1
        WEND

        Ptr1% = I% - 1 ' First character to delete
        N% = Count%
        WHILE (I% <= L%) AND (N% > 0)
            IF (FNTestDelim%(S$, Delim$, I%) = 1) THEN N% = N% - 1
            I% = I% + 1
        WEND

        IF (N% > 0) OR (I% > L%) THEN ' Delete to the end of string
            S$ = LEFT$(S$,Ptr1%-1)
        ELSE           ' Deletion ends before the end of string
            S$ = LEFT$(S$,Ptr1%) + MID$(S$,I%)
        END IF
    END IF

END SUB

SUB InsertWord(S$, Delim$, NewWord$, Index%) STATIC
' Insert NewWord$ AFTER the Index%'th word in string S$

STATIC I%, N%, L%, Ptr%

IF Delim$ = "" THEN Delim$ = " "

' Search for the Index%'th word
L% = LEN(S$)
N% = Index%
I% = 1

' Loop until you find a non-Delim$ char or the end-of-string
WHILE (I% < L%) AND (INSTR(Delim$,MID$(S$,I%,1)) > 0)
    I% = I% + 1
WEND
```

```
    IF N% > 0 THEN I% = I% + 1

    WHILE (I% <= L%) AND (N% > 0)
        IF (FNTestDelim%(S$, Delim$, I%) = 1) THEN N% = N% - 1
        I% = I% + 1
    WEND

    IF (N% = 0) THEN ' found the Index%'th word
        Ptr% = I% - 1
        ' The same delimiter character at Ptr1% is used in the insertion
        S$ = LEFT$(S$,Ptr%) + NewWord$ + MID$(S$,Ptr%)
    END IF

END SUB

SUB ParseToArray(S$, Delim$, PS$(1), Count%) STATIC
' Parses string S$ into an array of strings PS$().
' Count% returns the parsed word Count%

STATIC I%, N%, L%, Ptr1%, Ptr2%

L% = LEN(S$)
IF L% = 0 THEN EXIT SUB
IF Delim$ = "" THEN Delim$ = " "

' Initialize pointers and counters
I% = 1
Count% = 0

' Loop until you find a non-Delim$ char or the end-of-string
WHILE (I% < L%) AND (INSTR(Delim$,MID$(S$,I%,1)) > 0)
    I% = I% + 1
WEND

Ptr1% = I%

IF (I% = 1) THEN I% = 2

WHILE I% <= L%
    IF (FNTestDelim%(S$, Delim$, I%) = 1) THEN
        Count% = Count% + 1
        Ptr2% = I% - 1
        IF Ptr1% = Ptr2% THEN
            PS$(Count%) = ""
        ELSE
            PS$(Count%) = MID$(S$,Ptr1%,Ptr2%-Ptr1%+1)
        END IF

        ' Loop until you find a non-Delim$ char or the end-of-string
        WHILE (I% < L%) AND (INSTR(Delim$,MID$(S$,I%,1)) > 0)
            I% = I% + 1
        WEND

        Ptr1% = I%
    END IF
    I% = I% + 1
```

```
WEND

IF Ptr1% < L% THEN
   Count% = Count% + 1
   PS$(Count%) = MID$(S$,Ptr1%)
END IF

END SUB
```

Listing 3.5 *Turbo BASIC source code for TOOLBOX1.BAS*

```
'-----------------------------------------------------------'
'                                                           '
'            String manipulation module TOOLBOX1            '
'                   Turbo BASIC version                     '
' Version 1.1                                       5/87    '
'       Copyright (c) 1987   Namir Clement Shammas          '
'                                                           '
'                                                           '
'-----------------------------------------------------------'


DEF FNPadLeft$(S$, C$, L%)
' Return a string that is padded to the left with L% numbers of C$ characters

IF L% < 1 THEN L% = 1
IF LEN(C$) > 1 THEN C$ = LEFT$(C$,1)
FNPadLeft$ = STRING$(L%,C$) + S$

END DEF

DEF FNPadRight$(S$, C$, L%)
'Return a string that is padded to the right with L% numbers of C$ characters

IF L% < 1 THEN L% = 1
IF LEN(C$) > 1 THEN C$ = LEFT$(C$,1)
FNPadRight$ = S$ + STRING$(L%,C$)

END DEF

DEF FNPadCenter$(S$, C$, L%, Index%)
' Return a string that is padded in the center with C$ characters

IF L% < 1 THEN L% = 1
IF Index% < 1 THEN Index% = 2

IF Index% < LEN(S$) THEN
   IF LEN(C$) > 1 THEN C$ = LEFT$(C$,1)
     FNPadCenter$ = LEFT$(S$,Index%-1) + STRING$(L%,C$) + MID$(S$,Index%)
  ELSE
```

```
        FNPadCenter$ = "" ' Bad Index% value
END IF

END DEF

DEF FNPadEnds$(S$, C$, L%)
' Return a string that is padded at both ends with C$ characters

LOCAL T$

IF L% < 1 THEN L% = 1
T$ = STRING$(L%,C$)
FNPadEnds$ = T$ + S$ + T$

END DEF

SUB DelLeft(S$, C$, KillC%) STATIC
' Scan string S$ and delete all characters from the left end and up
' to the first occurence of C$.
' The first occurence is also deleted if  KillC% is not zero.

LOCAL L%

IF LEN(C$) > 1 THEN C$ = LEFT$(C$,1)
L% = INSTR(S$,C$)
IF L% = 0 THEN EXIT SUB ' Boundary character not found
IF (KillC% = 0) THEN L% = L% - 1
S$ = MID$(S$,L%+1)

END SUB

SUB DelRight(S$, C$, KillC%) STATIC
' Scan string S$ and delete all characters from the right end and up
' to the first occurence of C$.
' The first occurence is also deleted if  KillC% is not zero.

LOCAL L%

IF LEN(C$) > 1 THEN C$ = LEFT$(C$,1)

L% = LEN(S$)
WHILE (MID$(S$,L%,1) <> C$) AND (L% > 0)
    L% = L% - 1
WEND

IF L% = 0 THEN EXIT SUB ' Boundary character not found
IF (KillC% <> 0) THEN L% = L% - 1
S$ = LEFT$(S$,L%)

END SUB

SUB LeftTrim(S$) STATIC
' Remove leading spaces from string S$

LOCAL L%, I%
```

```
LET L% = LEN(S$)
LET I% = 1

WHILE (MID$(S$,I%,1) = " ") AND (I% <= L%)
    INCR I%
WEND

IF I% = L% THEN S$ = ""  ' The entire string is full of blanks
IF I% > 1 THEN S$ = RIGHT$(S$,L%-I%+1)

END SUB

SUB RightTrim(S$) STATIC
' Remove trailing spaces from string S$

LOCAL L%, I%

LET L% = LEN(S$)
LET I% = L%

WHILE (MID$(S$,I%,1) = " ") AND (I% > 0)
    I% = I% - 1
WEND

IF I% = 0 THEN S$ = ""  ' The entire string is full of blanks
IF I% < L% THEN S$ = LEFT$(S$,I%)

END SUB


SUB RemoveStr(S$, SubStr$) STATIC
' Remove all occureneces of SubStr$ from string S$.

LOCAL L%, K%

K% = LEN(SubStr$)
L% = INSTR(S$, SubStr$)

WHILE L% > 0
    IF L% = 1 THEN
        S$ = MID$(S$,(L%+K%))
    ELSE
        S$ = MID$(S$,1,(L%-1)) + MID$(S$,(L%+K%))
    END IF
    L% = INSTR(S$, SubStr$)
WEND

END SUB


SUB RemoveCharRange(S$, FC$, LC$) STATIC
' Remove all characters that meet the following criterion:
'
'      ASCII(FC$) <=  ASCII(char)   <= ASCII(LC$)

LOCAL ASCII.LC%, ASCII.FC%, A%, L%, I%, J%
```

```
ASCII.LC% = ASC(LC$)
ASCII.FC% = ASC(FC$)

L% = LEN(S$)
J% = 0

FOR I% = 1 TO L%
    J% = J% + 1
    A% = ASC(MID$(S$,J%,1))
    IF (ASCII.FC% <= A%) AND (A% <= ASCII.LC%) THEN
        IF J% = 1 THEN
            S$ = MID$(S$,2)
        ELSEIF J% = LEN(S$) THEN
            S$ = LEFT$(S$,J%-1)
        ELSE
            S$ = LEFT$(S$,J%-1) + MID$(S$,J%+1)
        END IF
        J% = J% - 1
    END IF
NEXT I%

END SUB


SUB TypeOverStr(S$, SubStr$, Index%) STATIC
' The substring SubStr$ overwrites portions of S$ starting at Index%
' The substring may be trunctaed if it causes S$ to expand
' The subroutine is EXITed if
'      1) The Index% > length of string S$
'      2) The Substring is a null string.
'      3) The subtring SubStr$ itself is larger than the string S$

LOCAL J%, L%

L% = LEN(S$)
J% = LEN(SubStr$)

IF Index% < 1 THEN Index% = 1
IF (Index% > L%) OR (J% = 0) OR (J% > L%) THEN EXIT SUB
IF (Index% + J%) > L% THEN SubStr$ = LEFT$(SubStr$,(L% - Index%))

IF Index% = 1 THEN
    S$ = SubStr$ + MID$(S$,J%+1)
ELSEIF (Index% + J%) = L% THEN
    S$ = LEFT$(S$,Index%-1) + SubStr$
ELSE
    S$ = LEFT$(S$,Index%-1) + SubStr$ + MID$(S$,Index%+K%)
END IF

END SUB


SUB ReplaceStr(S$, SubStr$, Index%, C$) STATIC
' Replaces portions of S$ with SubStr$ where character C$ is found.
' Action starts at Index% position of string S$.
```

BASIC LIBRARIES

```
' The Substring is not scanned for C$ after it is inserted

LOCAL J%, L%

J% = LEN(SubStr$)
IF Index% < 1 THEN Index% = 1
IF Index% > LEN(S$) THEN EXIT SUB
IF LEN(C$) > 1 THEN C$ = LEFT$(C$,1)

L% = INSTR(Index%, S$, C$)
WHILE L% > 0

    Index% = L% + J%

    IF L% = 1 THEN
        S$ = SubStr$ + MID$(S$,2)
    ELSEIF L% = LEN(S$) THEN
        S$ = LEFT$(S$,L%-1) + SubStr$
    ELSE
        S$ = LEFT$(S$,L%-1) + SubStr$ + MID$(S$,L%+1)
    END IF

    L% = INSTR(Index%, S$, C$)
WEND

END SUB


SUB ReplaceChar(S$, OldChar$, NewChar$, Start%) STATIC
' Replaces all the occurences of OldChar$ with NewChar$

LOCAL I%

IF (OldChar$ = "") OR (NewChar$ = "") THEN EXIT SUB
IF Start% < 1 THEN Start% = 1
IF Start% > LEN(S$) THEN EXIT SUB

IF LEN(OldChar$) > 1 THEN OldChar$ = LEFT$(OldChar$,1)
IF LEN(NewChar$) > 1 THEN NewChar$ = LEFT$(NewChar$,1)

FOR I% = Start% TO LEN(S$)
    IF MID$(S$,I%,1) = OldChar$ THEN MID$(S$,I%,1) = NewChar$
NEXT I%

END SUB


SUB ReplaceCharRange(S$, FirstChar$, LastChar$, NewChar$, Start%) STATIC
' Replaces any character between FirstChar$ and LastChar$ with NewChar$

LOCAL ASCII.LC%, ASCII.FC%, A%, L%, I%, J%

IF (FirstChar$ = "") OR (LastChar$ = "") OR (NewChar$ = "") THEN EXIT SUB
IF LEN(NewChar$)  > 1 THEN NewChar$ = LEFT$(NewChar$,1)

IF Start% < 1 THEN Start% = 1
```

```
IF Start% > LEN(S$) THEN EXIT SUB

ASCII.FC% = ASC(FirstChar$)
ASCII.LC% = ASC(LastChar$)

FOR I% = Start% TO LEN(S$)
    A% = ASC(MID$(S$,I%,1))
    IF (ASCII.FC% <= A%) AND (A% <= ASCII.LC%) THEN
        MID$(S$,I%,1) = NewChar$
    END IF
NEXT I%

END SUB

'-----------------------------------------------------------
' The following routines are inspired by the REXX language
'-----------------------------------------------------------

DEF FNTestDelim%(S$,D$,I%)
' Local function used to test delimiter characters
IF (INSTR(D$,MID$(S$,I%-1,1)) = 0) AND (INSTR(D$,MID$(S$,I%,1)) > 0)
THEN
    FNTestDelim% = 1
ELSE
    FNTestDelim% = 0
END IF

END DEF


DEF FNGetWord$(S$, Delim$, GetNum%)
' Scans string S$ and obtain the 'GetNum%' word.
' String Delim$ provides the set of delimiter characters

LOCAL I%, N%, L%, Ptr1%

IF GetNum% < 1 THEN GetNum% = 1
IF Delim$ = "" THEN Delim$ = " "

N% = GetNum% - 1
I% = 1
L% = LEN(S$)

' Loop until you find a non-Delim$ char or the end-of-string
WHILE (I% < L%) AND (INSTR(Delim$,MID$(S$,I%,1)) > 0)
    INCR I%
WEND

IF I% > L% THEN
    FNGetWord$ = ""
    EXIT DEF
END IF

IF N% > 0 THEN INCR I%

WHILE (I% <= L%) AND (N% > 0)
```

BASIC LIBRARIES 165

```
        IF (FNTestDelim%(S$, Delim$, I%) = 1) THEN DECR N%
        INCR I%
WEND

IF (N% > 0) THEN
    FNGetWord$ = ""
ELSE

    ' Loop until you find a non-Delim$ char or the end-of-string
    WHILE (I% < L%) AND (INSTR(Delim$,MID$(S$,I%,1)) > 0)
        INCR I%
    WEND

    Ptr1% = I%
    N% = 1
    WHILE (I% <= L%) AND (N% > 0)
        IF (FNTestDelim%(S$, Delim$, I%) = 1) THEN DECR N%
        INCR I%
    WEND
    FNGetWord$ = MID$(S$,Ptr1%,I%-Ptr1%)
END IF

END DEF

DEF FNWordPos(S$, Delim$, Search$, Index%)
' Returns the "word" Count% of Search$ in S$, starting at the Index%'th word

LOCAL I%, N%, L%, Ptr%

IF (INSTR(S$,Search$) = 0) THEN   ' sought word is not is string
    FNWordPos = 0
    EXIT DEF
END IF

IF Delim$ = "" THEN Delim$ = " "

' Search for the Index%'th word
L% = LEN(S$)
N% = Index% - 1
I% = 1

' Loop until you find a non-Delim$ char or the end-of-string
WHILE (I% < L%) AND (INSTR(Delim$,MID$(S$,I%,1)) > 0)
    INCR I%
WEND

IF I% > L% THEN
    FNWordPos = 0
    EXIT DEF
END IF

IF N% > 0 THEN INCR I%

WHILE (I% <= L%) AND (N% > 0)
    IF (FNTestDelim%(S$, Delim$, I%) = 1) THEN DECR N%
    INCR I%
```

```
    WEND

IF N% > 0 THEN
    FNWordPos = 0
ELSE
    IF I% > 1 THEN I% = I% - 1
    Ptr% = INSTR(I%, S$, Search$)
    Count% = 1
    WHILE (I% < Ptr%)
        IF (FNTestDelim%(S$, Delim$, I%) = 1) THEN INCR Count%
        INCR I%
    WEND
    FNWordPos = Count% + Index% - 1
END IF

END DEF


SUB DelWord(S$, Delim$, Start%, Count%) STATIC
' Delete 'Count%' words starting from the Start%'th word.
' If more words are specified there are to delete, the extra number
' is ignored.

LOCAL I%, L%, N%, Ptr1%

IF Delim$ = "" THEN Delim$ = " "

' Search for the Start%'th word
L% = LEN(S$)
N% = Start% - 1
I% = 1

' Loop until you find a non-Delim$ char or the end-of-string
WHILE (I% < L%) AND (INSTR(Delim$,MID$(S$,I%,1)) > 0)
    INCR I%
WEND

IF N% > 0 THEN INCR I%

WHILE (I% <= L%) AND (N% > 0)
    IF (FNTestDelim%(S$, Delim$, I%) = 1) THEN DECR N%
    INCR I%
WEND

IF (N% = 0) THEN ' found the Start%'th word

    ' Loop until you find a non-Delim$ char or the end-of-string
    WHILE (I% < L%) AND (INSTR(Delim$,MID$(S$,I%,1)) > 0)
       INCR I%
    WEND

    Ptr1% = I% - 1 ' First character to delete
    N% = Count%
    WHILE (I% <= L%) AND (N% > 0)
        IF (FNTestDelim%(S$, Delim$, I%) = 1) THEN DECR N%
        INCP I%
```

```
        WEND

        IF (N% > 0) OR (I% > L%) THEN  ' Delete to the end of string
            S$ = LEFT$(S$,Ptr1%-1)
        ELSE                ' Deletion ends before the end of string
            S$ = LEFT$(S$,Ptr1%) + MID$(S$,I%)
        END IF
    END IF

END SUB

SUB InsertWord(S$, Delim$, NewWord$, Index%) STATIC
' Insert NewWord$ AFTER the Index%'th word in string S$

LOCAL I%, N%, L%, Ptr%

IF Delim$ = "" THEN Delim$ = " "

' Search for the Index%'th word
L% = LEN(S$)
N% = Index%
I% = 1

' Loop until you find a non-Delim$ char or the end-of-string
WHILE (I% < L%) AND (INSTR(Delim$,MID$(S$,I%,1)) > 0)
    INCR I%
WEND

IF N% > 0 THEN INCR I%

WHILE (I% <= L%) AND (N% > 0)
    IF (FNTestDelim%(S$, Delim$, I%) = 1) THEN DECR N%
    INCR I%
WEND

IF (N% = 0) THEN ' found the Index%'th word
    Ptr% = I% - 1
    ' The same delimiter character at Ptr1% is used in the insertion
    S$ = LEFT$(S$,Ptr%) + NewWord$ + MID$(S$,Ptr%)
END IF

END SUB

SUB ParseToArray(S$, Delim$, PS$(1), Count%) STATIC
' Parses string S$ into an array of strings PS$().
' Count% returns the parsed word Count%

LOCAL I%, N%, L%, Ptr1%, Ptr2%

L% = LEN(S$)
IF L% = 0 THEN EXIT SUB
IF Delim$ = "" THEN Delim$ = " "

' Initialize pointers and counters
I% = 1
Count% = 0
```

```
' Loop until you find a non-Delim$ char or the end-of-string
WHILE (I% < L%) AND (INSTR(Delim$,MID$(S$,I%,1)) > 0)
    INCR I%
WEND

Ptr1% = I%

IF (I% = 1) THEN I% = 2

WHILE I% <= L%
    IF (FNTestDelim%(S$, Delim$, I%) = 1) THEN
        INCR Count%
        Ptr2% = I% - 1
        IF Ptr1% = Ptr2% THEN
            PS$(Count%) = ""
        ELSE
            PS$(Count%) = MID$(S$,Ptr1%,Ptr2%-Ptr1%+1)
        END IF

        ' Loop until you find a non-Delim$ char or the end-of-string
        WHILE (I% < L%) AND (INSTR(Delim$,MID$(S$,I%,1)) > 0)
            INCR I%
        WEND

        Ptr1% = I%
    END IF
    INCR I%
WEND

IF Ptr1% < L% THEN
    INCR Count%
    PS$(Count%) = MID$(S$,Ptr1%)
END IF

END SUB
```

Listing 3.6. *True BASIC source code for TOOLBOX1.TRU*

```
MODULE TOOLBOX1

!-----------------------------------------------------------!
!                                                           !
!          String manipulation module TOOLBOX1              !
!                 True BASIC version                        !
! Version 1.1                                     5/87      !
!       Copyright (c) 1987    Namir Clement Shammas         !
!                                                           !
!                                                           !
!-----------------------------------------------------------!
```

BASIC LIBRARIES

```
DECLARE DEF PadLeft$, PadRight$, PadEnds$
DECLARE DEF TestDelim, GetWord$, WordPos
PRIVATE TestDelim

DEF PadLeft$(S$, C$, L)
! Return a string that is padded to the left with L numbers of C$ characters
   IF L < 1 THEN LET L = 1
   IF LEN(C$) > 1 THEN LET C$ = C$[1:1]
   LET PadLeft$ = REPEAT$(C$,L) & S$
END DEF

DEF PadRight$(S$, C$, L)
! Return a string that is padded to the right with L numbers of C$ characters
   IF L < 1 THEN LET L = 1
   IF LEN(C$) > 1 THEN LET C$ = C$[1:1]
   LET PadRight$ = S$ & REPEAT$(C$,L)
END DEF

DEF PadCenter$(S$, C$, L, Index)
! Return a string that is padded in the center with C$ characters
   IF L < 1 THEN LET L = 1
   IF Index < 1 THEN LET Index = 2
   IF Index < LEN(S$) THEN
      IF LEN(C$) > 1 THEN LET C$ = C$[1:1]
      LET PadCenter$ = S$[1:Index-1] & REPEAT$(C$,L) & S$[Index:MAXNUM]
   ELSE
      LET PadCenter$ = ""  ! Bad Index value
   END IF
END DEF

DEF PadEnds$(S$, C$, L)
! Return a string that is padded at both ends with C$ characters
   IF L < 1 THEN LET L = 1
   LET T$ = REPEAT$(C$,L)
   LET PadEnds$ = T$ & S$ & T$
END DEF


SUB DelLeft(S$, C$, KillC)
! Scan string S$ and delete all characters from the left end and up
! to the first occurence of C$.
! The first occurence is also deleted if  KillC is not zero.

IF LEN(C$) > 1 THEN LET C$ = C$[1:1]
LET L = POS(S$,C$)
IF L = 0 THEN EXIT SUB ! Boundary character not found
IF KillC = 0 THEN LET L = L - 1
LET S$ = S$[L+1:MAXNUM]
END SUB


SUB DelRight(S$, C$, KillC)
! Scan string S$ and delete all characters from the right end and up
! to the first occurence of C$.
```

```
    ! The first occurence is also deleted if  KillC is not zero.

IF LEN(C$) > 1 THEN LET C$ = C$[1:1]
LET L = LEN(S$)
DO WHILE (S$[L:L] <> C$) AND (L > 0)
    LET L = L - 1
LOOP
IF L = 0 THEN EXIT SUB ! Boundary character not found
IF KillC <> 0 THEN LET L = L - 1
LET S$ = S$[1:L]
END SUB

SUB LeftTrim(S$)
! Remove leading spaces from string S$
LET S$ = LTRIM$(S$)
END SUB

SUB RightTrim(S$)
! Remove trailing spaces from string S$
LET S$ = RTRIM$(S$)
END SUB

SUB RemoveStr(S$, SubStr$)
! Remove all occureneces of SubStr$ from string S$.

LET K = LEN(SubStr$)
LET L = POS(S$, SubStr$)
DO WHILE L > 0
    IF L = 1 THEN
        LET S$ = S$[L+K:MAXNUM]
    ELSE
        LET S$ = S$[1:L-1] & S$[L+K:MAXNUM]
    END IF
    LET L = POS(S$, SubStr$)
LOOP
END SUB

SUB RemoveCharRange(S$, FC$, LC$)
! Remove all characters that meet the following criterion:
!
!     ASCII(FC$) <=  ASCII(char)   <= ASCII(LC$)

LET ASCII_LC = ORD(LC$)
LET ASCII_FC = ORD(FC$)

LET L = LEN(S$)
LET J = 0
FOR I = 1 TO L
    LET J = J + 1
    LET A = ORD(S$[J:J])
    IF (ASCII_FC <= A) AND (A <= ASCII_LC) THEN
        IF J = 1 THEN
            LET S$ = S$[2:MAXNUM]
        ELSEIF J = LEN(S$) THEN
            LET S$ = S$[1:J-1]
        ELSE
```

BASIC LIBRARIES

```
                LET S$ = S$[1:J-1] & S$[J+1:MAXNUM]
            END IF
            LET J = J - 1
        END IF
    NEXT I

END SUB

SUB TypeOverStr(S$, SubStr$, Index)
! The substring SubStr$ overwrites portions of S$ starting at Index
! The substring may be trunctaed if it causes S$ to expand
! The subroutine is EXITed if
!       1) The Index > length of string S$.
!       2) The Substring is a null string.
!       3) The subtring SubStr$ itself is larger than the string S$

LET L = LEN(S$)
LET J = LEN(SubStr$)
IF Index < 1 THEN LET Index = 1
IF (Index > L) OR (J = 0) OR (J > L) THEN EXIT SUB
IF (Index + J) > L THEN LET SubStr$ = SubStr$[1:(L - Index)]

IF Index = 1 THEN
    LET S$ = SubStr$ & S$[J+1:MAXNUM]
ELSEIF (Index + J) = L THEN
    LET S$ = S$[1:Index-1] & SubStr$
ELSE
    LET S$ = S$[1:Index-1] & SubStr$ & S$[Index+K:MAXNUM]
END IF

END SUB

SUB ReplaceStr(S$, SubStr$, Index, C$)
! Replaces portions of S$ with SubStr$ where character C$ is found.
! Action starts at Index position of string S$.
! The Substring is not scanned for C$ after it is inserted

LET J = LEN(SubStr$)
IF Index < 1 THEN LET Index = 1
IF Index > LEN(S$) THEN EXIT SUB
IF LEN(C$) > 1 THEN LET C$ = C$[1:1]

LET L = POS(S$, C$, Index)
DO WHILE L > 0

    LET Index = L + J

    IF L = 1 THEN
        LET S$ = SubStr$ & S$[2:MAXNUM]
    ELSEIF L = LEN(S$) THEN
        LET S$ = S$[1:L-1] & SubStr$
    ELSE
        LET S$ = S$[1:L-1] & SubStr$ & S$[L+1:MAXNUM]
    END IF

    LET L = POS(S$, C$, Index)
```

```
    LOOP

END SUB

SUB ReplaceChar(S$, OldChar$, NewChar$, Start)
! Replaces all the occurences of OldChar$ with NewChar$

IF (OldChar$ = "") OR (NewChar$ = "") THEN EXIT SUB
IF Start < 1 THEN LET Start = 1
IF Start > LEN(S$) THEN EXIT SUB

IF LEN(OldChar$) > 1 THEN LET OldChar$ = OldChar$[1:1]
IF LEN(NewChar$) > 1 THEN LET NewChar$ = NewChar$[1:1]

FOR I = Start TO LEN(S$)
    IF S$[I:I] = OldChar$ THEN LET S$[I:I] = NewChar$
NEXT I

END SUB


SUB ReplaceCharRange(S$, FirstChar$, LastChar$, NewChar$, Start)
! Replaces any character between FirstChar$ and LastChar$ with
NewChar$

IF (FirstChar$ = "") OR (LastChar$ = "") OR (NewChar$ = "") THEN
EXIT SUB
IF LEN(NewChar$)  > 1 THEN LET NewChar$ = NewChar$[1:1]

IF Start < 1 THEN LET Start = 1
IF Start > LEN(S$) THEN EXIT SUB

LET ASCII_FC = ORD(FirstChar$)
LET ASCII_LC = ORD(LastChar$)

FOR I = Start TO LEN(S$)
    LET A = ORD(S$[I:I])
    IF (ASCII_FC <= A) AND (A <= ASCII_LC) THEN
        LET S$[I:I] = NewChar$
    END IF
NEXT I

END SUB

!---------------------------------------------------------
! The following routines are inspired by the REXX language
!---------------------------------------------------------

DEF TestDelim(S$,Delim$,I)
! Local function used to test delimiter characters
 IF (POS(Delim$,S$[I-1:I-1]) = 0) AND (POS(Delim$,S$[I:I]) > 0) THEN
    LET TestDelim = 1
  ELSE
    LET TestDelim = 0
 END IF
```

```
END DEF


DEF GetWord$(S$, Delim$, GetNum)
! Scans string S$ and obtain the 'GetNum' word.
! String Delim$ provides the set of delimiter characters

IF GetNum < 1 THEN LET GetNum = 1
IF Delim$ = "" THEN LET Delim$ = " "
LET N = GetNum - 1
LET I = 1
LET L = LEN(S$)

! Loop until you find a non-Delim$ char or the end-of-string
DO WHILE (I <= L) AND (POS(Delim$,S$[I:I]) > 0)
   LET I = I + 1
LOOP

IF I > L THEN
   LET GetWord$ = ""
   EXIT DEF
END IF

IF N > 0 THEN LET I = I + 1

DO WHILE (I <= L) AND (N > 0)
    IF TestDelim(S$, Delim$, I) = 1 THEN LET N = N - 1
    LET I = I + 1
LOOP

IF N > 0 THEN
   LET GetWord$ = ""
ELSE

   DO WHILE (I <= L) AND (POS(Delim$,S$[I:I]) > 0)
      LET I = I + 1
   LOOP

   LET Ptr1 = I
   LET N = 1
   DO WHILE (I <= L) AND (N > 0)
      IF TestDelim(S$, Delim$, I) = 1 THEN LET N = N - 1
      LET I = I + 1
   LOOP
   LET GetWord$ = S$[Ptr1:I-2]
END IF

END DEF

DEF WordPos(S$, Delim$, Search$, Index)
! Returns the "word" count of Search$ in S$, starting at the Index'th word

IF POS(S$,Search$) = 0 THEN ! sought word is not is string
   LET WordPos = 0
   EXIT DEF
END IF
```

```
IF Delim$ = "" THEN LET Delim$ = " "

! Search for the Index'th word
LET L = LEN(S$)
LET N = Index - 1
LET I = 1

! Loop until you find a non-Delim$ char or the end-of-string
DO WHILE (I <= L) AND (POS(Delim$,S$[I:I]) > 0)
   LET I = I + 1
LOOP

IF I > L THEN
   LET WordPos = 0
   EXIT DEF
END IF

IF N > 0 THEN LET I = I + 1

DO WHILE (I <= L) AND (N > 0)
   IF TestDelim(S$, Delim$, I) = 1 THEN LET N = N - 1
   LET I = I + 1
LOOP

IF N > 0 THEN
   LET WordPos = 0
ELSE
   IF I > 1 THEN LET I = I - 1
   LET Ptr = POS(S$, Search$, I)
   LET Count = 1
   DO WHILE (I < Ptr)
      IF TestDelim(S$, Delim$, I) = 1 THEN LET Count = Count + 1
      LET I = I + 1
   LOOP
   LET WordPos = Count + Index - 1
END IF

END DEF


SUB DelWord(S$, Delim$, Start, Count)
! Delete 'Count' words starting from the Start'th word.
! If more words are specified there are to delete, the extra number
! is ignored.


IF Delim$ = "" THEN LET Delim$ = " "

! Search for the Start'th word
LET L = LEN(S$)
LET N = Start - 1
LET I = 1

! Loop until you find a non-Delim$ char or the end-of-string
DO WHILE (I <= L) AND (POS(Delim$,S$[I:I]) > 0)
```

```
        LET I = I + 1
LOOP

IF N > 0 THEN LET I = I + 1

DO WHILE (I <= L) AND (N > 0)
    IF TestDelim(S$, Delim$, I) = 1 THEN LET N = N - 1
    LET I = I + 1
LOOP

IF N = 0 THEN ! found the Start'th word

    ! Loop until you find a non-Delim$ char or the end-of-string
    DO WHILE (I <= L) AND (POS(Delim$,S$[I:I]) > 0)
      LET I = I + 1
    LOOP

    LET Ptr1 = I - 1 ! First character to delete
    LET N = Count
    DO WHILE (I <= L) AND (N > 0)
        IF TestDelim(S$, Delim$, I) = 1 THEN LET N = N - 1
        LET I = I + 1
    LOOP

    IF (N > 0) OR (I > L) THEN ! Delete to the end of string
        LET S$ = S$[1:Ptr1-1]
    ELSE           ! Deletion ends before the end of string
        LET S$ = S$[1:Ptr1] & S$[I:MAXNUM]
    END IF
END IF

END SUB


SUB InsertWord(S$, Delim$, NewWord$, Index)
! Insert NewWord$ AFTER the Index'th word in string S$

IF Delim$ = "" THEN LET Delim$ = " "

! Search for the Index'th word
LET L = LEN(S$)
LET N = Index
LET I = 1

! Loop until you find a non-Delim$ char or the end-of-string
DO WHILE (I <= L) AND (POS(Delim$,S$[I:I]) > 0)
   LET I = I + 1
LOOP

IF N > 0 THEN LET I = I + 1

DO WHILE (I <= L) AND (N > 0)
    IF TestDelim(S$, Delim$, I) = 1 THEN LET N = N - 1
    LET I = I + 1
LOOP
```

```
    IF N = 0 THEN ! found the Index'th word
       LET Ptr = I - 1
       ! The same delimiter character at Ptr1 is used in the insertion
       LET S$ = S$[1:Ptr] & NewWord$ & S$[Ptr:L]
    END IF

END SUB


SUB ParseToArray(S$, Delim$, PS$(), Count)
! Parses string S$ into an array of strings PS$().
! Count returns the parsed word count

LET L = LEN(S$)
IF L = 0 THEN EXIT SUB
IF Delim$ = "" THEN LET Delim$ = " "

! Initialize pointers and counters
LET I = 1
LET Count = 0

! Loop until you find a non-Delim$ char or the end-of-string
DO WHILE (I <= L) AND (POS(Delim$,S$[I:I]) > 0)
    LET I = I + 1
LOOP

LET Ptr1 = I ! assign to first non-delimiter char

IF I = 1 THEN LET I = 2

DO WHILE I <= L
    IF TestDelim(S$, Delim$, I) =   THEN
        LET Count = Count + 1
        MAT REDIM PS$(Count) ! Adjust dimension size
        LET Ptr2 = I - 1
        IF Ptr1 = Ptr2 THEN
            LET PS$(Count) = ""
        ELSE
            LET PS$(Count) = S$[Ptr1:Ptr2]
        END IF

        ! Loop until you find a non-Delim$ char or the end-of-string
        DO WHILE (I <= L) AND (POS(Delim$,S$[I:I]) > 0)
            LET I = I + 1
        LOOP

        LET Ptr1 = I

    END IF
    LET I = I + 1
LOOP

IF Ptr1 < L THEN
    LET Count = Count + 1
    MAT REDIM PS$(Count)
    LET PS$(Count) = S$[Ptr1:L]
    END IF
```

END SUB

END MODULE

Library Module NUMANAL

PURPOSE: The NUMANAL library module provides six BASIC subroutines to perform the following numerical analysis tasks:

1. numerical integration using Simpson's rule

2. numerical Lagrangian interpolation

3. numerical differentiation

4. solving a system of linear equations using LU decomposition

5. solving for all real and imaginary roots of a polynomial using the Lin-Bairstow method

Listings 3.7, 3.8, and 3.9 contain the library source code for the QuickBASIC, Turbo BASIC, and True BASIC versions, respectively.

ROUTINES

The following is a list of headings for function and subroutine definitions borrowed from the QuickBASIC listing. They are identical to those of Turbo BASIC. However, they contain minor syntactical differences compared to those of True BASIC, including:

1. subroutines in True BASIC need no STATIC declarations

2. no % or # is needed with numeric-typed parameters

SUB Integrate(Y#(1), First%, Last%, DeltaX#, Area#) STATIC
SUB Integrate(Y(), First, Last, DeltaX, Area) ! True BASIC

This subroutine implements Simpson's method for numerical integration using equidistant data. The number of data points (= *Last - First* + 1) must be an odd integer, otherwise the subroutine assigns *1.0E+30* to the area before exiting.

Y()	the array of curve values [INPUT]
First	the index of array *Y()* such that *Y(First)* is at the lower integration limit [INPUT]
Last	the index of array *Y()* such that *Y(Last)* is at the upper integration limit [INPUT]
Delta	step size for the independent variable [INPUT]
Area	area under the curve. [OUTPUT]

SUB   Interpolate(X#(1),Y#(1),First%,Last%,XInt#,YInt#)   STATIC
SUB   Interpolate(X(), Y(), First, Last, XInt, YInt) ! True BASIC

This subroutine implements the Lagrangian interpolation. The arrays of *X()* and *Y()* are supplied as reference points. The *First* and *Last* parameters assist in selecting a set of members in the array to be used in interpolating *XInt*. This type of choice gives the routine more flexibility by including or excluding points when necessary. This feature is very useful when handling a large array that covers a wide range of functions that are not smooth. The Lagrangian method does not require the data to be equidistant. However, avoid passing data with duplicate data in array *X()*.

X()	array of values for the independent variable [INPUT]
Y()	array of values for the dependent variable (i.e., function) [INPUT]
First	index of the first data point to enter interpolation [INPUT]
Last	index of the last data point to enter interpolation [INPUT]
XInt	value for interpolation [INPUT]
YInt	the interpolated value for the dependent variable [OUTPUT]

**SUB Differentiate(Y#(1),First%,Last%,DeltaX#,Slope#(1))
STATIC**

**SUB Differentiate(Y(), First, Last, DeltaX, Slope()) ! True
BASIC**

This routine performs numerical differentiation on equidistant data. The results are assigned to the *Slope()* array. Keep in mind that numerical differentiation is NOT a smooth operation: expect more errors than in numerical integration.

Y()	array of function values [INPUT]
First	index of first member of array *Y()* entering the numerical differentiation [INPUT]
Last	index of last member of array *Y()* entering the numerical differentiation [INPUT]
DeltaX	step size for the independent variable [INPUT]
Slope()	array of numerical slopes [OUTPUT]

**SUB Decomp(N%, SmallNum#, A#(2), LU#(2), RowIndex%(1),
Status#, Pivot%, S#(1)) STATIC**

**SUB Decomp(N,SmallNum,A(,),LU(,),RowIndex(),
Status,Pivot,S())! True BASIC**

This subroutine is the first of two routines that enable you to solve a system for simultaneous linear equations. The LU-decomposition is performed by this subroutine on matrix *A(,)* to return matrix *LU(,)*.

N	the number of equations (= unknown variables) [INPUT]
SmallNum	the small EPSILON value (use 1E-30) [INPUT]
A(,)	the input matrix [INPUT]

LU(,)	the LU-decomposed matrix [OUTPUT]
RowIndex()	the array of row orders [OUTPUT]
Status	the status of the decomposition [OUTPUT] If equal to zero, then the matrix is singular or nearly singular.
Pivot	Index of *RowIndex()* with largest pivot ratio [OUTPUT]
S()	array of largest absolute value of rows in matrix *A(,)* [OUTPUT]

SUB Solve(N%, LU#(2), RowIndex%(1), B#(1), X#(1)) STATIC
SUB Solve(N, LU(,), RowIndex(), B(), X()) ! True BASIC

This subroutine is used with routine *Decomp* to solve the matrix equation $AX = B$. The input to the routine is the *LU(,)* matrix and *RowIndex()* array, obtained from *Decomp*. The array *B()* supplies the solution vector and the solution to the system of equations is returned by array *X()*.

N	the size of the LU(,) matrix [INPUT]
LU(,)	LU-decomposed matrix [INPUT]
RowIndex()	the array of row order [INPUT]
B()	the array containing the solution vector [INPUT]
X()	the array returning the sought solution [OUTPUT]

BASIC LIBRARIES

SUB PolyRoots(Coeff#(1), RealRoot#(1), ImagRoot#(1), PolyOrder%, Accuracy#) STATIC

SUB PolyRoots(Coeff(),RealRoot(),ImagRoot(),PolyOrder, Accuracy)! True BASIC

This subroutine implements the Lin-Bairstow algorithm to solve for all the roots (real and imaginary) of polynomials with real coefficients. The solution is returned using the *RealRoot()* and *ImagRoot()* arrays. The first stores the real components of a root. The second contains the imaginary part. When the subroutine finds a real root, it stores a zero in the corresponding imaginary part. Thus, your application programs should test each member of the *ImagRoot()* array to determine whether or not the obtained root is real or complex.

The solution may be hampered by high accuracy requirements and supplying coefficients of an *unstable* polynomial.

Coeff()	the coefficient of the polynomial [INPUT]
	Y = Coeff(0) + Coeff(1) X + Coeff(2) X^2 + ...
RealRoot()	the array of real parts of real or complex roots [OUTPUT]
ImagRoot()	the array of imaginary parts of complex roots [OUTPUT]
PolyOrder	the order of the polynomial [INPUT]
Accuracy	the accuracy of solution [INPUT]

Listing 3.7. *QuickBASIC source code for the NUMANAL.BAS library.*

```
' Numerical analysis module
' QuickBASIC verion 3.0
' Copyright (c) 1987 Namir Clement Shammas


SUB Integrate(Y#(1), First%, Last%, DeltaX#, Area#) STATIC
' obtain Area# under curve using Simpson's rule
' Y#() is the array of data
' N% is the number of equidistant data points
' DeltaX# = Y#(2) - Y#(1) = Y#(3) - Y#(2) = ... = Y#(N%) - Y#(N%-1)
' Area# is the sought Area# under the curve

STATIC N%, Shift%, I%, SumOdd#, SumEven#

N% = Last% - First% + 1
Shift% = First% - 1

IF ((N% - (N%\2)*2) = 0) THEN ' N% is even
    Area# = 1.0E+30
    EXIT SUB
END IF

SumOdd# = Y#(Shift%+2)
SumEven# = Y#(Shift%+3)

FOR I% = Shift%+4 TO Shift%+N% STEP 2
    SumOdd# = SumOdd# + Y#(I%)
    SumEven# = SumEven# + Y#(I%+1)
NEXT I%

Area# = DeltaX#/3 * (Y#(Shift%+1) + 4*SumOdd# + 2*SumEven# - Y#(Shift%+N%))

END SUB


SUB Interpolate(X#(1), Y#(1), First%, Last%, XInt#, YInt#)  STATIC
' use Lagrangian interpolation to interpolate XInt# on YInt#

STATIC Term#, I%, J%

YInt# = 0 ' Initialize interpolated value

FOR I% = First% TO Last%
    Term# = 1 ' Initialize term value
    FOR J% = First% TO Last%
        IF I% <> J% THEN Term# = Term# * (XInt# - X#(J%))/(X#(I%) - X#(J%))
    NEXT J%
```

```
        YInt# = YInt# + Y#(I%) * Term#
NEXT I%

END SUB



SUB Differentiate(Y#(1), First%, Last%, DeltaX#, Slope#(1))   STATIC
' perform numerical differentiation using equidistant data
' array Slope returns the slopes

STATIC I%, N%, NN%, M%, Shift%, H#

N% = Last% - First% + 1
Shift% = First% - 1
M% = N% - (N% \ 3) * 3
H# = 2 * DeltaX#

FOR I% = Shift%+1 TO Shift%+N%-M% STEP 3
    Slope#(I%)   = (-3*Y#(I%) + 4*Y#(I%+1) - Y#(I%+2)) / H#
    Slope#(I%+1) = (Y#(I%+2) - Y#(I%)) / H#
    Slope#(I%+2) = (Y#(I%) - 4*Y#(I%+1) + 3*Y#(I%+2)) / H#
NEXT I%

NN% = Shift%+N%
IF M% > 0 THEN Slope#(NN%) = (Y#(NN%-2) - 4*Y#(NN%-1) + 3*Y#(NN%)) / H#
IF M% > 1 THEN Slope#(NN%-1) = (Y#(NN%) - Y#(NN%-2)) / H#

END SUB


SUB
Decomp(N%,SmallNum#,A#(2),LU#(2),RowIndex%(1),Status#,Pivot%,S#(1))
STATIC
' Decompses matrix A#(N%,N%) into LU#(N%,N%) matrix
' LU#() is the LU decomposition matrix
' RowIndex%() is the array of Row order
' Status# contains the result of the decomposition. A zero value signals
'        a singular matrix

STATIC Singular%, I%, J%, K%, M%, Index%, StopIndex%, StartIndex%
STATIC Ratio#, Sum#

Singular% = 0  ' Set sigular flag

' Initialize RowIndex%() and S#() arrays
FOR I% = 1 TO N%
    RowIndex%(I%) = I%
    S#(I%) = 0
    FOR J% = 1 TO N%
        IF (S#(I%) < ABS(A#(I%,J%))) THEN S#(I%) = ABS(A#(I%,J%))
    NEXT J%
NEXT I%

' Form the LU#(,) matrix
FOR M% = 1 TO N%
```

```
    StopIndex% = M% - 1
    FOR I% = M% TO N%
        Index% = RowIndex%(I%)
        Sum# = A#(Index%,M%)
        IF M% <> 1 THEN
            FOR K% = 1 TO StopIndex%
                Sum# = Sum# - LU#(Index%,K%)*LU#(RowIndex%(K%),M%)
            NEXT K%
        END IF
        LU#(Index%,M%) = Sum#
    NEXT I%

    ' Get Status#
    Status# = 0
    FOR K% = M% TO N%
        Index% = RowIndex%(K%)
        Ratio# = ABS(LU#(Index%,M%) / S#(Index%))
        IF Ratio# > Status# THEN
            Status# = Ratio#
            Pivot% = K%
        END IF
    NEXT K%

    Index% = RowIndex%(Pivot%)
    IF Pivot% <> M% THEN ' Swap rows M% and Pivot%
        RowIndex%(Pivot%) = RowIndex%(M%)
        RowIndex%(M%) = Index%
    END IF
    ' Quit if A is nearly singular or M% = N%
    LUPivot = LU#(Index%,M%)
    IF (Status# > SmallNum#) AND (ABS(LUPivot) > SmallX) THEN
        IF (Singular% <> 0) OR (M% = N%) THEN EXIT SUB
    ELSE
        Singular% = 1
    END IF

    ' Get entries of roe M% of upper matrix
    StartIndex% = M%+1
    FOR J% = StartIndex% TO N%
        Sum# = A#(Index%,J%)
        IF M% <> 1 THEN
            FOR K% = 1 TO StopIndex%
                Sum# = Sum# - LU#(Index%,K%)*LU#(RowIndex%(K%),J%)
            NEXT K%
        END IF
        LU#(Index%,J%) = Sum# / LUPivot
    NEXT J%
 NEXT M%

END SUB

SUB Solve(N%, LU#(2), RowIndex%(1), B#(1), X#(1)) STATIC
' The second routine that is used in solving A X = B
' B#() is the solution vector
' X#() is the array containing the solution to A X = B
```

BASIC LIBRARIES 185

```
        STATIC I%, J%, K%, Index%, StopIndex%, StartIndex%
        STATIC Sum#

        ' Start forward substitution
        FOR I% = 1 TO N%
            Index% = RowIndex%(I%)
            Pivot# = LU#(Index%,I%)
            StopIndex% = I% - 1
            Sum# = B#(Index%)
            IF I% <> 1 THEN
                FOR K% = 1 TO StopIndex%
                    Sum# = Sum# - LU#(Index%,K%)*X#(K%)
                NEXT K%
            END IF
            X#(I%) = Sum# / Pivot#
        NEXT I%

        IF N% = 1 THEN EXIT SUB

        ' Start backward substitution
        FOR I% = 2 TO N%
            J% = N% - I% + 1
            StartIndex% = J% + 1
            Sum# = X#(J%)
            FOR K% = StartIndex% TO N%
                Sum# = Sum# - LU#(RowIndex%(J%),K%)*X#(K%)
            NEXT K%
            X#(J%) = Sum#
        NEXT I%

        END SUB


        SUB PolyRoots(Coeff#(1), RealRoot#(1), ImagRoot#(1), PolyOrder%, Accuracy#) STATIC
        ' Subroutine that solves all the roots of a polynomial with real
        ' coefficients.  The Lin-Bairstow method is used.
        ' Coeff#() is the array of polynomial coefficients.  They are not altered.
        '
        ' polynomial is:
        '   Y = Coeff#(0) + Coeff#(1) X + Coeff#(2) X^2 + ... + Coeff#(N%) X^N%
        '
        ' RealRoot#() is the array of real parts of the roots
        ' ImagRoot#() is the array of the imaginary parts of the roots
        ' PolyOrder% is the order of the polynomial
        ' Accuracy# is the solution Accuracy# used

        STATIC Count%, N%, I%
        STATIC ALFA1#, ALFA2#, BETA1#, BETA2#, DELTA1#, DELTA2#, DELTA3#

        REM $DYNAMIC
        DIM CHS%(2)

        CHS%(1) = 1
        CHS%(2) = -1
        N% = PolyOrder%
```

```
DIM A#(N%+1), B#(N%+1), D#(N%+1)

FOR I% = 0 TO N%
    A#(N%-I%+1) = Coeff#(I%)
NEXT I%

IF A#(1) <> 1 THEN ' Adjust coefficients if needed
    FOR I% = N%+1 TO 1 STEP - 1
        A#(I%) = A#(I%) / A#(1)
    NEXT I%
END IF

Count% = 0

DO
    ' Start the main Lin-Bairstow iteration loop
      Initialize the counter and guesses for the coefficients of the
    ' quadratic factor,
    '
    '   p(x) = X^2 + ALFA1# * X + BETA1#
    '

    ALFA1# = 1 : BETA1# = 1

    DO
        B#(0) = 0 : D#(0) = 0
        B#(1) = 1 : D#(1) = 1

        FOR I% = 2 TO N%+1
            B#(I%) = A#(I%) - ALFA1# * B#(I%-1) - BETA1# * B#(I%-2)
            D#(I%) = B#(I%) - ALFA1# * D#(I%-1) - BETA1# * D#(I%-2)
        NEXT I%

        DELTA1# = D#(N%-1)^2 - (D#(N%) - B#(N%)) * D#(N%-2)
        ALFA2# = (B#(N%) * D#(N%-1) - B#(N%+1) * D#(N%-2)) / DELTA1#
        BETA2# = (B#(N%+1) * D#(N%-1) - (D#(N%) - B#(N%)) * B#(N%)) / DELTA1#
        ALFA1# = ALFA1# + ALFA2#
        BETA1# = BETA1# + BETA2#

    LOOP UNTIL ( (ABS(ALFA2#) <= Accuracy#) AND (ABS(BETA2#) <= Accuracy#) )

    DELTA1# = ALFA1#^2 - 4 * BETA1#

    IF DELTA1# < 0 THEN ' imaginary roots
        DELTA2# = SQR(ABS(DELTA1#)) / 2
        DELTA3# = ALFA1# / 2
        FOR I% = 1 TO 2
            RealRoot#(Count%+I%) = DELTA2#
            ImagRoot#(Count%+I%) = CHS%(I%) * DELTA3#
        NEXT I%
    ELSE ' Real roots
        FOR I% = 1 TO 2
            ImagRoot#(Count%+I%) = 0
        NEXT I%
        RealRoot#(Count%+1) = (SQR(DELTA1#) - ALFA1#) / 2
        RealRoot#(Count%+2) = (SQR(DELTA1#) + ALFA1#) / (-2)
```

```
        END IF

        ' Update root counter
        Count% = Count% + 2

        ' Reduce polynomial order
        N% = N% - 2

        ' For N% > 2 calculate coefficients of the new polynomial
        IF N% >= 2 THEN
            FOR I% = 1 TO N%+1
                A#(I%) = B#(I%)
            NEXT I%
        END IF

LOOP UNTIL N% < 2

IF N% = 1 THEN   ' Obtain last signle real root
    RealRoot#(Count%+1) = -B#(2)
    ImagRoot#(Count%+1) = 0
END IF

Erase A#, B#, D#, CHS%  ' Erase local arrays before exiting
subroutine

END SUB
```

Listing 3.8. *Turbo BASIC source code for the NUMANAL.BAS library*

```
' Numerical analysis module
' Turbo BASIC verion 1.0
' Copyright (c) 1987 Namir Clement Shammas


SUB Integrate(Y#(1), First%, Last%, DeltaX#, Area#) STATIC
' obtain Area# under curve using Simpson's rule
' Y#() is the array of data
' N% is the number of equidistant data points
' DeltaX# = Y#(2) - Y#(1) = Y#(3) - Y#(2) = ... = Y#(N%) - Y#(N%-1)
' Area# is the sought Area# under the curve

LOCAL N%, Shift%, I%, SumOdd#, SumEven#

N% = Last% - First% + 1
Shift% = First% - 1

IF (N% - (N%\2)*2) = 0 THEN  ' N% is even
    Area# = 1.0E+30
```

```
        EXIT SUB
END IF

SumOdd# = Y#(Shift%+2)
SumEven# = Y#(Shift%+3)

FOR I% = Shift%+4 TO Shift%+N% STEP 2
    SumOdd# = SumOdd# + Y#(I%)
    SumEven# = SumEven# + Y#(I%+1)
NEXT I%

Area# = DeltaX#/3 * (Y#(Shift%+1) + 4*SumOdd# + 2*SumEven# -
Y#(Shift%+N%))

END SUB


SUB Interpolate(X#(1), Y#(1), First%, Last%, XInt#, YInt#)   STATIC
' use Lagrangian interpolation to interpolate XInt# on YInt#

LOCAL Term#, I%, J%

YInt# = 0 ' Initialize interpolated value

FOR I% = First% TO Last%
    Term# = 1# ' Initialize term value
    FOR J% = First% TO Last%
        IF I% <> J% THEN Term# = Term# * (XInt# - X#(J%))/(X#(I%) -
X#(J%))
    NEXT J%
    YInt# = YInt# + Y#(I%) * Term#
NEXT I%

END SUB



SUB Differentiate(Y#(1), First%, Last%, DeltaX#, Slope#(1))   STATIC
' perform numerical differentiation using equidistant data
' array Slope returns the slopes

LOCAL I%, N%, NN%, M%, Shift%, H#

N% = Last% - First% + 1
Shift% = First% - 1
M% = N% - (N% \ 3) * 3
H# = 2 * DeltaX#

FOR I% = Shift%+1 TO Shift%+N%-M% STEP 3
    Slope#(I%)   = (-3*Y#(I%) + 4*Y#(I%+1) - Y#(I%+2)) / H#
    Slope#(I%+1) = (Y#(I%+2) - Y#(I%)) / H#
    Slope#(I%+2) = (Y#(I%) - 4*Y#(I%+1) + 3*Y#(I%+2)) / H#
NEXT I%

NN% = Shift%+N%
IF M% > 0 THEN Slope#(NN%) = (Y#(NN%-2) - 4*Y#(NN%-1) + 3*Y#(NN%)) / H#
```

BASIC LIBRARIES

```
    IF M% > 1 THEN Slope#(NN%-1) = (Y#(NN%) - Y#(NN%-2)) / H#

END SUB


SUB
Decomp(N%,SmallNum#,A#(2),LU#(2),RowIndex%(1),Status#,Pivot%,S#(1))
STATIC
' Decompses matrix A#(N%,N%) into LU#(N%,N%) matrix
' LU#() is the LU decomposition matrix
' RowIndex%() is the array of Row order
' Status# contains the result of the decomposition. A zero value signals
'       a singular matrix

LOCAL Singular%, I%, J%, K%, M%, Index%, StopIndex%, StartIndex%
LOCAL Ratio#, Sum#

Singular% = 0  ' Set sigular flag

' Initialize RowIndex%() and S#() arrays
FOR I% = 1 TO N%
    RowIndex%(I%) = I%
    S#(I%) = 0
    FOR J% = 1 TO N%
        IF (S#(I%) < ABS(A#(I%,J%))) THEN S#(I%) = ABS(A#(I%,J%))
    NEXT J%
NEXT I%

' Form the LU#(,) matrix
FOR M% = 1 TO N%
    StopIndex% = M% - 1
    FOR I% = M% TO N%
        Index% = RowIndex%(I%)
        Sum# = A#(Index%,M%)
        IF M% <> 1 THEN
            FOR K% = 1 TO StopIndex%
                Sum# = Sum# - LU#(Index%,K%)*LU#(RowIndex%(K%),M%)
            NEXT K%
        END IF
        LU#(Index%,M%) = Sum#
    NEXT I%

    ' Get Status#
    Status# = 0
    FOR K% = M% TO N%
        Index% = RowIndex%(K%)
        Ratio# = ABS(LU#(Index%,M%) / S#(Index%))
        IF Ratio# > Status# THEN
            Status# = Ratio#
            Pivot% = K%
        END IF
    NEXT K%

    Index% = RowIndex%(Pivot%)
    IF Pivot% <> M% THEN  ' Swap rows M% and Pivot%
        RowIndex%(Pivot%) = RowIndex%(M%)
```

```
            RowIndex%(M%) = Index%
        END IF
        ' Quit if A is nearly singular or M% = N%
        LUPivot = LU#(Index%,M%)
        IF (Status# > SmallNum#) AND (ABS(LUPivot) > SmallX) THEN
            IF (Singular% <> 0) OR (M% = N%) THEN EXIT SUB
        ELSE
            Singular% = 1
        END IF

        ' Get entries of roe M% of upper matrix
        StartIndex% = M%+1
        FOR J% = StartIndex% TO N%
            Sum# = A#(Index%,J%)
            IF M% <> 1 THEN
                FOR K% = 1 TO StopIndex%
                    Sum# = Sum# - LU#(Index%,K%)*LU#(RowIndex%(K%),J%)
                NEXT K%
            END IF
            LU#(Index%,J%) = Sum# / LUPivot
        NEXT J%
    NEXT M%

END SUB

SUB Solve(N%, LU#(2), RowIndex%(1), B#(1), X#(1)) STATIC
' The second routine that is used in solving A X = B
' B#() is the solution vector
' X#() is the array containing the solution to A X = B

LOCAL I%, J%, K%, Index%, StopIndex%, StartIndex%
LOCAL Sum#

' Start forward substitution
FOR I% = 1 TO N%
    Index% = RowIndex%(I%)
    Pivot# = LU#(Index%,I%)
    StopIndex% = I% - 1
    Sum# = B#(Index%)
    IF I% <> 1 THEN
        FOR K% = 1 TO StopIndex%
            Sum# = Sum# - LU#(Index%,K%)*X#(K%)
        NEXT K%
    END IF
    X#(I%) = Sum# / Pivot#
NEXT I%

IF N% = 1 THEN EXIT SUB

' Start backward substitution
FOR I% = 2 TO N%
    J% = N% - I% + 1
    StartIndex% = J% + 1
    Sum# = X#(J%)
    FOR K% = StartIndex% TO N%
        Sum# = Sum# - LU#(RowIndex%(J%),K%)*X#(K%)
```

```
        NEXT K%
        X#(J%) = Sum#
NEXT I%

END SUB



SUB PolyRoots(Coeff#(1), RealRoot#(1), ImagRoot#(1), PolyOrder%,
Accuracy#) STATIC
' Subroutine that solves all the roots of a polynomial with real
' coefficients.  The Lin-Bairstow method is used.
' Coeff#() is the array of polynomial coefficients.  They are not altered.
'
' polynomial is:
'    Y = Coeff#(0) + Coeff#(1) X + Coeff#(2) X^2 + ... + Coeff#(N%) X^N%
'
' RealRoot#() is the array of real parts of the roots
' ImagRoot#() is the array of the imaginary parts of the roots
' PolyOrder% is the order of the polynomial
' Accuracy# is the solution Accuracy# used

LOCAL A#(), B#(), D#(), CHS%(), Count%, N%, I%
LOCAL ALFA1#, ALFA2#, BETA1#, BETA2#, DELTA1#, DELTA2#, DELTA3#
DIM CHS%(2)

CHS%(1) = 1
CHS%(2) = -1
N% = PolyOrder%

DIM A#(N%+1), B#(N%+1), D#(N%+1)

FOR I% = 0 TO N%
    A#(N%-I%+1) = Coeff#(I%)
NEXT I%

IF A#(1) <> 1 THEN ' Adjust coefficients if needed
    FOR I% = N%+1 TO 1 STEP - 1
        A#(I%) = A#(I%) / A#(1)
    NEXT I%
END IF

Count% = 0

DO
    ' Start the main Lin-Bairstow iteration loop
    ' Initialize the counter and guesses for the coefficients of the
    ' quadratic factor,
    '
    '    p(x) = X^2 + ALFA1# * X + BETA1#
    '
    ALFA1# = 1 : BETA1# = 1

    DO
        B#(0) = 0 : D#(0) = 0
        B#(1) = 1 : D#(1) = 1
```

```
            FOR I% = 2 TO N%+1
                B#(I%) = A#(I%) - ALFA1# * B#(I%-1) - BETA1# * B#(I%-2)
                D#(I%) = B#(I%) - ALFA1# * D#(I%-1) - BETA1# * D#(I%-2)
            NEXT I%

            DELTA1# = D#(N%-1)^2 - (D#(N%) - B#(N%)) * D#(N%-2)
            ALFA2# = (B#(N%) * D#(N%-1) - B#(N%+1) * D#(N%-2)) / DELTA1#
            BETA2# = (B#(N%+1) * D#(N%-1) - (D#(N%) - B#(N%)) * B#(N%)) / DELTA1#
            ALFA1# = ALFA1# + ALFA2#
            BETA1# = BETA1# + BETA2#

        LOOP UNTIL ( (ABS(ALFA2#) <= Accuracy#) AND (ABS(BETA2#) <= Accuracy#) )

        DELTA1# = ALFA1#^2 - 4 * BETA1#

        IF DELTA1# < 0 THEN ' imaginary roots
            DELTA2# = SQR(ABS(DELTA1#)) / 2
            DELTA3# = ALFA1# / 2
            FOR I% = 1 TO 2
                RealRoot#(Count%+I%) = DELTA2#
                ImagRoot#(Count%+I%) = CHS%(I%) * DELTA3#
            NEXT I%
        ELSE ' Real roots
            FOR I% = 1 TO 2
                ImagRoot#(Count%+I%) = 0
            NEXT I%
            RealRoot#(Count%+1) = (SQR(DELTA1#) - ALFA1#) / 2
            RealRoot#(Count%+2) = (SQR(DELTA1#) + ALFA1#) / (-2)
        END IF

        ' Update root counter
        Count% = Count% + 2

        ' Reduce polynomial order
        N% = N% - 2

        ' For N% > 2 calculate coefficients of the new polynomial
        IF N% >= 2 THEN
            FOR I% = 1 TO N%+1
                A#(I%) = B#(I%)
            NEXT I%
        END IF

LOOP UNTIL N% < 2

IF N% = 1 THEN ' Obtain last signle real root
    RealRoot#(Count%+1) = -B#(2)
    ImagRoot#(Count%+1) = 0
END IF

Erase A#, B#, D#, CHS% ' Erase local arrays before leaving subroutine

END SUB
```

Listing 3.9. *True BASIC source code for the NUMANAL.TRU module*

```
MODULE Numerical_Analysis

! Numerical analysis module
! True BASIC verion
! Copyright (c) 1987 Namir Clement Shammas


SUB Integrate(Y(),First,Last,DeltaX,Area)
! obtain area under curve using Simpson's rule
! Y() is the array of data
! N is the number of equidistant data points
! Deltax = Y(2) - Y(1) = Y(3) - Y(2) = ... = Y(N) - Y(N-1)
! Area is the sought area under the curve

LET N = Last - First + 1
LET Shift = First - 1

IF (N - INT(N/2)*2) = 0 THEN ! N is even
    LET Area = MAXNUM
    EXIT SUB
END IF

LET SumOdd  = Y(Shift+2)
LET SumEven = Y(Shift+3)

FOR I = Shift+4 TO Shift+N STEP 2
    LET SumOdd = SumOdd + Y(I)
    LET SumEven = SumEven + Y(I+1)
NEXT I

LET Area = DeltaX/3 * (Y(Shift+1) + 4*SumOdd + 2*SumEven - Y(Shift+N))

END SUB


SUB Interpolate(X(),Y(),First,Last,XInt,YInt)
! Perform Lagrangian interpolation

LET YInt = 0

FOR I = First TO Last
    LET Term = 1
    FOR J = First TO Last
        IF I <> J THEN LET Term = Term * (XInt - X(J))/(X(I) - X(J))
    NEXT J
    LET YInt = YInt + Y(I) * Term
NEXT I

END SUB
```

```
SUB Differentiate(Y(),First,Last,DeltaX,Slope())
! perform numerical differentiation using equidistant data
! array Slope returns the slopes
LET N = Last - First + 1
LET Shift = First - 1
LET M = N - INT(N/3)*3
LET H = 2 * DeltaX
FOR I = Shift+1 TO Shift+N-M STEP 3
    LET Slope(I)   = (-3*Y(I) + 4*Y(I+1) - Y(I+2)) / H
    LET Slope(I+1) = (Y(I+2) - Y(I)) / H
    LET Slope(I+2) = (Y(I) - 4*Y(I+1) + 3*Y(I+2)) / H
NEXT I

LET NN = Shift + N
IF M > 0 THEN LET Slope(NN) = (Y(NN-2) - 4*Y(NN-1) + 3*Y(NN)) / H
IF M > 1 THEN LET Slope(NN-1) = (Y(NN) - Y(NN-2)) / H

END SUB


SUB Decomp(N, SmallNum, A(,), LU(,), RowIndex(), Status, Pivot, S())
! Decompses matrix A(N,N) into LU(N,N) matrix
! LU() is the LU decomposition matrix
! RowIndex() is the array of Row order
! Status contains the result of the decomposition. A zero value signals
!       a singular matrix

MAT LU = ZER(N,N) ! Ensure correct size of LU(,) matrix
MAT REDIM RowIndex(N), S(N)

LET Singular = 0 ! Set sigular flag
! Initialize RowIndex() and S() arrays
FOR I = 1 TO N
    LET RowIndex(I) = I
    LET S(I) = 0
    FOR J = 1 TO N
        LET S(I) = MAX(S(I),ABS(A(I,J)))
    NEXT J
NEXT I

! Form the LU(,) matrix
FOR M = 1 TO N
    LET StopIndex = M - 1
    FOR I = M TO N
        LET Index = RowIndex(I)
        LET Sum = A(Index,M)
        IF M <> 1 THEN
            FOR K = 1 TO StopIndex
                LET Sum = Sum - LU(Index,K)*LU(RowIndex(K),M)
            NEXT K
        END IF
        LET LU(Index,M) = Sum
    NEXT I
```

```
        ! Get Status
        LET Status = 0
        FOR K = M TO N
            LET Index = RowIndex(K)
            LET Ratio = ABS(LU(Index,M) / S(Index))
            IF Ratio > Status THEN
                LET Status = Ratio
                LET Pivot = K
            END IF
        NEXT K

        LET Index = RowIndex(Pivot)
        IF Pivot <> M THEN ! Swap rows M and Pivot
            LET RowIndex(Pivot) = RowIndex(M)
            LET RowIndex(M) = Index
        END IF
        ! Quit if A is nearly singular or M = N
        LET LUPivot = LU(Index,M)
        IF (Status > SmallNum) AND (ABS(LUPivot) > SmallX) THEN
            IF (Singular <> 0) OR (M = N) THEN EXIT SUB
        ELSE
            LET Singular = 1
        END IF

        ! Get entries of roe M of upper matrix
        LET StartIndex = M+1
        FOR J = StartIndex TO N
            LET Sum = A(Index,J)
            IF M <> 1 THEN
                FOR K = 1 TO StopIndex
                    LET Sum = Sum - LU(Index,K)*LU(RowIndex(K),J)
                NEXT K
            END IF
            LET LU(Index,J) = Sum / LUPivot
        NEXT J
    NEXT M

END SUB

SUB Solve(N, LU(,), RowIndex(), B(), X())
! The second routine that is used in solving A X = B
! B() is the solution vector
! X() is the array containing the solution to A X = B

! Start forward substitution
FOR I = 1 TO N
    LET Index = RowIndex(I)
    LET Pivot = LU(Index,I)
    LET StopIndex = I - 1
    LET Sum = B(Index)
    IF I <> 1 THEN
        FOR K = 1 TO StopIndex
            LET Sum = Sum - LU(Index,K)*X(K)
        NEXT K
    END IF
    LET X(I) = Sum / Pivot
```

```
    NEXT I

    IF N = 1 THEN EXIT SUB

    ! Start backward substitution
    FOR I = 2 TO N
        LET J = N - I + 1
        LET StartIndex = J + 1
        LET Sum = X(J)
        FOR K = StartIndex TO N
            LET Sum = SUm - LU(RowIndex(J),K)*X(K)
        NEXT K
        LET X(J) = Sum
    NEXT I

END SUB


SUB PolyRoots(Coeff(), RealRoot(), ImagRoot(), PolyOrder, Accuracy)
! Subroutine that solves all the roots of a polynomial with real
! coefficients.  The Lin-Bairstow method is used.
! Coeff() is the array of polynomial coefficients.  They are not altered.
!
! polynomial is:
!   Y = Coeff(0) + Coeff(1) X + Coeff(2) X^2 + ... + Coeff(N) X^N
!
! RealRoot() is the array of real parts of the roots
! ImagRoot() is the array of the imaginary parts of the roots
! PolyOrder is the order of the polynomial
! Accuracy is the solution accuracy used
OPTION BASE 0

DIM A(10), B(10), D(10), CHS(2)

LET CHS(1) = 1
LET CHS(2) = -1
LET N = PolyOrder

MAT REDIM A(N+1), B(N+1), D(N+1)

FOR I = 0 TO N
    LET A(N-I+1) = Coeff(I)
NEXT I

IF A(1) <> 1 THEN  ! Adjust coefficients if needed
    FOR I = N+1 TO 1 STEP - 1
        LET A(I) = A(I) / A(1)
    NEXT I
END IF

LET Count = 0

DO
    ! Start the main Lin-Bairstow iteration loop
    ! Initialize the counter and guesses for the coefficients of the
    ! quadratic factor,
```

```
    !
    !   p(x) = X^2 + ALFA1 * X + BETA1
    !

    LET ALFA1, BETA1 = 1

    DO
        LET B(0), D(0) = 0
        LET B(1), D(1) = 1

        FOR I = 2 TO N+1
            LET B(I) = A(I) - ALFA1 * B(I-1) - BETA1 * B(I-2)
            LET D(I) = B(I) - ALFA1 * D(I-1) - BETA1 * D(I-2)
        NEXT I
        LET DELTA1 = D(N-1)^2 - (D(N) - B(N)) * D(N-2)
        LET ALFA2 = (B(N) * D(N-1) - B(N+1) * D(N-2)) / DELTA1
        LET BETA2 = (B(N+1) * D(N-1) - (D(N) - B(N)) * B(N)) / DELTA1
        LET ALFA1 = ALFA1 + ALFA2
        LET BETA1 = BETA1 + BETA2

    LOOP UNTIL ( (ABS(ALFA2) <= Accuracy) AND (ABS(BETA2) <= Accuracy) )

    LET DELTA1 = ALFA1^2 - 4 * BETA1

    IF DELTA1 < 0 THEN ! imaginary roots
        LET DELTA2 = SQR(ABS(DELTA1)) / 2
        LET DELTA3 = ALFA1 / 2
        FOR I = 1 TO 2
            LET RealRoot(Count+I) = DELTA2
            LET ImagRoot(Count+I) = CHS(I) * DELTA3
        NEXT I
    ELSE ! Real roots
        FOR I = 1 TO 2
            LET ImagRoot(Count+I) = 0
        NEXT I
        LET RealRoot(Count+1) = (SQR(DELTA1) - ALFA1) / 2
        LET RealRoot(Count+2) = (SQR(DELTA1) + ALFA1) / (-2)
    END IF

    ! Update root counter
    LET Count = Count + 2

    ! Reduce polynomial order
    LET N = N - 2

    ! For N > 2 calculate coefficients of the new polynomial
    IF N >= 2 THEN
        FOR I = 1 TO N+1
            LET A(I) = B(I)
        NEXT I
    END IF

LOOP UNTIL N < 2

IF N = 1 THEN ! Obtain last signle real root
    LET RealRoot(Count+1) = -B(2)
```

```
        LET ImagRoot(Count+1) = 0
    END IF

END SUB

END MODULE
```

In comparing the listings of the three versions, notice that they are very similar and easily converted from one version to another. This is generally true for number-crunching routines. In subroutine *Decomp*, there is one functional difference between True BASIC and the others. The True BASIC subroutine version is able to expand the size of the parameter matrix $LU(,)$ to match the size of parameter matrix $A(,)$. This exempts the application program from ensuring adequate dimension space for the $LU(,)$ matrix. This is not the case with QuickBASIC and Turbo BASIC, because you cannot redimension a matrix parameter. In the *PolyRoots* subroutine, the True BASIC first DIMensions the local routines with integer constant limits and then adjusts their sizes with MAT REDIM. By contrast, QuickBASIC and Turbo BASIC simply dimension the local arrays using one of the routine parameters.

The following set of programs uses various parts of library NUMANAL and TOOLBOX0. The first two programs will have listings in all three BASIC implementations. The rest will be listed for Turbo BASIC (they are also compatible with QuickBASIC).

The first application enables you to solve for the roots of a polynomial. The program consists of two nested loops. The inner loop is used to obtain data from the keyboard and to confirm the data. The outer loop performs the following:

+obtains the data using the inner loop

+performs the needed subroutine calls

+displays the results

+queries the user for additional calculation

First, I will show how the program works. Next, I will present the listings and discuss the differences between the three versions.

When the program starts running, it clears the screen and displays the centered title *ROOTS OF A POLYNOMIAL*. The program proceeds to request the polynomial order and the polynomial coefficients. Figure 3.1.1 shows the input screen when solving for the roots of:

```
P(X) = X^3 + 10
```

```
                     ROOTS OF A POLYNOMIAL
                     ---------------------

        Enter polynomial degree (2->10)? 3

        Enter X( 0 ) ? 10
        Enter X( 1 ) ? 0
        Enter X( 2 ) ? 0
        Enter X( 3 ) ? 1

        Information correct (Y/N) ? y
```

Figure 3.1.1 *Input screen image when running TESTNUM1.BAS with Turbo BASIC.*

The screen clears and the results are displayed as shown in Figure 3.1.2. The solution yields two complex roots and one real root:

```
             1.86580 +/- i 1.07722

                 -2.15532
```

```
            ROOTS OF A POLYNOMIAL
            --------------------

        Root #      Real    part      Imaginary part
        ------      ------------      --------------
          1         +1.86580E+00      -107722E+00

          2         +1.86580E+00      +1.07722E+00

          3         -2.15532E+00      +0.00000E+00




Want to process another polynomial (Y/N) ? n
```

Figure 3.1.2 *Output screen image when running TESTNUM1.BAS with Turbo BASIC.*

Now that we have seen the application running, here are the listings.

Listing 3.10. *QuickBASIC source code for TESTNUM1.BAS application program to solve for the roots of a polynomial.*

```
'PROGRAM Test_NUMANAL_Module

' QuickBASIC 3.0 program to test NUMANAL.BAS module.
' General-purpose module TOOLBOX0.BAS is also used.
' This program solves for all the roots of a polynomial
' Copyright (c) 1987 Namir Clement Shammas

OPTION BASE 0

DIM Coeff#(20), RealRoot#(20), ImagRoot#(20)
```

```
' include libraries NUMANAL.BAS and TOOLBOX0.BAS
REM $INCLUDE: 'NUMANAL.BAS'
REM $INCLUDE: 'TOOLBOX0.BAS'

DO ' Outer loop

 DO ' Inner loop for data entry

    CALL Display.Heading
    PolyOrder% = FNInteger.In.Range%("Enter polynomial degree (2->10)",2,10)
    PRINT
    FOR I% = 0 TO PolyOrder%
        PRINT "Enter X(";I%;
        INPUT   ") "; Coeff#(I%)
    NEXT I%
    PRINT
    ' use FNYesNo$ function in TOOLBOX0
    OK$ = FNYesNo$("Information correct")

 LOOP UNTIL OK$ = "Y"

 Accuracy# = 0.001 ' assign accuracy
 ' call routine in library NUMANAL.BAS
 CALL PolyRoots(Coeff#(), RealRoot#(), ImagRoot#(), PolyOrder%, Accuracy#)

 ' display results
 CALL Display.Heading

 PRINT "            Root #         Real   part      Imaginary part"
 PRINT "            ------         -------------    --------------"
 Img$ = "             ##           +#.#####^^^^      +#.#####^^^^"

 FOR I% = 1 TO PolyOrder%
    PRINT USING Img$ ; I%, RealRoot#(I%), ImagRoot#(I%)
 NEXT I%

 ' use FNYesNo$ function in TOOLBOX0
 LOCATE 22,1
 OK$ = FNYesNo$("Want to process another polynomial")

LOOP UNTIL OK$ = "N"


SUB Display.Heading STATIC

CLS
' use Center_Message and Blank_Lines in TOOLBOX0
CALL Center.Message("ROOTS OF A POLYNOMIAL",1)
CALL Center.Message("---------------------",2)
CALL Blank.Lines(3)

END SUB

END
```

Listing 3.11. *Turbo BASIC source code for TESTNUM1.BAS application program to solve for the roots of a polynomial*

```
'PROGRAM Test.NUMANAL.Module

' Turbo BASIC 1.0 program to test NUMANAL.BAS module.
' General-purpose module TOOLBOX0.BAS is also used.
' This program solves for all the roots of a polynomial
' Copyright (c) 1987 Namir Clement Shammas

OPTION BASE 0

DIM Coeff#(20),RealRoot#(20),ImagRoot#(20)

' include libraries NUMANAL.BAS and TOOLBOX0.BAS
$INCLUDE "NUMANAL.BAS"
$INCLUDE "TOOLBOX0.BAS"

DO ' Outer loop

  DO ' Inner loop for data entry
     CALL Display.Heading
     PolyOrder% = FNInteger.In.Range%("Enter polynomial degree (2->10)",2,10)
     PRINT
     FOR I% = 0 TO PolyOrder%
         PRINT "Enter X(";I%;
         INPUT    ") "; Coeff#(I%)
     NEXT I%
     PRINT
     ' use FNYesNo$ function in TOOLBOX0
     OK$ = FNYesNo$("Information correct")

  LOOP UNTIL OK$ = "Y"

  Accuracy# = 0.001 ' assign accuracy
  ' call routine in library NUMANAL.BAS
  CALL PolyRoots(Coeff#(), RealRoot#(), ImagRoot#(), PolyOrder%, Accuracy#)

  ' display results
  CALL Display.Heading

  PRINT "              Root #        Real    part     Imaginary part"
  PRINT "              ------        -------------    ---------------"
  Img$ = "              ##          +#.#####^^^^    +#.#####^^^^"

  FOR I% = 1 TO PolyOrder%
     PRINT USING Img$ ; I%, RealRoot#(I%), ImagRoot#(I%)
  NEXT I%

  ' use FNYesNo$ function in TOOLBOX0
  LOCATE 22,1
```

```
    OK$ = FNYesNo$("Want to process another polynomial")

LOOP UNTIL OK$ = "N"


SUB Display.Heading STATIC

CLS
' use Center_Message and Blank_Lines in TOOLBOX0
CALL Center.Message("ROOTS OF A POLYNOMIAL",1)
CALL Center.Message("--------------------",2)
CALL Blank.Lines(3)

END SUB

END
```

Listing 3.12. *True BASIC source code for TESTNUM1.TRU application program to solve for the roots of a polynomial*

```
PROGRAM Test_NUMANAL_Module

! True BASIC program to test NUMANAL.TRU module.
! General-purpose module TOOLBOX0.TRU is also used.
! This program solves for all the roots of a polynomial
! Copyright (c) 1987 Namir Clement Shammas

OPTION BASE 0

! include modules NUMANAL.TRU and TOOLBOX0.TRU
Library "NUMANAL.TRU","TOOLBOX0.TRU"

! Declare imported function(s)
DECLARE DEF YesNo$, Integer_In_Range

DIM Coeff(20),RealRoot(20),ImagRoot(20)

DO ! Outer loop

  DO ! Inner loop for data entry
     CALL Display_Heading
     LET PolyOrder = Integer_In_Range("Enter polynomial degree(2->10)",2,10)
     PRINT
     FOR I = 0 TO PolyOrder
         PRINT "Enter X(";I;
         INPUT PROMPT ") : ": Coeff(I)
     NEXT I
     PRINT
     ! use YesNo$ function in TOOLBOX0
     LET OK$ = YesNo$("Information correct")
```

```
LOOP UNTIL OK$ = "Y"

LET Accuracy = 0.001 ! assign accuracy
! call routine in module NUMANAL.TRU
CALL PolyRoots(Coeff(), RealRoot(), ImagRoot(), PolyOrder, Accuracy)

! display results
CALL Display_Heading

PRINT "            Root #          Real    part    Imaginary part"
PRINT "            ------          -------------    --------------"
LET Img$ = "             ##          +#.#####^^^^^    +#.#####^^^^^"

FOR I = 1 TO PolyOrder
   PRINT USING Img$ : I, RealRoot(I), ImagRoot(I)
NEXT I

! use YesNo$ function in TOOLBOX0
SET CURSOR 22,1
LET OK$ = YesNo$("Want to process another polynomial")

LOOP UNTIL OK$ = "N"

SUB Display_Heading
! internal subroutine to display centered message
CLEAR ! clear screen
! use Center_Message and Blank_Lines in TOOLBOX0
CALL Center_Message("ROOTS OF A POLYNOMIAL",1)
CALL Center_Message("---------------------",2)
CALL Blank_Lines(3)

END SUB

END
```

Looking at listings 3.10, 3.11, and 3.12, notice the following:

1. QuickBASIC and Turbo BASIC have the libraries included in the program. True BASIC uses the LIBRARY declaration. An alternate route for invoking the subroutines in library NUMANAL is to create NUMANAL.EXE library and invoke it as the alternate library. I chose to use QuickBASIC metacommands because they are a bit clearer. All library files are assumed to be located on the current directory.

2. The functions imported from True BASIC modules must be listed in a DECLARE DEF statement. Since function names in the other BASICs start with the letters *FN*, no similar declaration is needed.

3. QuickBASIC 3.0 is used in writing the QuickBASIC version. If you have QuickBASIC 2.0, you must convert all DO LOOPs into WHILE-WEND loops. Notice that the other BASICs also use the same DO LOOPs.

4. The *FNInteger.In.Range%()* function (*Integer_In_Range()* in True BASIC), found in TOOLBOX0, is used to control integer input. The program uses this function to ensure that you type a number between two and ten.

5. The *FNYesNo$()* function (*YesNo$* in True BASIC), imported from TOOLBOX0, is used in prompting you for a Yes/No answer.

6. By virtue of using the INCLUDE directives in QuickBASIC and Turbo BASIC, the compiled program contains the code of many unused routines. You can minimize this waste by creating your own working library versions that include routines you frequently use. The True BASIC compiler optimizes the running code by importing only those routines used by the application program.

The above comments may be generalized for similar comparisons involving other application programs.

The second sample application program solves systems of simultaneous linear equations. The program consists of two DO-LOOPs. The inner DO-LOOP is used to enter and confirm data. The outer DO-LOOP also invokes the NUMANAL subroutines *Decomp* and *Solve*, displays the results, and queries the user for more calculations.

Following is a sample run used to solve the equations:

$$X1 + X2 = 10$$

$$2\ X1 - X2 = 2$$

```
            SOLVING A SYSTEM OF LINEAR EQUATIONS
         ---------------------------------------

Enter number of equation ? 2

Enter A( 1 , 1 ) ? 1
Enter A( 1 , 2 ) ? 1

Enter B( 1 ) ? 10


Enter A( 2 , 1 ) ? 2
Enter A( 2 , 2 ) ? -1

Enter B( 2 ) ? 2



Information correct (Y/N) ? y
```

Figure 3.2.1 *Input screen image when running TESTNUM2.BAS with Turbo BASIC.*

After you confirm the correctness of the data, the screen is cleared and the output is displayed, as shown in figure 3.2.2. The solution is:

$$X1 = 4$$

$$X2 = 6$$

```
            SOLVING A SYSTEM OF LINEAR EQUATIONS
            ------------------------------------

    X( 1 ) =   4
    X( 2 ) =   6




    Want to solve another set of equations (Y/N) ? n
```

Figure 3.2.2 *Output screen image when running TESTNUM2.BAS with Turbo BASIC.*

Listings 3.13, 3.14, and 3.15 present the three versions of the above program for QuickBASIC, Turbo BASIC, and True BASIC, respectively.

Listing 3.13. *QuickBASIC source code for application TESTNUM2.BAS that solves a system of simultaneous equations.*

```
' PROGRAM Test.NUMANAL.Module.2

' QuickBASIC 3.0 program to test NUMANAL.BAS module.
' General-purpose module TOOLBOX0.BAS is also used.
' This program solves a system of linear equations
' Copyright (c) 1987 Namir Clement Shammas

OPTION BASE 0

DIM A#(20,20), LU#(20,20), X#(20), B#(20), S#(20), RowIndex%(20)

' include libraries NUMANAL.BAS and TOOLBOX0.BAS
REM $INCLUDE: 'NUMANAL.BAS'
```

```
REM $INCLUDE: 'TOOLBOX0.BAS'

DO ' Outer loop

 DO ' Inner loop for data entry

    CALL Display.Heading
    INPUT  "Enter number of equation "; N%
    PRINT
    FOR I% = 1 TO N%
        FOR J% = 1 TO N%
            PRINT "Enter A(";I%;",";J%;
            INPUT   ") "; A#(I%,J%)
        NEXT J%
        PRINT
         PRINT "Enter B(";I%;
         INPUT   ") ";B#(I%)
         CALL Blank.Lines(2)
    NEXT I%
    PRINT
    ' use YesNo$ function in TOOLBOX0
    OK$ = FNYesNo$("Information correct")

 LOOP UNTIL OK$ = "Y"

 SmallNum = 1e-30 ' assign epsilon
 ' call routines in module NUMANAL.BAS
 CALL Decomp(N%, SmallNum, A#(), LU#(), RowIndex%(), Status, Pivot, S#())
 IF Status <> 0 THEN
     CALL Solve(N%, LU#(), RowIndex%(), B#(), X#())

     ' display results
     CALL Display.Heading

     FOR I% = 1 TO N%
             PRINT "X(";I%;") = ";X#(I%)
     NEXT I%
 ELSE
    PRINT
    PRINT "The matrix is singular or nearly-singular"
 END IF

 ' use YesNo$ function in TOOLBOX0
 LOCATE 22,1
 OK$ = FNYesNo$("Want to solve another set of equations")

LOOP UNTIL OK$ = "N"

SUB Display.Heading STATIC
' internal subroutine to display centered message
CLS ' clear screen
' use Center.Message and Blank.Lines in TOOLBOX0
CALL Center.Message("SOLVING A SYSTEM OF LINEAR EQUATIONS",1)
CALL Center.Message("-----------------------------------",2)
CALL Blank.Lines(3)
```

```
END SUB

END
```

Listing 3.14. *Turbo BASIC source code for application TESTNUM2.BAS that solves a system of simultaneous equations.*

```
' PROGRAM Test.NUMANAL.Module.2

' Turbo BASIC program to test NUMANAL.BAS module.
' General-purpose module TOOLBOX0.BAS is also used.

' This program solves a system of linear equations
' Copyright (c) 1987 Namir Clement Shammas

OPTION BASE 0

DIM A#(20,20), LU#(20,20), X#(20), B#(20), S#(20), RowIndex%(20)

' include libraries NUMANAL.BAS and TOOLBOX0.BAS
$INCLUDE "NUMANAL.BAS"
$INCLUDE "TOOLBOX0.BAS"

DO ' Outer loop

  DO ' Inner loop for data entry

      CALL Display.Heading
      INPUT  "Enter number of equation "; N%
      PRINT
      FOR I% = 1 TO N%
          FOR J% = 1 TO N%
              PRINT "Enter A(";I%;",";J%;
              INPUT  ") "; A#(I%,J%)
          NEXT J%
          PRINT
          PRINT "Enter B(";I%;
          INPUT  ") ";B#(I%)
          CALL Blank.Lines(2)
      NEXT I%
      PRINT
      ' use YesNo$ function in TOOLBOX0
      OK$ = FNYesNo$("Information correct")

  LOOP UNTIL OK$ = "Y"

  SmallNum# = 1e-30 ' assign epsilon
  ' call routines in module NUMANAL.BAS
  CALL Decomp(N%, SmallNum#, A#(), LU#(), RowIndex%(), Status#, Pivot%, S#())
  IF Status# <> 0 THEN
```

```
           CALL Solve(N%, LU#(), RowIndex%(), B#(), X#())

           ' display results
           CALL Display.Heading

           FOR I% = 1 TO N%
              PRINT "X(";I%;") = ";X#(I%)
           NEXT I%
      ELSE
         PRINT
         PRINT "The matrix is singular or nearly-singular"
      END IF

      ' use YesNo$ function in TOOLBOX0
      LOCATE 22,1
      OK$ = FNYesNo$("Want to solve another set of equations")

   LOOP UNTIL OK$ = "N"

   SUB Display.Heading STATIC
   ' internal subroutine to display centered message
   CLS ' clear screen
   ' use Center.Message and Blank.Lines in TOOLBOX0
   CALL Center.Message("SOLVING A SYSTEM OF LINEAR EQUATIONS",1)
   CALL Center.Message("------------------------------------",2)
   CALL Blank.Lines(3)

   END SUB

   END
```

Listing 3.15. *True BASIC source code for application TESTNUM2.TRU that solves a system of simultaneous equations*

```
PROGRAM Test_NUMANAL_Module_2

! True BASIC program to test NUMANAL.TRU module.
! General-purpose module TOOLBOX0.TRU is also used.
! This program solves a system of linear equations
! Copyright (c) 1987 Namir Clement Shammas

OPTION BASE 0

! include modules NUMANAL.TRU and TOOLBOX0.TRU
Library "NUMANAL.TRU","TOOLBOX0.TRU"

! Declare imported function(s)
DECLARE DEF YesNo$

DIM A(20,20), LU(20,20), X(20), B(20), S(20), RowIndex(20)
```

BASIC LIBRARIES 211

```
DO ! Outer loop

 DO ! Inner loop for data entry
    CALL Display_Heading
    INPUT PROMPT "Enter number of equation : ": N
    PRINT
    FOR I = 1 TO N
        FOR J = 1 TO N
            PRINT "Enter A(";I;",";J;
            INPUT PROMPT ") : ": A(I,J)
        NEXT J
        PRINT
        PRINT "Enter B(";I;
        INPUT PROMPT ") : ":B(I)
        CALL Blank_Lines(2)
    NEXT I
    PRINT
    ! use YesNo$ function in TOOLBOX0
    LET OK$ = YesNo$("Information correct")

 LOOP UNTIL OK$ = "Y"

 LET SmallNum = 1e-30 ! assign epsilon
 ! call routine in module NUMANAL.TRU
 CALL Decomp(N, SmallNum, A(,), LU(,), RowIndex(), Status, Pivot, S())
 IF Status <> 0 THEN
     CALL Solve(N, LU(,), RowIndex(), B(), X())

     ! display results
     CALL Display_Heading

     FOR I = 1 TO N
        PRINT "X(";I;") = ";X(I)
     NEXT I
 ELSE
     PRINT
     PRINT "Matrix is singular or nearly-singular"
 END IF

 ! use YesNo$ function in TOOLBOX0
 SET CURSOR 22,1
 LET OK$ = YesNo$("Want to solve another set of equations")

LOOP UNTIL OK$ = "N"

SUB Display_Heading
! internal subroutine to display centered message
CLEAR ! clear screen
! use Center_Message and Blank_Lines in TOOLBOX0
CALL Center_Message("SOLVING A SYSTEM OF LINEAR EQUATIONS",1)
CALL Center_Message("-----------------------------------",2)
CALL Blank_Lines(3)

END SUB
```

```
END
```

The next three applications will be listed for Turbo BASIC only. You can easily run them with QuickBASIC or True BASIC by studying the first two applications and comparing the listings.

The next application program demonstrates numerical integration. The mathematical Error function, erf(x), may be evaluated by using several series of approximations or numerical integration. The Error function has the following properties:

```
erf(0) = 0

erf(infinity) = 1

erf(-x) = - erf(x)
```

The series approximation used to evaluate erf(x) for (x < 3) is:

```
erf(X) = 2/SQRT(Pi) (X  - X^3/3 + X^5 /(5*2!) - X^7/(7*3!) + ...)
```

The Error function is evaluated using integration:

```
erf(X) = 2/SQRT(Pi) * (Area under EXP(-t^2) for t = 0 to t = X)
```

Program *TESTNUM3.BAS* prompts the user for an argument for the Error function. The value of the Error function is calculated using the above two methods and is displayed on the screen. The program is set to use eleven points for Simpson's rule of numerical integration. The values of EXP(-t^2) are taken at equal intervals between zero and the supplied argument. Figure 3.3 shows the screen when TESNUM3.BAS runs and is requested to calculate erf(1).

BASIC LIBRARIES   213

```
                    EVALUATING THE ERROR FUNCTION
                    -------------------------------


    Enter argument for error function ? 1

    Erf( 1 ) =   .8427007583124242   using series approximation

    Erf( 1 ) =   .8427016772990493   using integration with
                 11 points








    Want to evaluate erf() using other arguments (Y/N) ? n
```

Figure 3.3 *Screen image for program TESTNUM3.BAS.*

Listing 3.16 shows the Turbo BASIC source code for TESTNUM3.BAS.

Listing 3.16. *Turbo BASIC source code for application TESTNUM3.TBAS that evaluates the Error function using numerical integration and series approximation*

```
' PROGRAM Test.NUMANAL.Module.3

' Turbo BASIC program to test NUMANAL.BAS module.
' General-purpose module TOOLBOX0.BAS is also used.

' This program evaluates the Error Function by two methods:
'
'    1) Series approximation.
'
'    2) Numerical integration.
'
```

```
    Copyright (c) 1987 Namir Clement Shammas

OPTION BASE 0

NumDiv% = 10 ' the number of data points used for integration
PI# = 355# / 113#

DIM Y#(NumDiv%)

' include modules NUMANAL.BAS and TOOLBOX0.BAS
$INCLUDE "NUMANAL.BAS"
$INCLUDE "TOOLBOX0.BAS"

' define error function
DEF FNErrorFun#(X#)
' evaluate error function using series approximation
' if argument is greater than 3 the assymptotic value
' of 1 is returned

IF ABS(X#) >= 3 THEN

    Sum# = SGN(X#)

ELSE

    Sum# = X#
    CHS% = -1
    Numerator# = X#^3
    Factorial# = 1
    J% = 1
    I% = 3

    DO
        Term# = CHS% * Numerator# / Factorial# / I%
        Sum# = Sum# + Term#

        ' update factors
        CHS% = -CHS%
        J% = J% + 1
        I% = I% + 2
        Numerator# = Numerator# * X# * X#
        Factorial# = Factorial# * J%

    LOOP UNTIL ABS(Term#) < 1.0E-07

    Sum# = 2# / SQR(PI#) * Sum#

END IF

FNErrorFun# = Sum# ' return result of series approximation

END DEF

DO
```

BASIC LIBRARIES

```
        CALL Display.Heading
        INPUT "Enter argument for error function "; X#
        F# = FNErrorFun#(X#)
        PRINT
        PRINT "Erf(";X#;") = ";F#;" using series approximation"
        PRINT

        ' Prepare array of data for integration
        Y#(0) = 1
        XX# = 0
        Delta# = X# / NumDiv%

        ' loop to calculate values for array Y#()
        FOR I% = 1 TO NumDiv%
            XX# = XX# + Delta#
            Y#(I%) = EXP(-XX#^2)
        NEXT I%

        ' call routines in module NUMANAL.BAS
        ' Note: number of data points MUST BE ODD
        '       Number of points = NumDiv% - 0 + 1
        '                        = NumDiv% + 1
        '                        ( = 11 in this case)
        CALL Integrate(Y#(), 0, NumDiv%, Delta#, Area#)
        Area# = 2 / SQR(PI#) * Area#
        PRINT "Erf(";X#;") = ";Area#;" using integration with";(NumDiv%+1);
        PRINT "points"
        ' use YesNo$ function in TOOLBOX0
        LOCATE 22,1
        OK$ = FNYesNo$("Want to evaluate erf() using other arguments")

LOOP UNTIL OK$ = "N"

SUB Display.Heading STATIC
' internal subroutine to display centered message
CLS ' clear screen
' use Center.Message and Blank.Lines in TOOLBOX0
CALL Center.Message("EVALUATING THE ERROR FUNCTION",1)
CALL Center.Message("-----------------------------",2)
CALL Blank.Lines(3)

END SUB

END
```

In the above listing the series approximation for the Error function is evaluated using function *FNErrorFun#()*. For arguments equal to or greater than three, the function returns plus or minus one, the asymptotic values. Otherwise, a DO-LOOP is used to calculate the series. The loop is exited when the magnitude of a calculated term is less than 1.E-07.

To use the numerical integration routine in library NUMANAL.BAS, the application program takes the argument and calculates eleven equidistant values for EXP(-XX#^2). The number of data points supplied to subroutine *Integrate* MUST be odd. The calculated area is then multiplied by (2/SQRT(Pi)) to obtain the sought value of the Error function.

The next application program demonstrates calling the numerical interpolation subroutine *Interpolate()* in NUMANAL. The application also uses the Error function discussed above. Interpolation is used when only discrete data points are available or when the original functions require much computing to evaluate them. Thus, the idea behind program TESTNUM4.BAS is to pre-calculate values of the Error function and use them to interpolate at any requested value. In this case, ten equidistant points, in the range of 0.3 to 3, were used for the interpolation. This is not a requirement for the Lagrangian interpolation algorithm being used. However, well-spread data points generally give better results than clustered data points. The program also displays the value of the Error function obtained using series approximations.

Figure 3.4 shows the screen image for program TESTNUM4.BAS, shown in listing 3.17, when running under Turbo BASIC.

BASIC LIBRARIES

```
            EVALUATING THE ERROR FUNCTION
            -------------------------------

  Enter argument for error function ? 1

  Erf( 1 ) = .8427007583124242 using series approximation

  Erf( 1 ) = .8427001049309899 using interpolation with
             10 points




  Want to evaluate erf() using other arguments (Y/N) ? n
```

Figure 3.4 *Screen image for program TESTNUM4.BAS.*

The above result shows that the interpolated value is in good agreement with the value obtained by series approximation.

Listing 3.17. *Turbo BASIC source code for application TESTNUM4.TBAS that evaluates the Error function using numerical integrations and series approximation*

```
' PROGRAM Test.NUMANAL.Module.4

' Turbo BASIC program to test NUMANAL.BAS module.
' General-purpose module TOOLBOX0.BAS is also used.

' This program evaluates the Error Function by series approximation
' at specific points and then compares interpolated values with
' exact values.
'
' Copyright (c) 1987 Namir Clement Shammas
```

```
OPTION BASE 0

NumDiv% = 10   ' the number of data points used for interpolation
PI# = 355# / 113#

DIM Y#(NumDiv%),X#(NumDiv%)

' include modules NUMANAL.BAS and TOOLBOX0.BAS
$INCLUDE "NUMANAL.BAS"
$INCLUDE "TOOLBOX0.BAS"


' define error function
DEF FNErrorFun#(X#)
' evaluate error function using series approximation
' if argument is greater than 3 the assymptotic value
' of 1 is returned

IF ABS(X#) >= 3 THEN

    Sum# = SGN(X#)

ELSE

    Sum# = X#
    CHS% = -1
    Numerator# = X#^3
    Factorial# = 1
    J% = 1
    I% = 3

    DO
        Term# = CHS% * Numerator# / Factorial# / I%
        Sum# = Sum# + Term#

        ' update factors
        CHS% = -CHS%
        J% = J% + 1
        I% = I% + 2
        Numerator# = Numerator# * X# * X#
        Factorial# = Factorial# * J%

    LOOP UNTIL ABS(Term#) < 1.0E-07

    Sum# = 2# / SQR(PI#) * Sum#

END IF

FNErrorFun# = Sum#   ' return result of series approximation

END DEF


' Prepare array of data for interpolation
X#(0) = 0#
```

BASIC LIBRARIES

```
Delta# = 0.3#
' loop to calculate values for arrays Y#() and X#()
FOR K% = 1 TO NumDiv%
    X#(K%) = X#(K% - 1) + Delta#
    Y#(K%) = FNErrorFun#(X#(K%))
NEXT K%

DO

    CALL Display.Heading
    INPUT "Enter argument for error function "; XInt#
    F# = FNErrorFun#(XInt#)
    PRINT
    PRINT "Erf(";XInt#;") = ";F#;" using series approximation"
    PRINT

    ' call routines in module NUMANAL.BAS
    CALL Interpolate(X#(), Y#(), 1, NumDiv%, XInt#, YInt#)
    PRINT "Erf(";XInt#;") = ";YInt#;" using intepolation with";NumDiv%;
    PRINT "points"
    ' use YesNo$ function in TOOLBOX0
    LOCATE 22,1
    OK$ = FNYesNo$("Want to evaluate erf() using other arguments")

LOOP UNTIL OK$ = "N"

SUB Display.Heading STATIC
' internal subroutine to display centered message
CLS ' clear screen
' use Center.Message and Blank.Lines in TOOLBOX0
CALL Center.Message("EVALUATING THE ERROR FUNCTION",1)
CALL Center.Message("------------------------------",2)
CALL Blank.Lines(3)

END SUB

END
```

In listing 3.17 the FOR K%-NEXT loop is used to calculate values for the *X#()* and *Y#()* arrays. The number of points need not be specifically odd or even. Notice that the FOR-NEXT loop uses K% and not I% or J% as its loop control variable. Why? This is due to the fact that function *FNErrorFun#()*, which is called in the FOR-NEXT loop body, also uses I% and J%. Thus, using K% avoids the undesirable side effects of simultaneous employment of the same variable.

The last application program demonstrates calling the *Differentiate()* subroutine in library NUMANAL. The program TESTNUM5.BAS, shown in listing 3.18, takes no user input. Instead, it displays a table of results that includes the argument values, the values for the slope of the Error function obtained numerically, and the exact slope values. A percent difference column is also shown. Figure 3.5 shows the screen image for Turbo BASIC running TESTNUM5.BAS.

```
          EVALUATING THE SLOPE OF THE ERROR FUNCTION
          -------------------------------------------


Point #     X     Slope by subr     Slope by formula     % Diff
-------    ----   -------------     ----------------     -------
   1       0.30   +1.054393069      +1.031260866          +2.24
   2       0.60   +0.780469050      +0.787243398          -0.86
   3       0.90   +0.506545031      +0.501968553          +0.91
   4       1.20   +0.240647013      +0.267344336          -9.99
   5       1.50   +0.131294195      +0.118930284         +10.40
   6       1.80   +0.021941377      +0.044191721         -50.35
   7       2.10   +0.010531136      +0.013715649         -23.22
   8       2.40   +0.004741880      +0.003555649         +33.37
   9       2.70   -0.001047376      +0.000769925        -236.04
  10       3.00   -0.000362310      +0.000139253        -360.18
```

Figure 3.5 *Screen image for TESTNUM5.BAS.*

The results reflect and increasing error in the slope values as the argument values go from 0.3 to 3. This also speaks of how error-sensitive numerical differentiation is.

Listing 3.18. *Turbo BASIC source code for application TESTNUM5.TBAS that evaluates the slope of the Error function using numerical differentiation*

```
' PROGRAM Test.NUMANAL.Module.5

' Turbo BASIC program to test NUMANAL.BAS module.
' General-purpose module TOOLBOX0.BAS is also used.

' This program evaluates the slope of the error function
' by two methods:
'
'     1) Exact values = 2/SQRT(PI) * EXP(-X^2)
'
'     2) Using numerical interpolation with equidistant points
'
' Copyright (c) 1987 Namir Clement Shammas

OPTION BASE 0

NumDiv% = 10 ' the number of data points used for interpolation
PI# = 355# / 113#

DIM Y#(NumDiv%),X#(NumDiv%),Slope#(NumDiv%)

' include modules NUMANAL.BAS and TOOLBOX0.BAS
$INCLUDE "NUMANAL.BAS"
$INCLUDE "TOOLBOX0.BAS"


' define error function
DEF FNErrorFun#(X#)
' evaluate error function using series approximation
' if argument is greater than 3 the assymptotic value
' of 1 is returned

IF ABS(X#) >= 3 THEN

    Sum# = SGN(X#)

ELSE

    Sum# = X#
    CHS% = -1
    Numerator# = X#^3
    Factorial# = 1
    J% = 1
    I% = 3
```

```
            DO
                Term# = CHS% * Numerator# / Factorial# / I%
                Sum# = Sum# + Term#

                ' update factors
                CHS% = -CHS%
                J% = J% + 1
                I% = I% + 2
                Numerator# = Numerator# * X# * X#
                Factorial# = Factorial# * J%

            LOOP UNTIL ABS(Term#) < 1.0E-07

            Sum# = 2# / SQR(PI#) * Sum#

    END IF

    FNErrorFun# = Sum# ' return result of series approximation

    END DEF

    DEF FNDeriv#(X#) = 2# / SQR(PI#) / EXP(X# * X#)


    ' Prepare array of data for interpolation
    X#(0) = 0#
    Delta# = 0.3#

    ' loop to calculate values for arrays Y#() and X#()
    FOR K% = 1 TO NumDiv%
        X#(K%) = X#(K% - 1) + Delta#
        Y#(K%) = FNErrorFun#(X#(K%))
    NEXT K%


    CALL Display.Heading

    ' call routines in module NUMANAL.BAS
    CALL Differentiate(Y#(), 1, NumDiv%, Delta#, Slope#())
    PRINT "     Point #    X     Slope by subr     Slope by formula     % Diff"
    PRINT "     -------   ----   -------------     ----------------     -------"
    Img$ ="        ##     #.##   +#.########       +#.########          +###.##"

    FOR K% = 1 TO NumDiv%
        F# = FNDeriv#(X#(K%))
        Diff# = 100# * (Slope#(K%) - F#)/F#
        PRINT USING Img$;K%,X#(K%),Slope#(K%),F#,Diff#
    NEXT K%


    SUB Display.Heading STATIC
    ' internal subroutine to display centered message
    CLS ' clear screen
    ' use Center.Message and Blank.Lines in TOOLBOX0
    CALL Center.Message("EVALUATING THE SLOPE OF THE ERROR FUNCTION",1)
    CALL Center.Message("-----------------------------------------",2)
```

```
CALL Blank.Lines(3)

END SUB

END
```

Library Module BASTAT

PURPOSE: The BASTAT library contains routines to perform basic descriptive statistics. This includes calculating the following:

+mean

+standard deviation

+variance

+third and fourth moments

+coefficient of kurtosis

+skewness coefficient

The routines permit observations to be processed as discrete data or to be associated with frequencies. The BASTAT library requires you to use *OPTION BASE 1* in your application programs.

The True BASIC version differs from the others in that the variables for statistical summation are NOT accessible to the application program. In a True BASIC module, SHARED variables are available to all the routines within the modules. In QuickBASIC and Turbo BASIC, SHARED variables declared within routines become global! You may alter the access of the statistical summation variables in True BASIC by replacing the SHARED keyword with PUBLIC, making them global. This must be accompanied by the insertion of a DECLARE PUBLIC *<list of variables>* statement in any True BASIC application program.

Listings 3.19, 3.20, and 3.21 contain the library source code for the QuickBASIC, Turbo BASIC, and True BASIC versions, respectively.

ROUTINES

The following is a list of headings for function and subroutine definitions borrowed from the QuickBASIC listing. They are identical to those of Turbo BASIC. However, they contain minor syntactical differences compared to those of True BASIC, including:

1. function names in True BASIC do not have to begin with the letters *FN*

2. subroutines in True BASIC need no STATIC declarations

SUB Initialize.Bastat STATIC
SUB Initialize_Bastat ! True BASIC

This subroutine initializes the statistical summations and the control variable. This routine must be the first called. The initialized variables are:

Sum	number of data points
SumX1	sum of the observation
SumX2	sum of the observations squared
SumX3	sum of the observations cubed
SumX4	sum of the observations raised to the fourth power
Control	control variable to monitor the proper logical progress of the different subroutine calls

SUB SUM.DATA(D#(2), Index%, IndxFreq%, N%) STATIC
SUB SUM_DATA(D(,), Index, IndxFreq, N) ! True BASIC

This subroutine is employed to accumulate data in the statistical summations. This routine must be called before the next two subroutines, *Mean.Sdev* and *Moments*. The observations are passed as a numerical matrix. Two indexes are supplied to select the variable (that is, matrix column) to enter the statistics and the frequency variable (optional). If the *Index* or *IndxFreq* arguments are outside the valid range column in matrix *D(,)*, the subroutine exits without performing any statistical summations.

The list of arguments is:

D	data matrix [INPUT]
Index	index used to select the matrix column containing the variable whose statistics are sought [INPUT]
IndxFreq	index used to select the matrix column containing the frequency data; a zero value indicates that no frequencies are used [INPUT]
N	number of observations [INPUT]

It was pointed out earlier that *OPTION BASE 1* must be used with the application programs employing library BASTAT. Variable *IndxFreq* is the reason: a zero value signals that no frequency (other than one) is used. You can easily change the zero values in the listing to whatever values suit your applications.

SUB Mean.Sdev(Mean#, Sdev#) STATIC
SUB Mean_Sdev(Mean, Sdev) ! True BASIC

This subroutine emulates a function returning two results, namely, the mean, *Mean*, and standard deviation, *Sdev*, values. No input parameters are involved.

SUB Moments(Mean#,Mom2#,Mom3#,Mom4#,SkewCoeff#, KurtCoeff#) STATIC

SUB Moments(Mean,Mom2,Mom3,Mom4,SkewCoeff,KurtCoeff) ! True BASIC

This subroutine returns the following six statistics:

Mean	the mean (first moment) [OUTPUT]
Mom2	the second moment (the variance) [OUTPUT]

Mom3	the third moment [OUTPUT]
Mom4	the fourth moment [OUTPUT]
SkewCoeff	the skewness coefficient [OUTPUT]
KurtCoeff	the kurtosis coefficient [OUTPUT]

Listing 3.19. *QuickBASIC source code for the BASTAT.BAS library*

```
' MODULE Bastat

' Module for Basic statistics
' QuickBASIC version
' Copyright (c) 1987 Namir Clement Shammas


SUB Initialize.Bastat STATIC
' Initialize summations and control variable

SHARED Sum#, SumX1#, SumX2#, SumX3#, SumX4#, Control%

Sum# = 0 : SumX1# = 0 : SumX2# = 0 : SumX3# = 0 : SumX4# = 0
Control% = 1

END SUB

SUB SUM.DATA(D#(2), Index%, IndxFreq%, N%) STATIC
' Accumlate statistical data

SHARED Sum#, SumX1#, SumX2#, SumX3#, SumX4#, Control%
STATIC Low%, Hi%, I%, Freq#, X#, SQRX#

IF Control% < 1 THEN CALL Initialize.Bastat

I% = IndxFreq%
IF ((I% < LBOUND(D#,2)) OR (I% > UBOUND(D#,2))) AND (I% <> 0) THEN EXIT SUB
IF (Index% < LBOUND(D#,2)) OR (Index% > UBOUND(D#,2)) THEN EXIT SUB

Low% = LBOUND(D#,1)
Hi%  = UBOUND(D#,1)
IF (Low% + N% - 1) > Hi% THEN N% = Hi% - Low% + 1
```

```
    FOR I% = Low% TO Low% + N% - 1
        X# = D#(I%,Index%)
        SQRX# = X#^2
        IF IndxFreq% = 0 THEN Freq# = 1# ELSE Freq# = D#(I%,IndxFreq%)
        Sum# = Sum# + Freq#
        SumX1# = SumX1# + X#         * Freq#
        SumX2# = SumX2# + SQRX#      * Freq#
        SumX3# = SumX3# + X * SQRX#  * Freq#
        SumX4# = SumX4# + SQRX#^2    * Freq#
    NEXT I%

    IF N% > 2 THEN Control% = 2

    END SUB


    SUB Mean.Sdev(Mean#, Sdev#) STATIC
    ' calculate basic statistics

    SHARED Sum#, SumX1#, SumX2#, SumX3#, SumX4#, Control%

    IF Control% > 1 THEN
        Mean# = SumX1# / Sum#
        Sdev# = SQR((SumX2# - SumX1#^2/Sum#)/(Sum#-1))
    ELSE
        Mean# = 1.0E+30
        Sdev# = 1.0E+30
    END IF

    END SUB


    SUB Moments(Mean#, Mom2#, Mom3#, Mom4#, SkewCoeff#, KurtCoeff#) STATIC
    ' routine to calculate the first four moments and the coefficients
    ' of skewness and kurtosis

    SHARED Sum#, SumX1#, SumX2#, SumX3#, SumX4#, Control%

    IF Control% > 1 THEN
        Mean# = SumX1# / Sum#
        Mom2# = SumX2#/Sum# - Mean#^2
        Mom3# = SumX3#/Sum# - 3/Sum#*Mean#*SumX2# + 2*Mean#^3
        Mom4# = SumX4#/Sum# - 4/Sum#*SumX3# + 6/Sum#*Mean#^2*SumX2# - 3*Mean#^4
        SkewCoeff# = Mom3# / Mom2#^1.5
        KurtCoeff# = Mom4# / Mom2#^2
    ELSE
        Mean#     = 1.0E+30 :  Mom2#     = 1.0E+30
        Mom3#     = 1.0E+30 :  Mom4#     = 1.0E+30
        SkewCoeff# = 1.0E+30 : KurtCoeff# = 1.0E+30
    END IF

    END SUB
```

Listing 3.20. *Turbo BASIC source code for the BASTAT.BAS library*

```
' MODULE Bastat

' Module for Basic statistics
' Turbo BASIC version
' Copyright (c) 1987 Namir Clement Shammas


SUB Initialize.Bastat STATIC
' Initialize summations and control variable

SHARED Sum#, SumX1#, SumX2#, SumX3#, SumX4#, Control%

Sum# = 0 : SumX1# = 0 : SumX2# = 0 : SumX3# = 0 : SumX4# = 0
Control% = 1

END SUB

SUB SUM.DATA(D#(2), Index%, IndxFreq%, N%) STATIC
' Accumlate statistical data

SHARED Sum#, SumX1#, SumX2#, SumX3#, SumX4#, Control%
LOCAL Low%, Hi%, I%, Freq#, X#, SQRX#

IF Control% < 1 THEN CALL Initialize.Bastat

I% = IndxFreq%
IF ((I% < LBOUND(D#(2))) OR (I% > UBOUND(D#(2)))) AND (I% <> 0) THEN EXIT SUB
IF (Index% < LBOUND(D#(2))) OR (Index% > UBOUND(D#(2))) THEN EXIT SUB

Low% = LBound(D#(1))
Hi%  = UBound(D#(1))
IF (Low% + N% - 1) > Hi% THEN N% = Hi% - Low% + 1


FOR I% = Low% TO Low% + N% - 1
    X# = D#(I%,Index%)
    SQRX# = X#^2
    IF IndxFreq% = 0 THEN Freq# = 1 ELSE Freq# = D#(I%,IndxFreq%)
    Sum# = Sum# + Freq#
    SumX1# = SumX1#  + X# * Freq#
    SumX2# = SumX2# + SQRX# * Freq#
    SumX3# = SumX3# + X * SQRX# * Freq#
    SumX4# = SumX4# + SQRX#^2 * Freq#
NEXT I%

IF N% > 2 THEN Control% = 2

END SUB


SUB Mean.Sdev(Mean#, Sdev#) STATIC
' calculate basic statistics
```

```
    SHARED Sum#, SumX1#, SumX2#, SumX3#, SumX4#, Control%

    IF Control% > 1 THEN
        Mean# = SumX1# / Sum#
        Sdev# = SQR((SumX2# - SumX1#^2/Sum#)/(Sum#-1))
    ELSE
        Mean# = 1.0E+30
        Sdev# = 1.0E+30
    END IF

    END SUB


    SUB Moments(Mean#, Mom2#, Mom3#, Mom4#, SkewCoeff#, KurtCoeff#)
    STATIC
    ' routine to calculate the first four moments and the coefficients
    ' of skewness and kurtosis

    SHARED Sum#, SumX1#, SumX2#, SumX3#, SumX4#, Control%

    IF Control% > 1 THEN
        Mean# = SumX1# / Sum#
        Mom2# = SumX2#/Sum# - Mean#^2
        Mom3# = SumX3#/Sum# - 3/Sum#*Mean#*SumX2# + 2*Mean#^3
        Mom4# = SumX4#/Sum# - 4/Sum#*SumX3# + 6/Sum#*Mean#^2*SumX2# - 3*Mean#^4
        SkewCoeff# = Mom3# / Mom2#^1.5
        KurtCoeff# = Mom4# / Mom2#^2
    ELSE
        Mean#      = 1.0E+30 :  Mom2#      = 1.0E+30
        Mom3#      = 1.0E+30 :  Mom4#      = 1.0E+30
        SkewCoeff# = 1.0E+30 :  KurtCoeff# = 1.0E+30
    END IF

    END SUB
```

Listing 3.21. *True BASIC source code for the BASTAT.TRU library*

```
MODULE Bastat

! Module for Basic statistics
! True BASIC version
! Copyright (c) 1987 Namir Clement Shammas

! List variables that are shared between module routines
SHARE Sum, SumX1, SumX2, SumX3, SumX4, Control


SUB Initialize_Bastat
! Initialize summations and control variable
```

```
    LET Sum, SumX1, SumX2, SumX3, SumX4 = 0
    LET Control = 1

END SUB


SUB SUM_DATA(D(,),Index,IndxFreq,N)
! Accumlate statistical data

IF Control < 1 THEN CALL Initialize_Bastat

LET  I = IndxFreq
IF ((I < LBOUND(D,2)) OR (I > UBOUND(D,2))) AND (I <> 0) THEN EXIT SUB
IF (Index < LBOUND(D,2)) OR (Index > UBOUND(D,2)) THEN EXIT SUB

LET Low = LBOUND(D,1)
LET Hi  = UBOUND(D,1)
IF (Low + N - 1) > Hi THEN LET N = Hi - Low + 1


FOR I = Low TO Low + N - 1
    LET X = D(I,Index)
    LET SQRX = X^2
    IF IndxFreq = 0 THEN LET Freq = 1 ELSE LET Freq = D(I,IndxFreq)
    LET Sum = Sum + Freq
    LET SumX1 = SumX1  + X * Freq
    LET SumX2 = SumX2 + SQRX * Freq
    LET SumX3 = SumX3 + X * SQRX * Freq
    LET SumX4 = SumX4 + SQRX^2 * Freq
NEXT I

IF N > 2 THEN LET Control = 2

END SUB



SUB Mean_Sdev(Mean, Sdev)
! calculate basic statistics

IF Control > 1 THEN
    LET Mean = SumX1 / Sum
    LET Sdev = SQR((SumX2 - SumX1^2/Sum)/(Sum-1))
ELSE
    LET Mean, Sdev = MAXNUM
END IF

END SUB


SUB Moments(Mean, Mom2, Mom3, Mom4, SkewCoeff, KurtCoeff)
! routine to calculate the first four moments and the coefficients
! of skewness and kurtosis

IF Control > 1 THEN
    LET Mean = SumX1 / Sum
    LET Mom2 = SumX2/Sum - Mean^2
```

```
    LET Mom3 = SumX3/Sum - 3/Sum*Mean*SumX2 + 2*Mean^3
    LET Mom4 = SumX4/Sum - 4/Sum*SumX3 + 6/Sum*Mean^2*SumX2 - 3*Mean^4
    LET SkewCoeff = Mom3 / Mom2^1.5
    LET KurtCoeff = Mom4 / Mom2^2
ELSE
    LET Mean, Mom2, Mom3, Mom4 = MAXNUM
    LET SkewCoeff, KurtCoeff = MAXNUM
END IF

END SUB

END MODULE
```

To demonstrate calling subroutines in library BASTAT, I have written an application program that returns the basic statistics for randomly generated numbers. The built-in BASIC random number generator (found in all implementations) is used. The user specifies the count of random numbers generated, in the range of 10 to 100. The QuickBASIC and Turbo BASIC program versions prompt you for a seed when the RANDOMIZE statement is encountered.

I have run the application program TESTSTAT.TRU with True BASIC. The screen image for a sample run is shown in Figure 3.6.

```
              BASIC STAT FOR RANDOM NUMBER
              ---------------------------

How many random numbers to generate (10->100) : 100

Mean =  49.2864

Sdev =  29.3034

Third moment =  1720.54

Fourth moment =  4.90462e+7

Skewness coefficient =  6.94158e-2

Kurtosis coefficient =  67.8677

Process another set (Y/N) ? n
```

Figure 3.6 *Screen image for program TESTSTAT.TRU running with True BASIC.*

Listings 3.22, 3.23, and 3.24 present the source code for the application program TESTSTAT.

Listing 3.22. *QuickBASIC source code for the TESTSTAT.BAS program to obtain basic statistics for random numnbers*

```
'PROGRAM Do.Stat

' QuickBASIC program to test module BASTAT.BAS
' Copyright (c) 1987  Namir C. Shammas

OPTION BASE 1

DIM X#(100,1)

REM $INCLUDE: 'TOOLBOX0.BAS'
```

BASIC LIBRARIES

```
REM $INCLUDE: 'BASTAT.BAS'

DO
  CLS ' clear screen
  CALL Center.Message("BASIC STAT FOR RANDOM NUMBER",1)
  CALL Center.Message("-----------------------------",2)
  CALL Blank.Lines(3)

  N% = FNInteger.In.Range%("How many random numbers to generate (10->100)",10,100)

  RANDOMIZE

  FOR I% = 1 TO N%
    X#(I%,1) = 100 * RND(1)
  NEXT I%


  ' Initialize summations and control variable
  CALL Initialize.Bastat

  ' Accumlate statistical data
  CALL SUM.DATA(X#(),1,0,N%)

  ' calculate basic statistics
  CALL Mean.Sdev(Mean#, Sdev#)

  PRINT
  PRINT "Mean = ";Mean#
  PRINT
  PRINT "Sdev = ";Sdev#

  ' Calculate the first four moments and the coefficients
  ' of skewness and kurtosis
  CALL Moments(Mean#, Mom2#, Mom3#, Mom4#, SkewCoeff#, KurtCoeff#)

  PRINT
  PRINT "Third moment = ";Mom3#
  PRINT
  PRINT "Fourth moment = ";Mom4#
  PRINT
  PRINT "Skewness coefficient = ";SkewCoeff#
  PRINT
  PRINT "Kurtosis coefficient = ";KurtCoeff#
  PRINT

  OK$ = FNYesNo$("Process another set")

LOOP UNTIL OK$ = "N"

END
```

Listing 3.23. *Turbo BASIC source code for the TESTSTAT.BAS program to obtain basic statistics for random numbers*

```
'PROGRAM Do.Stat

' Turbo BASIC program to test library BASTAT.BAS
' Copyright (c) 1987  Namir Clement Shammas

OPTION BASE 1

DIM X#(100,1)

$INCLUDE "TOOLBOX0.BAS"
$INCLUDE "BASTAT.BAS"

DO
   CLS ' clear screen
   CALL Center.Message("BASIC STAT FOR RANDOM NUMBER",1)
   CALL Center.Message("----------------------------",2)
   CALL Blank.Lines(3)

   N% = FNInteger.In.Range%("How many random numbers to generate (10->100)",10,100)

   RANDOMIZE

   FOR I% = 1 TO N%
      X#(I%,1) = 100 * RND(1)
   NEXT I%


   ' Initialize summations and control variable
   CALL Initialize.Bastat

   ' Accumlate statistical data
   CALL SUM.DATA(X#(),1,0,N%)

   ' calculate basic statistics
   CALL Mean.Sdev(Mean#, Sdev#)

   PRINT
   PRINT
   PRINT "Mean = ";Mean#
   PRINT
   PRINT "Sdev = ";Sdev#

   ' Calculate the first four moments and the coefficients
   ' of skewness and kurtosis
   CALL Moments(Mean#, Mom2#, Mom3#, Mom4#, SkewCoeff#, KurtCoeff#)

   PRINT
   PRINT "Third moment = ";Mom3#
   PRINT
   PRINT "Fourth moment = ";Mom4#
```

```
    PRINT
    PRINT "Skewness coefficient = ";SkewCoeff#
    PRINT
    PRINT "Kurtosis coefficient = ";KurtCoeff#
    PRINT

    OK$ = FNYesNo$("Process another set")

LOOP UNTIL OK$ = "N"

END
```

Listing 3.24. *True BASIC source code for the TESTSTAT.TRU program to obtain basic statistics for random numbers*

```
PROGRAM Do_Stat

! True BASIC program to test module BASTAT.TRU
! Copyright (c) 1987   Namir C. Shammas

OPTION BASE 1

! Declare modules used
LIBRARY "BASTAT.TRU","TOOLBOX0"

! Declare imported function
DECLARE DEF Integer_In_Range, YesNo$

DIM X(100,1)
DO
  CLEAR ! clear screen
  CALL Center_Message("BASIC STAT FOR RANDOM NUMBER",1)
  CALL Center_Message("----------------------------",2)
  CALL Blank_Lines(3)

  LET N = Integer_In_Range("How many random numbers to generate (10->100)",10,100)

  RANDOMIZE

  FOR I = 1 TO N
    LET X(I,1) = 100 * RND
  NEXT I


  ! Initialize summations and control variable
  CALL Initialize_Bastat

  ! Accumlate statistical data
```

```
    CALL SUM_DATA(X(,),1,0,N)

    ! calculate basic statistics
    CALL Mean_Sdev(Mean, Sdev)

    PRINT
    PRINT "Mean = ";Mean
    PRINT
    PRINT "Sdev = ";Sdev

    ! Calculate the first four moments and the coefficients
    ! of skewness and kurtosis
    CALL Moments(Mean, Mom2, Mom3, Mom4, SkewCoeff, KurtCoeff)

    PRINT
    PRINT "Third moment = ";Mom3
    PRINT
    PRINT "Fourth moment = ";Mom4
    PRINT
    PRINT "Skewness coefficient = ";SkewCoeff
    PRINT
    PRINT "Kurtosis coefficient = ";KurtCoeff
    PRINT

    LET OK$ = YesNo$("Process another set")
LOOP UNTIL OK$ = "N"

END
```

The correct use of library BASTAT requires that you call the routines in a certain logical order. If the calls to the subroutines in BASTAT were issued in discordance with the required sequence, the returned results would be large numbers. These numbers indicate that out-of-sequence calls were issued. Supplying bad values for the variable index or frequency index may yield the same effect.

Library Module LINREG

PURPOSE: The LINREG library contains routines to perform basic linear regression. The library is used to calculate the regression slope, intercept, and coefficient of determination. The library contains a function used to perform mathematical transformations on the data.

The True BASIC version differs from the others in that the variables for statistical summation are not accessible to the application program. In a True

BASIC module, SHARED variables are available to all the routines within the modules. In QuickBASIC and Turbo BASIC, SHARED variables declared within routines become global! You may alter the access of the statistical summation variables in True BASIC by replacing the SHARED keyword with PUBLIC, making them global. This must be accompanied by the insertion of a DECLARE PUBLIC <list of variables> statement in any True BASIC application program.

Listings 3.25, 3.26, and 3.27 contain the library source code for the QuickBASIC, Turbo BASIC, and True BASIC versions, respectively.

ROUTINES

The following is a list of headings for function and subroutine definitions borrowed from the QuickBASIC listing. They are identical to those of Turbo BASIC. However, they contain minor syntactical differences compared to those of True BASIC, including:

1. function names in True BASIC do not have to begin with the letters *FN*

2. subroutines in True BASIC need no STATIC declarations

DEF   FNFunc#(A#,I%,C1#,C2#,C3#,C4#)
DEF   Func(A,I,Coeff())   ! True BASIC

This function is used to perform temporary mathematical transformations on the statistical observations. You can expand the list of transformations. The function also accepts four coefficients that enable you to write more variant types of transformations.

In QuickBASIC and Turbo BASIC, the arguments are:

        A#   the input data

        I%   the transformation selection index

        C1# to C3#   the four coefficients

True BASIC allows arguments to be arrays, passed by value. This enables the True BASIC version to replace the four variables *C1* to *C4* with the array *Coeff()*. Another important difference between True BASIC and the other two BASIC implementations is that function *Func* is not exported by the LINREG.TRU module. The PRIVATE declaration makes the function local to the module and invisible to any application program. You may change that by simply deleting the PRIVATE declaration line.

SUB InitializeLR STATIC
SUB InitializeLR ! True BASIC

This subroutine initializes the statistical summations and the progress control variable. It must be called before any other subroutine in the library, except for *SetDefaultCoeff*.

	Sum	number of data points
	SumX	sum of the independent variables
	SumXX	sum of the squared values of the independent variables
	SumY	sum of the dependent variables
	SumYY	sum of the squared values of the dependent variables
	SumXY	sum of the cross products
	Control	control variable to monitor the proper logical progress of the different subroutine calls

SUB SetDefaultCoeff(Coeff#(1)) STATIC
SUB Set_Default_Coeff(Coeff(,)) ! True BASIC

This routine assigns default values to the transformation coefficients used by function *FNFunc#()*. The values assigned represent the most frequently used ones, making it more convenient for the application program. Prior to calling the next subroutine, your application must either call this subroutine or explicitly assign values for the transformation coefficients. This subroutine involves no input parameter.

SUB ADDDATA(D#(2),Yindex%,Xindex%,N%,XFunc%,
             YFunc%,Coeff#(1)) STATIC

SUB ADD_DATA(D(,),Yindex,Xindex,N,XFunc,YFunc,Coeff(,))
      ! True BASIC

This routine adds data to the statistical summations. It must be called before invoking the next subroutine. Temporary mathematical transformations are carried out by this routine.

D(,)	data matrix [INPUT]
Yindex	index to select the matrix column containing the dependent variable [INPUT]
Xindex	index to select the matrix column containing the independent variable [INPUT]
N	the number of observations [INPUT]
XFunc	index to select the transformations for the independent variable [INPUT]
YFunc	index to select the transformations for the dependent variable [INPUT]
Coeff(,)	the array of transformation coefficients [INPUT]

SUB LRSTAT(Slope#, Intercept#, R2#) STATIC
SUB LR_STAT(Slope, Intercept, R2) ! True BASIC

This subroutine returns the regression intercept, slope, and coefficient of determination (R2). No input parameter is involved. If the application program does not follow the correct logical sequence in calling the routines in LINREG, the argumentsof these routines return large numbers to indicate an "out-of-sequence" error.

Listing 3.25. *QuickBASIC source code for the LINREG>BAS library*

```
' Simple linear regression library
' QuickBASIC version
' Copyright (c) 1987 Namir Clement Shammas

DEF FNFunc#(A#,I%,C1#,C2#,C3#,C4#)
' Tranformations function

STATIC F#

SELECT CASE I%

   CASE 1
      F# = LOG(C1# + C2# * A#)
   CASE 2
      F# = EXP(C1# + C2# * A#)
   CASE 3
      F# = C1# + C2# * (A# + C3#)^C4#
   CASE ELSE
      F# = A#  ' default assignment
END SELECT

FNFunc# = F#

END DEF


SUB InitializeLR STATIC
' Initialize stat summations

SHARED Sum#, SumX#, SumXX#, SumY#, SumYY#, SumXY#, Control%

Sum#  = 0 : SumX#  = 0 : SumXX# = 0
SumY# = 0 : SumYY# = 0 : SumXY# = 0
Control% = 1

END SUB


SUB SetDefaultCoeff(Coeff#(1)) STATIC
' Assign default values to the C<n> coefficients

Coeff#(1) = 0 : Coeff#(3) = 0
Coeff#(2) = 1 : Coeff#(4) = 1
```

```
END SUB


SUB ADDDATA(D#(2),Yindex%,Xindex%,N%,XFunc%,YFunc%,Coeff#(1)) STATIC
' Subroutine to accumulate statistical summations

SHARED Sum#, SumX#, SumXX#, SumY#, SumYY#, SumXY#, Control%
STATIC Low%, Hi%, Y#, X#

IF Control% < 1 THEN CALL InitializeLR : CALL
SetDefaultCoeff(Coeff#())

' Check value of N%
Low% = LBOUND(D#,1)
Hi%  = UBOUND(D#,1)
IF (Low% + N% - 1) > Hi% THEN N% = Hi% - Low% + 1

Sum# = Sum# + N%

FOR I% = Low% TO Low% + N% - 1
    X# = FNFunc#(D#(I%,Xindex%),XFunc%,Coeff#(1),Coeff#(2),Coeff#(3),Coeff#(4))
    Y# = FNFunc#(D#(I%,Yindex%),YFunc%,Coeff#(1),Coeff#(2),Coeff#(3),Coeff#(4))
    SumX#  = SumX#  + X#
    SumY#  = SumY#  + Y#
    SumXX# = SumXX# + X#^2
    SumYY# = SumYY# + Y#^2
    SumXY# = SumXY# + X# * Y#
NEXT I%

IF N% > 2 THEN Control% = 2

END SUB

SUB LRSTAT(Slope#, Intercept#, R2#) STATIC
' Calculate regression statistics

SHARED Sum#, SumX#, SumXX#, SumY#, SumYY#, SumXY#, Control%
STATIC MeanX#, MeanY#, SdevX#, SdevY#

IF Control% > 1 THEN   ' Check for correct sequence
    MeanX# = SumX# / Sum#
    MeanY# = SumY# / Sum#
    SdevX# = SQR((SumXX# - SumX#^2/Sum#)/(Sum#-1))
    SdevY# = SQR((SumYY# - SumY#^2/Sum#)/(Sum#-1))
    Slope# = (SumXY# - MeanX# * MeanY# * Sum#)/(SdevX#^2)/(Sum#-1)
    Intercept# = MeanY# - Slope# * MeanX#
    R2# = (SdevX# / SdevY# * Slope#)^2
ELSE
    R2#       = 1.0E+30
    Slope#    = 1.0E+30
    Intercept# = 1.0E+30
END IF

END SUB
```

Listing 3.26. *Turbo BASIC source code for the LINREG.BAS library*

```
' Simple linear regression library
' Turbo BASIC 1.0 version
' Copyright (c) 1987 Namir Clement Shammas


DEF FNFunc#(A#,I%,C1#,C2#,C3#,C4#)
' Tranformations function

    SELECT CASE I%
      CASE 1
          F# = LOG(C1# + C2# * A#)
      CASE 2
          F# = EXP(C1# + C2# * A#)
      CASE 3
          F# = C1# + C2# * (A# + C3#)^C4#
      CASE ELSE
          F# = A#
    END SELECT

    FNFunc# = F#

END DEF



SUB InitializeLR STATIC
' Initialize stat summations

SHARED Sum#, SumX#, SumXX#, SumY#, SumYY#, SumXY#, Control%

Sum#  = 0 : SumX#  = 0 : SumXX# = 0
SumY# = 0 : SumYY# = 0 : SumXY# = 0
Control% = 1

END SUB



SUB SetDefaultCoeff(Coeff#(1)) STATIC
' Assign default values to the C<n> coefficients

Coeff#(1) = 0 : Coeff#(3) = 0
Coeff#(2) = 1 : Coeff#(4) = 1

END SUB



SUB ADDDATA(D#(2),Yindex%,Xindex%,N%,XFunc%,YFunc%,Coeff#(1)) STATIC
' Subroutine to accumulate statistical summations
```

BASIC LIBRARIES

```
SHARED Sum#, SumX#, SumXX#, SumY#, SumYY#, SumXY#, Control%
LOCAL Low%, Hi%, X#, Y#

IF Control% < 1 THEN CALL InitializeLR : CALL
SetDefaultCoeff(Coeff#())

' Check value of N%
Low%  = LBound(D#(1))
Hi%   = UBound(D#(1))
'IF (Low% + N% - 1) > Hi% THEN N% = Hi% - Low% + 1

Sum# = Sum# + N%

FOR I% = Low% TO Low% + N% - 1
    X# = FNFunc#(D#(I%,Xindex%),XFunc%,Coeff#(1),Coeff#(2),Coeff#(3),Coeff#(4))
    Y# = FNFunc#(D#(I%,Yindex%),YFunc%,Coeff#(1),Coeff#(2),Coeff#(3),Coeff#(4))
    SumX#  = SumX#  + X#
    SumY#  = SumY#  + Y#
    SumXX# = SumXX# + X#^2
    SumYY# = SumYY# + Y#^2
    SumXY# = SumXY# + X# * Y#
NEXT I%

IF N% > 2 THEN Control% = 2

END SUB

SUB LRSTAT(Slope#, Intercept#, R2#) STATIC
' Calculate regression statistics

SHARED Sum#, SumX#, SumXX#, SumY#, SumYY#, SumXY#, Control%
LOCAL MeanX#, MeanY#, SdevX#, SdevY#

IF Control% > 1 THEN  ' Check for correct sequence
    MeanX# = SumX# / Sum#
    MeanY# = SumY# / Sum#
    SdevX# = SQR((SumXX# - SumX#^2/Sum#)/(Sum#-1))
    SdevY# = SQR((SumYY# - SumY#^2/Sum#)/(Sum#-1))
    Slope# = (SumXY# - MeanX# * MeanY# * Sum#)/(SdevX#^2)/(Sum#-1)
    Intercept# = MeanY# - Slope# * MeanX#
    R2# = (SdevX# / SdevY# * Slope#)^2
ELSE
    R2#       = 1.0E+30
    Slope#    = 1.0E+30
    Intercept# = 1.0E+30
END IF

END SUB
```

Lisitng 3.27. *True BASIC source code for the LINREG.TRU module*

```
MODULE LinReg

! Simple linear regression module
! Copyright (c) 1987 Namir Clement Shammas

PRIVATE Func
DECLARE DEF Func
SHARE Sum, SumX, SumXX, SumY, SumYY, SumXY, Control

CALL InitializeLR ! Only module initialization step
DEF Func(A,I,Coeff())
! Tranformations function

    SELECT CASE INT(I)
        CASE 1
            LET F = LOG(Coeff(1) + Coeff(2) * A)
        CASE 2
            LET F = EXP(Coeff(1) + Coeff(2) * A)
        CASE 3
            LET F = Coeff(1) + Coeff(2) * (A+Coeff(3))^Coeff(4)
        CASE ELSE
            LET F = A
    END SELECT

    LET Func = F

END DEF


SUB InitializeLR
! Initialize stat summations

LET Sum, SumX, SumXX, SumY, SumYY, SumXY = 0
LET Control = 1

END SUB


SUB Set_Default_Coeff(Coeff())
! Assign default values to the Coeff() array

LET Coeff(1), Coeff(3) = 0
LET Coeff(2), Coeff(4) = 1

END SUB


SUB ADD_DATA(D(,),Yindex,Xindex,N,XFunc,YFunc,Coeff())
! Subroutine to accumulate statistical summations
```

```
IF Control < 1 THEN
    CALL InitializeLR
    CALL Set_Default_Coeff(Coeff())
END IF

! Check value of N
LET Low = LBOUND(D,1)
LET Hi  = UBOUND(D,1)
IF (Low + N - 1) > Hi THEN LET N = Hi - Low + 1

LET Sum = Sum + N

FOR I = LBOUND(D,1) TO LBOUND(D,1) + N - 1
    LET X = Func(D(I,Xindex),XFunc,Coeff())
    LET Y = Func(D(I,Yindex),YFunc,Coeff())
    LET SumX = SumX + X
    LET SumY = SumY + Y
    LET SumXX = SumXX + X^2
    LET SumYY = SumYY + Y^2
    LET SumXY = SumXY + X * Y
NEXT I

IF N > 2 THEN LET Control = 2

END SUB


SUB LR_STAT(Slope, Intercept, R2)
! Calculate regression statistics

IF Control < 2 THEN ! Check for correct sequence
    LET R2 = MAXNUM
    LET Slope = MAXNUM
    LET Intercept = MAXNUM
    EXIT SUB
END IF
LET MeanX = SumX / Sum
LET MeanY = SumY / Sum
LET SdevX = SQR((SumXX - SumX^2/Sum)/(Sum-1))
LET SdevY = SQR((SumYY - SumY^2/Sum)/(Sum-1))
LET Slope = (SumXY - MeanX * MeanY * Sum)/(SdevX^2)/(Sum-1)
LET Intercept = MeanY - Slope * MeanX
LET R2 = (SdevX / SdevY * Slope)^2

END SUB

END MODULE
```

I have written an application program that performs a simple form of automatic curve fitting. The program fits a data set with the linear, logarithmic, exponential, and power curves. The results are displayed on the screen, making it possible for you to compare models and select the best one for you.

To simplify data entry and editing, I elected to use DATA statements to become the source of statistical observations. You can edit the QuickBASIC and Turbo BASIC versions of the program to employ INCLUDE files containing the sought DATA statements (for example, $INCLUDE "MYDATA.DAT" in Turbo BASIC). This enables you to save the DATA sets in separate files and use them by editing the included file name before compiling.

The data used by program TESTLINR is taken from "$Y = X^2$" with a few errors deliberately added   Figure 3.7 shows the screen image when True BASIC runs program TESTLINR.TRU. The power fit is the best (highest R2 value) and reveals that the best fitted curve is indeed close to "$Y = X^2$". If the *error* or *noise* in the data had been greater, the above conclusion might not hold true.

```
             AUTOMATIC CURVE FITTING
             -----------------------

 RSqr =  .95188
 Y = (-22.0033 ) + ( 11.0182 ) * X


 RSqr =  .74902
 Y = (-22.3789 ) + ( 40.3696 ) * LN(X)


 RSqr =  .91301
 LN(Y) = ( .506463 ) + ( .458262 ) * X


 RSqr =  .99924
 LN(Y) = ( 3.61001e-2 ) + ( 1.98015 ) * LN(X)
```

Figure 3.7 *Screen image for program TESTLINR.TRU running with True BASIC.*

Listing 3.28, 3.29, and 3.30 show the three versions of program TESTLINR. The four curves are fitted by using two nested FOR-NEXT loops with *XFunc* and *YFunc* being the loop control variables. They are also passed as arguments to *ADDDATA* to select the transformation required. Notice that subroutine *SetDefaultCoeff* is called before the nested FOR loops. *SetDefaultCoeff* conveniently assigns the default (popular) values to the transformation coefficients.

The True BASIC version uses the *DO WHILE MORE DATA* loop to read all of the DATA statements. The number of DATA statements read is updated and stored in variable *N*. The versions of the other BASICs need to read *N* first and then use a FOR-NEXT loop to read the DATA statements.

Listing 3.28. *QuickBASIC source code for program TESTLINR.BAS that performs a simple automatic curve fitting.*

```
'PROGRAM Test.Linear.Regression

' QuickBASIC program that performs linear
' regression using the subroutines in module LINREG.BAS
' Copyright (c) 1987 Namir C. Shammas

OPTION BASE 1

DIM X#(100,2),Coeff#(4)

REM $INCLUDE: 'LINREG.BAS'
REM $INCLUDE: 'TOOLBOX0.BAS'

CLS
' Call routines from TOOLBOX0.BAS
CALL Center.Message("AUTOMATIC CURVE FITTING",1)
CALL Center.Message("----------------------",2)
CALL Blank.Lines(3)

' The following data statements list the observation in (X,Y) pairs
' First DATA statement has the (X,Y) pair count
DATA 10
DATA 1,1.1, 2,3.87, 3,9, 4,15, 5,26, 6,36, 7,50, 8,65, 9,80, 10,100

READ N%

FOR I% = 1 TO N%
    READ X#(I%,1),X#(I%,2)
NEXT I%

Xindex% = 1
Yindex% = 2

CALL SetDefaultCoeff(Coeff#())

FOR YFunc% = 0 TO 1
```

```
            IF YFunc% = 0 THEN Y$ = "Y = " ELSE Y$ = "LN(Y) = "

        FOR XFunc% = 0 TO 1

            IF XFunc% = 0 THEN X$ = "X" ELSE X$ = "LN(X)"

                CALL InitializeLR
                CALL ADDDATA(X#(),Yindex%,Xindex%,N%,XFunc%,YFunc%,Coeff#())
                CALL LRSTAT(Slope#, Intercept#, R2#)
                ' Display results
                PRINT
                PRINT USING "RSqr = #.#####";R2#
                PRINT Y$;"(";Intercept#;") + (";Slope#;") * ";X$

        NEXT XFunc%

    NEXT YFunc%

    END
```

Listing 3.29. *Turbo BASIC source code for program TESTLINR.BAS that performs a simple automatic curve fitting.*

```
'PROGRAM Test.Linear.Regression

' Turbo BASIC program that performs linear
' regression using the subroutines in module LINREG.BAS
' Copyright (c) 1987 Namir C. Shammas

OPTION BASE 1

DIM X#(100,2),Coeff#(4)

$INCLUDE "LINREG.BAS"
$INCLUDE "TOOLBOX0.BAS"

CLS
' Call routines from TOOLBOX0.BAS
CALL Center.Message("AUTOMATIC CURVE FITTING",1)
CALL Center.Message("-----------------------",2)
CALL Blank.Lines(3)

' The following data statements list the observation in (X,Y) pairs
' First DATA statement has the (X,Y) pair count
DATA 10
DATA 1,1.1, 2,3.87, 3,9, 4,15, 5,26, 6,36, 7,50, 8,65, 9,80, 10,100
```

```
READ N%

FOR I% = 1 TO N%
    READ X#(I%,1),X#(I%,2)
NEXT I%

Xindex% = 1
Yindex% = 2

CALL SetDefaultCoeff(Coeff#())

FOR YFunc% = 0 TO 1

    IF YFunc% = 0 THEN Y$ = "Y = " ELSE Y$ = "LN(Y) = "

    FOR XFunc% = 0 TO 1

        IF XFunc% = 0 THEN X$ = "X" ELSE X$ = "LN(X)"

        CALL InitializeLR
        CALL ADDDATA(X#(),Yindex%,Xindex%,N%,XFunc%,YFunc%,Coeff#())
        CALL LRSTAT(Slope#, Intercept#, R2#)
        ' Display results
        PRINT
        PRINT USING "RSqr = #.#####";R2#
        PRINT Y$;"(";Intercept#;") + (";Slope#;") * ";X$

    NEXT XFunc%

NEXT YFunc%

END
```

Listing 3.30. *True BASIC source code for program TESTLINR.TRU that performs a simple automatic curve fitting.*

```
PROGRAM Test_Linear_Regression

! True BASIC program that performs linear
! regression using the subroutines in module LINREG.TRU
! Copyright (c) 1987 Namir C. Shammas

OPTION BASE 1

DIM X(100,2),Coeff(4)

! Declare modules used
LIBRARY "LINREG.TRU","TOOLBOX0.TRU"
```

```
CLEAR
! Call routines from TOOLBOX0.TRU
CALL Center_Message("AUTOMATIC CURVE FITTING",1)
CALL Center_Message("----------------------",2)
CALL Blank_Lines(3)

! The following data statements list the observation in (X,Y) pairs
DATA 1,1.1, 2,3.87, 3,9, 4,15, 5,26, 6,36, 7,50, 8,65, 9,80, 10,100

LET N = 0
DO WHILE MORE DATA
   LET N = N + 1
   READ X(N,1),X(N,2)
LOOP

LET Xindex = 1
LET Yindex = 2

CALL Set_Default_Coeff(Coeff())

FOR YFunc = 0 TO 1

    IF YFunc = 0 THEN LET Y$ = "Y = " ELSE LET Y$ = "LN(Y) = "

    FOR XFunc = 0 TO 1

        IF XFunc = 0 THEN LET X$ = "X" ELSE LET X$ = "LN(X)"

        CALL InitializeLR
        CALL ADD_DATA(X(,),Yindex,Xindex,N,XFunc,YFunc,Coeff())
        CALL LR_STAT(Slope, Intercept, R2)
        ! Display results
        PRINT
        PRINT USING "RSqr = #.#####":R2
        PRINT Y$;"(";Intercept;") + (";Slope;") * ";X$

    NEXT XFunc

NEXT YFunc

END
```

Library Module SORT

PURPOSE: The SORT library offers routines for internal sorting and searching. Two sorting methods are implemented—namely, the Shell-Metzner and the QuickSort algorithms. In the Turbo and True BASIC library versions, the recursive QuickSort method is implemented. In QuickBASIC, the nonrecursive version of QuickSort is implemented, since the QuickBASIC version used does not support recursion.

The sorting routines are written with the following features and capabilities:

1. The sorted data are stored in one-dimensional arrays of strings declared using OPTION BASE 1.

2. The arrays of string "keys" are not rearranged, but instead an array of indexes (or pointers) is used. The array of indexes is used to access the keys in a sorted order.

The search routines are able to look up a sought key using a linear or binary search. The linear search is used with unsorted arrays, while the binary search is used to efficiently look through sorted arrays.

Indexed searching is taken one step further. The SORT library contains two subroutines, one to set up an index table, the other to use it. The index table is set up to handle names from A to z (that is, from A to Z and a to z). The index table works in conjunction with the arrays of indexes obtained from either sorting routines.

Listings 3.31, 3.32, and 3.33 contain the library source code for the QuickBASIC, Turbo BASIC, and True BASIC versions, respectively.

ROUTINES

The following is a list of headings for function and subroutine definitions borrowed from the QuickBASIC listing. They are identical to those of Turbo BASIC. However, they contain minor syntactical differences compared to those of True BASIC, including:

1. function names in True BASIC do not have to begin with the letters *FN*

2. subroutines in True BASIC need no STATIC declarations

SUB ResetIndices(RecIndex%(1), NData%) STATIC
SUB ResetIndices(RecIndex(), NData) ! True BASIC

This subroutine is called by the sorting routines to initialize the array of indexes *RecIndex()*. The parameter *NData* is the array size, assuming *OPTION BASE 1* is used in the application program.

SUB SwapThem(RecIndex%(1),I%,J%) STATIC
SUB SwapThem(RecIndex(),I,J) ! True BASIC

This subroutine is also used internally by the sorting routines. The *I*th and *J*th elements of array *RecIndex()* are swapped. In the True BASIC module, *SwapThem* is declared as PRIVATE and therefore not accessible to any application program.

SUB ShellSort(Kee$(1),RecIndex%(1),NData%,AscendingOrder%) STATIC

SUB ShellSort(Kee$(),RecIndex(),NData,AscendingOrder) !True BASIC

This subroutine performs the Shell-Metzner sort on a one-dimensional array of strings. The array of strings is not rearranged. Instead, an array of indexes is returned to give the sort order. The list of parameters is:

Kee$()	the arrays of data (that is, sort keys) [INPUT]
RecIndex()	the array of indexes [OUTPUT]
NData	the number of sorted keys (assume OPTION BASE 1)
AscendingOrder	if set to one, the indexes are set to provide an ascending order, otherwise they provide a descending order [INPUT]

SUB Sort(Kee$(1), RecIndex%(1), Left%, Right%) ' Turbo BASIC

SUB Sort(Kee$(), RecIndex(), Left, Right) ! True BASIC

This subroutine works as the inner engine for the recursive QuickSort versions. In True BASIC, it is appropriately declared as a PRIVATE routine to deny access to any application program using the module. The Turbo BASIC user should not call this subroutine, but should use the next one instead.

SUB QuickSort(Kee$(1), RecIndex%(1), NData%) STATIC
    'QuickBASIC

SUB QuickSort(Kee$(1), RecIndex%(1), NData%) 'Turbo BASIC
SUB QuickSort(Kee$(), RecIndex(), NData) ! True BASIC

This subroutine implements the QuickSort algorithm. The Turbo and True BASIC versions are the recursive versions of QuickSort. By contrast, the QuickBASIC version is the non-recursive one to accommodate the unsupported recursion. The list of arguments is:

    Kee$()   the arrays of data (that is, sort keys) [INPUT]

    RecIndex()   the array of indexes [OUTPUT]

    NData   the number of sorted keys
                    (assume OPTION BASE 1) [INPUT]

SUB Linear.Search(Item$,Kee$(1),RecIndex%(1),NData%,Index%)
    STATIC

SUB Linear_Search(Item$,Kee$(),RecIndex(),NData,Index)
    ! True BASIC

This routine searches through an array of strings. The search uses the array of indexes. However, these indexes need not reflect any sorted order (if they did, you would be better off using the binary search method anyway!). Why use them? Using indexex enables the subroutine to implement a system where the indexes are used for heuristic purposes. This gives the subroutine the ability to remember the most frequently matched keys and point to them. Thus, the most frequently matched keys are pointed to by *RecIndex(1)*, and so on. Gradually, the array of indexes creates a type of sorted order that is based on the frequency of key usage. The parameter *Index* returns the location of the matched array member, or zero if none is found. The list of parameters is:

    Item$ the search key [INPUT]

    Kee$()   the array of keys [INPUT]

RecIndex()   the array of indexes [IN/OUT].

NData   the number of elements in array *Kee$()* [INPUT]

Index   the index of the matching key; zero is returned
                  if no match is found [OUTPUT]

**SUB Binary.Search(Item$,Kee$(1),RecIndex%(1),NData%,Index%)
        STATIC**

**SUB Binary_Search(Item$,Kee$(),RecIndex(),NData,Index)
        ! True BASIC**

This routine searches quickly and efficiently through a sorted array. The binary search algorithm is implemented here to quickly determine whether a match is found, without scanning the entire array. The parameter *Index* returns the location of the matched array member, or zero if none is found. The list of parameters is:

Item$ the search key [INPUT]

Kee$()   the array of keys [INPUT]

RecIndex()   the array of indexes [INPUT].

NData   the number of elements in array *Kee$()* [INPUT]

Index   the index of the matching key; zero is returned
                  if no match is found [OUTPUT]

**SUB Set.Index.Table(Table%(1),Kee$(1),RecIndex%(1),NData%)
        STATIC**

**SUB Set_Index_Table(Table(),Kee$(),RecIndex(),NData) ! True
        BASIC**

This routine is used to set up an index table. The array of indexes must be arranged by either sorting routine (or any other routine you may write that builds the array identically). The entries are indexed for A to Z and a to z, a total of 52 elements. All entries are initialized to zero. Then the array of indexes is used to point out to the first element that accompanies each table entry. The list of arguments is:

Table()	the array of table entry indexes [OUTPUT]
Kee$()	the array of keys [INPUT]
RecIndex()	the array of indexes [INPUT].
NData	the number of elements in array *Kee$()* [INPUT]

SUB Search.Table(Item$,Kee$(1),RecIndex%(1),Table%(1), NData%,Index%) STATIC

SUB Search_Table(Item$,Kee$(),RecIndex(),Table(), NData,Index) ! True BASIC

Search operations that use indexed tables are even more efficient than binary searches. Using the indexes, the program knows where to start searching and when to stop. This subroutine enables you to perform searching using the indexed table set up by subroutine *Set.Index.Table*. The parameter *Index* returns the location of the matched array member, or zero if none is found. The list of parameters is:

Item$	the search key [INPUT]
Kee$()	the array of keys [INPUT]
RecIndex()t	the array of indexes [INPUT].
Table()	the array of table entry indexes [INPUT].
NData	the number of elements in array *Kee$()* [INPUT]
Index	the index of the matching key; zero is returned if no match is found [OUTPUT]

Listing 3.31. *QuickBASIC source code for library SORT.BAS*

```
' Library  Sort_Search
' Perform the following:
'
'     1) Shell-Metzner sort.
'     2) Non-recursive QuickSort.
'     3) Linear search.
'     4) Binary Indexed search.
'
' QuickBASIC version
' Copyright (c) 1987  Namir Clement Shammas
'

SUB ResetIndices(RecIndex%(1), NData%) STATIC
' Initialize record indices for the keys

STATIC I%

FOR I% = 1 TO NData%
    RecIndex%(I%) = I%
NEXT I%

END SUB


SUB SwapThem(RecIndex%(1),I%,J%) STATIC
' Local procedure to swap indices

SHARED InOrder%
STATIC Temporary%

InOrder% = 0
Temporary% = RecIndex%(I%)
RecIndex%(I%) = RecIndex%(J%)
RecIndex%(J%) = Temporary%

END SUB


SUB ShellSort(Kee$(1), RecIndex%(1), NData%, AscendingOrder%) STATIC
' Procedure to perform a Shell-Meztner sorting
' Assume lowbound is 1

SHARED InOrder%
STATIC Offset%, I%, J%

CALL ResetIndices(RecIndex%(), NData%)
Offset% = NData%

WHILE Offset% > 1
   Offset% = Offset% \ 2

   DO
```

BASIC LIBRARIES

```
            InOrder% = 1
            FOR J% = 1 TO (NData% - Offset%)
                I% = J% + Offset%
                IF AscendingOrder% = 1 THEN
                    IF Kee$(RecIndex%(I%)) < Kee$(RecIndex%(J%)) THEN
                        CALL SwapThem(RecIndex%(),I%,J%)
                    END IF
                ELSE
                    IF Kee$(RecIndex%(I%)) > Kee$(RecIndex%(J%)) THEN
                        CALL SwapThem(RecIndex%(),I%,J%)
                    END IF
                END IF
            NEXT J%
        LOOP WHILE InOrder% = 0

WEND
END SUB


SUB QuickSort(Kee$(1), RecIndex%(1), NData%) STATIC
' Procedure to perform a non-recursive QuickSort

STATIC Left%, Right%, I%, J%, Median$, Stack%
DIM LStack%(50), RStack%(50)

' Initialize record indices for the keys
CALL ResetIndices(RecIndex%(), NData%)
Stack.Height% = 1 : LStack%(1) = 1 : RStack%(1) = NData%

DO
    Left% = LStack%(Stack.Height%)
    Right% = RStack%(Stack.Height%)
    Stack.Height% = Stack.Height% - 1

    DO
        I% = Left% : J% = Right%
        Median$ = Kee$(RecIndex%((Left% + Right%) \ 2))
        DO

            WHILE Kee$(RecIndex%(I%)) < Median$
                I% = I% + 1
            WEND

            WHILE Median$ < Kee$(RecIndex%(J%))
                J% = J% - 1
            WEND

            IF I% <= J% THEN
                CALL SwapThem(RecIndex%(), I%, J%)
                I% = I% + 1 : J% = J% - 1
            END IF

        LOOP WHILE I% <= J%

        IF I% < Right% THEN
            Stack.Height% = Stack.Height% + 1
```

```
                LStack%(Stack.Height%) = I%
                RStack%(Stack.Height%) = Right%
            END IF
            Right% = J%

        LOOP WHILE Left% < Right%

    LOOP WHILE Stack.Height% <> 0

    ERASE LStack%, RStack%

END SUB


SUB Linear.Search(Item$, Kee$(1), RecIndex%(1), NData%, Index%)
STATIC
' Routine to search for Item$ in array Kee$()
' Index% returns zero if no match is found

STATIC I%, Tempo%

IF RecIndex%(1) = 0 THEN CALL ResetIndices(RecIndex%(), NData%)
Index% = 0
I% = 1

WHILE (Index% = 0) AND (I% <= NData%)
    IF Item$ = Kee$(RecIndex%(I%)) THEN
        IF I% > 1 THEN
            Tempo% = RecIndex%(I%)
            RecIndex%(I%) = RecIndex%(I%-1)
            RecIndex%(I%-1) = Tempo%
            Index% = RecIndex%(I%-1)
        ELSE
            Index% = RecIndex%(1)
        END IF
    ELSE
        I% = I% + 1
    END IF
WEND

END SUB


SUB Binary.Search(Item$, Kee$(1), RecIndex%(1), NData%, Index%)
STATIC
' Routine for binary search in an ordered list

STATIC First%, Last%, Range%, Median%

First% = 1  ' Assume lower bound is 1
Last% = NData%
Range% = Last%
Index% = 0

WHILE (Range% > 2) AND (Index% = 0)
    Median% = (First% + Last%) \ 2
```

BASIC LIBRARIES

```
            IF Item$ = Kee$(RecIndex%(Median%)) THEN
                Index% = RecIndex%(Median%)
            ELSE
                IF Item$ > Kee$(RecIndex%(Median%)) THEN
                    First% = Median%
                ELSE
                    Last% = Median%
                END IF
                Range% = Last% - First% + 1
            END IF
    WEND

END SUB


SUB Set.Index.Table(Table%(1),Kee$(1),RecIndex%(1),NData%) STATIC
' Set Index% table using the First% characters of the array Kee$()

STATIC I%, J%, Shift%

FOR I% = 1 TO 52 : Table%(I%) = 0 : NEXT I% ' Initialize Table()

Shift% = ASC("A") - 1

FOR I% = NData% TO 1 STEP -1
    J% = ASC(LEFT$(Kee$(RecIndex%(I%)),1)) - Shift%
    IF (J% > 0) AND (J% < 53) THEN Table%(J%) = I%
NEXT I%

END SUB


SUB Search.Table(Item$, Kee$(1), RecIndex%(1), Table%(1), NData%,
Index%) STATIC
' Search in the table set by Set.Index%.Table

STATIC Shift%, Key.Num%, I%

Shift% = ASC("A") - 1
Key.Num% = ASC(LEFT$(Item$,1)) - Shift%
Index% = 0

IF (Key.Num% < 1) OR (Key.Num% > 52) THEN EXIT SUB ' No matching entry
IF Table%(Key.Num%) = 0 THEN EXIT SUB ' No matching entry

I% = Table%(Key.Num%) ' Obtain First% table entry
GO.ON% = 1

WHILE (I% <= NData%) AND (Index% = 0) AND (GO.ON% = 1)
    IF Item$ = Kee$(RecIndex%(I%)) THEN
            Index% = RecIndex%(I%)
    ELSE
            I% = I% + 1
    END IF
    ' The tests checks if we are searching beyond the feasible Range%
    IF (ASC(LEFT$(Kee$(RecIndex%(I%)),1)) - Shift%) <> Key.Num% THEN
```

```
            GO.ON% = 0
    END IF
WEND

END SUB
```

Lisitng 3.32. *Turbo BASIC source code for library SORT.BAS*

```
' Library  Sort.Search
' Performs the following:
'
'    1) Shell-Metzner sort.
'    2) Non-recursive QuickSort.
'    3) Linear search.
'    4) Binary Indexed search.
'
' Turbo BASIC version
' Copyright (c) 1987  Namir Clement Shammas
'

SUB ResetIndices(RecIndex%(1), NData%) STATIC
' Initialize record indices for the keys

LOCAL I%

FOR I% = 1 TO NData%
    RecIndex%(I%) = I%
NEXT I%

END SUB

SUB SwapThem(RecIndex%(1),I%,J%) STATIC
' Local procedure to swap indices

SHARED InOrder%
LOCAL Temporary%

InOrder% = 0
Temporary% = RecIndex%(I%)
RecIndex%(I%) = RecIndex%(J%)
RecIndex%(J%) = Temporary%

END SUB

SUB ShellSort(Kee$(1), RecIndex%(1), NData%, AscendingOrder%) STATIC
' Procedure to perform a Shell-Meztner sorting
' Assume lowbound is 1

SHARED InOrder%
LOCAL Offset%, I%, J%
```

```
    CALL ResetIndices(RecIndex%(), NData%)
    Offset% = NData%
    DO WHILE Offset% > 1
        Offset% = Offset% \ 2
        DO
            InOrder% = 1
            FOR J% = 1 TO (NData% - Offset%)
                I% = J% + Offset%
                IF AscendingOrder% = 1 THEN
                    IF Kee$(RecIndex%(I%)) < Kee$(RecIndex%(J%)) THEN
                        CALL SwapThem(RecIndex%(),I%,J%)
                    END IF
                ELSE
                    IF Kee$(RecIndex%(I%)) > Kee$(RecIndex%(J%)) THEN
                        CALL SwapThem(RecIndex%(),I%,J%)
                    END IF
                END IF
            NEXT J%
        LOOP UNTIL InOrder% = 1
    LOOP

END SUB

SUB Sort(Kee$(1), RecIndex%(1), Left%, Right%)
' Recursive subroutine called by QuickSort

LOCAL I%, J%, Median%, Data1$

I% = Left%
J% = Right%
Median% = INT((Left% + Right%) / 2)
Data1$ = Kee$(RecIndex%(Median%))

DO

    DO WHILE Kee$(RecIndex%(I%)) < Data1$
        INCR I%
    LOOP

    DO WHILE Data1$ < Kee$(RecIndex%(J%))
        DECR J%
    LOOP

    IF I% <= J% THEN
        CALL SwapThem(RecIndex%(),I%,J%)
        INCR I%
        DECR J%
    END IF

LOOP UNTIL I% > J%

IF Left% < J%   THEN CALL Sort(Kee$(),RecIndex%(),Left%,J%)
IF I% < Right%  THEN CALL Sort(Kee$(),RecIndex%(),I%,Right%)

END SUB
```

```
SUB QuickSort(Kee$(1), RecIndex%(1), NData%) STATIC
' Procedure to perform a QuickSort

' Initialize record indices for the keys
CALL ResetIndices(RecIndex%(), NData%)

CALL Sort(Kee$(),RecIndex%(),1,NData%)

END SUB


SUB Linear.Search(Item$, Kee$(1), RecIndex%(1), NData%, Index%) STATIC
' Routine to search for Item$ in array Kee$()
' Index% returns zero if no match is found

LOCAL I%, Tempo%

IF RecIndex%(1) = 0 THEN CALL ResetIndices(RecIndex%(), NData%)
Index% = 0
I% = 1

DO WHILE (Index% = 0) AND (I% <= NData%)
   IF Item$ = Kee$(RecIndex%(I%)) THEN
      IF I% > 1 THEN
         Tempo% = RecIndex%(I%)
         RecIndex%(I%) = RecIndex%(I%-1)
         RecIndex%(I%-1) = Tempo%
         Index% = RecIndex%(I%-1)
      ELSE
         Index% = RecIndex%(1)
      END IF
   ELSE
      INCR I%
   END IF
LOOP

END SUB


SUB Binary.Search(Item$, Kee$(1), RecIndex%(1), NData%, Index%) STATIC
' Routine for binary search in an ordered list
LOCAL First%, Last%, Range%, Median%

First% = 1            ' Assume lower bound is 1
Last% = NData%
Range% = Last%
Index% = 0
DO WHILE (Range% > 2) AND (Index% = 0)

   Median% = (First% + Last%) \ 2

   IF Item$ = Kee$(RecIndex%(Median%)) THEN
      Index% = RecIndex%(Median%)
      EXIT LOOP
   END IF
```

```
        IF Item$ > Kee$(RecIndex%(Median%)) THEN
           First% = Median%
        ELSE
           Last% = Median%
        END IF

        Range% = Last% - First% + 1

LOOP

END SUB


SUB Set.Index.Table(Table%(1),Kee$(1),RecIndex%(1),NData%) STATIC
'Set Index% table using the First% characters of the array Kee$()

LOCAL I%, J%, Shift%

FOR I% = 1 TO 52 : Table%(I%) = 0 : NEXT I% ' Initialize Table()

Shift% = ASC("A") - 1

FOR I% = NData% TO 1 STEP -1
    J% = ASC(LEFT$(Kee$(RecIndex%(I%)),1)) - Shift%
    IF (J% > 0) AND (J% < 53) THEN Table%(J%) = I%
NEXT I%

END SUB


SUB Search.Table(Item$, Kee$(1), RecIndex%(1), Table%(1), NData%,
Index%) STATIC
' Search in the table set by Set.Index%.Table

LOCAL Shift%, Key.Num%, I%

Shift% = ASC("A") - 1
Key.Num% = ASC(MID$(Item$,1,1)) - Shift%
Index% = 0
IF (Key.Num% < 1) OR (Key.Num% > 52) THEN EXIT SUB ' No matching entry
IF Table%(Key.Num%) = 0 THEN EXIT SUB ' No matching entry

I% = Table%(Key.Num%) ' Obtain First% table entry

DO WHILE (I% <= NData%) AND (Index% = 0)
    IF Item$ = Kee$(RecIndex%(I%)) THEN
        Index% = RecIndex%(I%)
    ELSE
        INCR I%
    END IF
' The until clause test if we are searching beyond the feasible Range%
LOOP UNTIL (ASC(MID$(Kee$(RecIndex%(I%)),1,1)) - Shift%) <> Key.Num%

END SUB
```

Listing 3.33. *True BASIC source code for module SORT.TRU*

```
MODULE Sort_Search

! Module to perform:
!
!  1) Shell-Metzner sort
!  2) Recursive QuickSort
!  3) Linear search
!  4) Indexed binary search
!
!  True BASIC version
!  Copyright (c) 1987   Namir Clement Shammas
!

! List of local, unexported subroutines
PRIVATE SwapThem, Sort
SHARE InOrder

SUB ResetIndices(RecIndex(), NData)
! Initialize record indices for the keys

FOR I = 1 TO NData
    LET RecIndex(I) = I
NEXT I

END SUB

SUB SwapThem(RecIndex(),I,J)
! Local procedure to swap indices

LET InOrder = 0
LET Temporary = RecIndex(I)
LET RecIndex(I) = RecIndex(J)
LET RecIndex(J) = Temporary

END SUB

SUB ShellSort(Kee$(), RecIndex(), NData, AscendingOrder)
! Procedure to perform a Shell-Meztner sorting
! Assume lowbound is 1

CALL ResetIndices(RecIndex(), NData)
LET Offset = NData
DO WHILE Offset > 1
   LET Offset = INT(Offset / 2)
   DO
      LET InOrder = 1
      FOR J = 1 TO (NData - Offset)
         LET I = J + Offset
         IF AscendingOrder = 1 THEN
```

BASIC LIBRARIES

```
                    IF Kee$(RecIndex(I)) < Kee$(RecIndex(J)) THEN
                       CALL SwapThem(RecIndex(),I,J)
                    END IF
                 ELSE
                    IF Kee$(RecIndex(I)) > Kee$(RecIndex(J)) THEN
                       CALL SwapThem(RecIndex(),I,J)
                    END IF
                 END IF
         NEXT J
      LOOP UNTIL InOrder = 1
   LOOP

END SUB


SUB Sort(Kee$(), RecIndex(), Left, Right)
! Recursive subroutine called by QuickSort
LET I = Left
LET J = Right
LET Median = INT((Left + Right) / 2)
LET Data1$ = Kee$(RecIndex(Median))
DO
   DO WHILE Kee$(RecIndex(I)) < Data1$
      LET I = I + 1
   LOOP

   DO WHILE Data1$ < Kee$(RecIndex(J))
      LET J = J - 1
   LOOP

   IF I <= J THEN
      CALL SwapThem(RecIndex(),I,J)
      LET I = I + 1
      LET J = J - 1
   END IF
LOOP UNTIL I > J
IF Left < J THEN CALL Sort(Kee$(),RecIndex(),Left,J)
IF I < Right THEN CALL Sort(Kee$(),RecIndex(),I,Right)

END SUB                      ! Sort

SUB QuickSort(Kee$(), RecIndex(), NData)
! Procedure to perform a QuickSort

! Initialize record indices for the keys
CALL ResetIndices(RecIndex(), NData)

CALL Sort(Kee$(),RecIndex(),1,NData)

END SUB                      ! QuickSort


SUB Linear_Search(Item$, Kee$(), RecIndex(), NData, Index)
! Routine to search for Item$ in array Kee$()
! Index returns zero if no match is found
```

```
   IF RecIndex(1) = 0 THEN CALL ResetIndices(RecIndex(), NData)
   LET Index = 0
   LET I = 1

   DO WHILE (Index = 0) AND (I <= NData)
      IF Item$ = Kee$(RecIndex(I)) THEN
         IF I > 1 THEN
            LET Tempo = RecIndex(I)
            LET RecIndex(I) = RecIndex(I-1)
            LET RecIndex(I-1) = Tempo
            LET Index = RecIndex(I-1)
         ELSE
            LET Index = RecIndex(1)
         END IF
      ELSE
         LET I = I + 1
      END IF
   LOOP

END SUB

SUB Binary_Search(Item$, Kee$(), RecIndex(), NData, Index)
! Routine for binary search in an ordered list

LET First = 1             ! Assume lower bound is 1
LET Last = INT(NData)
LET Range = Last
LET Index = 0

DO WHILE (Range > 2) AND (Index = 0)
   LET Median = INT((First + Last) / 2)
   IF Item$ = Kee$(RecIndex(Median)) THEN
      LET Index = RecIndex(Median)
      EXIT DO
   END IF

   IF Item$ > Kee$(RecIndex(Median)) THEN
      LET First = Median
   ELSE
      LET Last = Median
   END IF
   LET Range = Last - First + 1
LOOP

END SUB

SUB Set_Index_Table(Table(),Kee$(),RecIndex(),NData)
! Set index table using the first characters of the array Kee$()
MAT Table = ZER(52)         ! initialize for 'A' to 'z'

LET Shift = ORD("A") - 1
FOR I = NData TO 1 STEP -1
   LET J = ORD(Kee$(RecIndex(I))[1:1]) - Shift
   IF (J > 0) AND (J < 53) THEN LET Table(J) = I
NEXT I
```

```
END SUB

SUB Search_Table(Item$, Kee$(), RecIndex(), Table(), NData, Index)
! Search in the table set by Set_Index_Table

LET Shift = ORD("A") - 1
LET Key_Num = ORD(Item$[1:1]) - Shift
LET Index = 0
IF (Key_Num < 1) OR (Key_Num > 52) THEN EXIT SUB ! No matching entry
IF Table(Key_Num) = 0 THEN EXIT SUB ! No matching entry

LET I = Table(Key_Num) ! Obtain first table entry
DO WHILE (I <= NData) AND (Index = 0)
   IF Item$ = Kee$(RecIndex(I)) THEN
      LET Index = RecIndex(I)
   ELSE
      LET I = I + 1
   END IF
! The until clause test if we are
! searching beyond the feasible range
LOOP UNTIL (ORD(Kee$(RecIndex(I))[1:1]) - Shift) <> Key_Num

END SUB

END MODULE
```

I have written an automatic demonstration application program to exercise the various parts of library SORT. The BASIC program reads DATA statements that contain keywords from the Pascal programming language. The program sorts the array of keywords using both Shell-Metzner and QuickSort and carries out searches.

The first aspect demonstrated by the application program TESTSORT is sorting the Pascal keywords using the Shell method. Figure 3.8.1 shows the screen image where the keywords are displayed in ascending order using the array of indexes.

```
            SORTED LIST PRODUCED BY SHELL SORT

                 Index #              Item
                 -------           -------------
                   10                 ABS
                    3                 ASSIGN
                    6                 ATAN
                   15                 BOOLEAN
                    7                 COS
                   12                 FUNCTION
                   14                 INTEGER
                   11                 PROCEDURE
                    1                 READ
                   13                 REAL
                    4                 RESET
                    5                 REWRITE
                    8                 SIN
                    9                 SQRT
                    2                 WRITE

         press any key to continue
```

Figure 3.8.1 *First screen image for program TESTSORT.TRU running under True BASIC.*

Next, the program calls on the QuickSort subroutine to sort the same list. Figure 3.8.2 shows the sorted list. In addition, the screen also shows the result of calling the binary search subroutine to locate "COS". The correct index, 7, is returned.

```
           SORTED LIST PRODUCED BY QUICKSORT

              Index #                 item
              -------             --------------
                10                    ABS
                 3                    ASSIGN
                 6                    ATAN
                15                    BOOLEAN
                 7                    COS
                12                    FUNCTION
                14                    INTEGER
                11                    PROCEDURE
                 1                    READ
                13                    REAL
                 4                    RESET
                 5                    REWRITE
                 8                    SIN
                 9                    SQRT
                 2                    WRITE

   A binary search for 'COS' returns an array index of  7

   press any key to continue
```

Figure 3.8.2 *Second screen image for program TESTSORT.TRU.*

The third screen, shown in figure 3.8.3, displays the portions of the index table that have entries assigned to them. Fewer keywords are displayed because the index points only to the first keys encountered. The screen also shows the results of searching for "COS", "READ", and "REZO" (not a Pascal keyword).

```
                      INDEX TABLE

    Entry #        Character       Array Index         Item
    -------        ---------       -----------         ----

       1               A               10              ABS
       2               B               15              BOOLEAN
       3               C                7              COS
       6               F               12              FUNCTION
       9               I               14              INTEGER
      16               P               11              PROCEDURE
      18               R                1              READ
      19               S                8              SIN
      23               W                2              WRITE


    Using the search table 'COS' is located at index  7
    Using the search table 'READ' is located at index  1
    Using the search table 'REZO' is located at index  0
```

Figure 3.8.3 *Third screen image for program TESTSORT.TRU.*

Listing 3.34, 3.35, and 3.36 show the three versions of program TESTSORT. The QuickBASIC version contains a definition for function *FNUCASE$()* to mimic the predefined *UCASE$()* function available in both Turbo and True BASIC. All three versions illustrate how the array of pointers is used to access the data in sorted order.

Listing 3.34. *QuickBASIC source code for program TESTSORT.BAS that demonstrates the sorting and searching features of library SORT.BAS*

```
'PROGRAM Test.Sort.Search

' Program to demonstrate using the SORT.BAS library
' This program provides a demo for sorting and indexed searching
```

```
' QuickBASIC version

OPTION BASE 1

DIM A$(15), Ptr%(15), Table%(52)

' include library used
REM $INCLUDE: 'SORT.BAS'

DATA 15
DATA READ, WRITE, ASSIGN, RESET, REWRITE, ATAN, COS, SIN, SQRT, ABS
DATA PROCEDURE, FUNCTION, REAL, INTEGER, BOOLEAN

READ NData%
FOR I% = 1 TO NData%
    READ A$(I%)
NEXT I%

CALL ShellSort(A$(), Ptr%(), NData%, 1)

CALL Center("Sorted list produced by Shell sort")

PRINT "                        Index #         Item"
PRINT "                        -------         --------------"
M$ = "                          ##           \              \"
FOR I% = 1 TO NData%
    PRINT USING M$;Ptr%(I%),A$(Ptr%(I%))
NEXT I%

LOCATE 22,1 : PRINT "press any key to continue ";

Z$ = INPUT$(1)

CALL QuickSort(A$(), Ptr%(), NData%)
CALL Center("Sorted list produced by QuickSort")
PRINT "                        Index #         Item"
PRINT "                        -------         --------------"
M$ = "                          ##           \              \"
FOR I% = 1 TO NData%
    PRINT USING M$;Ptr%(I%),A$(Ptr%(I%))
NEXT I%

Item$ = "COS"
CALL Binary.Search(Item$, A$(), Ptr%(), NData%, Index%)
PRINT
PRINT "A binary search for ";Item$;" returns an array Index of ";Index%
PRINT
LOCATE 22,1 : PRINT "press any key to continue ";
Z$ = INPUT$(1)

CALL Set.Index.Table(Table%(),A$(),Ptr%(),NData%)
CALL Center("Index table")
PRINT "        Entry #      Character      Array Index       Item"
PRINT "        -------      ---------      -----------       ------------"
M$ = "          ##            \\             ###           \            \"
FOR I% = 1 TO 52
```

```
        T = Table%(I%)
        IF T > 0 THEN PRINT USING M$;I%,CHR$(I%+64),Ptr%(T),A$(Ptr%(T))
NEXT I%
PRINT
PRINT

' test index searches
Item$ = "COS"
CALL Search.Table(Item$, A$(), Ptr%(), Table%(), NData%, Index%)
PRINT "Using the se
```

Listing 3.35. *Turbo BASIC source code for program TESTSORT.BAS that demonstrates the sorting and searching features of library SORT.BAS*

```
'PROGRAM Test.Sort.Search

' Program to demonstrate using the SORT.BAS library
' This program provides a demo for sorting and indexed searching
' Turbo BASIC version

OPTION BASE 1

DIM A$(15), Ptr%(15), Table%(52)

' include used libraries
$INCLUDE "SORT.BAS"
$INCLUDE "TOOLBOX0.BAS"

DATA 15
DATA READ, WRITE, ASSIGN, RESET, REWRITE, ATAN, COS, SIN, SQRT, ABS
DATA PROCEDURE, FUNCTION, REAL, INTEGER, BOOLEAN

READ NData%
FOR I% = 1 TO NData%
    READ A$(I%)
NEXT I%

CALL ShellSort(A$(), Ptr%(), NData%, 1)

CALL Center("Sorted list produced by Shell sort")
PRINT "                    Index #           Item"
PRINT "                    -------           ----------------"
M$ = "                      ##              \              \"
FOR I% = 1 TO NData%
    PRINT USING M$;Ptr%(I%),A$(Ptr%(I%))
NEXT I%
LOCATE 22,1 : PRINT "press any key to continue";
Z$ = INPUT$(1)

CALL QuickSort(A$(), Ptr%(), NData%)
```

BASIC LIBRARIES

```
CALL Center("Sorted list produced by QuickSort")
PRINT "                      Index #           Item"
PRINT "                      -------           ----------------"
    M$="                       ##              \              \"
FOR I% = 1 TO NData%
    PRINT USING M$;Ptr%(I%),A$(Ptr%(I%))
NEXT I%

Item$ = "COS"
CALL Binary.Search(Item$, A$(), Ptr%(), NData%, Index%)
PRINT
PRINT "A binary search ";Item$;" returns an array index of ";Index%
PRINT
LOCATE 22,1 : PRINT "press any key to continue";
Z$ = INPUT$(1)

CALL Set.Index.Table(Table%(),A$(),Ptr%(),NData%)
CALL Center("Index table")
PRINT "        Entry #      Character     Array Index      Item"
PRINT "        -------      ---------     -----------      ------------"
    M$="        ##           \\            ###              \            \"
FOR I% = 1 TO 52
    T = Table%(I%)
    IF T > 0 THEN PRINT USING M$;I%,CHR$(I%+64),Ptr%(T),A$(Ptr%(T))
NEXT I%
PRINT
PRINT

' test indexed table search
Item$ = "COS"
CALL Search.Table(Item$, A$(), Ptr%(), Table%(), NData%, Index%)
PRINT "Using the search table ";Item$;" is located at index ";Index%

Item$ = "READ"
CALL Search.Table(Item$, A$(), Ptr%(), Table%(), NData%, Index%)
PRINT "Using the search table ";Item$;" is located at index ";Index%

Item$ = "REZO"
CALL Search.Table(Item$, A$(), Ptr%(), Table%(), NData%, Index%)
PRINT "Using the search table ";Item$;" is located at index ";Index%

SUB Center(S$) STATIC
' Center message in uppercase
CLS
CALL Center.Message(UCASE$(S$),1)
PRINT : PRINT

END SUB

END
```

Listing 3.36. *True BASIC source code for program TESTSORT.TRU that demonstrates the sorting and searching features of module SORT.TRU*

```
PROGRAM Test_Sort_Search

OPTION BASE 1

DIM A$(15), Ptr(15), Table(52)

! Declare used modules
LIBRARY "SORT.TRU","TOOLBOX0.TRU"

DATA 15
DATA READ, WRITE, ASSIGN, RESET, REWRITE, ATAN, COS, SIN, SQRT, ABS
DATA PROCEDURE, FUNCTION, REAL, INTEGER, BOOLEAN

READ NData
FOR I = 1 TO NData
    READ A$(I)
NEXT I

CALL ShellSort(A$(), Ptr(), NData, 1)

CALL Center("Sorted list produced by Shell sort")
PRINT "                        Index #          Item"
PRINT "                        -------          --------------"
LET M$="                          ##            ############"
FOR I = 1 TO NData
    PRINT USING M$:Ptr(I),A$(Ptr(I))
NEXT I
SET CURSOR 22,1
PRINT "press any key to continue";
GET KEY A_KEY

CALL QuickSort(A$(), Ptr(), NData)
CALL Center("Sorted list produced by QuickSort")
PRINT "                        Index #          Item"
PRINT "                        -------          --------------"
LET M$="                          ##            ############"
FOR I = 1 TO NData
    PRINT USING M$:Ptr(I),A$(Ptr(I))
NEXT I

LET Item$ = "COS"
CALL Binary_Search(Item$, A$(), Ptr(), NData, Index)
PRINT
PRINT "A binary search for '";Item$;"' returns an array index of ";Index
PRINT
SET CURSOR 22,1
PRINT "press any key to continue";
GET KEY A_K
CALL Set_Index_Table(Table(),A$(),Ptr(),NData)
CALL Center("Index table")
```

```
    PRINT "      Entry #    Character    Array Index      Item"
    PRINT "      -------    ---------    -----------    ---------"
    LET M$="        ##          #           ###         ############"
    FOR I = 1 TO 52
        LET T = Table(I)
        IF T > 0 THEN PRINT USING M$:I,CHR$(I+64),Ptr(T),A$(Ptr(T))
    NEXT I
    PRINT
    PRINT
    ! test indexed searches
    LET Item$ = "COS"
    CALL Search_Table(Item$, A$(), Ptr(), Table(), NData, Index)
    PRINT "Using the search table '";Item$;"' is located at index ";Index

    LET Item$ = "READ"
    CALL Search_Table(Item$, A$(), Ptr(), Table(), NData, Index)
    PRINT "Using the search table '";Item$;"' is located at index ";Index

    LET Item$ = "REZO"
    CALL Search_Table(Item$, A$(), Ptr(), Table(), NData, Index)
    PRINT "Using the search table '";Item$;"' is located at index ";Index

SUB Center(S$)

    CLEAR
    LET S$ = UCASE$(S$)
    CALL Center_Message(S$,1)
    PRINT
    PRINT

END SUB

END
```

Library Module LISTS

PURPOSE: This library provides a set of routines to perform fundamental list manipulation in BASIC. This includes list insertion, deletion, and search. Since BASIC lacks Pascal-like pointers, arrays are used to implement lists. The lists are maintained in sorted order with the aid of an array of indexes. This makes searching through a sorted list more efficient. The physical sequence of the array storing the data maintains the chronological order of entries.

Listings 3.37, 3.38, and 3.39 contain the library source code for the QuickBASIC, Turbo BASIC, and True BASIC versions, respectively.

ROUTINES

The following is a list of headings for function and subroutine definitions borrowed from the QuickBASIC listing. They are identical to those of **Turbo BASIC**. However, they contain minor syntactical differences compared to those of True BASIC, including:

1. function names in True BASIC do not have to begin with the letters *FN*

2. subroutines in True BASIC need no STATIC declarations

```
' -------- QuickBASIC ------
TRUE2% = 1
FALSE2% = 0
NIL% = 0

' -------- Turbo BASIC ------
%TRUE2 = 1
%FALSE2 = 0
%NIL = 0

! -------- True BASIC ------
DEF TRUE2 = 1
DEF FALSE2 = 0
DEF NIL = 0
```

These constants and functions assign values for TRUE, FALSE, and NIL.

SUB INSERTNODE(ITEM$,HEAD%,LIST.SIZE%, LIST.ITEM$(1),LIST.PTR%(1)) STATIC

SUB InsertNode(Item$,Head,List_Size,List_Item$(),List_Ptr()) ! True BASIC

This subroutine is used to insert a string-type data into the list. The *Head* parameter is the index of the first list member. Normally, *Head* has a value of one. Other values assigned to *Head* enable you to bypass the actual list head and begin at another member. The *LIST.PTR()* array maintains the links between the members of the list and simultaneously supports a sorted order. The list of parameters is:

ITEM$ the inserted list member [INPUT]

HEAD   the index to the head of the list [IN/OUT]

LIST.SIZEt   the list size [IN/OUT]

LIST.ITEM$()   the array of string simulating the list [IN/OUT]

LIST.PTR()   the array of list pointers [IN/OUT]

SUB DELNODE(ITEM$,OK%,HEAD%,LIST.SIZE%,
    LIST.ITEM$(1),LIST.PTR%(1)) STATIC

SUB DelNode(Item$,OK,Head,List_Size,List_Item$(),List_Ptr())
    ! True BASIC

This subroutine searches array *LIST.ITEM$()* for *ITEM$* and deletes the latter. The parameter *OK* returns the outcome of the subroutine action. The list of parameters is:

ITEM$ the list member to be deleted [INPUT]

OK   a numeric flag to indicate the outcome of deletion; if OK = TRUE2 then *Item$* was found and deleted; otherwise, no deletion occurred [OUTPUT]

HEAD   the pointer to the head of the list [IN/OUT]

LIST.SIZE   the list size [IN/OUT]

LIST.ITEM$()   the array of strings simulating the list [IN/OUT]

LIST.PTR()   the array of list pointers [IN/OUT]

SUB FINDNODE(ITEM$, HEAD%, LIST.ITEM$(1),
              LIST.PTR%(1), FOUND%) STATIC

SUB FindNode(Item$, Head, List_Item$(), List_Ptr(), Found)
             ! True BASIC

This routine searches for *ITEM$* in array *LIST.ITEM$()* and returns a TRUE2/FALSE2 result with the parameter *Found*.

ITEM$	the inserted list member [INPUT]
HEAD	the pointer to the head of the list [INPUT]
LIST.ITEM$()	the array of strings simulating the list [INPUT]
LIST.PTR()	the array of list pointers [INPUT]
FOUND	the search outcome (TRUE or FALSE) [OUTPUT]

SUB GETORDEREDPTR(HEAD%, LIST.SIZE%, LISTPTR%(1),
              RANKPTR%(1)) STATIC

SUB GetOrderedPtr(Head, List_Size, ListPtr(), RankPtr())
             ! True BASIC

Recall that the array of list pointers is used to maintain a sorted list. This subroutine returns an array of ranks that enable you to access the list elements in ascending order. Thus, *RANKPTR(1)* is the index of the first sorted element, *RANKPTR(2)* is the index for the second one, and so on. Since the array of ranks is not automatically updated with the list insertion and deletion operations, this subroutine must be called to update the rank indexes. The list of parameters is:

HEAD	the pointer to the head of the list [INPUT]
LIST.SIZE	the list size [INPUT]
LISTPTR()	the array of list pointers [INPUT]

RANKPTR() the array of sorted ranks [OUTPUT].

SUB REVORDEREDPTR(HEAD%, LIST.SIZE%, LISTPTR%(1), RANKPTR%(1)) STATIC

**SUB RevOrderedPtr(Head, List_Size, ListPtr(), RankPtr())
! True BASIC**

This subroutine is similar to *GETORDEREDPTR*, except that the array of rank pointers returned enables you to access the list in descending order. Since the array of ranks is not automatically updated with the list insertion and deletion operations, this subroutine MUST be called to update the rank indices. The list of parameters is:

HEAD the index to the head of the list [INPUT]

LIST.SIZE the list size [INPUT]

LISTPTR() the array of list pointers [INPUT]

RANKPTR() the array of sorted ranks [OUTPUT]

Listing 3.37. *QuickBASIC source code for library LISTS.BAS.*

```
'-----------------------------------------------------------'
'                                                           '
'              SINGLE-LINKED LIST MODULE                    '
'              -------------------------                    '
'                                                           '
'         Copyright (c) 1987   Namir Clement Shammas        '
'                                                           '
' QUICKBASIC VERSION 3.0                        2/14/1987   '
'                                                           '
'-----------------------------------------------------------'

CONST TRUE2% = 1, FALSE2% = 0,  NIL2% = 0
```

```
SUB GETORDEREDPTR(HEAD%, LIST.SIZE%, LISTPTR%(1), RANKPTR%(1))
' Routine to return a rank index array for the list in ascending order

STATIC I%

RANKPTR%(1) = HEAD%

FOR I% = 2 TO LIST.SIZE%
    RANKPTR%(I%) = LISTPTR%(RANKPTR%(I%-1))
NEXT I%

END SUB


SUB REVORDEREDPTR(HEAD%, LIST.SIZE%, LISTPTR%(1), RANKPTR%(1)) STATIC
' Routine to return a rank index array for the list in descending
order

STATIC I%

RANKPTR%(LIST.SIZE%) = HEAD%

FOR I% = LIST.SIZE%-1 TO 1 STEP -1
    RANKPTR%(I%) = LISTPTR%(RANKPTR%(I%+1))
NEXT I%

END SUB


SUB FINDNODE(ITEM$, HEAD%, LIST.ITEM$(1), LIST.PTR%(1), FOUND%)
STATIC
' Search for ITEM$ in list LIST.ITEM$() starting with HEAD%
' HEAD% may not neccessarely be the actual head of the list.
' This feature is useful in "smart" searches

STATIC PTR%, GO.ON%

FOUND% = FALSE2%
PTR% = HEAD%
GO.ON% = TRUE2%

WHILE (PTR% <> NIL2%) AND (GO.ON% = TRUE2%)
  IF LIST.ITEM$(PTR%) >= ITEM$ THEN
     GO.ON% = FALSE2%
  ELSE
     PTR% = LIST.PTR%(PTR%)
  END IF
WEND

IF PTR% <> NIL2% THEN
    IF LIST.ITEM$(PTR%) = ITEM$ THEN FOUND% = TRUE2%
END IF

END SUB
```

BASIC LIBRARIES 281

```
SUB INSERTNODE(ITEM$, HEAD%, LIST.SIZE%, LIST.ITEM$(1),
LIST.PTR%(1)) STATIC
' Insert ITEM$ in list LIST.ITEM$()

STATIC PTR%, LASTPTR%, GO.ON%

IF (HEAD% = NIL2%) OR (LIST.SIZE% = 0) THEN
    LIST.SIZE% = 1
    HEAD% = 1
    LIST.ITEM$(1) = ITEM$
    LIST.PTR%(1) = NIL2%

 ELSE ' SEARCH IN LIST
    LASTPTR% = NIL2%
    PTR% = HEAD%
    GO.ON% = TRUE2%

    WHILE (PTR% <> NIL2%) AND (GO.ON% = TRUE2%)
      IF LIST.ITEM$(PTR%) >= ITEM$ THEN

          GO.ON% = FALSE2%
      ELSE
          LASTPTR% = PTR%
          PTR% = LIST.PTR%(PTR%)
      END IF
    WEND

    LIST.SIZE% = LIST.SIZE% + 1
    LIST.ITEM$(LIST.SIZE%) = ITEM$
    IF LASTPTR% = NIL2% THEN
        LIST.PTR%(LIST.SIZE%) = PTR%
        HEAD% = LIST.SIZE%
    ELSE
        LIST.PTR%(LASTPTR%) = LIST.SIZE%
        LIST.PTR%(LIST.SIZE%) = PTR%
    END IF

END IF

END SUB


SUB DELNODE(ITEM$, OK%, HEAD%, LIST.SIZE%, LIST.ITEM$(1),
LIST.PTR%(1)) STATIC
' Routine to delere node containing ITEM$

STATIC PTR%, LASTPTR%, GO.ON%

OK% = FALSE2%
LASTPTR% = NIL2%
PTR% = HEAD%
GO.ON% = TRUE2%

WHILE (PTR% <> NIL2%) AND (GO.ON% = TRUE2%)
    IF LIST.ITEM$(PTR%) >= ITEM$ THEN
```

```
            GO.ON% = FALSE2%
        ELSE
            LASTPTR% = PTR%
            PTR% = LIST.PTR%(PTR%)
        END IF
WEND

IF PTR% <> NIL2%   THEN
    IF LIST.ITEM$(PTR%) = ITEM$ THEN OK% = TRUE2%
END IF

IF OK% = TRUE2% THEN
    IF LASTPTR% = NIL2% THEN
        HEAD% = LIST.PTR%(PTR%)
    ELSE
        LIST.PTR%(LASTPTR%) = LIST.PTR%(PTR%)
    END IF
END IF

LIST.SIZE% = LIST.SIZE% - 1

END SUB
```

Listing 3.38. *Turbo BASIC source code for library LISTS.BAS*

```
'-----------------------------------------------------------'
'                                                           '
'               SINGLE-LINKED LIST MODULE                   '
'               ------------------------                    '
'                                                           '
'       Copyright (c) 1987   Namir Clement Shammas          '
'                                                           '
' TURBO BASIC VERSION 1.0                       2/14/1987   '
'                                                           '
'-----------------------------------------------------------'


%TRUE2 = 1
%FALSE2 = 0
%NIL2 = 0


SUB GETORDEREDPTR(HEAD%, LIST.SIZE%, LISTPTR%(1), RANKPTR%(1))
STATIC
' Routine to return a rank index array for the list in ascending order

LOCAL I%
```

```
RANKPTR%(1) = HEAD%

FOR I% = 2 TO LIST.SIZE%
    RANKPTR%(I%) = LISTPTR%(RANKPTR%(I%-1))
NEXT I%

END SUB



SUB REVORDEREDPTR(HEAD%, LIST.SIZE%, LISTPTR%(1), RANKPTR%(1))
STATIC
' Routine to return a rank index array for the list in descending order

LOCAL I%

RANKPTR%(LIST.SIZE%) = HEAD%

FOR I% = LIST.SIZE%-1 TO 1 STEP -1
    RANKPTR%(I%) = LISTPTR%(RANKPTR%(I%+1))
NEXT I%

END SUB



SUB FINDNODE(ITEM$, HEAD%, LIST.ITEM$(1), LIST.PTR%(1), FOUND%) STATIC
' Search for ITEM$ in list LIST.ITEM$() starting with HEAD%
' HEAD% may not neccessarely be the actual head of the list.
' This feature is useful in "smart" searches

LOCAL PTR%

FOUND% = %FALSE2
PTR% = HEAD%

DO WHILE PTR% <> %NIL2
  IF LIST.ITEM$(PTR%) >= ITEM$ THEN EXIT LOOP
  PTR% = LIST.PTR%(PTR%)
LOOP

IF PTR% <> %NIL2  THEN
    IF LIST.ITEM$(PTR%) = ITEM$ THEN FOUND% = %TRUE2
END IF

END SUB



SUB INSERTNODE(ITEM$, HEAD%, LIST.SIZE%, LIST.ITEM$(1), LIST.PTR%(1)) STATIC
' Insert ITEM$ in list LIST.ITEM$()

LOCAL PTR%, LASTPTR%

IF (HEAD% = %NIL2) OR (LIST.SIZE% = 0) THEN
    LIST.SIZE% = 1
    HEAD% = 1
    LIST.ITEM$(1) = ITEM$
    LIST.PTR%(1) = %NIL2
```

```
      ELSE ' SEARCH IN LIST
         LASTPTR% = %NIL2
         PTR% = HEAD%

         DO WHILE PTR% <> %NIL2
            IF LIST.ITEM$(PTR%) >= ITEM$ THEN EXIT LOOP
            LASTPTR% = PTR%
            PTR% = LIST.PTR%(PTR%)
         LOOP

         LIST.SIZE% = LIST.SIZE% + 1
         LIST.ITEM$(LIST.SIZE%) = ITEM$
         IF LASTPTR% = %NIL2 THEN
            LIST.PTR%(LIST.SIZE%) = PTR%
            HEAD% = LIST.SIZE%
         ELSE
            LIST.PTR%(LASTPTR%) = LIST.SIZE%
            LIST.PTR%(LIST.SIZE%) = PTR%
         END IF

   END IF

END SUB


SUB DELNODE(ITEM$, OK%, HEAD%, LIST.SIZE%, LIST.ITEM$(1), LIST.PTR%(1)) STATIC
' Routine to delere node containing ITEM$

LOCAL PTR%, LASTPTR%
OK% = %FALSE2
LASTPTR% = %NIL2
PTR% = HEAD%

DO WHILE PTR% <> %NIL2
    IF LIST.ITEM$(PTR%) >= ITEM$ THEN EXIT LOOP
    LASTPTR% = PTR%
    PTR% = LIST.PTR%(PTR%)
LOOP

IF PTR% <> %NIL2  THEN
    IF LIST.ITEM$(PTR%) = ITEM$ THEN OK% = %TRUE2
END IF

IF OK% = %TRUE2 THEN
    IF LASTPTR% = %NIL2 THEN
        HEAD% = LIST.PTR%(PTR%)
    ELSE
        LIST.PTR%(LASTPTR%) = LIST.PTR%(PTR%)
    END IF
END IF
LIST.SIZE% = LIST.SIZE% - 1

END SUB
```

Listing 3.39. *True BASIC source code for module LISTS.TRU*

```
MODULE Lists

!---------------------------------------------------------------!
!                                                               !
!              Single-Linked List Module                        !
!              -------------------------                        !
!                                                               !
!        Copyright (c) 1987   Namir Clement Shammas             !
!                                                               !
! True BASIC Version 1.0                        2/14/1987       !
!                                                               !
!---------------------------------------------------------------!

DECLARE DEF TRUE2, FALSE2, NIL2

DEF TRUE2 = 1
DEF FALSE2 = 0
DEF NIL2 = 0

SUB GetOrderedPtr(Head, List_Size, ListPtr(), RankPtr())
! Routine to return a rank index array for the list in ascending order

LET RankPtr(1) = Head

FOR I = 2 TO List_Size
    LET RankPtr(I) = ListPtr(RankPtr(I-1))
NEXT I

END SUB


SUB RevOrderedPtr(Head, List_Size, ListPtr(), RankPtr())
! Routine to return a rank index array for the list in descending order

LET RankPtr(List_Size) = Head

FOR I = List_Size-1 TO 1 STEP -1
    LET RankPtr(I) = ListPtr(RankPtr(I+1))
NEXT I

END SUB

SUB FindNode(Item$, Head, List_Item$(), List_Ptr(), Found)
! Search for Item$ in list List_Item$() starting with Head
! Head may not neccessarely be the actual head of the list
! This feature is useful in "smart" searches

LET Found = FALSE2
LET Ptr = Head
```

```
     DO WHILE Ptr <> NIL2
       IF List_Item$(Ptr) >= Item$ THEN EXIT DO
       LET Ptr = List_Ptr(Ptr)
     LOOP

     IF Ptr <> NIL2  THEN
         IF List_Item$(Ptr) = Item$ THEN LET Found = TRUE2
     END IF

END SUB


SUB InsertNode(Item$, Head, List_Size, List_Item$(), List_Ptr())
! Insert Item$ in list List_Item$()

IF (Head = NIL2) OR (List_Size = 0) THEN
     LET List_Size = 1
     LET Head = 1
     LET List_Item$(1) = Item$
     LET List_Ptr(1) = NIL2
 ELSE ! Search in list

     LET LastPtr = NIL2
     LET Ptr = Head

     DO WHILE Ptr <> NIL2
       IF List_Item$(Ptr) >= Item$ THEN EXIT DO
       LET LastPtr = Ptr
       LET Ptr = List_Ptr(Ptr)
     LOOP

     LET List_Size = List_Size + 1
     LET List_Item$(List_Size) = Item$
     IF LastPtr = NIL2 THEN
         LET List_Ptr(List_Size) = Ptr
         LET Head = List_Size
     ELSE
         LET List_Ptr(LastPtr) = List_Size
         LET List_Ptr(List_Size) = Ptr
     END IF

END IF

END SUB


SUB DelNode(Item$, OK, Head, List_Size, List_Item$(), List_Ptr())
! Routine to delete node containing Item$

LET OK = FALSE2
LET LastPtr = NIL2
LET Ptr = Head

DO WHILE Ptr <> NIL2
     IF List_Item$(Ptr) >= Item$ THEN EXIT DO
```

```
        LET LastPtr = Ptr
        LET Ptr = List_Ptr(Ptr)
LOOP

IF Ptr <> NIL2   THEN
    IF List_Item$(Ptr) = Item$ THEN LET OK = TRUE2
END IF

IF OK = TRUE2 THEN
    IF LastPtr = NIL2 THEN
        LET Head = List_Ptr(Ptr)
    ELSE
        LET List_Ptr(LastPtr) = List_Ptr(Ptr)
    END IF
END IF

LET List_Size = List_Size - 1

END SUB

END MODULE
```

I have written a demonstration program that reads DATA statements containing a list of keywords from the Pascal language. The program builds a list and displays it in ascending sorted order. To demonstrates the deletion process, four keywords are removed from the list and the new list is displayed in descending order. The last part prompts the user for a keyword and searches for it in the list. The above is performed using an open DO-LOOP with the EXIT condition set to true if the user's input is a null string.

Figure 3.9.1 shows the screen image when program TESTLIST.BAS starts running under Turbo BASIC. The DATA items inserted in the list are displayed in the order in which they are read.

```
Inserting a list of some Pascal keywords


Inserting PROCEDURE    in list
Inserting FUNCTION     in list
Inserting READLN       in list
Inserting WRITELN      in list
Inserting BEGIN        in list
Inserting WITH         in list
Inserting REPEAT       in list
Inserting UNTIL        in list
Inserting REAL         in list
Inserting INTEGER      in list
Inserting TYPE         in list
Inserting SEEK         in list
Inserting RESET        in list
Inserting REWRITE      in list
Inserting BLOCKREAD    in list
Inserting BLOCKWRITE   in list
Inserting COS          in list
Inserting SIN          in list


press any key
```

Figure 3.9.1 *Image of the first screen for program TESTLIST.BAS running with Turbo BASIC.*

The array of pointers maintains the list in a sorted order. Figure 3.9.2 shows the screen displaying the sorted list in ascending order. This is carried out using the array of ranks.

```
Full list of some Pascal keywords in ascending order

BEGIN
BLOCKREAD
BLOCKWRITE
COS
FUNCTION
INTEGER
PROCEDURE
READLN
REAL
REPEAT
RESET
REWRITE
SEEK
SIN
TYPE
UNTIL
WITH
WRITELN

press any key
```

Figure 3.9.2 *Image of the second screen for program TESTLIST.BAS.*

Between the screens displayed in figures 3.9.2 and 3.9.3, the program deletes four list members. They are the keywords BEGIN, REAL, INTEGER, and FUNCTION. The program then displays the new list in reverse sorted order.

```
Partial list of some Pascal keywords in descending order
(BEGIN, REAL, INTEGER and FUNCTION were deleted)

WRITELN
WITH
UNTIL
TYPE
SIN
SEEK
REWRITE
RESET
REPEAT
READLN
PROCEDURE
COS
BLOCKWRITE
BLOCKREAD

press any key
```

Figure 3.9.3 *Image of the third screen for program TESTLIST.BAS.*

Following the screen in figure 3.9.3, the user is prompted to test the list membership of keywords. Figure 3.9.4 shows the screen image when the keywords "TYPE", "type", and "COS" are entered. Notice that "type" is declared not a member, since case sensitive string comparison is used in the list library.

```
    Search for item (press [ENTER] to exit) ? TYPE

    IS TYPE IN THE LIST? YES

    Search for item (press [ENTER] to exit) ? type

    IS type IN THE LIST? NO

    Search for item (press [ENTER] to exit) ? COS

    IS COS IN THE LIST? YES

    Search for item (press [ENTER] to exit) ? <press [ENTER]>
```

Figure 3.9.4 *Image of the screen for program TESTLIST.BAS while prompting the user for search items.*

Listings 3.40, 3.41, and 3.42 contain the three versions of demonstration program TESTLIST.

Listing 3.40. *QuickBASIC source code for the list-manipulation demonstration program TESTLIST.BAS*

```
' PROGRAM Test.Lists
' QuickBASIC version

OPTION BASE 1

DIM LIST.ITEM$(50), LIST.PTR%(50), RANKPTR%(50)

' Include used library
REM $INCLUDE: 'LISTS.BAS'

DATA 18
DATA PROCEDURE, FUNCTION, READLN, WRITELN, BEGIN, WITH, REPEAT
DATA UNTIL, REAL, INTEGER, TYPE, SEEK, RESET, REWRITE, BLOCKREAD
DATA BLOCKWRITE, COS, SIN, SQRT, SQR, TAN, ATAN, HI, LO

DEF FNSAYYN$(I%)
IF SGN(I%) > 0 THEN FNSAYYN$ = "YES" ELSE FNSAYYN$ = "NO"
```

```
END DEF

LIST.SIZE% = 0
HEAD% = NIL2%
READ NDATA%

CLS
PRINT "Inserting a list of some Pascal keywords" : PRINT

FOR I% = 1 TO NDATA%
  READ ITEM$
  CALL INSERTNODE(ITEM$, HEAD%, LIST.SIZE%, LIST.ITEM$(), LIST.PTR%())
  PRINT USING "Inserting \        \ in list"; ITEM$
NEXT I%

PRINT : PRINT "press any key " : A$ = INPUT$(1)

CLS
PRINT "Full list of some Pascal keywords in ascending order" : PRINT
CALL SHOW.LIST(0)

' Delete BEGIN, REAL, INTEGER and FUNCTION
CALL DELNODE("BEGIN",    OK%, HEAD%, LIST.SIZE%, LIST.ITEM$(), LIST.PTR%())
CALL DELNODE("REAL",     OK%, HEAD%, LIST.SIZE%, LIST.ITEM$(), LIST.PTR%())
CALL DELNODE("INTEGER",  OK%, HEAD%, LIST.SIZE%, LIST.ITEM$(), LIST.PTR%())
CALL DELNODE("FUNCTION", OK%, HEAD%, LIST.SIZE%, LIST.ITEM$(), LIST.PTR%())

CLS
PRINT "Partial list of some Pascal keywords in descending order (BEGIN, ";
PRINT "REAL, INTEGER and FUNCTION were deleted)" : PRINT
CALL SHOW.LIST(1)

' Use open loop for prompt & search
DO
  INPUT "Search for item (press [Enter] to exit) ";ITEM$ : PRINT
  IF ITEM$ = "" THEN EXIT DO
  CALL FINDNODE(ITEM$, HEAD%, LIST.ITEM$(), LIST.PTR%(), FOUND%)
  PRINT "IS ";ITEM$;" IN THE LIST? ";FNSAYYN$(FOUND%)
  PRINT
LOOP


SUB SHOW.LIST(IN.REVERSE%) STATIC
' local subroutine to show linked list

SHARED HEAD%, LIST.SIZE%, LIST.ITEM$(), LIST.PTR%(), RANKPTR%()

IF (IN.REVERSE% = FALSE2%) THEN
  CALL GETORDEREDPTR(HEAD%, LIST.SIZE%, LIST.PTR%(), RANKPTR%())
ELSE
  CALL REVORDEREDPTR(HEAD%, LIST.SIZE%, LIST.PTR%(), RANKPTR%())
END IF

FOR I% = 1 TO LIST.SIZE%
  PRINT LIST.ITEM$(RANKPTR%(I%))
NEXT I%
```

```
PRINT
PRINT "press any key"; : A$ = INPUT$(1)
PRINT
PRINT

END SUB

END
```

Listing 3.41 *Turbo BASIC source code for the list-manipulation demonstration program TESTLIST.BAS*

```
' PROGRAM Test.Lists
' Turbo BASIC version

OPTION BASE 1

DIM LIST.ITEM$(50), LIST.PTR%(50), RANKPTR%(50)

' Include used library
$INCLUDE "LISTS.BAS"

DATA 18
DATA PROCEDURE, FUNCTION, READLN, WRITELN, BEGIN, WITH, REPEAT
DATA UNTIL, REAL, INTEGER, TYPE, SEEK, RESET, REWRITE, BLOCKREAD
DATA BLOCKWRITE, COS, SIN, SQRT, SQR, TAN, ATAN, HI, LO

LIST.SIZE% = 0
HEAD% = %NIL2
READ NDATA%

CLS
PRINT "Inserting a list of some Pascal keywords" : PRINT

FOR I% = 1 TO NDATA%
  READ ITEM$
  CALL INSERTNODE(ITEM$, HEAD%, LIST.SIZE%, LIST.ITEM$(),
LIST.PTR%())
    PRINT USING "Inserting \         \ in list"; ITEM$
NEXT I%

PRINT : PRINT "press any key " : A$ = INPUT$(1)

CLS
PRINT "Full list of some Pascal keywords in ascending order" : PRINT
CALL SHOW.LIST(0)

' Delete BEGIN, REAL, INTEGER and FUNCTION
CALL DELNODE("BEGIN",    OK%, HEAD%, LIST.SIZE%, LIST.ITEM$(), LIST.PTR%())
```

```
    CALL DELNODE("REAL",     OK%, HEAD%, LIST.SIZE%, LIST.ITEM$(), LIST.PTR%())
    CALL DELNODE("INTEGER",  OK%, HEAD%, LIST.SIZE%, LIST.ITEM$(), LIST.PTR%())
    CALL DELNODE("FUNCTION", OK%, HEAD%, LIST.SIZE%, LIST.ITEM$(), LIST.PTR%())

    CLS
    PRINT "Partial list of some Pascal keywords in descending order (BEGIN, ";
    PRINT "REAL, INTEGER and FUNCTION were deleted)" : PRINT
    CALL SHOW.LIST(1)

    ' Use open loop for prompt & search
    DO
      INPUT "Search for item (press [Enter] to exit) ";ITEM$ : PRINT
      IF ITEM$ = "" THEN EXIT LOOP
      CALL FINDNODE(ITEM$, HEAD%, LIST.ITEM$(), LIST.PTR%(), FOUND%)
      PRINT "IS ";ITEM$;" IN THE LIST? ";FNSAYYN$(FOUND%)
      PRINT
    LOOP


    SUB SHOW.LIST(IN.REVERSE%) STATIC
    ' Internal subroutine to show linked list

    SHARED HEAD%, LIST.SIZE%, LIST.ITEM$(), LIST.PTR%(), RANKPTR%()

    IF (IN.REVERSE% = %FALSE2) THEN
       CALL GETORDEREDPTR(HEAD%, LIST.SIZE%, LIST.PTR%(), RANKPTR%())
    ELSE
       CALL REVORDEREDPTR(HEAD%, LIST.SIZE%, LIST.PTR%(), RANKPTR%())
    END IF

    FOR I% = 1 TO LIST.SIZE%
       PRINT LIST.ITEM$(RANKPTR%(I%))
    NEXT I%
    PRINT : PRINT "press any key " : A$ = INPUT$(1)
    PRINT
    END SUB

    DEF FNSAYYN$(I%)
    IF SGN(I%) > 0 THEN FNSAYYN$ = "YES" ELSE FNSAYYN$ = "NO"
    END DEF

    END
```

Listing 3.42. *True BASIC source code for the list-manipulation demonstration program TESTLIST.TRU*

```
    PROGRAM Test_Lists
    ! True BASIC version

    OPTION BASE 1
```

BASIC LIBRARIES   295

```
DECLARE DEF SAYYN$

DIM List_Item$(50), List_Ptr(50), RankPtr(50)

! Declare used library
LIBRARY "LISTS.TRU"

! Declare imported function(s)
DECLARE DEF FALSE2, NIL2

DATA 18
DATA PROCEDURE, FUNCTION, READLN, WRITELN, BEGIN, WITH, REPEAT
DATA UNTIL, REAL, INTEGER, TYPE, SEEK, RESET, REWRITE, BLOCKREAD
DATA BLOCKWRITE, COS, SIN, SQRT, SQR, TAN, ATAN, HI, LO


LET List_Size = 0
LET Head = NIL2
READ NData
CLEAR
PRINT "Inserting a list of some Pascal keywords"
PRINT

FOR I = 1 TO NData
   READ Item$
   CALL InsertNode(Item$, Head, List_Size, List_Item$(), List_Ptr())
   PRINT USING "Inserting <############ in list":Item$
NEXT I

PRINT
PRINT "press any key";
GET KEY A_KEY

CLEAR
PRINT "Full list of some Pascal keywords in ascending order"
PRINT
CALL Show_List(0)

! Delete BEGIN, REAL, INTEGER and FUNCTION
CALL DelNode("BEGIN", OK, Head, List_Size, List_Item$(), List_Ptr())
CALL DelNode("REAL", OK, Head, List_Size, List_Item$(), List_Ptr())
CALL DelNode("INTEGER", OK, Head, List_Size, List_Item$(),
List_Ptr())
CALL DelNode("FUNCTION", OK, Head, List_Size, List_Item$(),
List_Ptr())

CLEAR
PRINT "Partial list of some Pascal keywords in descending order (BEGIN, ";
PRINT "REAL, INTEGER and FUNCTION were deleted)"
PRINT
CALL Show_List(1)
PRINT

! Use open loop for prompt & search
DO
   INPUT PROMPT "Search for item (type 2 double quotes to exit) ":Item$
   PRINT
   IF Item$ = "" THEN EXIT DO
```

```
    CALL FindNode(Item$, Head, List_Item$(), List_Ptr(), Found)
    PRINT "Is ";Item$;" in the list ? ";SAYYN$(Found)
    PRINT
LOOP

SUB Show_List(In_Reverse)
! Internal subroutine to show linked list

IF In_Reverse = FALSE2 THEN
   CALL GetOrderedPtr(Head, List_Size, List_Ptr(), RankPtr())
ELSE
   CALL RevOrderedPtr(Head, List_Size, List_Ptr(), RankPtr())
END IF

FOR I = 1 TO LIST_SIZE
   PRINT List_Item$(RankPtr(I))
NEXT I

PRINT
PRINT "press any key";
GET KEY A_KEY
PRINT
END SUB

DEF SAYYN$(I)
IF SGN(I) > 0 THEN LET SAYYN$ = "YES" ELSE LET SAYYN$ = "NO"
END DEF

END
```

Library Module SETS

PURPOSE: This library implements sets in BASIC in a manner similar to the Pascal language. The string data type is used to simulate the set types. A set, then, is nothing but a long string containing delimited strings. This is possible due to the fact that strings in the New BASICs can be as large as 32K, or 64K. The default delimiter for set members is the comma. It is assigned to the function *FNDELIMITCHAR$* (in True BASIC it is *DelimitChar$*). You may alter the delimiter character returned by this function to use a different delimiter character (CAUTION: Be consistent with the delimiter character to make sure you do not create incompatabilities).

The set operations implemented are extensive and include:

   1. two-way string-to-set conversions

   2. change delimiter character in sets

3. creating character sets whose characters fall in a specified range

4. test for membership in a set

5. add and remove a member from a set

6. find the successor and predecessor of a member in a set (this is similar to *SUCC()* and *PRED()* functions in Pascal)

7. find the ordinal value of a member in a set (this is similar to the *ORD()* function in Pascal)

8. find *i*th member in a set

9. determine the membership size in a set

10. perform union, intersection, and difference operations on sets

11. sort a set by rearranging the members in ascending order

12. compare set for equality and inequalities

Listings 3.43, 3.44, and 3.45 contain the library source code for the QuickBASIC, Turbo BASIC, and True BASIC versions, respectively.

ROUTINES

The following is a list of headings for function and subroutine definitions borrowed from the QuickBASIC listing. They are identical to those of Turbo BASIC. However, they contain minor syntactical differences compared to those of True BASIC, including:

1. Function names in True BASIC do not have to begin with the letters *FN*.

2. Subroutines in True BASIC need no STATIC declarations.

DEF FNDELIMITCHAR$
DEF DelimitChar$! True BASIC

This function returns the character for set delimiting.

DEF FNHICHAR%
DEF HiChar ! True BASIC

This function returns the upper limit of the ASCII code table. If you port the program to another system, you may need to decrease the currently assigned number (255).

SUB CREATE.NEW.SET(SETNAME$) STATIC
SUB Create_New_Set(SetName$) ! True BASIC

This subroutine initializes a string-type set *SetName$* by assigning a null string to it.

SUB ADD.MEMBER(MEMBER$, SETNAME$) STATIC
SUB Add_Member(Member$,SetName$) ! True BASIC

This subroutine is used to add NONDUPLICATE members to the set. The new *Member$* is the candidate for insertion in set *SetName$*. The member addition process is case sensitive.

EXAMPLE:

```
Week$ = "Mon,Tue,Wed,Thu,Fri"
CALL ADD.MEMBER("Sat", Week$)
PRINT Week$ ' displays "Mon,Tue,Wed,Thu,Fri,Sat"

 ' Subroutine is CASE sensitive
CALL ADD.MEMBER("SAT", Week$)
PRINT Week$ ' displays "Mon,Tue,Wed,Thu,Fri,Sat,SAT"

" Try to insert a duplicate
CALL ADD.MEMBER("Wed", Week$)

' displays "Mon,Tue,Wed,Thu,Fri,Sat,SAT"
' the duplicated member is NOT inserted
PRINT Week$
```

SUB REMOVE.MEMBER(MEMBER$, SETNAME$, OK%) STATIC

SUB Remove_Member(Member$, SetName$, OK) ! True BASIC

This subroutine attempts to remove member *Member$* from set *SetName$*. If the deletion is successful, the parameter *OK* returns one; otherwise, zero. The membership deletion is CASE sensitive.

EXAMPLE:

```
Week$ = "Mon,Tue,Wed,Thu,Fri,Sat,Sun"
CALL REMOVE.MEMBER("Sat", Week$, OK%)
' Since OK% = 1, the next IF test succeeds
IF OK% = 1 THEN
    PRINT Week$ ' displays "Mon,Tue,Wed,Thu,Fri,Sun"
END IF

CALL REMOVE.MEMBER("SUN", Week$, OK%)
PRINT OK% ' displays zero: deletion did not occur
PRINT Week$ ' displays "Mon,Tue,Wed,Thu,Fri,Sun"
```

SUB CHANGE.SET(SETNAME$,OLD.DELIMITCHAR$, NEW.DELIMITCHAR$) STATIC

SUB Change_Set(SetName$,Old_DelimitChar$, New_DelimitChar$) ! True BASIC

This function scans the set *SETNAME$* and replaces the old delimiter character with a new one. Make sure that the new delimiter character is not already present in the set as part of a set member!

EXAMPLE:

```
Old.Delim$ = ","
New.Delim$ = "|"
' set of weekdays delimited by commas
SetName$ = "Mon,Tue,Wed,Thu,Fri,Sat,Sun"
CALL CHANGE.SET(SetName$, Old.Delim$, New.Delim$)
PRINT SetName$ ' displays "Mon|Tue|Wed|Thu|Fri|Sat|Sun"
```

DEF FNSAYTF2$(N%)
DEF SayTF2$(N) ! True BASIC

A simple function that returns "TRUE" if *N* is not zero, or "FALSE" otherwise.

EXAMPLE:

```
PRINT FNSAYTF2$(0)  ' displays "FALSE"
PRINT FNSAYTF2$(1)  ' displays "TRUE"
```

DEF FNMAKE.CHARSET$(FIRSTASCII%,LASTASCII%)
DEF Make_CharSet$(FirstASCII,LastASCII) ! True BASIC

This function returns a character set. The range of characters included in the set is defined by the *FIRSTASCII* and *LASTASCII* ASCII code numbers.

EXAMPLE:

```
FNMAKE.CHARSET$(ASC("I"),ASC("O")) returns
"I,J,K,L,M,N,O"
```

DEF FNMAKE.MORE.CHARSET$(START$,FIRSTASCII%, LASTASCII%)

DEF Make_More_CharSet$(Start$,FirstASCII,LastASCII) ! True BASIC

This function returns an expanded character set. The original character set *Start$* is concatenated to a new character set. The range for the new character set is defined by the *FIRSTASCII* and *LASTASCII* ASCII code numbers.

EXAMPLE:

```
Start$ = "A,B,C,D"
NewSet$ = FNMAKE.MORE.CHARSET$(Start$, ASC("a"), ASC("d"))
PRINT NewSet$  ' displays "A,B,C,D,a,b,c,d"
```

DEF FNMAKE.STRING.FROM.SET$(SETNAME$)
DEF Make_String_From_Set$(SetName$) ! True BASIC

This function takes a string-type set and removes the set delimiter characters.

EXAMPLE:

```
SetName$ = "Hello, there, how, are, you"
Phrase$ = FNMAKE.STRING.FROM.SET(SetName$)
PRINT Phrase$ ' displays "Hello there how are you"
```

DEF FNMAKE.SET.FROM.STRING$(A$, MEMBER.SIZE%)
DEF Make_Set_From_String$(A$, Member_Size) ! True BASIC

The function creates a set from string *A$*. The resulting set contains members of equal length (specified by the member size parameter).

EXAMPLE

```
A.Str$ = "MonTueWedThuFriSatSun"
Week$ = FNMAKE.SET.FROM.STRING$(A.Str$, 3)
PRINT Week$ ' displays "Mon,Tue,Wed,Thu,Fri,Sat,Sun"
```

DEF FNINSET%(MEMBER$, SETNAME$)
DEF InSet(Member$,SetName$) ! True BASIC

This function verifies the membership of *Member$* in set *SetName$*. The outcome is returned as a numeric code. A value of one is returned if the membership is established; otherwise, the function yields zero. The membership test is case sensitive.

EXAMPLE:

```
FNINSET%("Mon", "Mon,Tue,Wed,Thu,Fri") returns 1
FNINSET%("mon", "Mon,Tue,Wed,Thu,Fri") returns 0
FNINSET%("Sat", "Mon,Tue,Wed,Thu,Fri") returns 0
```

DEF FNSUCC$(MEMBER$,SETNAME$)
DEF Succ$(Member$,SetName$) ! True BASIC

Returns the member that succeeds *Member$* in set *SetName$*. If *Member$* is the last member in the set, then a null string is returned by the function. A null string is also returned if *Member$* is not actually a member of the set in question.

EXAMPLE:

```
Week$ = "Mon,Tue,Wed,Thu,Fri"
PRINT FNSUCC$("Tue", Week$) ' displays "Wed"
PRINT FNSUCC$("Thu", Week$) ' displays "Fri"
PRINT FNSUCC$("Fri", Week$) ' displays nothing

' Use a non-member
PRINT FNSUCC$("Sun", Week$) ' displays nothing
```

DEF FNPRED$(MEMBER$,SETNAME$)
DEF Pred$(Member$,SetName$) ! True BASIC

Returns the member that precedes *Member$* in set *SetName$*. If *Member$* is the first member in the set, then a null string is returned by the function. A null string is also returned if *Member$* is not actually a member of the set in question.

EXAMPLE:

```
Week$ = "Mon,Tue,Wed,Thu,Fri"
PRINT FNPRED$("Tue", Week$) ' displays "Mon"
PRINT FNPRED$("Thu", Week$) ' displays "Wed"
PRINT FNPRED$("Mon", Week$) ' displays nothing

' Use a non-member
PRINT FNPRED$("Sun", Week$) ' displays nothing
```

DEF FNSET.SIZE%(SETNAME$)
DEF Set_Size(SetName$) ! True BASIC

This function counts the number of members in set *SetName$*.

EXAMPLE:

```
Week$ = "Mon,Tue,Wed,Thu,Fri,Sat,Sun"
N% = FNSET.SIZE%(Week$)
PRINT "There are ";N%;" days in a week "
```

DEF FNSET.ORD%(MEMBER$, SETNAME$)
DEF Set_Ord(Member$, SetName$) ! True BASIC

This function yields the ordinal number of member *Member$* in set *SetName$*. If *Member$* is not a set member, a zero value is returned. The numbering system is such that the first member is assigned an ordinal value of one (in Pascal the first member has an ordinal value of zero).

EXAMPLE:

```
Week$ = "Sun,Mon,Tue,Wed,Thu,Fri,Sat"
Day$ = "Mon"
N% = FNSET.ORD%(Day$,Week$)
PRINT Day$;" is weekday number ";N%

Weekend$ = "Sat,Sun"
Day$ = "Sun"
N% = FNSET.ORD%(Day$,Weekend$)
PRINT Day$;" is weekend day number ";N%

Day$ = "Mon" ' try a non-member
N% = FNSET.ORD%(Day$,Weekend$)
' the next PRINT displays "Mon is weekend day number 0"
PRINT Day$;" is weekend day number ";N%
```

DEF FNSET.VAL$(N%, SETNAME$)
DEF Set_Val$(N, SetName$) ! True BASIC

This function is the reverse of the ordinal value function. Given the ordinal number *N* and the set *SetName$*, the function attempts to return the sought member. If the ordinal value is too high, a null string is returned.

EXAMPLE:

```
LeColorSet$ = "Red,Blue,Green,Yellow"
N% = 2
```

```
LeColor$ = FNSET.VAL$(N%, LeColorSet$)
PRINT LeColor$;" is color number ";N%;" in the set"
```

DEF FNUNITE.SETS$(SETA$, SETB$)
DEF Unite_Sets$(SetA$, SetB$) ! True BASIC

This routine unites two sets and returns the new set. Duplicate members are filtered out. Uniting a set with its subset yields that same set! Keep in mind that the set union operation is case sensitive.

EXAMPLE:

```
WeekDay$ = "Mon,Tue,Wed,Thu,Fri"
WeekEnd$ = "Sat,Sun"
Week$ = FNUNITE.SETS$(WeekDay$, WeekEnd$)
PRINT Week$ ' displays "Mon,Tue,Wed,Thu,Fri,Sat,Sun"

' Test duplicate members
Week2$ = FNUNITE.SETS$(Week$, WeekEnd$)
PRINT Week2$ ' displays "Mon,Tue,Wed,Thu,Fri,Sat,Sun'
' Set Week2$ equal Week$ because we attempted to unite a
' set with its subset!
```

DEF FNINTERSECT.SETS$(SETA$, SETB$)
DEF Intersect_Sets$(SetA$, SetB$) ! True BASIC

This function intersects two sets, *SetA$* and *SetB$*. The string-type set returned contains the members common in both parent sets. The function yields a null string to indicate a null set. Intersecting a set with its subset returns the subset.

EXAMPLE:

```
' Define set of days when John has free time
Days.John.Free$ = "Mon,Thu,Sat"

' Define set of days when Tim has free time
Days.Tim.Free$ = "Tue,Wed,Thu,Sat"

' Obtain days when both John and Tim can go fishing
F$ = FNINTERSECT.SETS$(Days.John.Free$,Days.Tim.Free$)
' F$ contains "Thu,Sat", the common days.
```

DEF FNDIFFERENCE.SETS$(SETA$, SETB$)
DEF Difference_Sets$(SetA$, SetB$) ! True BASIC

This function returns a set of members not in common between sets *SetA$* and *SetB$*. If either set is a subset of the other, an empty set (that is, null string) is returned.

EXAMPLE:

```
' Define set of days when John has free time
Days.John.Free$ = "Mon,Thu,Sat"

' Define set of days when Tim has free time
Days.Tim.Free$ = "Tue,Wed,Thu,Sat"

' Obtain days when both John and Tim CANNOT go fishing
F$ = FNDIFFERENCE.SETS$(Days.John.Free$,Days.Tim.Free$)
' F$ contains "Mon,Tue,Wed", the 'un-common' days.
```

SUB SORT.SET(SOURCESET$, TARGETSET$) STATIC
SUB Sort_Set(SourceSet$, TargetSet$) ! True BASIC

This routine sorts the members of *SourceSet$* in ascending order and stores the ordered set in *TargetSet$*.

EXAMPLE:

```
Week$ = "Mon,Tue,Wed,Thu,Fri,Sat,Sun"
CALL SORT.SET(Week$, Sorted$)
PRINT Sorted$ ' displays "Fri,Mon,Sat,Sun,Thu,Tue,Wed"
```

DEF FNARE.SETS.EQ%(SETA$, SETB$)
DEF Are_Sets_EQ(SetA$, SetB$) ! True BASIC

This function tests the equality of sets *SetA$* and *SetB$* (that is, are they copies of each other?). If the outcome is positive, the function returns the value one, otherwise, zero. The equality test is case sensitive. Thus, if *SetA$* has its members all in upper case and *SetB$* the same members in lower case, then the sets are not equal. To make the test case insensitive, convert both strings to the same case and then use this function.

EXAMPLE:

```
Week1$ = "Mon,Tue,Wed,Thu,Fri,Sat,Sun"
Week2$ = "MON,TUE,WED,THU,FRI,SAY,SUN"
' test for set equality
N% = FNARE.SETS.EQ%(Week1$, Week2$)
PRINT "Are sets equal ? ";FNSAYTF$(N%) ' displays FALSE

'Convert Week1$ to uppercase
Week3$ = UCASE$(Week1$)
' now test for set equality
N% = FNARE.SETS.EQ%(Week3$, Week2$)
PRINT "Are sets equal ? ";FNSAYTF$(N%) ' displays TRUE
```

DEF FNARE.SETS.LEQ%(SETA$, SETB$)
DEF Are_Sets_LEQ(SetA$, SetB$) ! True BASIC

This function tests to determine whether or not set *SetA$* is less than or equal to *SetB$*. In other words, is *SetA$* equivalent to *SetB$* OR is it a subset of it? If *SetA$* is equivalent to *SetB$*, the function returns a value of one, otherwise it returns zero.

EXAMPLE:

```
Week$ = "Mon,Tue,Wed,Thu,Fri,Sat,Sun"
WeekEnd$ = "Sat,Sun"
N% = FNARE.SETS.LEQ%(WeekEnd$, Week$)
PRINT N% ' displays "1": WeekEnd$ is a subset of Week$

TripDay$ = "Sun, Mon, Tue"
N% = FNARE.SETS.LEQ%(WeekEnd$, TripDay$)
PRINT N% ' displays "0": WeekEnd$ is NOT a subset of TripDay$
```

DEF FNARE.SETS.LT%(SETA$, SETB$)
DEF Are_Sets_LT(SetA$, SetB$) ! True BASIC

This function tests if set *SetA$* is a subset of (but not equal to) *SetB$*. If the above condition is true, the function returns a value of one; otherwise, it returns zero.

BASIC LIBRARIES

EXAMPLE:

```
Week$ = "Mon,Tue,Wed,Thu,Fri,Sat,Sun"
WeekEnd$ = "Sat,Sun"
N% = FNARE.SETS.LEQ%(WeekEnd$, Week$)
PRINT N% ' displays "1": WeekEnd$ is a subset of Week$
```

The following popular sets are included in the library and are made accessible to the application program. These sets are constructed with the comma as the delimiter character. The relatively short sets are listed in their entirety. The longer sets are only commented.

YESNOSET$	= "YES,Yes,yes,NO,No,no,Y,y,N,n,"
YESSET$	= "YES,Yes,yes,Y,"
NOSET$	= "NO,No,no,N,n,"
TRUESET$	= "TRUE,True,true,T,t,"
FALSESET$	= "FALSE,False,false,F,f,"
BOOLSET$	= "TRUE,FALSE,true,false True,False,T,F,t,f,"
YNSET$	= "Y,N,y,n,"
TFSET$	= "F,T,f,t,"
WEEKENDSET$	= "SATURDAY,SUNDAY,"
WEEKSET$	set of all weekdays
WEEKDAYSET$	set of weekdays (Monday through Friday)
MONTHSET$	set of 12 months (January through December)
LOWERCASESET$	set of lowercase letters ("a" to "z")
UPPERCASESET$	set of uppercase letters ("A" to "Z")
DIGITSET$	set of digits ("0" to "9")

LETTERSET$ set of upper-case and lower-case letters

ALPHANUMSET$ set of letters and digits

CONTROLSET$ set of control characters (ASCII 0 to 31)

PUNCTSET$ set of punctuation letters

Listing 3.43. *QuickBASIC source code for library SETS.BAS*

```
'-----------------------------------------------------------'
'                                                           '
'                       BASIC SETS                          '
'                      ------------                         '
'                    QuickBASIC version                     '
' VERSION 1.0                                    12/86      '
'                                                           '
'           Copyright (c) 1987  Namir Clement Shammas       '
'                                                           '
'-----------------------------------------------------------'

'----------------------
DEF FNDELIMITCHAR$ = ","

DEF FNHICHAR% = 255   ' FOR THE IBM-PC

'----------------------
SUB CHANGE.SET(SETNAME$,OLD.DELIMITCHAR$, NEW.DELIMITCHAR$) STATIC
' CHANGE DELIMIT CHARACTERS IN SET SETNAME$
STATIC L%, I%

ODC$ = LEFT$(OLD.DELIMITCHAR$,1)
NDC$ = LEFT$(NEW.DELIMITCHAR$,1)
L% = LEN(SETNAME$)

IF L% > 0 THEN
    FOR I% = 1 TO L%
        IF MID$(SETNAME$,I%,1) = ODC$ THEN MID$(SETNAME$,I%,1) = NDC$
    NEXT I%
END IF

END SUB

'----------------------
DEF FNSAYTF2$(N%)
    IF SGN(N%) > 0 THEN FNSAYTF2$ = "TRUE" ELSE FNSAYTF2$ = "FALSE"
```

```
END DEF

'----------------------------------------
DEF FNMAKE.CHARSET$(FIRSTASCII%,LASTASCII%)
' CREATE A SET WITH SINGLE CHARACTERS RANGING FROM
' CHR$(FIRSTASCII) TO CHR$(LASTASCII)

STATIC FIRST%, LAST%, I%, A$

FIRST% = ABS(FIRSTASCII%)
LAST%  = ABS(LASTASCII%)
IF LAST% > FNHICHAR% THEN LAST% = FNHICHAR%
IF FIRST% > LAST% THEN LAST% = FIRST%
A$ = ""

FOR I% = FIRST% TO LAST%
    A$ = A$ + CHR$(I%) + FNDELIMITCHAR$
NEXT I%

FNMAKE.CHARSET$ = A$

END DEF

'--------------------------------
DEF FNMAKE.MORE.CHARSET$(START$,FIRSTASCII%,LASTASCII%)
' APPEND TO A SET BY ADDING A SUBSET OF SINGLE CHARACTERS
' RANGING FROM CHR$(FIRSTASCII) TO CHR$(LASTASCII)

STATIC FIRST%, LAST%, I%, A$

FIRST% = ABS(FIRSTASCII%)
LAST%  = ABS(LASTASCII%)
IF LAST% > FNHICHAR% THEN LAST% = FNHICHAR%
IF FIRST% > LAST% THEN LAST% = FIRST%

A$ = ""

FOR I% = FIRST% TO LAST%
    A$ = A$ + CHR$(I%) + FNDELIMITCHAR$
NEXT I%

FNMAKE.MORE.CHARSET$ = START$ + A$

END DEF

'--------------------------------
DEF FNMAKE.SET.FROM.STRING$(A$, MEMBER.SIZE%)
' CREATE A SET WHOSE MEMBERS ARE 'MEMBER.SIZE' LONGS

STATIC L%, B$

MEMBER.SIZE% = ABS(MEMBER.SIZE%)
L% = LEN(A$)
IF L% = 0 THEN
    FNMAKE.SET.FROM.STRING$ = ""
```

```
        ELSE
            IF MEMBER.SIZE% < 1  THEN MEMBER.SIZE% = 1
            IF MEMBER.SIZE% > L% THEN MEMBER.SIZE% = L%
            B$ = ""
            FOR I% = 1 TO L% STEP MEMBER.SIZE%
                B$ = B$ + MID$(A$,I%,MEMBER.SIZE%) + FNDELIMITCHAR$
            NEXT I%
            FNMAKE.SET.FROM.STRING$ = B$
        END IF

END DEF

'--------------------------------
DEF FNMAKE.STRING.FROM.SET$(SETNAME$)
' CREATE A STRING BY REMOVING SET-MEMBER DELIMITERS FROM A SET
STRING

STATIC A$, J%, I%, COUNT.DELIMIT$

J% = 0
A$ = ""
COUNT.DELIMIT% = 0

FOR I% = 1 TO LEN(SETNAME$)-1
    IF (MID$(SETNAME$,I%,1) <> FNDELIMITCHAR$) OR (COUNT.DELIMIT% = 2) THEN
        J% = J% + 1
        A$ = A$ + MID$(SETNAME$,I%,1)
        COUNT.DELIMIT% = 0
    ELSE
        COUNT.DELIMIT% = COUNT.DELIMIT% + 1
    END IF
NEXT I%

FNMAKE.STRING.FROM.SET$ = A$

END DEF

'--------------------------------
SUB CREATE.NEW.SET(SETNAME$) STATIC
' INITIALIZE A NEW SET

SETNAME$ = ""

END SUB

'----------------------------------
DEF FNINSET%(MEMBER$, SETNAME$)
' TEST IF MEMBER$ IS A MEMBER IS SET SETNAME$

STATIC M$, I%

M$ = MEMBER$ + FNDELIMITCHAR$
I% = INSTR(SETNAME$, M$)
FNINSET% = SGN(I%)

END DEF
```

BASIC LIBRARIES 311

```
'---------------------------------
SUB ADD.MEMBER(MEMBER$, SETNAME$) STATIC
' ADD MEMBER$ TO SET SETNAME$ IF IT IS A NEW MEMBER

IF FNINSET%(MEMBER$, SETNAME$) = 0 THEN
    SETNAME$ = SETNAME$ + MEMBER$ + FNDELIMITCHAR$
END IF

END SUB

'---------------------------------
SUB REMOVE.MEMBER(MEMBER$, SETNAME$, OK%) STATIC
' REMOVE MEMBER$ FROM SET SETNAME$

STATIC M$, I%

OK% = 0
M$ = MEMBER$ + FNDELIMITCHAR$
I% = INSTR(SETNAME$, M$)
IF I% > 0 THEN
    OK% = 1
    IF I% > 1 THEN
        SETNAME$ = MID$(SETNAME$,1,I%-1) + MID$(SETNAME$,I%+LEN(M$))
    ELSE
        SETNAME$ = MID$(SETNAME$,1+LEN(M$))
    END IF
END IF

END SUB

'---------------------------------
DEF FNSUCC$(MEMBER$,SETNAME$)
' RETURN THE SUCCESSOR OF MEMBER$ IN SETNAME$

STATIC HI%, M$, FIRST%, LAST%, I%

HI% = LEN(SETNAME$)
M$ = MEMBER$ + FNDELIMITCHAR$
I% = INSTR(SETNAME$, M$)

IF I% > 0 THEN
    I% = I% + LEN(M$)
    IF I% < HI% THEN
        FIRST% = I%
        LAST% = INSTR(FIRST%,SETNAME$,FNDELIMITCHAR$)
        FNSUCC$ = MID$(SETNAME$,FIRST%,LAST%-FIRST%)
    ELSE
        FNSUCC$ = ""
    END IF
ELSE
    FNSUCC$ = ""
END IF

END DEF
```

```
'--------------------------------
DEF FNPRED$(MEMBER$,SETNAME$)
' RETURNS THE PREDECCESOR

STATIC HI%, M$, I%, FIRST%, LAST%

HI% = LEN(SETNAME$)
M$ = MEMBER$ + FNDELIMITCHAR$
I% = INSTR(SETNAME$, M$)
IF I% > 0 THEN
    I% = I% - 2
    IF I% > 1 THEN
        LAST% = I%
        WHILE (MID$(SETNAME$,I%,1) <> ",") AND (I% > 1)
            I% = I% - 1
        WEND
        IF I% > 1 THEN FIRST% = I%+1 ELSE FIRST% = I%
        FNPRED$ = MID$(SETNAME$,FIRST%,LAST%-FIRST%+1)
    ELSE
    FNPRED$ = ""
    END IF
ELSE
    FNPRED$ = ""
END IF

END DEF

'--------------------------
DEF FNSET.SIZE%(SETNAME$)
' RETURN THE NUMBER OF MEMBERS IN SETNAME$

STATIC COUNT%, I%

COUNT% = 0
I% = INSTR(SETNAME$,FNDELIMITCHAR$)

WHILE I% > 0
    COUNT% = COUNT% + 1
    I% = INSTR(I%+1,SETNAME$, FNDELIMITCHAR$)
WEND

FNSET.SIZE% = COUNT%

END DEF

'--------------------------
DEF FNSET.ORD%(MEMBER$, SETNAME$)
' RETURN ORDINAL VALUE OF A SET MEMBER
' VALID RANGE OF VALUES IS 1 OR GREATER

STATIC M$, I%, COUNT%

M$ = MEMBER$ + FNDELIMITCHAR$
I% = INSTR(SETNAME$, M$)

IF I% > 0 THEN
```

```
        COUNT% = 1
        WHILE I% > 1
            IF (MID$(SETNAME$,I%,1) = FNDELIMITCHAR$) THEN COUNT% = COUNT% + 1
            I% = I% - 1
        WEND
        FNSET.ORD% = COUNT%
ELSE
    FNSET.ORD% = 0
END IF

END DEF

'-------------------------
DEF FNSET.VAL$(N%, SETNAME$)
' FIND THE N'TH SET MEMBER

STATIC COUNT%, I%, J%

COUNT% = N%-1
I% = INSTR(SETNAME$, FNDELIMITCHAR$)
J% = 1

WHILE (COUNT% > 0) AND (I% > 0)
    J% = I%+1
    I% = INSTR(J%, SETNAME$, FNDELIMITCHAR$)
    COUNT% = COUNT% - 1
WEND

IF (COUNT% = 0) AND (I% > 0) THEN
    FNSET.VAL$ = MID$(SETNAME$,J%,I%-J%)
ELSE
    FNSET.VAL$ = ""         ' INVALID ORDINAL VALUE
END IF

END DEF

'-------------------------
DEF FNUNITE.SETS$(SETA$, SETB$)
' UNITE TWO SETS

STATIC SIZEB%, B$, C$, I%

SIZEB% = FNSET.SIZE%(SETB$)
C$ = SETA$

FOR I% = 1 TO SIZEB%
    B$ = FNSET.VAL$(I%, SETB$)
    CALL ADD.MEMBER(B$, C$)
NEXT I%

FNUNITE.SETS$ = C$

END DEF

'-------------------------
```

```
DEF FNINTERSECT.SETS$(SETA$, SETB$)
' CREATE A SET WITH COMMON MEMBERS IN SETS SETA$ & SETB$

STATIC SIZEA%, SIZEB%, C$, B$, I%, J%

SIZEA% = FNSET.SIZE%(SETA$)
SIZEB% = FNSET.SIZE%(SETB$)
C$ = ""

FOR I% = 1 TO SIZEA%
    A$ = FNSET.VAL$(I%, SETA$)
    FOR J% = 1 TO SIZEB%
        B$ = FNSET.VAL$(J%, SETB$)
        IF A$ = B$ THEN CALL ADD.MEMBER(A$, C$)
    NEXT J%
NEXT I%

FNINTERSECT.SETS$ = C$

END DEF

'--------------------------
DEF FNDIFFERENCE.SETS$(SETA$, SETB$)
' Find set with members not common in both parent sets

STATIC SIZEA%, SIZEB%, MATCH%, C$, B$, I%, J%

SIZEA% = FNSET.SIZE%(SETA$)
SIZEB% = FNSET.SIZE%(SETB$)
C$ = ""

FOR I% = 1 TO SIZEA%
    A$ = FNSET.VAL$(I%, SETA$)
    MATCH% = 0
    FOR J% = 1 TO SIZEB%
        B$ = FNSET.VAL$(J%, SETB$)
        IF A$ = B$ THEN MATCH% = 1
    NEXT J%
    IF MATCH% = 0 THEN CALL ADD.MEMBER(A$, C$)
NEXT I%

FOR I% = 1 TO SIZEB%
    B$ = FNSET.VAL$(I%, SETB$)
    MATCH% = 0
    FOR J% = 1 TO SIZEA%
        A$ = FNSET.VAL$(J%, SETA$)
        IF A$ = B$ THEN MATCH% = 1
    NEXT J%
    IF MATCH% = 0 THEN CALL ADD.MEMBER(B$, C$)
NEXT I%

FNDIFFERENCE.SETS$ = C$

END DEF

'-------------------------------------
```

BASIC LIBRARIES 315

```
SUB SORT.SET(SOURCESET$, TARGETSET$) STATIC
' SORT THE ELEMENTS OF SET SORUCESET$ INTO TARGETSET$

REM $DYNAMIC

STATIC N%, OFFSET%, INORDER%, I%, J%

N% = FNSET.SIZE%(SOURCESET$)

DIM A$(N%)  ' create array to size

TARGETSET$ = ""

FOR I% = 1 TO N%
    A$(I%) = FNSET.VAL$(I%,SOURCESET$)
NEXT I%

OFFSET% = N%

WHILE OFFSET% > 1
    OFFSET% = OFFSET% \ 2
    DO
        INORDER% = 1
        FOR J% = 1 TO (N% - OFFSET%)
            I% = J% + OFFSET%
            IF A$(I%) < A$(J%) THEN INORDER% = 0 : SWAP A$(I%),A$(J%)
        NEXT J%
    LOOP UNTIL (INORDER% = 1)
WEND

FOR I% = 1 TO N%
    CALL ADD.MEMBER(A$(I%), TARGETSET$)
NEXT I%

Erase A$ ' erase local array

END SUB

'---------------------------------
DEF FNARE.SETS.EQ%(SETA$, SETB$)
' TEST IF SETA$ AND SETB$ ARE IDENTICAL

STATIC A%, B%, SAME.MEMBER%, I%

A% = FNSET.SIZE%(SETA$)
B% = FNSET.SIZE%(SETB$)

IF A% <> B% THEN
    FNARE.SETS.EQ% = 0
ELSE
    CALL SORT.SET(SETA$,A$)
    CALL SORT.SET(SETB$,B$)
    I% = 1
    SAME.MEMBER% = 1
    WHILE (I% <= A%) AND (SAME.MEMBER% = 1)
        IF FNSET.VAL$(I%,A$) <> FNSET.VAL$(I%,B$) THEN
```

```
                SAME.MEMBER% = 0
        ELSE
            I% = I% + 1
        END IF
    WEND
    FNARE.SETS.EQ% = SAME.MEMBER%
END IF

END DEF

'--------------------------------
DEF FNARE.SETS.LEQ%(SETA$, SETB$)
' TEST IF SETA$ IS A SUBSET OF SETB$ OR EQUAL TO IT
' EVERY MEMBER IN SETA$ MUST BE PRESENT IN SETB$

STATIC A%, B%, I%, J%

A% = FNSET.SIZE%(SETA$)
B% = FNSET.SIZE%(SETB$)

IF A% > B% THEN
    FNARE.SETS.LEQ% = 0
ELSE
    CALL SORT.SET(SETA$,A$)
    CALL SORT.SET(SETB$,B$)
    I% = 1
    J% = 1

    WHILE (I% <= A%) AND (J% <= B%)
        IF FNSET.VAL$(I%,A$) = FNSET.VAL$(J%,B$) THEN
            I% = I% + 1
            J% = J% + 1
        ELSE
            J% = J% + 1
        END IF
    WEND

    IF I% <= A% THEN
        FNARE.SETS.LEQ% = 0
    ELSE
        FNARE.SETS.LEQ% = 1
    END IF
END IF

END DEF

'--------------------------------
DEF FNARE.SETS.LT%(SETA$, SETB$)
' TEST IF SETA$ IS A SUBSET OF SETB$ BUT NO EQUAL TO IT.
' EVERY MEMBER OF SETA$ IS IN SETB$

STATIC A%, B%, I%, J%

A% = FNSET.SIZE%(SETA$)
B% = FNSET.SIZE%(SETB$)
IF A% >= B% THEN
```

```
            FNARE.SETS.LT% = 0
    ELSE
        CALL SORT.SET(SETA$,A$)
        CALL SORT.SET(SETB$,B$)
        I% = 1
        J% = 1

        WHILE (I% <= A%) AND (J% <= B%)
            IF FNSET.VAL$(I%,A$) = FNSET.VAL$(J%,B$) THEN
                I% = I% + 1
                J% = J% + 1
            ELSE
                J% = J% + 1
            END IF
        WEND

        I% = I% - 1
        IF (I% = A%) AND (I% < B%) THEN
            FNARE.SETS.LT% = 1
        ELSE
            FNARE.SETS.LT% = 0
        END IF
    END IF

END DEF


'------------- INITIALIZE SOME "POPULAR" SETS --------
YESNOSET$   = "YES,Yes,yes,NO,No,no,Y,y,N,n,"
YESSET$     = "YES,Yes,yes,Y,"
NOSET$      = "NO,No,no,N,n,"
TRUESET$    = "TRUE,True,true,T,t,"
FALSESET$   = "FALSE,False,false,F,f,"
BOOLSET$    = "TRUE,FALSE,true,false,True,False,T,F,t,f,"
YNSET$      = "Y,N,y,n,"
TFSET$      = "F,T,f,t,"
WEEKENDSET$ = "SATURDAY,SUNDAY,"
WEEKSET$ = ""
WEEKDAYSET$ = ""
FOR K% = 1 TO 7
    READ A$
    B$ = A$ + FNDELIMITCHAR$
    WEEKSET$ = WEEKSET$ + B$
    IF (K% > 1) AND (K% < 7) THEN WEEKDAYSET$ = WEEKDAYSET$ + B$
NEXT K%

'----- DATA FOR WEEKSET$ -----
DATA SUNDAY, MONDAY, TUESDAY, WEDNESDAY, THURSDAY, FRIDAY, SATURDAY

MONTHSET$ = ""
FOR K% = 1 TO 12
    READ A$
    MONTHSET$ = MONTHSET$ + A$ + FNDELIMITCHAR$
NEXT K%

'----- DATA FOR MONTHSET$ -----
```

```
DATA JANUARY, FEBRUARY, MARCH, APRIL, MAY, JUNE, JULY, AUGUST
DATA SEPTEMBER, OCTOBER, NOVEMBER, DECEMBER

LOWERCASESET$ = FNMAKE.CHARSET$(ASC("a"),ASC("z"))
UPPERCASESET$ = FNMAKE.CHARSET$(ASC("A"),ASC("Z"))
DIGITSET$ = "0,1,2,3,4,5,6,7,8,9,"
LETTERSET$ = FNUNITE.SETS$(UPPERCASESET$, LOWERCASESET$)
ALPHANUMSET$ = FNUNITE.SETS$(LETTERSET$, DIGITSET$)
CONTROLSET$ = FNMAKE.CHARSET$(0,31)

'------ BUILD PUNCTUATION SET --------
PUNCTSET$ = FNMAKE.CHARSET$(ASC(" "),ASC("/"))
PUNCTSET$ = FNMAKE.MORE.CHARSET$(PUNCTSET$,ASC(":"),ASC("@"))
PUNCTSET$ = FNMAKE.MORE.CHARSET$(PUNCTSET$,ASC("["),ASC("`"))
PUNCTSET$ = FNMAKE.MORE.CHARSET$(PUNCTSET$,ASC("{"),ASC("~"))
```

Listing 3.44. *Turbo BASIC source code for library SETS.BAS*

```
'--------------------------------------------------------------'
'                                                              '
'                      BASIC SETS                              '
'                      ----------                              '
'                   Turbo BASIC version                        '
'    VERSION 1.0                                    12/86      '
'                                                              '
'          Copyright (c) 1987  Namir Clement Shammas           '
'                                                              '
'--------------------------------------------------------------'

'---------------------

DEF FNDELIMITCHAR$ = ","

DEF FNHICHAR% = 255  ' FOR THE IBM-PC

'---------------------
SUB CHANGE.SET(SETNAME$,OLD.DELIMITCHAR$, NEW.DELIMITCHAR$) STATIC
' CHANGE DELIMIT CHARACTERS IN SET SETNAME$

LOCAL L%, I%

ODC$ = LEFT$(OLD.DELIMITCHAR$,1)
NDC$ = LEFT$(NEW.DELIMITCHAR$,1)
L% = LEN(SETNAME$)

IF L% > 0 THEN
    FOR I% = 1 TO L%
        IF MID$(SETNAME$,I%,1) = ODC$ THEN MID$(SETNAME$,I%,1) = NDC$
    NEXT I%
END IF
```

```
END SUB

'-----------------------
DEF FNSAYTF2$(N%)
    IF SGN(N%) > 0 THEN FNSAYTF2$ = "TRUE" ELSE FNSAYTF2$ = "FALSE"
END DEF

'---------------------------------------
DEF FNMAKE.CHARSET$(FIRSTASCII%,LASTASCII%)
' CREATE A SET WITH SINGLE CHARACTERS RANGING FROM
' CHR$(FIRSTASCII) TO CHR$(LASTASCII)

LOCAL FIRST%, LAST%, I%, A$

FIRST% = ABS(FIRSTASCII%)
LAST%  = ABS(LASTASCII%)

IF LAST% > FNHICHAR% THEN LAST% = FNHICHAR%
IF FIRST% > LAST% THEN LAST% = FIRST%
A$ = ""

FOR I% = FIRST% TO LAST%
    A$ = A$ + CHR$(I%) + FNDELIMITCHAR$
NEXT I%

FNMAKE.CHARSET$ = A$

END DEF

'--------------------------------
DEF FNMAKE.MORE.CHARSET$(START$,FIRSTASCII%,LASTASCII%)
' APPEND TO A SET BY ADDING A SUBSET OF SINGLE CHARACTERS
' RANGING FROM CHR$(FIRSTASCII) TO CHR$(LASTASCII)

LOCAL FIRST%, LAST%, I%, A$

FIRST% = ABS(FIRSTASCII%)
LAST%  = ABS(LASTASCII%)

IF LAST% > FNHICHAR% THEN LAST% = FNHICHAR%
IF FIRST% > LAST% THEN LAST% = FIRST%

A$ = ""

FOR I% = FIRST% TO LAST%
    A$ = A$ + CHR$(I%) + FNDELIMITCHAR$
NEXT I%

FNMAKE.MORE.CHARSET$ = START$ + A$

END DEF

'-----------------------------
DEF FNMAKE.SET.FROM.STRING$(A$, MEMBER.SIZE%)
' CREATE A SET WHOSE MEMBERS ARE 'MEMBER.SIZE' LONGS
```

```
    LOCAL L%, B$

    MEMBER.SIZE% = ABS(MEMBER.SIZE%)
    L% = LEN(A$)

    IF L% = 0 THEN
        FNMAKE.SET.FROM.STRING$ = ""
    ELSE
        IF MEMBER.SIZE% < 1 THEN MEMBER.SIZE% = 1
        IF MEMBER.SIZE% > L% THEN MEMBER.SIZE% = L%
        B$ = ""
        FOR I% = 1 TO L% STEP MEMBER.SIZE%
            B$ = B$ + MID$(A$,I%,MEMBER.SIZE%) + FNDELIMITCHAR$
        NEXT I%
        FNMAKE.SET.FROM.STRING$ = B$
    END IF

END DEF

'--------------------------------
DEF FNMAKE.STRING.FROM.SET$(SETNAME$)
' CREATE A STRING BY REMOVING SET-MEMBER DELIMITERS FROM A SET
STRING

LOCAL A$, J%, I%, COUNT.DELIMIT$

J% = 0
A$ = ""
COUNT.DELIMIT% = 0

FOR I% = 1 TO LEN(SETNAME$)-1
    IF (MID$(SETNAME$,I%,1) <> FNDELIMITCHAR$) OR (COUNT.DELIMIT% = 2) THEN
        J% = J% + 1
        A$ = A$ + MID$(SETNAME$,I%,1)
        COUNT.DELIMIT% = 0
    ELSE
        COUNT.DELIMIT% = COUNT.DELIMIT% + 1
    END IF
NEXT I%

FNMAKE.STRING.FROM.SET$ = A$

END DEF

'--------------------------------
SUB CREATE.NEW.SET(SETNAME$) STATIC
' INITIALIZE A NEW SET

SETNAME$ = ""

END SUB

'--------------------------------
DEF FNINSET%(MEMBER$, SETNAME$)
' TEST IF MEMBER$ IS A MEMBER IS SET SETNAME$
```

```
    LOCAL M$, I%

    M$ = MEMBER$ + FNDELIMITCHAR$
    I% = INSTR(SETNAME$, M$)

    FNINSET% = SGN(I%)

    END DEF

    '---------------------------------
    SUB ADD.MEMBER(MEMBER$, SETNAME$) STATIC
    ' ADD MEMBER$ TO SET SETNAME$ IF IT IS A NEW MEMBER

    IF FNINSET%(MEMBER$, SETNAME$) = 0 THEN
        SETNAME$ = SETNAME$ + MEMBER$ + FNDELIMITCHAR$
    END IF

    END SUB

    '---------------------------------
    SUB REMOVE.MEMBER(MEMBER$, SETNAME$, OK%) STATIC
    ' REMOVE MEMBER$ FROM SET SETNAME$

    LOCAL M$, I%

    OK% = 0
    M$ = MEMBER$ + FNDELIMITCHAR$
    I% = INSTR(SETNAME$, M$)

    IF I% > 0 THEN
        OK% = 1
        IF I% > 1 THEN
            SETNAME$ = MID$(SETNAME$,1,I%-1) + MID$(SETNAME$,I%+LEN(M$))
        ELSE
            SETNAME$ = MID$(SETNAME$,1+LEN(M$))
        END IF
    END IF

    END SUB

    '---------------------------------
    DEF FNSUCC$(MEMBER$,SETNAME$)
    ' RETURN THE SUCCESSOR OF MEMBER$ IN SETNAME$

    LOCAL HI%, M$, FIRST%, LAST%, I%

    HI% = LEN(SETNAME$)
    M$ = MEMBER$ + FNDELIMITCHAR$
    I% = INSTR(SETNAME$, M$)

    IF I% > 0 THEN
        I% = I% + LEN(M$)
        IF I% < HI% THEN
            FIRST% = I%
            LAST% = INSTR(FIRST%,SETNAME$,FNDELIMITCHAR$)
```

```
                FNSUCC$ = MID$(SETNAME$,FIRST%,LAST%-FIRST%)
        ELSE
                FNSUCC$ = ""
        END IF
ELSE
    FNSUCC$ = ""
END IF

END DEF

'--------------------------------
DEF FNPRED$(MEMBER$,SETNAME$)
' RETURNS THE PREDECCESOR

LOCAL HI%, M$, I%, FIRST%, LAST%

HI% = LEN(SETNAME$)
M$ = MEMBER$ + FNDELIMITCHAR$
I% = INSTR(SETNAME$, M$)

IF I% > 0 THEN
    I% = I% - 2
    IF I% > 1 THEN
        LAST% = I%
        WHILE (MID$(SETNAME$,I%,1) <> ",") AND (I% > 1)
            I% = I% - 1
        WEND
        IF I% > 1 THEN FIRST% = I%+1 ELSE FIRST% = I%
        FNPRED$ = MID$(SETNAME$,FIRST%,LAST%-FIRST%+1)
    ELSE
    FNPRED$ = ""
    END IF
ELSE
    FNPRED$ = ""
END IF

END DEF

'--------------------------
DEF FNSET.SIZE%(SETNAME$)
' RETURN THE NUMBER OF MEMBERS IN SETNAME$

LOCAL COUNT%, I%

COUNT% = 0
I% = INSTR(SETNAME$,FNDELIMITCHAR$)

WHILE I% > 0
    COUNT% = COUNT% + 1
    I% = INSTR(I%+1,SETNAME$, FNDELIMITCHAR$)
WEND

FNSET.SIZE% = COUNT%

END DEF
```

```
'---------------------------
DEF FNSET.ORD%(MEMBER$, SETNAME$)
' RETURN ORDINAL VALUE OF A SET MEMBER
' VALID RANGE OF VALUES IS 1 OR GREATER

LOCAL M$, I%, COUNT%

M$ = MEMBER$ + FNDELIMITCHAR$
I% = INSTR(SETNAME$, M$)

IF I% > 0 THEN
    COUNT% = 1

    WHILE I% > 1
        IF (MID$(SETNAME$,I%,1) = FNDELIMITCHAR$) THEN COUNT% - COUNT% + 1
        I% = I% - 1
    WEND

    FNSET.ORD% = COUNT%
ELSE
    FNSET.ORD% = 0
END IF

END DEF

'---------------------------
DEF FNSET.VAL$(N%, SETNAME$)
' FIND THE N'TH SET MEMBER

LOCAL COUNT%, I%, J%

COUNT% = N%-1
I% = INSTR(SETNAME$, FNDELIMITCHAR$)
J% = 1

WHILE (COUNT% > 0) AND (I% > 0)
    J% = I%+1
    I% = INSTR(J%, SETNAME$, FNDELIMITCHAR$)
    COUNT% = COUNT% - 1
WEND

IF (COUNT% = 0) AND (I% > 0) THEN
    FNSET.VAL$ = MID$(SETNAME$,J%,I%-J%)
ELSE
    FNSET.VAL$ = ""         ' INVALID ORDINAL VALUE
END IF

END DEF

'---------------------------
DEF FNUNITE.SETS$(SETA$, SETB$)
' UNITE TWO SETS

LOCAL SIZEB%, B$, C$, I%
```

```
    SIZEB% = FNSET.SIZE%(SETB$)
    C$ = SETA$

    FOR I% = 1 TO SIZEB%
        B$ = FNSET.VAL$(I%, SETB$)
        CALL ADD.MEMBER(B$, C$)
    NEXT I%

    FNUNITE.SETS$ = C$

    END DEF

    '--------------------------
    DEF FNINTERSECT.SETS$(SETA$, SETB$)
    ' CREATE A SET WITH COMMON MEMBERS IN SETS SETA$ & SETB$

    LOCAL SIZEA%, SIZEB%, C$, B$, I%, J%

    SIZEA% = FNSET.SIZE%(SETA$)
    SIZEB% = FNSET.SIZE%(SETB$)
    C$ = ""

    FOR I% = 1 TO SIZEA%
        A$ = FNSET.VAL$(I%, SETA$)
        FOR J% = 1 TO SIZEB%
            B$ = FNSET.VAL$(J%, SETB$)
            IF A$ = B$ THEN CALL ADD.MEMBER(A$, C$)
        NEXT J%
    NEXT I%

    FNINTERSECT.SETS$ = C$

    END DEF

    '--------------------------
    DEF FNDIFFERENCE.SETS$(SETA$, SETB$)
    ' Find set with members not common in both parent sets

    LOCAL SIZEA%, SIZEB%, MATCH%, C$, B$, I%, J%

    SIZEA% = FNSET.SIZE%(SETA$)
    SIZEB% = FNSET.SIZE%(SETB$)
    C$ = ""

    FOR I% = 1 TO SIZEA%
        A$ = FNSET.VAL$(I%, SETA$)
        MATCH% = 0
        FOR J% = 1 TO SIZEB%
            B$ = FNSET.VAL$(J%, SETB$)
            IF A$ = B$ THEN MATCH% = 1
        NEXT J%
        IF MATCH% = 0 THEN CALL ADD.MEMBER(A$, C$)
    NEXT I%

    FOR I% = 1 TO SIZEB%
        B$ = FNSET.VAL$(I%, SETB$)
```

BASIC LIBRARIES 325

```
        MATCH% = 0
        FOR J% = 1 TO SIZEA%
            A$ = FNSET.VAL$(J%, SETA$)
            IF A$ = B$ THEN MATCH% = 1
        NEXT J%
        IF MATCH% = 0 THEN CALL ADD.MEMBER(B$, C$)
    NEXT I%

    FNDIFFERENCE.SETS$ = C$

    END DEF

'--------------------------------------
SUB SORT.SET(SOURCESET$, TARGETSET$) STATIC
' SORT THE ELEMENTS OF SET SORUCESET$ INTO TARGETSET$

    LOCAL A$(), N%, OFFSET%, INORDER%, I%, J%

    N% = FNSET.SIZE%(SOURCESET$)

    DIM DYNAMIC A$(N%)  ' dimension to size

    TARGETSET$ = ""

    FOR I% = 1 TO N%
        A$(I%) = FNSET.VAL$(I%,SOURCESET$)
    NEXT I%

    OFFSET% = N%

    WHILE OFFSET% > 1
        OFFSET% = OFFSET% \ 2
        REPEAT.LOOP1:
            INORDER% = 1
            FOR J% = 1 TO (N% - OFFSET%)
                I% = J% + OFFSET%
                IF A$(I%) < A$(J%) THEN INORDER% = 0 : SWAP A$(I%),A$(J%)
            NEXT J%
        IF INORDER% = 0 THEN GOTO REPEAT.LOOP1
    WEND

    FOR I% = 1 TO N%
        CALL ADD.MEMBER(A$(I%), TARGETSET$)
    NEXT I%

    Erase A$  ' erase local array

    END SUB

'---------------------------------
DEF FNARE.SETS.EQ%(SETA$, SETB$)
' TEST IF SETA$ AND SETB$ ARE IDENTICAL

    LOCAL A%, B%, SAME.MEMBER%, I%
```

```
    A% = FNSET.SIZE%(SETA$)
    B% = FNSET.SIZE%(SETB$)

    IF A% <> B% THEN
        FNARE.SETS.EQ% = 0
    ELSE
        CALL SORT.SET(SETA$,A$)
        CALL SORT.SET(SETB$,B$)
        I% = 1
        SAME.MEMBER% = 1
        WHILE (I% <= A%) AND (SAME.MEMBER% = 1)
            IF FNSET.VAL$(I%,A$) <> FNSET.VAL$(I%,B$) THEN
                SAME.MEMBER% = 0
            ELSE
                I% = I% + 1
            END IF
        WEND
        FNARE.SETS.EQ% = SAME.MEMBER%
    END IF

END DEF

'---------------------------------
DEF FNARE.SETS.LEQ%(SETA$, SETB$)
' TEST IF SETA$ IS A SUBSET OF SETB$ OR EQUAL TO IT
' EVERY MEMBER IN SETA$ MUST BE PRESENT IN SETB$

LOCAL A%, B%, I%, J%

A% = FNSET.SIZE%(SETA$)
B% = FNSET.SIZE%(SETB$)

IF A% > B% THEN
    FNARE.SETS.LEQ% = 0
ELSE
    CALL SORT.SET(SETA$,A$)
    CALL SORT.SET(SETB$,B$)
    I% = 1
    J% = 1
    WHILE (I% <= A%) AND (J% <= B%)
        IF FNSET.VAL$(I%,A$) = FNSET.VAL$(J%,B$) THEN
            I% = I% + 1
            J% = J% + 1
        ELSE
            J% = J% + 1
        END IF
    WEND
    IF I% <= A% THEN
        FNARE.SETS.LEQ% = 0
    ELSE
        FNARE.SETS.LEQ% = 1
    END IF
END IF

END DEF
```

```
'--------------------------------
DEF FNARE.SETS.LT%(SETA$, SETB$)
' TEST IF SETA$ IS A SUBSET OF SETB$ BUT NO EQUAL TO IT.
' EVERY MEMBER OF SETA$ IS IN SETB$

LOCAL A%, B%, I%, J%

A% = FNSET.SIZE%(SETA$)
B% = FNSET.SIZE%(SETB$)
IF A% >= B% THEN
    FNARE.SETS.LT% = 0
ELSE
    CALL SORT.SET(SETA$,A$)
    CALL SORT.SET(SETB$,B$)
    I% = 1
    J% = 1
    WHILE (I% <= A%) AND (J% <= B%)
        IF FNSET.VAL$(I%,A$) = FNSET.VAL$(J%,B$) THEN
            I% = I% + 1
            J% = J% + 1
        ELSE
            J% = J% + 1
        END IF
    WEND
    I% = I% - 1
    IF (I% = A%) AND (I% < B%) THEN
        FNARE.SETS.LT% = 1
    ELSE
        FNARE.SETS.LT% = 0
    END IF
END IF

END DEF


'------------- INITIALIZE SOME "POPULAR" SETS --------
YESNOSET$   = "YES,Yes,yes,NO,No,no,Y,y,N,n,"
YESSET$     = "YES,Yes,yes,Y,"
NOSET$      = "NO,No,no,N,n,"
TRUESET$    = "TRUE,True,true,T,t,"
FALSESET$   = "FALSE,False,false,F,f,"
BOOLSET$    = "TRUE,FALSE,true,false,True,False,T,F,t,f,"
YNSET$      = "Y,N,y,n,"
TFSET$      = "F,T,f,t,"
WEEKENDSET$ = "SATURDAY,SUNDAY,"

WEEKSET$ = ""
WEEKDAYSET$ = ""

FOR K% = 1 TO 7
    READ A$
    B$ = A$ + FNDELIMITCHAR$
    WEEKSET$ = WEEKSET$ + B$
    IF (K% > 1) AND (K% < 7) THEN WEEKDAYSET$ = WEEKDAYSET$ + B$
NEXT K%
```

```
'----- DATA FOR WEEKSET$ -----
DATA SUNDAY, MONDAY, TUESDAY, WEDNESDAY, THURSDAY, FRIDAY, SATURDAY

MONTHSET$ = ""
FOR K% = 1 TO 12
   READ A$
   MONTHSET$ = MONTHSET$ + A$ + FNDELIMITCHAR$
NEXT K%

'----- DATA FOR MONTHSET$ -----
DATA JANUARY, FEBRUARY, MARCH, APRIL, MAY, JUNE, JULY, AUGUST
DATA SEPTEMBER, OCTOBER, NOVEMBER, DECEMBER

LOWERCASESET$ = FNMAKE.CHARSET$(ASC("a"),ASC("z"))
UPPERCASESET$ = FNMAKE.CHARSET$(ASC("A"),ASC("Z"))
DIGITSET$ = "0,1,2,3,4,5,6,7,8,9,"
LETTERSET$ = FNUNITE.SETS$(UPPERCASESET$, LOWERCASESET$)
ALPHANUMSET$ = FNUNITE.SETS$(LETTERSET$, DIGITSET$)
CONTROLSET$ = FNMAKE.CHARSET$(0,31)

'------ BUILD PUNCTUATION SET --------
PUNCTSET$ = FNMAKE.CHARSET$(ASC(" "),ASC("/"))
PUNCTSET$ = FNMAKE.MORE.CHARSET$(PUNCTSET$,ASC(":"),ASC("@"))
PUNCTSET$ = FNMAKE.MORE.CHARSET$(PUNCTSET$,ASC("["),ASC("`"))
PUNCTSET$ = FNMAKE.MORE.CHARSET$(PUNCTSET$,ASC("{"),ASC("~"))
```

Listing 3.45. *True BASIC source code for module SETS.TRU*

```
MODULE Sets

!-------------------------------------------------------------!
!                                                             !
!                    MODULE SETS                              !
!                    -----------                              !
!                 True BASIC version                          !
! Version 1.0                                      12/86      !
!                                                             !
.         Copyright (c) 1987  Namir Clement Shammas           !
!                                                             !
!-------------------------------------------------------------!

PUBLIC YesNoSet$, BoolSet$, YesSet$, NoSet$, TrueSet$, FalseSet$
PUBLIC YNSet$, TFSet$, WeekSet$, WeekEndSet$, WeekdaySet$, MonthSet$
PUBLIC LowerCaseSet$, UpperCaseSet$, LetterSet$, DigitSet$
PUBLIC AlphanumSet$, ControlSet$, PunctSet$

DECLARE DEF DelimitChar$, InSet, Succ$, Pred$, Set_Size, Set_Val$
DECLARE DEF Set_Ord, SayTF2$, Make_CharSet$, Make_More_CharSet$
```

```
DECLARE DEF Make_Set_From_String$, Make_String_From_Set$
DECLARE DEF Unite_Sets$, HiChar
DECLARE DEF Are_Sets_EQ, Are_Sets_LEQ, Are_Sets_LT

SHARE TRUE, FALSE

LET TRUE = 1
LET FALSE = 0

!------------ initialize some "popular" sets --------
LET YesNoSet$  = "YES,Yes,yes,NO,No,no,Y,y,N,n,"
LET YesSet$    = "YES,Yes,yes,y,"
LET NoSet$     = "NO,No,no,N,n,"
LET TrueSet$   = "TRUE,True,true,T,t,"
LET FalseSet$  = "FALSE,False,false,F,f,"
LET BoolSet$   = "TRUE,FALSE,True,False,true,false,T,F,t,f,"
LET YNSet$     = "Y,N,"
LET TFSet$     = "F,T,"
LET WeekEndSet$ = "Saturday,Sunday,"
LET WeekSet$ = ""
LET WeekdaySet$ = ""
FOR I = 1 TO 7
READ A$
LET B$ = A$ & DelimitChar$
LET WeekSet$ = WeekSet$ & B$
IF (I > 1) AND (I < 7) THEN LET WeekdaySet$ = WeekdaySet$ & B$
NEXT I

!----- Data for WeekSet$ -----
DATA Sunday, Monday, Tuesday, Wednesday, Thursday, Friday, Saturday

LET MonthSet$ = ""
FOR I = 1 TO 12
    READ A$
    LET MonthSet$ = MonthSet$ & A$ & DelimitChar$
NEXT I

!----- Data for MonthSet$ -----
DATA January, February, March, April, May, June, July, August
DATA September, October, November, December

LET LowerCaseSet$ = Make_CharSet$(ORD("a"),ORD("z"))
LET UpperCaseSet$ = Make_CharSet$(ORD("A"),ORD("Z"))
LET DigitSet$ = "0,1,2,3,4,5,6,7,8,9,"
LET LetterSet$ = Unite_Sets$(UpperCaseSet$, LowerCaseSet$)
LET AlphaNumSet$ = Unite_Sets$(LetterSet$,DigitSet$)
LET ControlSet$ = Make_CharSet$(0,31)

!------ Build punctuation set --------
LET PunctSet$ = Make_CharSet$(ORD(" "),ORD("/"))
LET PunctSet$ = Make_More_CharSet$(PunctSet$,ORD(":"),ORD("@"))
LET PunctSet$ = Make_More_CharSet$(PunctSet$,ORD("["),ORD("`"))
LET PunctSet$ = Make_More_CharSet$(PunctSet$,ORD("{"),ORD("~"))

!---------------------
DEF DelimitChar$ = ","
```

```
DEF HiChar = 255              ! for the IBM-PC

!---------------------
SUB Change_Set(SetName$,Old_DelimitChar$, New_DelimitChar$)
! change delimit characters in set SetName$

LET ODC$ = Old_DelimitChar$[1:1]
LET NDC$ = New_DelimitChar$[1:1]
LET L = LEN(SetName$)

IF L > 0 THEN
   FOR I = 1 TO L
       IF SetName$[I:I] = ODC$ THEN LET SetName$[I:I] = NDC$
   NEXT I
END IF

END SUB

!---------------------
DEF SayTF2$(N)
  IF SGN(N) > 0 THEN LET SayTF2$ = "TRUE" ELSE LET SayTF2$ = "FALSE"
END DEF

!--------------------------------
DEF Make_CharSet$(FirstASCII,LastASCII)
! create a set with single characters ranging from
! chr$(FirstASCII) to chr$(LastASCII)

LET First = INT(ABS(FirstASCII))
LET Last  = INT(ABS(LastASCII))

IF Last > HiChar THEN LET Last = HiChar
IF First > Last THEN LET Last = First

LET A$ = ""

FOR I = First TO Last
    LET A$ = A$ & CHR$(I) & DelimitChar$
NEXT I

LET Make_CharSet$ = A$

END DEF

!----------------------------------
DEF Make_More_CharSet$(Start$,FirstASCII,LastASCII)
! Append to a set by adding a subset of single characters
! ranging from chr$(FirstASCII) to chr$(LastASCII)

LET First = INT(ABS(FirstASCII))
LET Last  = INT(ABS(LastASCII))

IF Last > HiChar THEN LET Last = HiChar
IF First > Last THEN LET Last = First
LET A$ = ""
```

```
    FOR I = First TO Last
        LET A$ = A$ & CHR$(I) & DelimitChar$
    NEXT I

    LET Make_More_CharSet$ = Start$ & A$

END DEF

!--------------------------------
DEF Make_Set_From_String$(A$, Member_Size)
! Create a set whose members are 'Member_Size' longs

LET Member_Size = INT(ABS(Member_Size))
LET L = LEN(A$)

IF L = 0 THEN
   LET Make_Set_From_String$ = ""
ELSE
   IF Member_Size < 1 THEN LET Member_Size = 1
   IF Member_Size > L THEN LET Member_Size = L
   LET B$ = ""
   FOR I = 1 TO L STEP Member_Size
       LET B$ = B$ & A$[I:I+Member_Size-1] & DelimitChar$
   NEXT I
   LET Make_Set_From_String$ = B$
END IF

END DEF

!--------------------------------
DEF Make_String_From_Set$(SetName$)
! create a string by removing set-member delimiters from a set string

LET J = 0
LET A$ = ""
LET CountDelimit = 0

FOR I = 1 TO LEN(SetName$)-1
    IF (SetName$[I:I] <> DelimitChar$) OR (CountDelimit = 2) THEN
       LET J = J + 1
       LET A$ = A$ & SetName$[I:I]
       LET CountDelimit = 0
    ELSE
       LET CountDelimit = CountDelimit + 1
    END IF
NEXT I

LET Make_String_From_Set$ = A$

END DEF

!--------------------------------
SUB Create_New_Set(SetName$)
! Initialize a new set

LET SetName$ = ""
```

```
END SUB

!---------------------------------
SUB Add_Member(Member$,SetName$)
! Add Member$ to set SetName$ if it is a new member

IF Inset(Member$, SetName$) = 0 THEN
   LET SetName$ = SetName$ & Member$ & DelimitChar$
END IF

END SUB

!---------------------------------
DEF InSet(Member$,SetName$)
! Test if Member$ is a member is set SetName$

LET M$ = Member$ & DelimitChar$
LET I = POS(SetName$, M$)

IF I > 0 THEN LET InSet = 1 ELSE LET InSet = 0

END DEF

!---------------------------------
SUB Remove_Member(Member$, SetName$, OK)
! Remove Member$ from set SetName$

LET OK = 0
LET M$ = Member$ & DelimitChar$
LET I = POS(SetName$, M$)

IF I > 0 THEN
   LET OK = 1
   IF I > 1 THEN
     LET SetName$ = SetName$[1:I-1] & SetName$[I+LEN(M$):LEN(SetName$)]
   ELSE
     LET SetName$ = SetName$[1+LEN(M$):LEN(SetName$)]
   END IF
END IF

END SUB

!---------------------------------
DEF Succ$(Member$,SetName$)
! Find successor of member Member$

LET Hi = LEN(SetName$)
LET M$ = Member$ & DelimitChar$
LET I = POS(SetName$, M$)

IF I > 0 THEN
   LET I = I + LEN(M$)
   IF I < Hi THEN
      LET First = I
      LET Last = POS(SetName$,DelimitChar$,First) - 1
```

```
            LET Succ$ = SetName$[First:Last]
      ELSE
            LET Succ$ = ""
      END IF
ELSE
      LET Succ$ = ""
END IF

END DEF

!-------------------------------
DEF Pred$(Member$,SetName$)
! Find the predecessor

LET Hi = LEN(SetName$)
LET M$ = Member$ & DelimitChar$
LET I = POS(SetName$, M$)

IF I > 0 THEN
   LET I = I - 2
   IF I > 1 THEN
      LET Last = I
      DO WHILE (SetName$[I:I] <> ",") AND (I > 1)
         LET I = I - 1
      LOOP
      IF I > 1 THEN LET First = I+1 ELSE LET First = I
      LET Pred$ = SetName$[First:Last]
   ELSE
      LET Pred$ = ""
   END IF
ELSE
   LET Pred$ = ""
END IF

END DEF

!-------------------------
DEF Set_Size(SetName$)
! Return the set size

LET Count = 0
LET I = POS(SetName$,DelimitChar$)

DO WHILE I > 0
   LET Count = Count + 1
   LET I = POS(SetName$, DelimitChar$,I+1)
LOOP

LET Set_Size = Count

END DEF

!-------------------------
DEF Set_Ord(Member$, SetName$)
! Return ordinal value of a set member
! Valid range of value is 1 or greater
```

```
      LET M$ = Member$ & DelimitChar$
      LET I = POS(SetName$, M$)

      IF I > 0 THEN
         LET Count = 1
         DO WHILE I > 1
            IF SetName$[I:I] = DelimitChar$ THEN LET Count = Count + 1
            LET I = I - 1
         LOOP
         LET Set_Ord = Count
      ELSE
         LET Set_Ord = 0
      END IF

      END DEF

      !---------------------------
      DEF Set_Val$(N, SetName$)
      ! Return the N'th member of the set

      LET Count = N-1
      LET I = POS(SetName$, DelimitChar$)

      DO WHILE (Count > 0) AND (I > 0)
         LET J = I
         LET I = POS(SetName$, DelimitChar$, I+1)
         LET Count = Count - 1
      LOOP

      IF (Count = 0) AND (I > 0) THEN
         LET Set_Val$ = SetName$[J+1:I-1]
      ELSE
         LET Set_Val$ = ""         ! Invalid ordinal value
      END IF

      END DEF

      !---------------------------
      DEF Unite_Sets$(SetA$, SetB$)
      ! Unite sets SetA$ and SetB$

      LET SizeB = Set_Size(SetB$)
      LET C$ = SetA$

      FOR I = 1 TO SizeB
         LET B$ = Set_Val$(I, SetB$)
         CALL Add_Member(B$,C$)
      NEXT I

      LET Unite_Sets$ = C$

      END DEF

      !---------------------------
      DEF Intersect_Sets$(SetA$, SetB$)
```

```
    ! Return the set of members common in both sets
LET SizeA = Set_Size(SetA$)
LET SizeB = Set_Size(SetB$)
LET C$ = ""

FOR I = 1 TO SizeA
    LET A$ = Set_Val$(I, SetA$)
    FOR J = 1 TO SizeB
        LET B$ = Set_Val$(J, SetB$)
        IF A$ = B$ THEN CALL Add_Member(A$, C$)
    NEXT J
NEXT I

LET Intersect_Sets$ = C$

END DEF

!---------------------------
DEF Difference_Sets$(SetA$, SetB$)
    ! Return the set contain members not common to both sets
LET SizeA = Set_Size(SetA$)
LET SizeB = Set_Size(SetB$)
LET C$ = ""

FOR I = 1 TO SizeA
    LET A$ = Set_Val$(I, SetA$)
    LET Match = 0
    FOR J = 1 TO SizeB
        LET B$ = Set_Val$(J, SetB$)
        IF A$ = B$ THEN LET Match = 1
    NEXT J
    IF Match = 0 THEN CALL Add_Member(A$, C$)
NEXT I

FOR I = 1 TO SizeB
    LET B$ = Set_Val$(I, SetB$)
    LET Match = 0
    FOR J = 1 TO SizeA
        LET A$ = Set_Val$(J, SetA$)
        IF A$ = B$ THEN LET Match = 1
    NEXT J
    IF Match = 0 THEN CALL Add_Member(B$, C$)
NEXT I

LET Difference_Sets$ = C$

END DEF

!----------------------------------------
SUB Sort_Set(SourceSet$, TargetSet$)
    ! Sort the elements of set SoruceSet$ into TargetSet$

DIM A$(1)
```

```
LET N = Set_Size(SourceSet$)

MAT REDIM A$(N)  ! adjust matrix size

LET TargetSet$ = ""

FOR I = 1 TO N
    LET A$(I) = Set_Val$(I,SourceSet$)
NEXT I

LET Offset = N
DO WHILE Offset > 1
   LET Offset = INT(Offset/2)
   DO
      LET InOrder = TRUE
      FOR J = 1 TO (N - Offset)
          LET I = J + Offset
          IF A$(I) < A$(J) THEN
             LET InOrder = FALSE
             LET T$ = A$(I)
             LET A$(I) = A$(J)
             LET A$(J) = T$
          END IF
      NEXT J
   LOOP UNTIL InOrder = TRUE
LOOP                      ! End of while-loop

FOR I = 1 TO N
    CALL Add_Member(A$(I), TargetSet$)
NEXT I
END SUB

!--------------------------------

DEF Are_Sets_EQ(SetA$, SetB$)
! Test if SetA$ and SetB$ are identical

LET A = Set_Size(SetA$)
LET B = Set_Size(SetB$)

IF A <> B THEN
   LET Are_Sets_EQ = 0
ELSE
   CALL Sort_Set(SetA$,A$)
   CALL Sort_Set(SetB$,B$)
   LET I = 1
   LET Same_Member = TRUE
   DO WHILE (I <= A) AND (Same_Member = TRUE)
      IF Set_Val$(I,A$) <> Set_Val$(I,B$) THEN
         LET Same_Member = FALSE
      ELSE
         LET I = I + 1
      END IF
   LOOP
   LET Are_Sets_EQ = Same_Member
```

```
      END IF

   END DEF

   !---------------------------------
   DEF Are_Sets_LEQ(SetA$, SetB$)
   ! Test if SetA$ is a subset of SetB$ or equal to it
   ! Every member in SetA$ must be present in SetB$

   LET A = Set_Size(SetA$)
   LET B = Set_Size(SetB$)

   IF A > B THEN
      LET Are_Sets_LEQ = 0
   ELSE
      CALL Sort_Set(SetA$,A$)
      CALL Sort_Set(SetB$,B$)
      LET I = 1
      LET J = 1
      DO WHILE (I <= A) AND (J <= B)
         IF Set_Val$(I,A$) = Set_Val$(J,B$) THEN
            LET I = I + 1
            LET J = J + 1
         ELSE
            LET J = J + 1
         END IF
      LOOP
      IF I <= A THEN
         LET Are_Sets_LEQ = FALSE
      ELSE
         LET Are_Sets_LEQ = TRUE
      END IF

   END IF

   END DEF

   !---------------------------------
   DEF Are_Sets_LT(SetA$, SetB$)
   ! Test if SetA$ is a subset of SetB$ but no equal to it.
   ! Every member of SetA$ is in SetB$

   LET A = Set_Size(SetA$)
   LET B = Set_Size(SetB$)

   IF A >= B THEN
      LET Are_Sets_LT = 0
   ELSE
      CALL Sort_Set(SetA$,A$)
      CALL Sort_Set(SetB$,B$)
      LET I = 1
      LET J = 1
      DO WHILE (I <= A) AND (J <= B)
         IF Set_Val$(I,A$) = Set_Val$(J,B$) THEN
            LET I = I + 1
            LET J = J + 1
         ELSE
```

```
        LET J = J + 1
     END IF
LOOP
     LET I = I - 1
     IF (I = A) AND (I < B) THEN
        LET Are_Sets_LT = TRUE
     ELSE
        LET Are_Sets_LT = FALSE
     END IF
  END IF

  END DEF

  END MODULE
```

In comparing the library source code, you will notice that the True BASIC module "exports" the popular sets. This means that a True BASIC application has the option to import them using DECLARE PUBLIC statements. By contrast, Quickbasic and Turbo BASIC applications that INCLUDE the library files end up with these sets anyway! To avoid conflicts with other sets you create with the same name, make sure that your sets are initialized. This will overwrite the set names with your new members.

The applications for sets are indeed numerous. I have written a short application program TESTSETS that performs the following:

1. returns the names of the weekdays

2. returns the number of days in a week, number of months in a year, and the number of letters in the alphabet

3. prompts the user for a keyboard entry and classifies the first character as being:

    + A lowercase letter.
    + An uppercase letter.
    + A digit.
    + A letter.
    + An alphanumeric character.
    + A control character.
    + A punctuation character.

The program reprompts you until you press the [ENTER] key (in True BASIC you must first type two quotes). Figure 3.10 shows the screen image for the TESTSETS.BAS program running under Turbo BASIC. The figure shows the output for the input classification when 'A', 'a', '1', and '+' are keyed-in.

```
               DEMONSTRATION PROGRAM FOR SETS
               -------------------------------

TESTING THE DAYS OF THE PREDEFINED WEEK SET
Day # 1 ; of the week is SUNDAY
Day # 2 ; of the week is MONDAY
Day # 3 ; of the week is TUESDAY
Day # 4 ; of the week is WEDNESDAY
Day # 5 ; of the week is THURSDAY
Day # 6 ; of the week is FRIDAY
Day # 7 ; of the week is SATURDAY

TESTING THE SIZE OF THE PREDEFINED WEEK, MONTH AND
CHARACTER SETS
There are   7   days in a week
There are   12  month in a year
There are   26  letters in the alphabet

Enter one character (press [ENTER] to exit) ? a
Is character lowercase ?       : TRUE
Is character uppercase ?       : FALSE
Is character a digit ?         : FALSE
Is character a letter ?        : TRUE
Is character alphanumeric ?    : TRUE
Is character a Ctrl-char ?     : FALSE
Is character a punctuation ? : FALSE

Enter one character (press [ENTER] to exit) ? A
Is character lowercase ?       : FALSE
Is character uppercase ?       : TRUE
Is character a digit ?         : FALSE
Is character a letter ?        : TRUE
Is character alphanumeric ?    : TRUE
Is character a Ctrl-char ?     : FALSE
Is character a punctuation ? : FALSE

Enter one character (press [ENTER] to exit) ? 1
Is character lowercase ?       : FALSE
Is character uppercase ?       : FALSE
Is character a digit ?         : TRUE
Is character a letter ?        : FALSE
Is character alphanumeric ?    : TRUE
Is character a Ctrl-char ?     : FALSE
Is character a punctuation ? : FALSE

Enter one character (press [ENTER] to exit) ? +
Is character lowercase ?       : FALSE
Is character uppercase ?       : FALSE
Is character a digit ?         : FALSE
Is character a letter ?        : FALSE
Is character alphanumeric ?    : FALSE
Is character a Ctrl-char ?     : FALSE
Is character a punctuation ? : TRUE

Enter one character (press [ENTER] to exit) ? <[ENTER]>
```

Figure 3.10 *Screen image for program TESTSETS.BAS running under Turbo BASIC*

Listings 3.46, 3.47, and 3.48 present the three BASIC versions for the TESTSETS program. The QuickBASIC and Turbo BASIC versions import the entire SETS library using the INCLUDE directive. In True BASIC, this is done in three steps: using the LIBRARY, DECLARE DEF, and DECLARE PUBLIC declarations. While this is a bit more elaborate, it gives the application program more control over the imported functions and imported PUBLIC variables.

Listing 3.46. *QuickBASIC source code for program TESTSETS.BAS to demonstrate a few aspects of the SETS library*

```
' PROGRAM Test.Sets
' QuickBASIC version

' Include libraries used
REM $INCLUDE: 'SETS.BAS'
REM $INCLUDE: 'TOOLBOX0.BAS'

CLS

CALL Center.Message("DEMONSTRATION PROGRAM FOR SETS",1)
CALL Center.Message("-----------------------------",2)
CALL Blank.Lines(3)

PRINT "TESTING THE DAYS OF THE PREDEFINED WEEK SET"

FOR JOUR% = 1 TO 7
    PRINT "Day #";JOUR%;" of the week is ";FNSET.VAL$(JOUR%,WEEKSET$)
NEXT JOUR%

PRINT
PRINT "TESTING THE SIZE OF THE PREDEFINED WEEK, MONTH AND CHARACTER SETS"
PRINT "There are ";FNSET.SIZE%(WEEKSET$);" days in a week"
PRINT "There are ";FNSET.SIZE%(MONTHSET$);" month in a year"
PRINT "There are ";FNSET.SIZE%(UPPERCASESET$);" letters in the alphabet"

DO
    INPUT "Enter one character (press [Enter] to exit) ";A$
    IF A$ = "" THEN EXIT DO
    A$ = LEFT$(A$,1)
    PRINT "Is character lowercase ?      : ";FNSAYTF$(FNINSET%(A$,LOWERCASESET$))
    PRINT "Is character uppercase ?      : ";FNSAYTF$(FNINSET%(A$,UPPERCASESET$))
    PRINT "Is character a digit ?        : ";FNSAYTF$(FNINSET%(A$,DIGITSET$))
    PRINT "Is character a letter ?       : ";FNSAYTF$(FNINSET%(A$,LETTERSET$))
    PRINT "Is character alphanumeric ?   : ";FNSAYTF$(FNINSET%(A$,ALPHANUMSET$))
    PRINT "Is character a Ctrl-char ?    : ";FNSAYTF$(FNINSET%(A$,CONTROLSET$))
    PRINT "Is character a punctuation ?  : ";FNSAYTF$(FNINSET%(A$,PUNCTSET$))
```

```
     PRINT : PRINT

LOOP

END
```

Listing 3.47. *Turbo BASIC source code for program TESTSETS.BAS to demonstrate a few aspects of the SETS library*

```
' PROGRAM Test.Sets
' Turbo BASIC version

' Include library used
$INCLUDE "SETS.BAS"
$INCLUDE "TOOLBOX0.BAS"

CLS

CALL Center.Message("DEMONSTRATION PROGRAM FOR SETS",1)
CALL Center.Message("------------------------------",2)
CALL Blank.Lines(3)

PRINT "TESTING THE DAYS OF THE PREDEFINED WEEK SET"

FOR JOUR% = 1 TO 7
   PRINT "Day #";JOUR%"; of the week is ";FNSET.VAL$(JOUR%,WEEKSET$)
NEXT JOUR%

PRINT
PRINT "TESTING THE SIZE OF THE PREDEFINED WEEK, MONTH AND CHARACTER SETS"
PRINT "There are ";FNSET.SIZE%(WEEKSET$);" days in a week"
PRINT "There are ";FNSET.SIZE%(MONTHSET$);" month in a year"
PRINT "There are ";FNSET.SIZE%(UPPERCASESET$);" letters in the alphabet"
PRINT

DO
   INPUT "Enter one character (press [Enter] to exit) ";A$
   IF A$ = "" THEN EXIT LOOP
   A$ = LEFT$(A$,1)
   PRINT "Is character lowercase ?      : ";FNSAYTF$(FNINSET%(A$,LOWERCASESET$))
   PRINT "Is character uppercase ?      : ";FNSAYTF$(FNINSET%(A$,UPPERCASESET$))
   PRINT "Is character a digit ?        : ";FNSAYTF$(FNINSET%(A$,DIGITSET$))
   PRINT "Is character a letter ?       : ";FNSAYTF$(FNINSET%(A$,LETTERSET$))
   PRINT "Is character alphanumeric ?   : ";FNSAYTF$(FNINSET%(A$,ALPHANUMSET$))
   PRINT "Is character a Ctrl-char ?    : ";FNSAYTF$(FNINSET%(A$,CONTROLSET$))
   PRINT "Is character a punctuation ?  : ";FNSAYTF$(FNINSET%(A$,PUNCTSET$))
   PRINT : PRINT
LOOP

END
```

Listing 3.48. *True BASIC source code for program TESTSETS.TRU to demonstrate a few of the SETS module*

```
PROGRAM Test_Sets
! True BASIC version

! Include library used
LIBRARY "SETS.TRU","TOOLBOX0.TRU"

! Declare imported functions
DECLARE DEF SayTF$, InSet, Set_Size, Set_Val$

! Declare imported sets
DECLARE PUBLIC YesNoSet$, BoolSet$, YesSet$, NoSet$, TrueSet$,
FalseSet$
DECLARE PUBLIC YNSet$, TFSet$, WeekSet$, WeekEndSet$, WeekdaySet$,
MonthSet$
DECLARE PUBLIC LowerCaseSet$, UpperCaseSet$, LetterSet$, DigitSet$
DECLARE PUBLIC AlphanumSet$, ControlSet$, PunctSet$

CLEAR

CALL Center_Message("DEMONSTRATION PROGRAM FOR SETS",1)
CALL Center_Message("------------------------------",2)
CALL Blank_Lines(3)

PRINT "TESTING THE DAYS OF THE PREDEFINED WEEK SET"

FOR JOUR = 1 TO 7
   PRINT "Day #";JOUR;" of the week is ";Set_Val$(JOUR,WeekSet$)
NEXT JOUR

PRINT
PRINT "TESTING THE SIZE OF THE PREDEFINED WEEK, MONTH AND CHARACTER
SETS"
PRINT "There are ";Set_Size(WeekSet$);" days in a week"
PRINT "There are ";Set_Size(MonthSet$);" month in a year"
PRINT "There are ";Set_Size(UpperCaseSet$);" letters in the alphabet"
PRINT

DO
   INPUT PROMPT "Enter one character (2 quotes and [Enter] to exit) ":A$
   IF A$ = "" THEN EXIT DO
   LET A$ = A$[1:1]
   PRINT "Is character lowercase ?      : ";SayTF$(InSet(A$,LOWERCASESET$))
   PRINT "Is character uppercase ?      : ";SayTF$(InSet(A$,UpperCaseSet$))
   PRINT "Is character a digit ?        : ";SayTF$(InSet(A$,DIGITSET$))
   PRINT "Is character a letter ?       : ";SayTF$(InSet(A$,LETTERSET$))
   PRINT "Is character alphanumeric ?   : ";SayTF$(InSet(A$,ALPHANUMSET$))
   PRINT "Is character a Ctrl-char ?    : ";SayTF$(InSet(A$,CONTROLSET$))
```

```
    PRINT "Is character a punctuation ? : ";SayTF$(InSet(A$,PUNCTSET$))
    PRINT
    PRINT

LOOP

END
```

Library Module BINTREE

PURPOSE: The BINTREE library implements a single "instance" of a binary tree. Binary tree structures are more frequently discussed in Pascal, Modula-2, and C books than in BASIC books. The implementation of a binary tree structure lends itself more naturally to using pointers (available in Pascal and other structured languages). Another building tool for binary trees is dynamic allocation. Unfortunately, pointers and dynamic allocation (Pascal style) are not supported in BASIC. This leaves us using arrays to maintain binary trees.

The routines for this library were first written in True BASIC to use a few special features of that implementation. The first is the ability to hide module data from the application program. This enables a True BASIC module to maintain its internal array of pseudo-pointers (or indexes, if you like), hidden from the application programs. The fact that these PRIVATE variables are static (that is, they maintain their values between calls) makes the entire mechanism possible. The second feature used is True BASIC's MAT REDIM, which is capable of expanding an array without erasing its contents. This feature comes very close to dynamic allocation in Pascal.

There is a drawback to using hidden variables in True BASIC modules: you can only create one "instance" of that hidden variable. This leaves the following choices for a module developer:

1. Create a data structure that may be used in multiple instances (for example, using several binary trees in the same program). The entire collection of variables (scalars and arrays) supporting the data structure must be subroutine parameters.

2. Hide some internal data structures. This dictates that one instance (i.e., occurrence) of the data structure is allowed. This also makes the list of subroutine arguments shorter.

I have chosen to present a True BASIC version of module BINTREE that implements data hiding. I have translated the module into QuickBASIC and True

BASIC versions. Since these implementations do not support modules or data hiding, the variables supporting the single binary tree are global.

The BINTREE library offers the following capabilities:

1. initializing a binary tree

2. inserting new nodes

3. searching for data items in the tree

4. obtaining an array of indexed ranks for the tree nodes

5. rebalancing the binary tree

Listings 3.49, 3.50, and 3.51 contain the library source code for the QuickBASIC, Turbo BASIC, and True BASIC versions, respectively.

ROUTINES

I will now present the True BASIC version of module BINTREE.

The following is a list of PUBLIC variables that are exported to the application programs:

PUBLIC Tree_Ptr(1), Num_Nodes, Tree_Size, Bin_Tree$(1)

where:

Tree_Ptr()	is the array of sorted rank indices
Num_Nodes	is the number of data items in the binary tree
Tree_Size	is the size of the nearest full balanced tree
Bin_Tree$()	is the array of data items

The following is a list of internal variables shared among module routines only:

SHARE Left(1), Right(1), Node_Count, Copy_Item$(1)

Left()	the array of left node pointers
Right()	the array of right node pointers
Node_Count	a counter used by the routines
Copy_Item$()	an array to store the copy of the tree items

DEF NIL3 = MAXNUM
DEF TRUE3 = 1
DEF FALSE3 = 0

These constants and functions define values used in the binary tree system.

SUB Initialize(Item$)

This subroutine is used to initialize the binary tree by assigning its root node. Notice that no other arguments are needed, since a combination of PUBLIC and static PRIVATE variables is used.

SUB Insert(Item$)

Insertion of additional data items in the binary tree is carried out using this subroutine. The binary tree array is automatically expanded to accommodate incoming data. Thus, no array is wasted.

SUB Search(Item$, Found, Index)

This routine is used to search for *Item$* in the binary tree. If the search is successful, the parameter *Found* returns the value of function *TRUE2* (equal to 1). The *Index* parameter also returns the index of array *Bin_Tree$()* where the matching occurred. On the other hand, if *Item$* has no match in the binary tree, *Found* returns the value of function *FALSE2* (equal to 0). The value of *Index* in this case is irrelevant to the search.

SUB Traverse(Root)   ! RECURSIVE

This routine is an internal one (declared PRIVATE in the module), used to traverse the binary tree.

SUB Get_Sorted_List

This routine is employed to return an array of indexed ranks (the array used is *Tree_Ptr()*). Thus, *Tree_Ptr(1)* is the index of the first element, *Tree_Ptr(2)* is the index for the second, and so on. Using this routine is essential in True BASIC, since access to the left/right pointer arrays is denied.

SUB Rebalance_Tree

This subroutine is used to rebalance a binary tree. It should be used to improve searching performance of a large skewed binary tree. When in doubt about the balance of the binary tree, do not hesitate to use this routine.

SUB Rebalance_List(First,Last,Median,Node_Ptr)

This subroutine is an internal one (declared PRIVATE), used in implementing a recursive algorithm for tree rebalancing.

The following routines are taken from the Turbo BASIC library version.

```
'----- QuickBASIC -----
NIL3% = 0
TRUE3% = 1
FALSE% = 0

'----- Turbo BASIC
%NIL3 = 0
%TRUE3 = 1
%FALSE3 = 0
```

These constants are used in the binary tree system.

SUB INITIALIZE(ITEM$) STATIC

This subroutine is used to initialize the binary tree by assigning its root node. Notice that no other arguments are needed, since global variables are used.

SUB INSERT(ITEM$) STATIC

Insertion of additional data items in the binary tree is carried out using this subroutine. Unlike the True BASIC version, the binary tree array is not automatically expanded to accommodate incoming data. Adequate array space must be supplied.

SUB SEARCH(ITEM$, FOUND%, INDEX%) STATIC

This routine is used to search for *ITEM$* in the binary tree. If the search is successful, the parameter *Found* returns the value of function *FNTRUE2%* (equal to 1). The *INDEX* parameter also returns the index of array *BIN.TREE$()* where the matching occurred. On the other hand, if *ITEM$* has no match in the binary tree, *Found* returns the value of function *FNFALSE2%* (equal to 0). The value of *INDEX* in this case is irrelevant to the search.

SUB Traverse(ROOT%)

This internal routine is used to traverse the binary tree. The Turbo BASIC version is recursive; the QuickBASIC version is not.

SUB GET.SORTED.LIST STATIC

This routine is employed to return an array of indexed ranks (the array used is *TREE.PTR()*). Thus, *TREE.PTR(1)* is the index of the first element, *TREE.PTR(2)* is the index for the second, and so on.

SUB REBALANCE.TREE STATIC

This subroutine is used to rebalance a binary tree. It should be used to improve searching performance of a large skewed binary tree. When in doubt about the balance of the binary tree, do not hesitate to use this routine.

SUB REBAL.LST(FIRST%,LAST%,MEDIAN%,NODE%)

This internal subroutine is used by subroutine *REBALANCE.TREE*. The Turbo BASIC version is recursive and similar to that of True BASIC. The QuickBASIC version is non-recursive.

Rebalancing a binary tree requires the use of a top-down node access scheme. The new root is the sought first element, followed by the root's left and right branches. This process is repeated for all the other nodes systematically, going from a higher tree level to the one below it. The recursive version of the algorithm attempts to recursively balance the main left and right subtrees.

The nonrecursive algorithm balances M levels of a binary tree using two nested FOR-NEXT loops: one counts the levels, the other counts the number of nodes at the current level. At any level L, there can be at most $2^{(M-L)}$ nodes. At any level L, the first node is fetched from the array location $2^{(L-1)}$. Subsequent nodes on the same level are 2^L members apart.

There are two facts to observe in using either method of rebalancing. The first is that the rebalanced tree is most likely not a full tree. The next fullest tree size must be calculated. The second is that all nodes at the tree level 1 are leaves and have nil left and right pointers.

Listing 3.49. *QuickBASIC source code for library BINTREE.BAS.*

```
' BINARY.TREE LIBRARY
' QuickBASIC version of a binary tree library
```

```basic
' Copyright (c) 1987 Namir Clement Shammas

CONST NIL3% = 0, FALSE3% = 0, TRUE3% = 1


SUB INITIALIZE(ITEM$) STATIC
' SUBROUTINE TO INITIALIZE THE BINARY TREE

SHARED N.NODES%, BIN.TREE$(), LPTR%(), RPTR%()

N.NODES% = 1
BIN.TREE$(1) = ITEM$
LPTR%(1) = NIL3%
RPTR%(1) = NIL3%

END SUB


SUB SEARCH(ITEM$, FOUND%, INDEX%) STATIC
' SEARCH FOR ITEM$ AND RETURN INDEX% IF FOUND%.

SHARED N.NODES%, BIN.TREE$(), LPTR%(), RPTR%()

FOUND% = FALSE3%
INDEX% = 1

WHILE (INDEX% <> NIL3%) AND (FOUND% = FALSE3%)
   IF BIN.TREE$(INDEX%) = ITEM$ THEN
      FOUND% = TRUE3%
   ELSE
      IF BIN.TREE$(INDEX%) < ITEM$ THEN
         INDEX% = RPTR%(INDEX%)
      ELSE
         INDEX% = LPTR%(INDEX%)
      END IF
   END IF
WEND

END SUB


SUB INSERT(ITEM$) STATIC
' INSERT ITEM$ IN THE "DYNAMIC" BINARY TREE STRUCTURE
SHARED N.NODES%, BIN.TREE$(), LPTR%(), RPTR%()
STATIC INDEX%, FOUND%

N.NODES% = N.NODES% + 1
INDEX% = 1
FOUND% = FALSE3%

WHILE INDEX% <> NIL3%
   IF BIN.TREE$(INDEX%) < ITEM$ THEN
      IF RPTR%(INDEX%) <> NIL3% THEN
         INDEX% = RPTR%(INDEX%)
      ELSE
         RPTR%(INDEX%) = N.NODES%
```

```
                    INDEX% = NIL3%
            END IF
        ELSE
            IF LPTR%(INDEX%) <> NIL3% THEN
                INDEX% = LPTR%(INDEX%)
            ELSE
                LPTR%(INDEX%) = N.NODES%
                    INDEX% = NIL3%
            END IF
        END IF
WEND

BIN.TREE$(N.NODES%) = ITEM$
RPTR%(N.NODES%) = NIL3%
LPTR%(N.NODES%) = NIL3%

END SUB


SUB TRAVERSE(ROOT%) STATIC
' NON-RECURSIVE SUBROUTINE TO TRAVERSE THE BINARY TREE

SHARED N.NODES%, BIN.TREE$(), LPTR%(), RPTR%(),  NODE.COUNT%, TREE.PTR%()
SHARED TREE.SIZE%, STACK.SIZE%, STACK%()
STATIC TNODE%, MOVE.UP%

FOR TNODE% = 1 TO TREE.SIZE%
    TREE.PTR%(TNODE%) = NIL3%
NEXT TNODE%

TNODE% = ROOT%
STACK.SIZE% = 0
MOVE.UP% = FALSE3%

WHILE NODE.COUNT% < N.NODES%
    IF (LPTR%(TNODE%) <> NIL3%) AND (MOVE.UP% = FALSE3%) THEN
        STACK.SIZE% = STACK.SIZE% + 1
        STACK%(STACK.SIZE%) = TNODE%
        TNODE% = LPTR%(TNODE%)
    ELSE
        ' ACCESS NODE TNODE%
        NODE.COUNT% = NODE.COUNT% + 1
        TREE.PTR%(NODE.COUNT%) = TNODE%
        MOVE.UP% = FALSE3%

        IF (RPTR%(TNODE%) <> NIL3%) THEN
            TNODE% = RPTR%(TNODE%)
        ELSE
            IF STACK.SIZE% > 0 THEN
                TNODE% = STACK%(STACK.SIZE%)
                STACK.SIZE% = STACK.SIZE% - 1
                MOVE.UP% = TRUE3%
            END IF
        END IF
    END IF
WEND
```

BASIC LIBRARIES

```
END SUB


SUB GET.SORTED.LIST STATIC
' SUBROUTINE TO OBTAIN AN ARRAY OF POINTERS FOR THE SORTED LIST

SHARED NODE.COUNT%, TREE.SIZE%, TREE.PTR%()
STATIC I%

FOR I% = 1 TO TREE.SIZE% : TREE.PTR%(I%) = NIL3% : NEXT I%

NODE.COUNT% = 0  ' INITIALIZE NODE COUNT

' START AT THE ROOT OF THE BINARY TREE
CALL TRAVERSE(1)

END SUB


SUB REBALANCE.TREE STATIC
' SUBROUTINE TO REBALANCE BINARY TREE POINTERS

SHARED N.NODES%, BIN.TREE$(), LPTR%(), RPTR%(), COPY.ITEM$(), TREE.PTR%()
SHARED TREE.SIZE%

STATIC I%, L%, MAX.LEVELS%, OFFSET%, LOG.TREE!
STATIC DELTA%, DELTA2%, INDEX%, NODE%, PTR%

CALL GET.SORTED.LIST

FOR I% = 1 TO N.NODES%
   COPY.ITEM$(I%) = BIN.TREE$(I%)
   BIN.TREE$(I%) = ""
   LPTR%(I%) = NIL3%
   RPTR%(I%) = NIL3%
NEXT I%

LOG.TREE# = LOG(N.NODES%)/LOG(2)
IF (LOG.TREE# - INT(LOG.TREE#)) > 1E-8 THEN OFFSET% = 1 ELSE OFFSET% = 0
MAX.LEVELS% = INT(LOG.TREE#) + OFFSET%
NODE.NUM% = 0

FOR L% = MAX.LEVELS% TO 1 STEP -1

   INDEX% = 2^(L% - 1)
   DELTA% = 2^L%
   DELTA2% = DELTA% \ 4

   FOR I% = 1 TO 2^(MAX.LEVELS% - L%)

      NODE.NUM% = NODE.NUM% + 1

      IF (INDEX% <= N.NODES%) THEN
              BIN.TREE$(NODE.NUM%) = COPY.ITEM$(TREE.PTR%(INDEX%))
      END IF
```

```
            IF (L% > 1) THEN
                    LPTR%(NODE.NUM%) = 2 * NODE.NUM%
                    RPTR%(NODE.NUM%) = LPTR%(NODE.NUM%) + 1
            ELSE
                    LPTR%(NODE.NUM%) = NIL3%
                    RPTR%(NODE.NUM%) = NIL3%
            END IF

            INDEX% = INDEX% + DELTA%

        NEXT I%

    NEXT L%

END SUB
```

Listing 3.50. *Turbo BASIC souce code for library BINTREE.BAS*

```
' BINARY.TREE LIBRARY
' Turbo BASIC version of the binary tree library
' Copyright (c) 1987  Namir Clement Shammas

' Define pseudo constants
%NIL3 = 0
%TRUE3 = 1
%FALSE3 = 0

SUB INITIALIZE(ITEM$) STATIC
' Subroutine to initialize the binary tree

SHARED N.NODES%, BIN.TREE$(), LPTR%(), RPTR%()

N.NODES% = 1
BIN.TREE$(1) = ITEM$
LPTR%(1) = %NIL3
RPTR%(1) = %NIL3

END SUB


SUB SEARCH(ITEM$, FOUND%, INDEX%) STATIC
' Search for ITEM$ and return INDEX% if found.

SHARED N.NODES%, BIN.TREE$(), LPTR%(), RPTR%()

FOUND% = %FALSE3
INDEX% = 1

WHILE (INDEX% <> %NIL3) AND (FOUND% = %FALSE3)
```

```
         IF BIN.TREE$(INDEX%) = ITEM$ THEN
            FOUND% = %TRUE3
         ELSE
            IF BIN.TREE$(INDEX%) < ITEM$ THEN
               INDEX% = RPTR%(INDEX%)
            ELSE
               INDEX% = LPTR%(INDEX%)
            END IF
         END IF
   WEND

END SUB


SUB INSERT(ITEM$) STATIC
' Insert ITEM$ in the binary tree structure

SHARED N.NODES%, BIN.TREE$(), LPTR%(), RPTR%()
LOCAL INDEX%, FOUND%

N.NODES% = N.NODES% + 1
INDEX% = 1
FOUND% = %FALSE3

WHILE INDEX% <> %NIL3
   IF BIN.TREE$(INDEX%) < ITEM$ THEN
      IF RPTR%(INDEX%) <> %NIL3 THEN
         INDEX% = RPTR%(INDEX%)
      ELSE
         RPTR%(INDEX%) = N.NODES%
         INDEX% = %NIL3
      END IF
   ELSE
      IF LPTR%(INDEX%) <> %NIL3 THEN
         INDEX% = LPTR%(INDEX%)
      ELSE
         LPTR%(INDEX%) = N.NODES%
         INDEX% = %NIL3
      END IF
   END IF
WEND

BIN.TREE$(N.NODES%) = ITEM$
RPTR%(N.NODES%) = %NIL3
LPTR%(N.NODES%) = %NIL3

END SUB

SUB TRAVERSE(ROOT%) 'RECURSIVE
' Recursive subroutine to traverse the binary tree

SHARED N.NODES%, BIN.TREE$(), LPTR%(), RPTR%(),  NODE.COUNT%,
TREE.PTR%()

IF ROOT% <> %NIL3 THEN
   CALL TRAVERSE(LPTR%(ROOT%))
```

```
            NODE.COUNT% = NODE.COUNT% + 1
            TREE.PTR%(NODE.COUNT%) = ROOT%
            CALL TRAVERSE(RPTR%(ROOT%))
         END IF

      END SUB

      SUB GET.SORTED.LIST STATIC
      ' Subroutine to obtain an array of pointers for the sorted list

      SHARED NODE.COUNT%, TREE.SIZE%, TREE.PTR%()
      LOCAL I%

      FOR I% = 1 TO TREE.SIZE% : TREE.PTR%(I%) = %NIL3 : NEXT I%

      NODE.COUNT% = 0          ' INITIALIZE NODE COUNT
      ' START AT THE ROOT OF THE BINARY TREE
      CALL TRAVERSE(1)

      END SUB

      SUB REBALANCE.TREE STATIC
      ' Subroutine to rebalance binary tree pointers

      SHARED N.NODES%, BIN.TREE$(), LPTR%(), RPTR%(), COPY.ITEM$(), TREE.PTR%()
      LOCAL I%, FIRST%

      CALL GET.SORTED.LIST
      FOR I% = 1 TO N.NODES%
         COPY.ITEM$(I%) = BIN.TREE$(I%)
         BIN.TREE$(I%) = ""
         LPTR%(I%) = %NIL3
         RPTR%(I%) = %NIL3
      NEXT I%
      ROOT.MEDIAN% = (1 + N.NODES%) \ 2
      FIRST% = 1
      CALL REBAL.LST(FIRST%,N.NODES%,ROOT.MEDIAN%,FIRST%)
      END SUB

      SUB REBAL.LST(FIRST%,LAST%,MEDIAN%,NODE%) 'RECURSIVE
      ' Rebalance sorted sublists

      SHARED N.NODES%, BIN.TREE$(), LPTR%(), RPTR%(), COPY.ITEM$(), TREE.PTR%()
      LOCAL LMEDIAN%, RMEDIAN%

      BIN.TREE$(NODE%) = COPY.ITEM$(TREE.PTR%(MEDIAN%))

      IF FIRST% < LAST% THEN

        IF FIRST% <= (MEDIAN%-1) THEN
            LMEDIAN% = (FIRST% + MEDIAN% - 1) \ 2
            LPTR%(NODE%) = 2 * NODE%
            CALL REBAL.LST(FIRST%,MEDIAN%-1,LMEDIAN%,LPTR%(NODE%))
        END IF

          IF (MEDIAN%+1) <= LAST% THEN
```

```
            RMEDIAN% = (MEDIAN% + 1 + LAST%) \ 2
            RPTR%(NODE%) = 2 * NODE% + 1
            CALL REBAL.LST(MEDIAN%+1,LAST%,RMEDIAN%,RPTR%(NODE%))
      END IF

   END IF

   END SUB
```

Listing 3.51. *True BASIC source code for BINTREE.TRU*

```
MODULE  Binary_Tree

! TRUE BASIC module that implements a single binary tree
! Copyright (c) 1987  Namir Clement Shammas

PUBLIC Tree_Ptr(1), Num_Nodes, Tree_Size, Bin_Tree$(1)
DECLARE DEF NIL3, TRUE3, FALSE3
PRIVATE Traverse, Rebalance_List
SHARE Left(1), Right(1), Node_Count, Copy_Item$(1)

!------------ Module initialization ---------
LET Num_Nodes = 0

!----------- local functions -----------
DEF NIL3 = MAXNUM
DEF TRUE3 = 1
DEF FALSE3 = 0


SUB Initialize(Item$)
! Subroutine to initialize the binary tree

LET Num_Nodes = 1
LET Tree_Size = 1
LET Bin_Tree$(1) = Item$
LET Left(1) = NIL3
LET Right(1) = NIL3

END SUB


SUB Search(Item$, Found, Index)
! Search for Item$ and return Index if found.

LET Found = FALSE3
LET Index = 1

DO WHILE (Index <> NIL3) AND (Found = FALSE3)
   IF Bin_Tree$(Index) = Item$ THEN
```

```
            LET Found = TRUE3
         ELSE
            IF Bin_Tree$(Index) < Item$ THEN
               LET Index = Right(Index)
            ELSE
               LET Index = Left(Index)
            END IF
         END IF
LOOP

END SUB


SUB Insert(Item$)
! Insert Item$ in the "dynamic" binary tree structure

LET Num_Nodes = Num_Nodes + 1

IF Num_Nodes > Tree_Size THEN
   LET Tree_Size = Num_Nodes
   MAT REDIM Bin_Tree$(Tree_Size), Left(Tree_Size), Right(Tree_Size)
END IF

LET Index = 1
LET Found = FALSE3

DO WHILE Index <> NIL3
   IF Bin_Tree$(Index) < Item$ THEN
      IF Right(Index) <> NIL3 THEN
         LET Index = Right(Index)
      ELSE
         LET Right(Index) = Num_Nodes
         LET Index = NIL3
      END IF
   ELSE
      IF Left(Index) <> NIL3 THEN
         LET Index = Left(Index)
      ELSE
         LET Left(Index) = Num_Nodes
         LET Index = NIL3
      END IF
   END IF
LOOP

LET Bin_Tree$(Num_Nodes) = Item$
LET Right(Num_Nodes) = NIL3
LET Left(Num_Nodes) = NIL3

END SUB

SUB Traverse(Root)                ! RECURSIVE
! Recursive subroutine to traverse the binary tree

IF Root <> NIL3 THEN
   CALL Traverse(Left(Root))
   LET Node_Count = Node_Count + 1
```

```
            LET Tree_Ptr(Node_Count) = Root
            CALL Traverse(Right(Root))
         END IF

      END SUB

      SUB Get_Sorted_List
      ! Subroutine to obtain an array of pointers for the sorted list

         MAT REDIM Tree_Ptr(Tree_Size)
         LET Node_Count = 0        ! Initialize node count
         CALL Traverse(1)          ! Start at the root of the binary tree

      END SUB

      SUB Rebalance_Tree
      ! Subroutine to rebalance binary tree pointers

         LET L = 1
         LET Sum = 1

         DO WHILE Sum < Num_Nodes
            LET Sum = Sum + 2^L
            LET L = L + 1
         LOOP

         IF Sum > Tree_Size THEN
            LET Tree_Size = Sum
            MAT REDIM Bin_Tree$(Tree_Size), Left(Tree_Size), Right(Tree_Size)
         END IF

         CALL Get_Sorted_List
         MAT Copy_Item$ = Bin_Tree$
         MAT Bin_Tree$ = ""
         MAT Left = NIL3
         MAT Right = NIL3
         LET Root_Median = INT((1+Num_Nodes)/2)
         CALL Rebalance_List(1,Num_Nodes,Root_Median,1)
         MAT REDIM Copy_Item$(1)

      END SUB

      SUB Rebalance_List(First,Last,Median,Node_Ptr)
      ! Rebalance sorted sublists
      ! This subroutine is recursive

         LET Bin_Tree$(Node_Ptr) = Copy_Item$(Tree_Ptr(Median))

         IF First < Last THEN

            IF First <= (Median-1) THEN
               LET LMedian = INT((First+Median-1)/2)
               LET Left(Node_Ptr) = 2 * Node_Ptr
               CALL Rebalance_List(First,Median-1,LMedian,(Left(Node_Ptr)))
            END IF
```

```
        IF (Median+1) <= Last THEN
        LET RMedian = INT((Median+1+Last)/2)
        LET Right(Node_Ptr) = 2 * Node_Ptr + 1
        CALL Rebalance_List(Median+1,Last,RMedian,(Right(Node_Ptr)))
        END IF

END IF

END SUB

END MODULE
```

Since binary trees are data structures often used in sorting, I have written an application program that reads a textfile, sorts it, and writes the ordered text to an output file.

Figure 3.11.1 shows screen image for the TESTBIN program. The input file used is ELEMENTS.DAT (see figure 3.11.2), which contains basic chemistry data. The output is file SORTELEM.DAT, shown in figure 3.11.3.

BASIC LIBRARIES

```
          TEXTFILE SORTING UTILITY
          ------------------------


Enter input text file name ? elements.dat


Reading and sorting....


Enter output text file name ? sortelem.dat

text saved in file sortelem.dat



Sort another file (Y/N) ? n
```

Figure 3.11.1 *Screen image for program TESTBIN.TRU running under True BASIC.*

```
BASIC ELEMENT RECORD
! 9/22/1986
!Name Short_Name Sym AN Num_Val Val_Array AW
Hydrogen Hydr H 1 2 1 -1 1.00
Helium Helium He 2 1 0 4.00
Lithium Lithium Li 3 1 1 6.939
Berylium Berylium 4 1 2 9.01
Boron Bor 5 1 3 10.811
Carbon Carbon 6 3 -4 2 4 12.01
Nitrogen Nitr 7 5 -3 2 3 4 5 14.00
Oxygen Ox 8 1 -2 16.00
Flouride Flour 9 1 -1 19.00
Neon Neon Ne 10 1 0 21.183
Sodium Sodium Na 11 1 1 23.00
Magnesium Magnesium Mg 12 1 2 24.32
Aluminum Alum Al 13 1 3 26.98
Silicon Silic Si 14 1 4 28.09
Phosphorus Phosph P 15 4 -3 3 4 5 30.97
Sulfur Sulf S 16 4 -2 2 4 6 32.06
Chlorine Chlor Cl 17 5 -1 1 3 5 7 35.45
Potassium Potassium K 19 1 1 39.10
Calcium Calcium Ca 20 1 2 40.08
Chromium Chrom Cr 24 3 2 3 6 52.00
Manganese Mangan Mn 25 5 2 3 4 6 7 54.94
Iron Ferr Fe 26 3 2 3 55.84
Cobalt Cobalt Co 27 2 2 3 58.93
Nickel Nickel Ni 28 2 2 3 58.71
Copper Cupp Cu 29 2 1 2 63.55
Zinc Zinc Zn 30 1 2 35.37
Bromine Brom Br 35 3 -1 1 5
Silver Silver Ag 47 1 1 107.87
Cadmium Cadm Cd 48 1 2 112.40
Tin Stann Sn 50 2 2 4 118.69
Iodine Iod I 53  4 -1 1 5 7
Barium Barium Ba 56 1 2 137.34
Gold Aur Au 79 2 1 3 196.96
Mercury Mercur Hg 80 2 1 2 200.59
Lead Plumb Pb 82 2 2 4 207.19
Bismuth Bismuth Bi 83 2 3 5 208.98
! End of list
```

Figure 3.11.2 *Contents of textfile ELEMENTS.DAT.*

BASIC LIBRARIES

```
! 9/22/1986
! End of list
!Name Short_Name Sym AN Num_Val Val_Array AW
Aluminum Alum Al 13 1 3 26.98
Barium Barium Ba 56 1 2 137.34
BASIC ELEMENT RECORD
Berylium Berylium 4 1 2 9.01
Bismuth Bismuth Bi 83 2 3 5 208.98
Boron Bor 5 1 3 10.811
Bromine Brom Br 35 3 -1 1 5
Cadmium Cadm Cd 48 1 2 112.40
Calcium Calcium Ca 20 1 2 40.08
Carbon Carbon 6 3 -4 2 4 12.01
Chlorine Chlor Cl 17 5 -1 1 3 5 7 35.45
Chromium Chrom Cr 24 3 2 3 6 52.00
Cobalt Cobalt Co 27 2 2 3 58.93
Copper Cupp Cu 29 2 1 2 63.55
Flouride Flour 9 1 -1 19.00
Gold Aur Au 79 2 1 3 196.96
Helium Helium He 2 1 0 4.00
Hydrogen Hydr H 1 2 1 -1 1.00
Iodine Iod I 53  4 -1 1 5 7
Iron Ferr Fe 26 3 2 3 55.84
Lead Plumb Pb 82 2 2 4 207.19
Lithium Lithium Li 3 1 1 6.939
Magnesium Magnesium Mg 12 1 2 24.32
Manganese Mangan Mn 25 5 2 3 4 6 7 54.94
Mercury Mercur Hg 80 2 1 2 200.59
Neon Neon Ne 10 1 0 21.183
Nickel Ni 28 2 2 3 58.71
Nitrogen 7 5 -3 2 3 4 5 14.00
Oxygen 8 1 -2 16.00
Phosphorous P 15 4 -3 3 4 5 30.97
Potassium K 19 1 1 39.10
Silicon Si 14 1 4 28.09
Silver Ag 47 1 1 107.87
Sodium Na 11 1 1 23.00
Sulfur S 16 4 -2 2 4 6 32.06
Tin Sn 50 2 2 4 118.69
Zinc Zn 30 1 2 35.37
```

Figure 3.11.3 *Contents of textfile SORTELEM.DAT.*

Listings 3.52, 3.53, and 3.54 show the source code for versions of the application program TESTBIN. The programs include error handling code to deal with bad input and output file names. Notice that the arrays for the left and right pointer are hidden to the True BASIC application program, while they are global in the other BASIC versions. The QuickBASIC and Turbo BASIC source code shows how the application programs must deal with these arrays.

Listing 3.52. *QuickBASIC source code for program TESTBIN.BAS that sorts text files*

```
' PROGRAM TEST.BINARY.TREE

' Program that uses library BINTREE.BAS to sort a text file
' QuickBASIC version
' Copyright (c) 1987 Namir Clement Shammas

OPTION BASE 1

REM $DYNAMIC
DIM TREE.PTR%(10), BIN.TREE$(10), STACK%(10)
DIM LPTR%(10), RPTR%(10), COPY.ITEM$(10)


' Declare libraries
REM $INCLUDE: 'TOOLBOX0.BAS'
REM $INCLUDE: 'BINTREE.BAS'

DO

  CLS

  CALL Center.Message("TEXTFILE SORTING UTILITY",1)
  CALL Center.Message("------------------------",2)
  CALL Blank.Lines(3)

  ' Obtain input file
  DO

      ON ERROR GOTO Handle.Input

      INPUT "Enter input text filename ";F$
      PRINT
      OPEN "I",1,F$

      EXIT DO

Handle.Input:

      ' Error handler
```

BASIC LIBRARIES

```
            PRINT "Error: Cannot access file ";F$
            PRINT
            INPUT "Enter input text filename ";F$ : PRINT
            RESUME

LOOP

ON ERROR GOTO 0 ' disable error handling

PRINT
PRINT "Reading and sorting ..."
PRINT : PRINT

' Count text lines in the file
NData% = 0
DO UNTIL EOF(1)
    LINE INPUT #1, L$
    NData% = NData% + 1
LOOP

CLOSE #1

' Calculate the size of the smallest "complete" tree
LOG.TREE! = LOG(NData%)/LOG(2)
IF (LOG.TREE! - INT(LOG.TREE!)) > 1E-8 THEN OFFSET% = 1 ELSE OFFSET% = 0
TREE.SIZE% = 2^(OFFSET% + INT(LOG.TREE!)) - 1

' rediemnsion arrays
Erase TREE.PTR%, BIN.TREE$, STACK%
Erase LPTR%, RPTR%, COPY.ITEM$

DIM TREE.PTR%(TREE.SIZE%), BIN.TREE$(TREE.SIZE%), STACK%(TREE.SIZE%)
DIM LPTR%(TREE.SIZE%), RPTR%(TREE.SIZE%), COPY.ITEM$(TREE.SIZE%)

OPEN "I",1,F$
LINE INPUT #1, Text.Line$
' Initialize the binary tree with the firt text line
CALL Initialize(Text.Line$)

FOR I% = 2 TO NData%
    LINE INPUT #1, Text.Line$
    CALL Insert(Text.Line$)
NEXT I%

CLOSE #1

' Obtain pointers for the sorted tree
CALL Get.Sorted.List

' Obtain output file
DO

    ON ERROR GOTO Handle.Output

    INPUT "Enter output text filename ";F$
    PRINT
```

```
        OPEN "O",1,F$
        EXIT DO

Handle.Output:

        ' Error handler
        PRINT "Error: Cannot open file ";F$
        PRINT
        INPUT "Enter output text filename ";F$ : PRINT
        RESUME

    LOOP

    ON ERROR GOTO 0 ' disable error handling

    ' Loop to write sorted text file
    FOR I% = 1 TO Tree.Size%
        IF Tree.Ptr%(I%) <> NIL3% THEN PRINT #1, Bin.Tree$(Tree.Ptr%(I%))
    NEXT I%

    CLOSE #1

    PRINT "text saved in file ";F$
    CALL Blank.Lines(4)
    OK$ = FNYesNo$("Sort another file")

LOOP UNTIL OK$ = "N"

END
```

Listing 3.53. *Turbo BASIC source code for program TESTBIN.BAS that sorts text files*

```
' PROGRAM TEST.BINARY.TREE

' Program that uses module BINTREE.BAS to sort a text file
' Turbo BASIC version
' Copyright (c) 1987 Namir Clement Shammas

' Declare modules used
$INCLUDE "BINTREE.BAS"
$INCLUDE "TOOLBOX0.BAS"

DO

    CLS

    CALL Center.Message("TEXTFILE SORTING UTILITY",1)
    CALL Center.Message("------------------------",2)
```

BASIC LIBRARIES

```
    CALL Blank.Lines(3)

' Obtain input file
DO

    ON ERROR GOTO Handle.Input

    INPUT "Enter input text filename ";F$
    PRINT
    OPEN "I",1,F$

    EXIT LOOP

Handle.Input:

    ' Error handler
    PRINT "Error: Cannot access file ";F$
    PRINT
    INPUT "Enter input text filename ";F$
    PRINT
    RESUME

LOOP

ON ERROR GOTO 0 ' disable error handling

PRINT
PRINT "Reading and sorting ..."
PRINT : PRINT

' Count text lines in the file
NData% = 0
DO UNTIL EOF(1)
    LINE INPUT #1, L$
    INCR NData%
LOOP

CLOSE #1

' Calculate the size of the smallest "complete" tree
LOG.TREE! = LOG(NData%)/LOG(2)
IF (LOG.TREE! - INT(LOG.TREE!)) > 1E-8 THEN OFFSET% = 1 ELSE OFFSET% = 0
TREE.SIZE% = 2^(OFFSET% + INT(LOG.TREE!)) - 1

DIM TREE.PTR%(TREE.SIZE%), BIN.TREE$(TREE.SIZE%), STACK%(TREE.SIZE%)
DIM LPTR%(TREE.SIZE%), RPTR%(TREE.SIZE%), COPY.ITEM$(TREE.SIZE%)

OPEN "I",1,F$
LINE INPUT #1, Text.Line$
' Initialize the binary tree with the firt text line
CALL Initialize(Text.Line$)

FOR I% = 2 TO NData%
    LINE INPUT #1, Text.Line$
    CALL Insert(Text.Line$)
```

```
    NEXT I%

    CLOSE #1

    ' Obtain pointers for the sorted tree
    CALL Get.Sorted.List

    ' Obtain output file
    DO

        ON ERROR GOTO Handle.Output

        INPUT "Enter output text filename ";F$
        PRINT
        OPEN "O",1,F$
        EXIT LOOP

Handle.Output:

        ' Error handler
        PRINT "Error: Cannot open file ";F$
        PRINT
        INPUT "Enter output text filename ";F$
        PRINT
        RESUME

    LOOP

    ON ERROR GOTO 0 ' disable error handling

    ' Loop to write sorted text file
    FOR I% = 1 TO Tree.Size%
        IF Tree.Ptr%(I%) <> %NIL3 THEN PRINT #1, Bin.Tree$(Tree.Ptr%(I%))
    NEXT I%

    CLOSE #1

    PRINT "text saved in file ";F$
    CALL Blank.Lines(4)
    OK$ = FNYesNo$("Sort another file")

LOOP UNTIL OK$ = "N"

END
```

Listing 3.54. *True BASIC source code for program TESTBIN.TRU that sorts text files*

```
PROGRAM TEST_BINARY_TREE_MODULE
```

```
! Program that uses module BINTREE.TRU to sort a text file
! Copyright (c) 1987 Namir Clement Shammas

! Declare modules used
LIBRARY "BINTREE.TRU","TOOLBOX0.TRU"

! Declare public data
DECLARE PUBLIC Tree_Ptr(), Num_Nodes, Tree_Size, Bin_Tree$()

! Declare imported functions
DECLARE DEF NIL3, YesNo$

DO

   CLEAR

   CALL Center_Message("TEXTFILE SORTING UTILITY",1)
   CALL Center_Message("------------------------",2)
   CALL Blank_Lines(3)

   ! Obtain input file
   DO

      WHEN ERROR IN

           INPUT PROMPT "Enter input text filename ? ":F$
           PRINT
           OPEN #1: name F$, access input, organization text, create old
           LINE INPUT #1: Text_Line$
           ! Initialize the binary tree with the firt text line
           CALL Initialize(Text_Line$)
           LET OK$ = "Y"

      USE
           ! Error handler
           PRINT "Error: Cannot access file ";F$
           PRINT
           LET OK$ = "N"

      END WHEN

   LOOP UNTIL OK$ = "Y"

   PRINT
   PRINT "Reading and sorting....."
   PRINT
   PRINT

   ! Read text lines from the file
   DO WHILE MORE #1
       LINE INPUT #1: Text_Line$
       CALL Insert(Text_Line$)
   LOOP

   CLOSE #1
```

```
! Obtain pointers for the sorted tree
CALL Get_Sorted_List

! Obtain output file
DO

    WHEN ERROR IN

        INPUT PROMPT "Enter output text filename ? ":F$
        PRINT
        OPEN #1: name F$, access output, organization text, create newold
        ERASE #1
        LET OK$ = "Y"

    USE
        ! Error handler
        PRINT "Error: Cannot open file ";F$
        PRINT
        LET OK$ = "N"

    END WHEN

LOOP UNTIL OK$ = "Y"

! Loop to write sorted text file
FOR I = 1 TO Tree_Size
    IF Tree_Ptr(I) <> NIL3 THEN PRINT #1 : Bin_Tree$(Tree_Ptr(I))
NEXT I

CLOSE #1

PRINT "text saved in file ";F$
CALL Blank_Lines(4)
LET OK$ = YesNo$("Sort another file")

LOOP UNTIL OK$ = "N"

END
```

Library Module DOSFILE

PURPOSE: The DOSFILE library contains a set of routines to perform the following:

1. invoke a MS-DOS shell from within a BASIC application program

2. obtain the file entries of a particular directory

3. filter the files according to size, time, and date

4. create batch files

5. carry out multi-file text find/replace

Invoking the MS-DOS shell enables you to issue an MS-DOS command from within a running BASIC program. The "DIR" is perhaps the most popular command issue, used to inspect file names and directories. The predefined *SHELL()* command in QuickBASIC and Turbo BASIC is used. In True BASIC you must have file "SHELL TRC" in the same directory with the libraries.

I have chosen to use the *SHELL()* command, instead of inline code, or peeks and pokes. This makes the libraries and sample applications portable between the three implementations.

Accessing the files in a directory is performed by issuing the following BASIC statement:

```
DIR [directory name] > DOSFILE.DAT
```

which redirects the output of "DIR" to file DOSFILE.DAT. The latter file is then opened and read to extract the file names. The directory entries are saved in a string matrix with five columns, as shown:

	File name	Extension	Size	Time	Date
Column number -->	1	2	3	4	5

With the file information in the string matrix, a subroutine is provided to filter the selection according to any of the five attributes

Listings 3.55, 3.56, and 3.57 contain the library source code for the QuickBASIC, Turbo BASIC, and True BASIC versions, respectively.

ROUTINES

The following is a list of headings for function and subroutine definitions borrowed from the QuickBASIC listing. They are identical to those of Turbo BASIC. However, they contain minor syntactical differences compared to those of True BASIC, including:

1. Function names in True BASIC do not have to begin with the letters *FN*.

2. Subroutines in True BASIC need no STATIC declarations.

SUB CallDos STATIC
SUB CallDos ! True BASIC

This subroutine calls a simple MS-DOS shell. You are able to issue as many MS-DOS commands as needed. When an MS-DOS command is terminated, the routines wait for any key to be pressed. This prevents the screen from clearing before you are able to read the display. To exit the MS-DOS shell, you type *Q*.

SUB ToBLank(L$, P%) STATIC
SUB ToBLank(L$, P) ! True BASIC

SUB ToChar(L$, P%) STATIC
SUB ToChar(L$, P) ! True BASIC

These are internal subroutines used to scan for either a nonspace character or a space character.

SUB Parse(L$, Flname$(2), I%) STATIC
SUB Parse(L$, Flname$(,), I) ! True BASIC

This internal subroutine is used to extract the file name, extension name, size, time, and date from string *L$*. The results are stored in the *I*th row of string matrix *Flname$()*.

SUB GetFiles(LePath$, Flname$(2), NFile%) STATIC
SUB GetFiles(LePath$, Flname$(,), NFile) ! True BASIC

This subroutine scans the directory specified by string *LePath$* and returns the file entries, if any are found. The *LePath$* string may also contain file name wildcards to select specific files in the directory.

The Turbo and True BASIC versions employ their error-handling mechanism inside the subroutine. Supplying a bad path name results in prompting the user for a correct file name. Since QuickBASIC does not allow error-handling routines to be placed inside a subroutine, errors must be handled by the application program.

The list of parameters is:

    LePath$ the sought directory [INPUT].

    Flname$()   the matrix of file entries [OUTPUT]

    NFile   the number of files found [OUTPUT];
                    a zero value signals one of the following:

                    1) empty directory
                    2) bad directory name
                    3) wildcard file name specified has no match

SUB SelectFiles(InFlname$(2),OutFlname$(2),
       InFile%,OutFile%,AttrNum%,Attr$,Oper$) STATIC

SUB SelectFiles(InFlname$(,),OutFlname$(,),
       InFile,OutFile,AttrNum,Attr$,Oper$) ! True BASIC

This subroutine selects files using a particular file entry attribute. The selection criterion is:

```
<file entry(,AttrNum)> Oper$ Attr$
```

    InFlname$(,)   the input matrix containing file names [INPUT]

    OutFlname$(,)   the output matrix containing selected files
                      [OUTPUT]

    InFile   number of rows in matrix *InFlname$()* [INPUT]

    OutFile   number of selected files (also number of rows in
                      matrix *OutFlname$()*) [OUTPUT]

AttrNum	attribute number [INPUT] 1 ---> file name 2 ---> extension name 3 ---> file size 4 ---> time 5 ---> date
Attr$	the comparison value [INPUT]
Oper$	the comparison operator [INPUT] = ---> equal <>, #, /= ---> not equal < ---> less than <=, =< ---> less than or equal > ---> greater than >=, => ---> greater than or equal

SUB MakeBat(Flname$(2),NFile%,Bat$,DosCom$, LePath$,Tail$) STATIC

SUB MakeBat(Flname$(,),NFile,Bat$,DosCom$,LePath$,Tail$) ! True BASIC

This subroutine creates a batch file using a file entry matrix and a set of commands to be used in the batch file. The Turbo and True BASIC versions will prompt you for a correct batch file name if a bad one is supplied.

Flname$()	the matrix of file names [INPUT]
NFile	the number of batch commands [INPUT]
Bat$	the batch file name (may include drive and path names) [INPUT]
DosCom$	the leading DOS command; cannot be a null string.[INPUT]
LePath$	the (optional) path name used with the file entries; may be a null string [INPUT]

Tail$ the tail DOS command. May be a null string; may also contain spaces [INPUT]

The batch file *Bat$* will contain *NFile* lines of commands in the following format:

```
DosCom$  LePath$<file name> Tail$
```

To create a batch file for copying the "selected" files from directory "\MYDIR" to "\HISDIR" on drive "B:", set the following:

EXAMPLE:

```
DosCom$ = "COPY"
LePath$ = "\MYDIR\" ' don't forget the trailing '\
Tail$   = "B:\HISDIR"
```

Using the above parameters, the subroutine creates a batch file containing lines in this format:

```
COPY \MYDIR\<file name> B:\HISDIR
```

SUB EditFiles(LePath$(1),Flname$(1),Ext$(1),NFile%,FindStr$(1),ReplaceStr$(1),NStr%,EchoPrint%) STATIC

SUB EditFiles(LePath$(),Flname$(),Ext$(),NFile,FindStr$(), ReplaceStr$(),NStr,EchoPrint) ! True BASIC

This subroutines reads one or more files to find/replace text. The printer may be used to trace the find/replace operation. However, the print trace is required to keep record of the strings found.

Error handling is more elaborate in this subroutine. The Turbo and True BASIC versions use the internal error-handling mechanism to tackle bad file names. Supplying a bad file name will cause a prompt requesting a correct file name.

LePath$()	the array of directories [INPUT]
Flname$()	the array of file names [INPUT]
Ext$()	the array of file name extensions [INPUT]
NFile	the number of files to process [INPUT]
FindStr$()	the array of strings to find [INPUT]
ReplaceStr$()	the array of string replacements; null strings are interpreted as find-only [INPUT]
NStr	the number of find/replace strings [INPUT]
EchoPrint	the print echo flag (0 = do not print, else print) [INPUT]

Each file name processed is constructed by using the array elements of *LePath$()*, *Flname$()*, and *Ext$()* with the same index.

```
I'th file to process = LePath$(I) + Flname$(I) + "." + Ext$(I)
```

SUB Read.Lines(TextFile$, Text.Line$(1), Num.Lines%)
          STATIC
SUB Read_Lines(TextFile$, Text_Line$(), Num_Lines)
          ! True BASIC

Here is an internal subroutine used by the *EditFiles* subroutines. It reads the lines of a sequential textfile.

SUB Write.Lines(TextFile$, Text.Line$(1), Num.Lines%)
          STATIC
SUB Write_Lines(TextFile$, Text_Line$(), Num_Lines)
          ! True BASIC

This is an internal subroutine used by the *EditFiles* subroutines. It writes the lines of a sequential textfile.

Listing 3.55. *QuickBASIC source code for library DOSFILE.BAS.*

```
' LIBRARY DOS.Files

' QuickBASIC library to perform directory manipulations.
' Copyright (c) 1987   Namir Clement Shammas

SUB CallDos STATIC
' Invoke DOS from within BASIC program

DO

    CLS
    INPUT   "Enter DOS command [q = quit] ";DOS$
    PRINT
    IF (INSTR("Qq",DOS$) > 0) THEN EXIT DO
    Shell(DOS$)
    PRINT "press any key "
    A.KEY$ = INPUT$(1)

LOOP

END SUB

SUB ToBLank(L$, P%) STATIC
' Scan string until a blank is Found%

DO UNTIL MID$(L$,P%,1) = " "
    P% = P% + 1
LOOP
END SUB

SUB ToChar(L$, P%) STATIC
' Scan string until a non-blank is Found%

DO WHILE MID$(L$,P%,1) = " "
    P% = P% + 1
LOOP
END SUB


SUB Parse(L$, Flname$(2), I%) STATIC
' Parse string L$ into filename, extension, size, time and date.

Ptr% = INSTR(L$," ")
Flname$(I%,1) = LEFT$(L$,Ptr%-1)

CALL ToChar(L$, Ptr%)
```

```
    Ptr1% = Ptr%  ' index to first char of extension
    CALL ToBlank(L$, Ptr%)
    Ptr2% = Ptr% - 1  ' Index to last char of extension
    Flname$(I%,2) = MID$(L$,Ptr1%,Ptr2%-Ptr1%+1)

    CALL ToChar(L$, Ptr%)
    Ptr1% = Ptr%  ' index to first char of file size
    CALL ToBlank(L$, Ptr%)
    Ptr2% = Ptr% - 1  ' Index to last char of file size
    Flname$(I%,3) = MID$(L$,Ptr1%,Ptr2%-Ptr1%+1)

    CALL ToChar(L$, Ptr%)
    Ptr1% = Ptr%  ' index to first char of time
    CALL ToBlank(L$, Ptr%)
    Ptr2% = Ptr% - 1  ' Index to last char of time
    Flname$(I%,4) = MID$(L$,Ptr1%,Ptr2%-Ptr1%+1)

    CALL ToChar(L$, Ptr%)
    Ptr1% = Ptr%  ' index to first char of date
    Flname$(I%,5) = MID$(L$,Ptr1%)

END SUB


    SUB GetFiles(LePath$, Flname$(2),NFile%) STATIC
    ' Return array of filenames, extensions, file sizes, times and date
    '
    ' LePath$    is the directory path and file selection
    ' Flname$(,1) array of filenames.
    ' Flname$(,2) array of file extension names.
    ' Flname$(,3) array of file sizes
    ' Flname$(,4) array of file creation/update times
    ' Flname$(,5) array of file creation.update dates
    ' NFile%     number of member is arrays.

    Shell("DIR " + LePath$ + " > DOSFILE.DAT")

    OPEN "I",1,"DOSFILE.DAT"

    ' Read first four lines of headings.
    I% = 1
    DO WHILE (NOT EOF(1)) AND (I% < 5)
        LINE INPUT #1, L$
        I% = I% + 1
    LOOP

    I% = 0 ' reset line counter
    DO UNTIL EOF(1)
        LINE INPUT #1, L$
        IF INSTR(" .",LEFT$(L$,1)) = 0 THEN
            I% = I% + 1
                CALL Parse(L$, Flname$(), I%)
        END IF
    LOOP

    CLOSE #1
```

BASIC LIBRARIES 377

```
    IF I% > 0 THEN NFile% = I% ELSE NFile% = 0

END SUB


SUB SelectFiles(InFlname$(2),OutFlname$(2),
                InFile%,OutFile%,AttrNum%,Attr$,Oper$) STATIC
'

IF (InFile% <= 0) OR (Attr$ = "") OR (Oper$ = "") THEN EXIT SUB
IF (AttrNum% < 1) OR (AttrNum% > 5) THEN EXIT SUB

OutFile% = 0

FOR I% = 1 TO InFile%

    SELECT CASE Oper$

        CASE "="
            IF InFlname$(I%,AttrNum%) = Attr$ THEN
                OutFile% = OutFile% + 1
                FOR J% = 1 TO 5
                    OutFlname$(OutFile%,J%) = InFlname$(I%,J%)
                NEXT J%
            END IF

        CASE "<>", "#", "/="
            IF InFlname$(I%,AttrNum%) <> Attr$ THEN
                OutFile% = OutFile% + 1
                FOR J% = 1 TO 5
                    OutFlname$(OutFile%,J%) = InFlname$(I%,J%)
                NEXT J%
            END IF

        CASE "<"
            IF InFlname$(I%,AttrNum%) < Attr$ THEN
                OutFile% = OutFile% + 1
                FOR J% = 1 TO 5
                    OutFlname$(OutFile%,J%) = InFlname$(I%,J%)
                NEXT J%
            END IF

        CASE "<=","=<"
            IF InFlname$(I%,AttrNum%) <= Attr$ THEN
                OutFile% = OutFile% + 1
                FOR J% = 1 TO 5
                    OutFlname$(OutFile%,J%) = InFlname$(I%,J%)
                NEXT J%
            END IF

        CASE ">"
            IF InFlname$(I%,AttrNum%) > Attr$ THEN
                OutFile% = OutFile% + 1
                FOR J% = 1 TO 5
                    OutFlname$(OutFile% J%) = InFlname$(I%,J%)
```

```
                        NEXT J%
                    END IF

                CASE "=>",">="
                    IF InFlname$(I%,AttrNum%) >= Attr$ THEN
                        OutFile% = OutFile% + 1
                        FOR J% = 1 TO 5
                            OutFlname$(OutFile%,J%) = InFlname$(I%,J%)
                        NEXT J%
                    END IF

                CASE ELSE
                    PRINT
                    PRINT "Bad operator: ";Oper$
                    PRINT
            END SELECT

    NEXT I%

END SUB



SUB MakeBat(Flname$(2), NFile%, Bat$, DosCom$, LePath$, Tail$) STATIC

' create a batch file

OPEN "O",1,Bat$

Tail$ = " " + Tail$
Head$ = DosCom$ + " " + LePath$
I% = 1

DO WHILE I% <= NFile%
    L$ = Head$ + Flname$(I%,1) + "." + Flname$(I%,2) + Tail$
    PRINT #1, L$
    I% = I% + 1
LOOP

CLOSE #1

END SUB


SUB EditFiles(LePath$(1),Flname$(1),Ext$(1),NFile%,
              FindStr$(1),ReplaceStr$(1),NStr%,EchoPrint%) STATIC

REM $DYNAMIC
DIM Text.Line$(500)

FOR K = 1 TO NFile%
    F$ = LePath$(K) + Flname$(K) + "." + Ext$(K)
    CALL Read.Lines(F$, Text.Line$(), Num.Lines%)
    IF Num.Lines% > 0 THEN
       Changed% = 0 ' initialize chnage status flag
```

BASIC LIBRARIES

```
            FOR I% = 1 TO NStr%
                Found% = 0
                FOR J% = 1 TO Num.Lines%
                    Ptr% = INSTR(Text.Line$(J%),FindStr$(I%))
                    DO WHILE Ptr% > 0
                        IF (Found% = 0) THEN
                            Found% = 1
                            IF EchoPrint% <> 0 THEN
                                LPRINT
                                LPRINT "KEYWORD ; ";FindStr$(I%)
                            END IF
                        END IF
                        IF EchoPrint% <> 0 THEN LPRINT J%;";";Text.Line$(J%)

                        IF (ReplaceStr$(I%) <> "") THEN
                            Changed% = 1
                            First$ = ""
                            IF Ptr% > 1 THEN First$ = LEFT$(Text.Line$(J%),Ptr%-1)
                            Last$ = ""
                            IF (Ptr%+LEN(FindStr$(I%))) <= LEN(Text.Line$(J%)) THEN
                                Last$ = MID$(Text.Line$(J%),Ptr%+LEN(FindStr$(I%)))
                            END IF
                            Text.Line$(J%) = First$ + ReplaceStr$(I%) + Last$
                        END IF
                        Ptr% = INSTR(Ptr%+1,Text.Line$(J%),FindStr$(I%))
                    LOOP
                NEXT J%
            NEXT I%
            IF (Changed% = 1) THEN CALL Write.Lines(F$, Text.Line$(), Num.Lines%)
      END IF ' Num.Lines% > 0
NEXT K

IF EchoPrint% <> 0 THEN LPRINT CHR$(140) ' form feed

END SUB


SUB Read.Lines(TextFile$, Text.Line$(1), Num.Lines%) STATIC
' Subroutines to read text lines

Num.Lines% = 0

OPEN "I",1,TextFile$

DO UNTIL EOF(1)
   Num.Lines% = Num.Lines% + 1
'  MAT REDIM Text.Line$(Num.Lines%)
   LINE INPUT#1, Text.Line$(Num.Lines%)
LOOP

' clean close and exit.
CLOSE #1

END SUB
```

```
SUB Write.Lines(TextFile$, Text.Line$(1), Num.Lines%) STATIC
' Subroutines to write text lines

IF Num.Lines% < 1 THEN EXIT SUB

OPEN "O",1,TextFile$

FOR I% = 1 TO Num.Lines%
  PRINT #1, Text.Line$(I%)
NEXT I%

CLOSE #1

END SUB
```

Listing 3.56. *Turbo BASIC source code for library DOSFILE.BAS*

```
' LIBRARY DOS.Files

' Turbo BASIC library to perform directory manipulations.
' Copyright (c) 1987  Namir Clement Shammas

SUB CallDos STATIC
' Invoke DOS from within BASIC program

DO

    CLS
    INPUT   "Enter DOS command [q = quit] ";DOS$
    PRINT
    IF (INSTR("Qq",DOS$) > 0) THEN
        PRINT "press any key "
        EXIT LOOP
    END IF
    Shell(DOS$)
    A.KEY$ = INPUT$(1)

LOOP

END SUB

SUB ToBLank(L$, P%) STATIC
' Scan string until a blank is Found%

DO UNTIL MID$(L$,P%,1) = " "
    P% = P% + 1
LOOP
END SUB
```

```
SUB ToChar(L$, P%) STATIC
' Scan string until a non-blank is Found%

DO WHILE MID$(L$,P%,1) = " "
    P% = P% + 1
LOOP
END SUB


SUB Parse(L$, Flname$(2), I%) STATIC
' Parse string L$ into filename, extension, size, time and date.

Ptr% = INSTR(L$," ")
Flname$(I%,1) = LEFT$(L$,Ptr%-1)

CALL ToChar(L$, Ptr%)
Ptr1% = Ptr% ' index to first char of extension
CALL ToBlank(L$, Ptr%)
Ptr2% = Ptr% - 1 ' Index to last char of extension
Flname$(I%,2) = MID$(L$,Ptr1%,Ptr2%-Ptr1%+1)

CALL ToChar(L$, Ptr%)
Ptr1% = Ptr% ' index to first char of file size
CALL ToBlank(L$, Ptr%)
Ptr2% = Ptr% - 1 ' Index to last char of file size
Flname$(I%,3) = MID$(L$,Ptr1%,Ptr2%-Ptr1%+1)

CALL ToChar(L$, Ptr%)
Ptr1% = Ptr% ' index to first char of time
CALL ToBlank(L$, Ptr%)
Ptr2% = Ptr% - 1 ' Index to last char of time
Flname$(I%,4) = MID$(L$,Ptr1%,Ptr2%-Ptr1%+1)

CALL ToChar(L$, Ptr%)
Ptr1% = Ptr% ' index to first char of date
Flname$(I%,5) = MID$(L$,Ptr1%)

END SUB


SUB GetFiles(LePath$, Flname$(2),NFile%) STATIC
' Return array of filenames, extensions, file sizes, times and dates
'
' LePath$    is the directory path and file selection
' Flname$(,1) array of filenames.
' Flname$(,2) array of file extension names.
' Flname$(,3) array of file sizes
' Flname$(,4) array of file creation/update times
' Flname$(,5) array of file creation.update dates
' NFile%     number of member is arrays.

ON ERROR GOTO Exc.GetFiles

Shell("DIR " + LePath$ + " > DOSFILE.DAT")

OPEN "I",1,"DOSFILE.DAT"
```

```
' Read first four lines of headings.
I% = 1
DO WHILE (NOT EOF(1)) AND (I% < 5)
    LINE INPUT #1, L$
    I% = I% + 1
LOOP

I% = 0 ' reset line counter
DO UNTIL EOF(1)
    LINE INPUT #1, L$
    IF (INSTR(" .",LEFT$(L$,1)) = 0) THEN
        I% = I% + 1
        CALL Parse(L$, Flname$(), I%)
    END IF
LOOP

CLOSE #1

IF I% > 0 THEN NFile% = I% ELSE NFile% = 0

ON ERROR GOTO 0

EXIT SUB

Exc.GetFiles:
NFile% = 0
CLOSE#1
ON ERROR GOTO 0


END SUB



SUB
SelectFiles(InFlname$(2),OutFlname$(2),InFile%,OutFile%,AttrNum%,Attr
$,Oper$) STATIC
'

IF (InFile% <= 0) OR (Attr$ = "") OR (Oper$ = "") THEN EXIT SUB
IF (AttrNum% < 1) OR (AttrNum% > 5) THEN EXIT SUB

OutFile% = 0

FOR I% = 1 TO InFile%

    SELECT CASE Oper$

        CASE "="
            IF InFlname$(I%,AttrNum%) = Attr$ THEN
                OutFile% = OutFile% + 1
                FOR J% = 1 TO 5
                    OutFlname$(OutFile%,J%) = InFlname$(I%,J%)
                NEXT J%
            END IF
```

BASIC LIBRARIES

```
            CASE "<>", "#", "/="
                IF InFlname$(I%,AttrNum%) <> Attr$ THEN
                    OutFile% = OutFile% + 1
                    FOR J% = 1 TO 5
                        OutFlname$(OutFile%,J%) = InFlname$(I%,J%)
                    NEXT J%
                END IF

            CASE "<"
                IF InFlname$(I%,AttrNum%) < Attr$ THEN
                    OutFile% = OutFile% + 1
                    FOR J% = 1 TO 5
                        OutFlname$(OutFile%,J%) = InFlname$(I%,J%)
                    NEXT J%
                END IF

            CASE "<=","=<"
                IF InFlname$(I%,AttrNum%) <= Attr$ THEN
                    OutFile% = OutFile% + 1
                    FOR J% = 1 TO 5
                        OutFlname$(OutFile%,J%) = InFlname$(I%,J%)
                    NEXT J%
                END IF

            CASE ">"
                IF InFlname$(I%,AttrNum%) > Attr$ THEN
                    OutFile% = OutFile% + 1
                    FOR J% = 1 TO 5
                        OutFlname$(OutFile%,J%) = InFlname$(I%,J%)
                    NEXT J%
                END IF

            CASE "=>",">="
                IF InFlname$(I%,AttrNum%) >= Attr$ THEN
                    OutFile% = OutFile% + 1
                    FOR J% = 1 TO 5
                        OutFlname$(OutFile%,J%) = InFlname$(I%,J%)
                    NEXT J%
                END IF

            CASE ELSE
                PRINT
                PRINT "Bad operator: ";Oper$
                PRINT

        END SELECT

    NEXT I%

END SUB



SUB MakeBat(Flname$(2), NFile%, Bat$, DosCom$, LePath$, Tail$) STATIC
' create a batch file
```

```
ON ERROR GOTO Err.MakeBat

OPEN "O",1,Bat$

Tail$ = " " + Tail$
Head$ = DosCom$ + " " + LePath$
I% = 1

DO WHILE I% <= NFile%
    L$ = Head$ + Flname$(I%,1) + "." + Flname$(I%,2) + Tail$
    PRINT #1, L$
    I% = I% + 1
LOOP

CLOSE #1
ON ERROR GOTO 0

EXIT SUB

Err.MakeBat:
  PRINT
  PRINT "Error : Cannot open file ";Bat$ : PRINT
  INPUT "Enter correct batch filename ";Bat$ : PRINT
  RESUME

END SUB


SUB EditFiles(LePath$(1),Flname$(1),Ext$(1),NFile%,
              FindStr$(1),ReplaceStr$(1),NStr%,EchoPrint%) STATIC

DIM DYNAMIC Text.Line$(500)

FOR K = 1 TO NFile%
    F$ = LePath$(K) + Flname$(K) + "." + Ext$(K)
    CALL Read.Lines(F$, Text.Line$(), Num.Lines%)
    IF Num.Lines% > 0 THEN
      Changed% = 0 ' initialize chnage status flag
      FOR I% = 1 TO NStr%
          Found% = 0
          FOR J% = 1 TO Num.Lines%
              Ptr% = INSTR(Text.Line$(J%),FindStr$(I%))
              DO WHILE Ptr% > 0
                 IF (Found% = 0) THEN
                    Found% = 1
                    IF EchoPrint% <> 0 THEN
                       LPRINT
                       LPRINT "KEYWORD ; ";FindStr$(I%)
                    END IF
                 END IF
                 IF EchoPrint% <> 0 THEN LPRINT  J%;";";Text.Line$(J%)
                 IF (ReplaceStr$(I%) <> "") THEN
                    Changed% = 1
                    First$ = ""
                    IF Ptr% > 1 THEN First$ = LEFT$(Text.Line$(J%),Ptr%-1)
```

BASIC LIBRARIES   385

```
                          Last$ = ""
                          IF (Ptr%+LEN(FindStr$(I%)') <= LEN(Text.Line$(J%)) THEN
                             Last$ =
MID$(Text.Line$(J%),Ptr%+LEN(FindStr$(I%)))
                          END IF
                          Text.Line$(J%) = First$ + ReplaceStr$(I%) + Last$
                       END IF
                       Ptr% = INSTR(Ptr%+1,Text.Line$(J%),FindStr$(I%))
                LOOP
          NEXT J%
      NEXT I%
      IF (Changed% = 1) THEN CALL Write.Lines(F$, Text.Line$(), Num.Lines%)
   END IF ' Num.Lines% > 0
NEXT K

IF EchoPrint% <> 0 THEN LPRINT CHR$(140) ' form feed

Erase Text.Line$

END SUB


SUB Read.Lines(TextFile$, Text.Line$(1), Num.Lines%) STATIC
' Subroutines to read text lines

Num.Lines% = 0
ON ERROR GOTO Err.Read.Lines

OPEN "I",1,TextFile$

DO UNTIL EOF(1)
   Num.Lines% = Num.Lines% + 1
   LINE INPUT#1, Text.Line$(Num.Lines%)
LOOP

' clean close and exit.
CLOSE #1
ON ERROR GOTO 0
EXIT SUB

Err.Read.Lines:
   PRINT
   PRINT "Error : Cannot open file ";TextFile$ : PRINT
   INPUT "Enter correct filename ";TextFile$ : PRINT
   RESUME

END SUB


SUB Write.Lines(TextFile$, Text.Line$(1), Num.Lines%) STATIC
' Subroutines to write text lines

IF Num.Lines% < 1 THEN EXIT SUB

OPEN "O",1,TextFile$
```

```
FOR I% = 1 TO Num.Lines%
   PRINT #1, Text.Line$(I%)
NEXT I%

CLOSE #1

END SUB
```

Listing 3.57. *True BASIC source code for module DOSFILE.TRU*

```
MODULE DOS_Files

! True BASIC module to perform directory manipulations.
! Copyright (c) 1987  Namir Clement Shammas

LIBRARY "SHELL.TRU"

SUB CallDos
! Invoke DOS from within BASIC program
DO

    CLEAR
    INPUT PROMPT "Enter DOS command [q = quit] : ":DOS$
    PRINT
    IF UCASE$(DOS$) = "Q" THEN
        PRINT "press any key "
        EXIT DO
    END IF
    CALL Shell(DOS$)
    GET KEY A_KEY

LOOP

END SUB

SUB ToBLank(L$, P)
! Scan string until a blank is found

DO UNTIL L$[P:P] = " "
    LET P = P + 1
LOOP
END SUB

SUB ToChar(L$, P)
! Scan string until a non-blank is found

DO WHILE L$[P:P] = " "
    LET P = P + 1
LOOP
END SUB
```

```
SUB Parse(L$, Flname$(,), I)
! Parse string L$ into filename, extension, size, time and date.

LET Ptr = POS(L$," ")
LET Flname$(I,1) = L$[1:Ptr-1]

CALL ToChar(L$, Ptr)
LET Ptr1 = Ptr ! index to first char of extension
CALL ToBlank(L$, Ptr)
LET Ptr2 = Ptr - 1 ! Index to last char of extension
LET Flname$(I,2) = L$[Ptr1:Ptr2]

CALL ToChar(L$, Ptr)
LET Ptr1 = Ptr ! index to first char of file size
CALL ToBlank(L$, Ptr)
LET Ptr2 = Ptr - 1 ! Index to last char of file size
LET Flname$(I,3) = L$[Ptr1:Ptr2]

CALL ToChar(L$, Ptr)
LET Ptr1 = Ptr ! index to first char of time
CALL ToBlank(L$, Ptr)
LET Ptr2 = Ptr - 1 ! Index to last char of time
LET Flname$(I,4) = L$[Ptr1:Ptr2]

CALL ToChar(L$, Ptr)
LET Ptr1 = Ptr ! index to first char of date
LET Ptr2 = LEN(L$) ! Index to last char of date
LET Flname$(I,5) = L$[Ptr1:Ptr2]

END SUB


SUB GetFiles(LePath$, Flname$(,),NFile)
! Return array of filenames, extensions, file sizes, times and dates
!
! LePath$    is the directory path and file selection
! Flname$(,1) array of filenames.
! Flname$(,2) array of file extension names.
! Flname$(,3) array of file sizes
! Flname$(,4) array of file creation/update times
! Flname$(,5) array of file creation.update dates
! NFile      number of member is arrays.

CALL Shell("DIR " & LePath$ & " > DOSFILE.DAT")

OPEN #99: name "DOSFILE.DAT", organization text, create old, access input

! Read first four lines of headings.
LET I = 1
DO WHILE (MORE #99) AND (I < 5)
    LINE INPUT #99: L$
    LET I = I + 1
LOOP
```

```
        LET I = 0 ! reset line counter
        DO WHILE MORE #99
            LINE INPUT #99: L$
            IF POS(" .",L$[1:1]) = 0 THEN
                LET I = I + 1
                CALL Parse(L$, Flname$(,), I)
            END IF
        LOOP

        CLOSE #99

        IF I > 0 THEN LET NFile = I ELSE LET NFile = 0

        END SUB


        SUB SelectFiles(InFname$(,),OutFname$(,),InFile,
                        OutFile,AttrNum,Attr$,Oper$)
        !

        IF (InFile <= 0) OR (Attr$ = "") OR (Oper$ = "") THEN EXIT SUB
        IF (AttrNum < 1) OR (AttrNum > 5) THEN EXIT SUB

        LET OutFile = 0

        FOR I = 1 TO InFile

            SELECT CASE Oper$

                CASE "="
                    IF InFname$(I,AttrNum) = Attr$ THEN
                        LET OutFile = OutFile + 1
                        FOR J = 1 TO 5
                            LET OutFname$(OutFile,J) = InFname$(I,J)
                        NEXT J
                    END IF

                CASE "<>", "#", "/="
                    IF InFname$(I,AttrNum) <> Attr$ THEN
                        LET OutFile = OutFile + 1
                        FOR J = 1 TO 5
                            LET OutFname$(OutFile,J) = InFname$(I,J)
                        NEXT J
                    END IF

                CASE "<"
                    IF InFname$(I,AttrNum) < Attr$ THEN
                        LET OutFile = OutFile + 1
                        FOR J = 1 TO 5
                            LET OutFname$(OutFile,J) = InFname$(I,J)
                        NEXT J
                    END IF

                CASE "<=","=<"
                    IF InFname$(I,AttrNum) <= Attr$ THEN
```

BASIC LIBRARIES

```
                    LET OutFile = OutFile + 1
                    FOR J = 1 TO 5
                        LET OutFname$(OutFile,J) = InFname$(I,J)
                    NEXT J
                END IF

            CASE ">"
                IF InFname$(I,AttrNum) > Attr$ THEN
                    LET OutFile = OutFile + 1
                    FOR J = 1 TO 5
                        LET OutFname$(OutFile,J) = InFname$(I,J)
                    NEXT J
                END IF

            CASE "=>",">="
                IF InFname$(I,AttrNum) >= Attr$ THEN
                    LET OutFile = OutFile + 1
                    FOR J = 1 TO 5
                        LET OutFname$(OutFile,J) = InFname$(I,J)
                    NEXT J
                END IF

            CASE ELSE
                PRINT
                PRINT "Bad operator: ";Oper$
                PRINT

        END SELECT

    NEXT I

END SUB



SUB MakeBat(Flname$(,), NFile, Bat$, DosCom$, LePath$, Tail$)
! create a batch file

DO
 WHEN ERROR IN

    OPEN #99: name Bat$, access output, create newold, organization text
    ERASE #99

    LET Tail$ = " " & Tail$
    LET Head$ = DosCom$ & " " & LePath$
    LET I = 1

    DO WHILE I <= NFile
        LET L$ = Head$ & Flname$(I,1) & "." & Flname$(I,2) & Tail$
        PRINT #99: L$
        LET I = I + 1
    LOOP
    LET OK = 1

 USE
```

```
         PRINT
         PRINT "Error: Cannot open file ";Bat$
         PRINT
         INPUT PROMPT "Enter correct filename ? ":Bat$
         PRINT
         LET OK = 0

      END WHEN

   LOOP UNTIL OK = 1

   CLOSE #99

   END SUB


   SUB EditFiles(LePath$(),Flname$(),Ext$(),NFile,FindStr$(),
       ReplaceStr$(), NStr, EchoPrint)

   DIM Text_Line$(10)

   IF EchoPrint <> 0 THEN OPEN #98: PRINTER

   FOR K = 1 TO NFile
      LET F$ = LePath$(K) & Flname$(K) & "." & Ext$(K)
      CALL Read_Lines(F$, Text_Line$(), Num_Lines)
      IF Num_Lines > 0 THEN
        LET Changed = 0 ! initialize chnage status flag
        FOR I = 1 TO NStr
           LET Found = 0
           FOR J = 1 TO Num_Lines
              LET Ptr = POS(Text_Line$(J),FindStr$(I))
              DO WHILE Ptr > 0
                 IF (Found = 0) THEN
                    LET Found = 1
                    IF EchoPrint <> 0 THEN
                       PRINT #98
                       PRINT #98 : "KEYWORD : ";FindStr$(I)
                    END IF
                 END IF
                 IF EchoPint <> 0 THEN PRINT #98 : J;":";Text_Line$(J)
                 IF (ReplaceStr$(I) <> "") THEN
                    LET Changed = 1
                    LET First$ = ""
                    IF Ptr > 1 THEN LET First$ = Text_Line$(J)[1:(Ptr-1)]
                    LET Last$ = ""
                    IF (Ptr+LEN(FindStr$(I))) <= LEN(Text_Line$(J)) THEN
                       LET Last$ = Text_Line$(J)[Ptr+LEN(FindStr$(I)):MAXNUM]
                    END IF
                    LET Text_Line$(J) = First$ & ReplaceStr$(I) & Last$
                 END IF
                 LET Ptr = POS(Text_Line$(J),FindStr$(I),Ptr+1)
              LOOP
           NEXT J
        NEXT I
```

```
         IF (Changed = 1) THEN CALL Write_Lines(F$, Text_Line$(), Num_LInes)
   END IF ! Num_Lines > 0
NEXT K

IF EchoPrint <> 0 THEN
    PRINT #98 : CHR$(140) ! form feed
    CLOSE #98
END IF

END SUB


SUB Read_Lines(TextFile$, Text_Line$(), Num_Lines)
! Subroutines to read text lines

LET Num_Lines = 0
DO
 WHEN ERROR IN

    OPEN #99: name TextFile$, access input, create old, organization text

    DO WHILE  MORE #99
       LET Num_Lines = Num_Lines + 1
       MAT REDIM Text_Line$(Num_Lines)
       LINE INPUT#99: Text_Line$(Num_Lines)
    LOOP
    LET OK = 1
 USE
    PRINT
    PRINT "Error: Cannot open file ";TextFile$
    PRINT
    INPUT PROMPT "Enter correct filename ? ":TextFile$
    PRINT
    LET OK = 0
 END WHEN
LOOP UNTIL OK = 1

CLOSE #99

END SUB


SUB Write_Lines(TextFile$, Text_Line$(), Num_Lines)
! Subroutines to write text lines

IF Num_Lines < 1 THEN EXIT SUB

OPEN #99: name TextFile$, access output, create old, organization text
ERASE #99

FOR I = 1 TO Num_Lines
  PRINT #99 : Text_Line$(I)
NEXT I

CLOSE #99
```

```
END SUB

END MODULE
```

I have written two application programs to demonstrate the use of library DOSFILE. The first application creates a batch file. The second performs a translation (that is, find/replace strings) operation on the batch file.

The first application, TESTDOS1, has a simple menu with three options: exit, invoke the MS-DOS shell, and create a batch file. Figure 3.12.1 shows the screen image when the True BASIC version begins to run. The figure also reveals that option one is selected to invoke the MS-DOS shell.

```
            BATCH FILE CREATION PROGRAM
            ---------------------------

0) Exit.

1) Invoke the DOS shell.

2) Create a batch file.




Enter choice by number : 1
```

Figure 3.12.1 *First screen image for program TESTDOS1.TRU running under True BASIC.*

Once in the MS-DOS shell, I select to issue a "dir t*.*" command to display all file names starting with the letter *t*. Figure 3.12.2 shows the command typed and the displayed directory (your displayed directories may be different). After examining the information, press any key to return to the BASIC DOS shell prompt. Type *Q* to exit to the main menu.

```
Enter DOS command [q = quit] : dir t* *
  Volume in drive U is Hard Dsk 20
  Directory of   U:\

TOOLBOX0  TRU       8246   1-14-87     :57a
TOOLBOX1  TRU       9651   1-11-87    9:32p
TESTNUM1  TRU       1783   1-12-87    7:27a
TESTNUM2  TRU       1866   1-12-87    1:59a
TESTNUM3  TRU       2527   1-12-87    2:38a
TESTSTAT  TRU       1303   1-12-87    3:47p
TESTLINR  TRU       1209   1-12-87    1:41p
TESTSORT  TRU       2359   1-12-87    8:14p
TESTDOS1  TRU       3197   1-14-87   10:07a
TESTBIN   TRU       2051   1-14-87    2:19a
TESTLIST  TRU       2108   1-13-87    7:06a
TESTSETS  TRU       1729   1-13-87    2:45p
TESTDOS2  TRU       2231   1-14-87   12:30a
       13 File(s)    6805504 bytes free
```

Figure 3.12.2 *Screen image for program TESTDOS1.TRU displaying a ' dir' command issued under the DOS shell.*

In the main menu, select option two to create a batch file. This BASIC application is written with a number of exit points. You may abort the operation if you realize that a batch file will be created with the wrong commands or specifications.

Figure 3.12.3 shows the screen display after the first step of the batch file creation. In this step you select a directory and you may specify wildcards for the file names. Notice that with True BASIC you must type two quotes to select all of the files in the current directory. By contrast, you just press the [ENTER] key with the other BASICs. The figure shows that the *t* * * wildcard is used to select those files with names starting with the letter *t*.

Once the list is displayed, you are asked whether or not you wish to continue (your first exit point). For the sake of the demonstration, enter *Y* to continue.

```
Enter directory (two quotes for current directory) ? t*.*

TOOLBOX0    TRU   8246    1-14-87    5:57a
TOOLBOX1    TRU   9651    1-11-87    9:32p
TESTNUM1    TRU   1783    1-12-87    7:27a
TESTNUM2    TRU   1866    1-12-87    1:59a
TESTNUM3    TRU   2527    1-12-87    2:38a
TESTSTAT    TRU   1303    1-12-87    3:47p
TESTLINR    TRU   1209    1-12-87    1:41p
TESTSORT    TRU   2359    1-12-87    8:14p
TESTDOS1    TRU   3197    1-14-87    10:07a
TESTBIN     TRU   2051    1-14-87    2:19a
TESTLIST    TRU   2108    1-13-87    7:06a
TESTSETS    TRU   1729    1-13-87    2:45p
TESTDOS2    TRU   2231    1-14-87    12:30a


Continue (Y/N) ? y
```

Figure 3.12.3 *Screen image for program TESTDOS1.TRU to display the files obtained by calling subroutine 'GetFile'.*

The second stage in the program is to filter the files at hand and obtain a subset that conforms to some desired criteria. The selection prompts are placed in an open DO-LOOP. This enables you to select files using multiple logically ANDed conditions.

I will choose to select only those files that are greater than 3,000 bytes in size. Looking at the one-line menu, type *1* and enter *3000* and *>* for the attribute value and operator, respectively. This is translated internally into:

```
Select files such that: file size > 3000
```

Figure 3.12.4 shows the screen image for the above selection.

BASIC LIBRARIES

```
Select files by size, time or date (Y/N) ? y

Select by  0) Escape   1) Size    2) Time    3) Date

Select by number : 1

Enter attribute value : 3000

Enter attribute operator : >

Select files by size, time or date (Y/N) ? n
```

Figure 3.12.4 *Screen image for program TESTDOS1.TRU to display the file selection query.*

Next, the BASIC program lists the file selected, as shown in figure 3.12.5. There are only three entries that satisfy the selection criteria. At this point, the program asks whether or not to continue the batch file creation. This is your second and last chance to back out of the operation. Type *Y* to continue.

```
The following files have been selected for the batch file

TOOLBOX0    TRU   8246      1-14-87    5:57a
TOOLBOX1    TRU   9651      1-11-87    9:32p
TESTDOS1    TRU   3197      1-14-87    10:07a

Continue (Y/N) ? y
```

Figure 3.12.5 *Screen image for program TESTDOS1.TRU displaying the selected files.*

The third and last step in the batch file creation is specifying the batch file name and its contents. I will use my RAM-disk (drive D:) as the location where the batch file KOPY.BAT is created. I want to use the batch file to copy the selected files from directory C:\TRUE to the main directory in drive *A*. Figure 3.12.6 shows the program's prompts and my input.

```
Enter name (and directory path) for batch file ? D:\KOPY.BAT

Enter leading DOS command : COPY

Enter directory for files : C:\TRUE\

Enter tail DOS command : A:\

Information correct (Y/N) ? y
```

Figure 3.12.6 *Screen image for program TESTDOS1.TRU displaying the selected files.*

After the last input, the batch file is created and the main menu is displayed. Select option zero to exit the program. Figure 3.12.7 lists the contents of the KOPY.BAT batch file.

```
COPY C:\TRUE\TOOLBOX0.TRU A:\

COPY C:\TRUE\TOOLBOX1.TRU A:\

COPY C:\TRUE\TESTDOS1.TRU A:\
```

Figure 3.12.7 *Contents of batch file KOPY.BAT.*

Listing 3.58. *QuickBASIC source code for program TESTDOS1.BAS that creates batch files*

```
'PROGRAM Test.DOS1

' QuickBASIC program that uses module DOSFILE.BAS
' to create batch files.
' Copyright (c) 1987 Namir Clement Shammas

OPTION BASE 1

DIM F$(200,5),G$(200,5)

' Include libraries used
REM $INCLUDE: 'DOSFILE.BAS'
REM $INCLUDE: 'TOOLBOX0.BAS'

DO
    CLS
    CALL Center.Message("BATCH FILE CREATION PROGRAM",1)
    CALL Center.Message("--------------------------",2)
    CALL Blank.Lines(3)
    PRINT TAB(10);"0) Exit."
    PRINT
    PRINT TAB(10);"1) Invoke the DOS shell."
    PRINT
    PRINT TAB(10);"2) Create a batch file."
    LOCATE 15,10
    Choice% = FNInteger.In.Range%("Enter choice by number",0,2)

    SELECT CASE Choice%
      CASE 0
        CLS
        PRINT "End of program"

      CASE 1
        CALL CallDos

      CASE 2
        GOSUB Create.Batch

      CASE ELSE
        ' do nothing
    END SELECT

LOOP UNTIL Choice% = 0

END

Create.Batch:
' Subroutine to create batch files
```

```
CLS
INPUT "Enter directory (press the [Enter] key for current directory) ";LePath$
PRINT
CALL GetFiles(LePath$, F$(), NFile%)
IF NFile% > 0 THEN
    FOR I% = 1 TO NFile%
        IF ((I% MOD 20) = 0) THEN
            PRINT "press any key to continue.....";
            A.KEY$ = INPUT$(1)
            CLS
        END IF

        PRINT F$(I%,1);TAB(13);F$(I%,2);TAB(18);F$(I%,3);
        PRINT TAB(30);F$(I%,4);TAB(40);F$(I%,5)

        FOR J% = 1 TO 5
            G$(I%,J%) = F$(I%,J%)
        NEXT J%
    NEXT I%
ELSE
    RETURN
END IF

CALL Blank.Lines(2)
OK$ = FNYesNo$("Continue")
PRINT
IF OK$ = "N" THEN RETURN ' stop here

OutFile% = NFile%

DO
 OK$ = FNYesNo$("Select files by size, time or date")
 PRINT
 IF OK$ = "Y" THEN
    PRINT "Select by  0) Escape  1) Size   2) Time   3) Date"
    PRINT
    AttrNum% = FNInteger.In.Range%("Select by number",0,3)
    IF AttrNum% > 0 THEN
        AttrNum% = AttrNum% + 2 ' adjust to correct value
        PRINT
        INPUT  "Enter attribute value ";Attr$
        PRINT
        INPUT  "Enter attribute operator ";Oper$
        PRINT
        CALL SelectFiles(F$(),G$(),NFile%,OutFile%,AttrNum%,Attr$,Oper$)
    ELSE
        OK$ = "N"
    END IF
  END IF

LOOP UNTIL OK$ = "N"

CLS
PRINT "The following files have been selected for the batch file'
PRINT
FOR I% = 1 TO OutFile%
```

```
    IF ((I% MOD 20) = 0) THEN
        PRINT "press any key to continue.....";
        A.KEY$ = INPUT$(1)
        CLS
    END IF
    PRINT G$(I%,1);TAB(13);G$(I%,2);TAB(17);G$(I%,3);
    PRINT TAB(30);G$(I%,4);TAB(40);G$(I%,5)

NEXT I%

PRINT
OK$ = FNYesNo$("Continue")
PRINT
IF OK$ = "N" THEN RETURN ' stop here

DO

  PRINT
  INPUT "Enter name (and directory path) for batch file ";LePath$
  PRINT
  INPUT "Enter leading DOS command ";DosCom$
  PRINT
  INPUT "Enter directory for files ";LeDir$
  PRINT
  INPUT "Enter tail DOS command ";Tail$
  PRINT
  OK$ = FNYesNo$("Information correct")

LOOP UNTIL OK$ = "Y"

DO
  ' Turn error handling on
  ON ERROR GOTO File.Err

  CALL MakeBat(G$(),OutFile%,LePath$,DosCom$,LeDir$,Tail$)

  Error.Flag% = 0

  ON ERROR GOTO 0

LOOP UNTIL Error.Flag% = 0

RETURN

File.Err:
  PRINT : PRINT "Bad filename ";LePath$ : PRINT
  INPUT "Enter new batch filename ";LePath$ : PRINT
  Error.Flag% = 1
  RESUME
```

Listing 3.59. *Turbo BASIC source code for program TESTDOS1.BAS that creates batch files*

```
'PROGRAM Test.DOS1

' Turbo BASIC program that uses module DOSFILE.BAS
' to create batch files.
' Copyright (c) 1987 Namir Clement Shammas

OPTION BASE 1

DIM F$(200,5),G$(200,5)

' Include libraries used
$INCLUDE "DOSFILE.BAS"
$INCLUDE "TOOLBOX0.BAS"

DO
    CLS
    CALL Center.Message("BATCH FILE CREATION PROGRAM",1)
    CALL Center.Message("---------------------------",2)
    CALL Blank.Lines(3)
    PRINT TAB(10);"0) Exit."
    PRINT
    PRINT TAB(10);"1) Invoke the DOS shell."
    PRINT
    PRINT TAB(10);"2) Create a batch file."
    LOCATE 15,10
    Choice% = FNInteger.In.Range%("Enter choice by number",0,2)

    SELECT CASE Choice%
      CASE 0
        CLS
        PRINT "End of program"

      CASE 1
        CALL CallDos

      CASE 2
        GOSUB Create.Batch

      CASE ELSE
        ' do nothing

    END SELECT

LOOP UNTIL Choice% = 0

END

Create.Batch:
' Subroutine to create batch files
```

BASIC LIBRARIES

```
CLS
INPUT "Enter directory (press the [Enter] key for current directory) ";LePath$
PRINT
CALL GetFiles(LePath$, F$(), NFile%)
IF NFile% > 0 THEN
    FOR I% = 1 TO NFile%
        IF ((I% MOD 20) = 0) THEN
            PRINT "press any key to continue.....";
            A.KEY$ = INPUT$(1)
            CLS
        END IF

        PRINT F$(I%,1);TAB(13);F$(I%,2);TAB(18);F$(I%,3);
        PRINT TAB(30);F$(I%,4);TAB(40);F$(I%,5)

        FOR J% = 1 TO 5
            G$(I%,J%) = F$(I%,J%)
        NEXT J%
    NEXT I%
ELSE
    RETURN
END IF

CALL Blank.Lines(2)
OK$ = FNYesNo$("Continue")
PRINT
IF OK$ = "N" THEN RETURN   ' stop here

OutFile% = NFile%

DO
 OK$ = FNYesNo$("Select files by size, time or date")
 PRINT
 IF OK$ = "Y" THEN
    PRINT "Select by  0) Escape  1) Size    2) Time    3) Date"
    PRINT
    AttrNum% = FNInteger.In.Range%("Select by number",0,3)
    IF AttrNum% > 0 THEN
        AttrNum% = AttrNum% + 2   ' adjust to correct value
        PRINT
        INPUT  "Enter attribute value ";Attr$
        PRINT
        INPUT   "Enter attribute operator ";Oper$
        PRINT
        CALL SelectFiles(F$(),G$(),NFile%,OutFile%,AttrNum%,Attr$,Oper$)
    ELSE
        OK$ = "N"
    END IF
  END IF

LOOP UNTIL OK$ = "N"

CLS
PRINT "The following files have been selected for the batch file"
PRINT
FOR I% = 1 TO OutFile%
```

```
      IF ((I% MOD 20) = 0) THEN
          PRINT "press any key to continue.... ";
          A.KEY$ = INPUT$(1)
          CLS
      END IF
      PRINT G$(I%,1);TAB(13);G$(I%,2);TAB(17);G$(I%,3);
      PRINT TAB(30);G$(I%,4);TAB(40);G$(I%,5)

NEXT I%

PRINT
OK$ = FNYesNo$("Continue")
PRINT
IF OK$ = "N" THEN RETURN ' stop here

DO

  PRINT
  INPUT "Enter name (and directory path) for batch file ";LePath$
  PRINT
  INPUT "Enter leading DOS command ";DosCom$
  PRINT
  INPUT "Enter directory for files ";LeDir$
  PRINT
  INPUT "Enter tail DOS command ";Tail$
  PRINT
  OK$ = FNYesNo$("Information correct")

LOOP UNTIL OK$ = "Y"

CALL MakeBat(G$(),OutFile%,LePath$,DosCom$,LeDir$,Tail$, ErrorFlag%)

RETURN
```

Listing 3.60. *Tru BASIC source code for program TESTDOS1.TRUE that creates batch files*

```
PROGRAM Test_DOS1

! True BASIC program that uses module DOSFILE.TRU
! to create batch files.
! Copyright (c) 1987 Namir Clement Shammas

OPTION BASE 1

DIM F$(200,5),G$(200,5)

! Declare libraries used
LIBRARY "DOSFILE.TRU","TOOLBOX0.TRU"
```

```
! Decalre imported functions
DECLARE DEF YesNo$, Integer_In_Range

DO
    CLEAR
    CALL Center_Message("BATCH FILE CREATION PROGRAM",1)
    CALL Center_Message("---------------------------",2)
    CALL Blank_Lines(3)
    PRINT TAB(10);"0) Exit."
    PRINT
    PRINT TAB(10);"1) Invoke the DOS shell."
    PRINT
    PRINT TAB(10);"2) Create a batch file."
    SET CURSOR 15,10
    LET Choice = Integer_In_Range("Enter choice by number",0,2)

    SELECT CASE Choice
       CASE 0
          CLEAR
          PRINT "End of program"

       CASE 1
          CALL CallDos

       CASE 2
          CALL Create_Batch

       CASE ELSE
          ! do nothing

    END SELECT

LOOP UNTIL Choice = 0


SUB Create_Batch
! Subroutine to create batch files

CLEAR
INPUT PROMPT "Enter directory (two quotes for current directory) ? ":LePath$
PRINT
CALL GetFiles(LePath$, F$(,),NFile)
IF NFile > 0 THEN
    FOR I = 1 TO NFILE
        IF MOD(I,20) = 0 THEN
            PRINT "press any key to continue.....";
            GET KEY A_KEY
            CLEAR
        END IF
        PRINT F$(I,1);TAB(13);F$(I,2);TAB(18);F$(I,3);
        PRINT TAB(30);F$(I,4);TAB(40);F$(I,5)
        FOR J = 1 TO 5
            LET G$(I,J) = F$(I,J)
        NEXT J
    NEXT I
ELSE
```

```
        EXIT SUB
    END IF

    CALL Blank_Lines(2)
    LET OK$ = YesNo$("Continue")
    PRINT
    IF OK$ = "N" THEN EXIT SUB ! stop here

    LET OutFile = NFile

    DO
       LET OK$ = YesNo$("Select files by size, time or date")
       PRINT
       IF OK$ = "Y" THEN
          PRINT "Select by  0) Escape  1) Size    2) Time    3) Date"
          PRINT
          LET AttrNum = Integer_In_Range("Select by number",0,3)
          IF AttrNum > 0 THEN
              LET AttrNum = AttrNum + 2 ! adjust to correct value
              PRINT
              INPUT PROMPT "Enter attribute value : ":Attr$
              PRINT
              INPUT PROMPT "Enter attribute operator : ":Oper$
              PRINT
              CALL SelectFiles(F$(,),G$(,),NFile,OutFile,AttrNum,Attr$,Oper$)
          ELSE
              LET OK$ = "N"
          END IF
       END IF

    LOOP UNTIL OK$ = "N"

    CLEAR
    PRINT "The following files have been selected for the batch file"
    PRINT
    FOR I = 1 TO OutFile
       IF MOD(I,20) = 0 THEN
           PRINT "press any key to continue.....";
           GET KEY A_KEY
           CLEAR
       END IF
       PRINT G$(I,1);TAB(13);G$(I,2);TAB(18);G$(I,3);
       PRINT TAB(30);G$(I,4);TAB(40);G$(I,5)
    NEXT I

    PRINT
    LET OK$ = YesNo$("Continue")
    PRINT
    IF OK$ = "N" THEN EXIT SUB ! stop here

    DO

       PRINT
       INPUT PROMPT "Enter name (and directory path) for batch file ? ":LePath$
       PRINT
       INPUT PROMPT "Enter leading DOS command : ":DosCom$
```

```
    PRINT
    INPUT PROMPT "Enter directory for files : ":LeDir$
    PRINT
    INPUT PROMPT "Enter tail DOS command : ":Tail$
    PRINT
    LET OK$ = YesNo$("Information correct")

LOOP UNTIL OK$ = "Y"

CALL MakeBat(G$(,),OutFile,LePath$,DosCom$,LeDir$,Tail$)

END SUB

END
```

The QuickBASIC version of TESTDOS1.BAS contains the error-handler to tackle a bad file name. The user is prompted for a correct batch file name and the execution RESUMEs at the offending BASIC line, inside the subroutine.

The second BASIC application program, TESTDOS2, is the driver for the multi-file text find/replace routine. The program runs in the following sequence:

1. offers the option to enter the MS-DOS shell

2. enters the default values for the directory name, file name, and file extension; this is useful in minimizing keystrokes (and typos) when entering similar file names

3. enters the number and file names to process

4. enters the search and replace strings; when a replacement string is assigned a null string, the corresponding search string is used in a find-only operation

I have run the TESDOS2.BAS under Turbo BASIC to replace the following strings in the KOPY.BAT file created earlier:

1. replace "\TRUE" with "\TURBO"

2. replace "TRU" with "BAS"

3. replace "A:\" with "B:\"

Figure 3.12.8 shows the screen image when program TESTDOS2.BAS starts running. The program prompts for the following:

1. entering the MS-DOS shell (type *n*)

2. the number of files (enter 1)

3. the default path name (enter *D:*)

4. the default file name (just press the [ENTER] key)

5. the default extension name (enter BAT)

6. confirmation of the data entered (type *Y* if correct, *N* to re-enter the above data)

```
                FAST MULTI-FILE EDITING PROGRAM
                ---------------------------------

Need to invoke DOS shell (Y/N) ? n

Number of files (1 to 20) ? 1

Enter default path name ? D:\

Enter default file name ?

Enter default file extension name ? BAT

Information correct (Y/N) ? y
```

Figure 3.12.8 *First screen image of program TESTDOS2.BAS running under Turbo BASIC.*

The program proceeds to prompt for file name data, as shown in figure 3.12.9. This includes the path name, file name, and extension name for each file. For our demonstration, press the [ENTER] key for the path name and extension to use the default names. Key in "KOPY" in response to the file name prompt.

```
For file #   1

Enter path name [ [ENTER] = default] ?

Enter file name [ [ENTER] = default] ? KOPY

Enter extension file name [ [ENTER] = default] ?
```

Figure 3.12.9 *Screen image of program TESTDOS2.BAS display file name query.*

In the next screen, shown in figure 3.12.10, the program prompts for the search strings. I am replacing three strings: "\TRUE" with "\TURBO", "TRU" with "BAS", and "A:\" with "B:\". Type these strings and enter *n* for the echo-to-printer prompt.

```
Number of find/replace strings (1 to 20) ? 3

For Find/Replace string #  1
Enter search string ? \TRUE
Enter replace string ([ENTER] for find only) ? \TURBO

For Find/Replace string #  2
Enter search string ? TRU
Enter replace string ([ENTER] for find only) ? BAS

For Find/Replace string #  3
Enter search string ? A:\
Enter replace string ([ENTER] for find only) ? B:\

Echo to printer (Y/N) ? n
```

Figure 3.12.10 *Screen image of program TESTDOS2.BAS display search string queries.*

The program terminates successfully. Figure 3.12.11 lists the contents of the modified batch file KOPY.BAT. The three MS-DOS command lines comply with the changes.

```
COPY C:\TURBO\TOOLBOX0.BAS B:\
COPY C:\TURBO\TOOLBOX1.BAS B:\
COPY C:\TURBO\TESTDOS1.BAS B:\
```

Figure 3.12.11 *Contents of the modified KOPY.BAT file.*

The library subroutines of Turbo and True BASIC are able to directly handle bad file names. They prompt the user for correct file names and then continue. However, QuickBASIC does not allow an error-handler to reside entirely within a subroutine. In this case, we are able to work around the problem. Since the file names are requested by the application program, the QuickBASIC version verifies their existence in the main program. When the library subroutines are called, they are supplied with existing file names!

Listing 3.61. *QucikBASIC source code for program TESTDOS2.BAS that performs multi-file text find/replace*

```
'PROGRAM Test.DOS2

' QuickBASIC program that uses module DOSFILE.BAS
' to perform fast editing on a collection of files.
' Copyright (c) 1987 Namir Clement Shammas

OPTION BASE 1

DIM LePath$(20), F$(20), Ext$(20), FindStr$(20), ReplaceStr$(20)

' Declare libraries used
REM $INCLUDE: 'DOSFILE.BAS'
```

```
REM $INCLUDE: 'TOOLBOX0.BAS'

CALL Display.Heading
OK$ = FNYesNo$("Need to invoke DOS shell")

IF OK$ = "Y" THEN
    CALL CallDos
    CALL Display.Heading
ELSE
    PRINT
END IF

NFile% = FNInteger.In.Range%("Number of files (1 to 20)",1,20)
PRINT

DO

    INPUT "Enter default pathname ";DefPath$
    PRINT
    INPUT "Enter default filename ";DefName$
    PRINT
    INPUT "Enter default file extension name ";DefExt$
    PRINT
    OK$ = FNYesNo$("Information correct")
    PRINT

LOOP UNTIL OK$ = "Y"

ON ERROR GOTO BAD.FILES

' Obtain filenames
FOR I% = 1 TO NFile%
    CLS
    PRINT "For file # ";I%
    PRINT
    INPUT "Enter pathname [ [Enter] = default] ";LePath$(I%)
    IF LePath$(I%) = "" THEN LePath$(I%) = DefPath$
    PRINT
    INPUT  "Enter filename [ [Enter] = default] ";F$(I%)
    IF F$(I%) = "" THEN F$(I%) = DefName$
    PRINT
    INPUT  "Enter extension filename [ [Enter] = default] ";Ext$(I%)
    IF Ext$(I%) = "" THEN Ext$(I%) = DefExt$
    PRINT
    TF$ = LePath$(I%) + F$(I%) + "." + Ext$(I%)
    OPEN "I",1,TF$ ' test if present
    CLOSE #1
NEXT I%

ON ERROR GOTO 0

CLS
' Obtain find/replace strings
NStr% = FNInteger.In.Range%("Number of find/replace strings (1 to 20)",1,20)
```

```
   FOR I% = 1 TO NStr%
      PRINT
      PRINT "For Find/Replace string # ";I%
      INPUT "Enter search string ";FindStr$(I%)
      INPUT "Enter replace string ([Enter] for find only) ";ReplaceStr$(I%)
   NEXT I%

   PRINT
   OK$ = FNYesNo$("Echo to printer")
   PRINT
   IF OK$ = "Y" THEN EchoPrint% = 1 ELSE EchoPrint% = 0

   CALL EditFiles(LePath$(),F$(),Ext$(),NFile%,
              FindStr$(),ReplaceStr$(),NStr%,EchoPrint%)

   PRINT
   PRINT "Program terminated"


   SUB Display.Heading STATIC
   ' Subroutine to clear screen and display heading
   CLS
   CALL Center.Message("FAST MULTI-FILE EDITING PROGRAM",1)
   CALL Center.Message("-------------------------------",2)
   CALL Blank.Lines(3)

   END SUB

   END

   ' Bad filename error handler
   BAD.FILES:
      PRINT
      PRINT "Error: Cannot find file ";TF$
      PRINT
      PRINT "Please re-enter information"
      PRINT
      PRINT "press any key to continue "; : A.KEY$ = INPUT$(1)
      I% = I% - 1 ' decrement FOR loop counter to re-enter data
      RESUME NEXT
```

Listing 3.62. *Turbo BASIC source code for program TESTDOS2.BAS that performs multi-file text find/replace*

```
'PROGRAM Test.DOS2

' Turbo BASIC program that uses module DOSFILE.BAS
' to perform fast editing on a collection of files.
```

BASIC LIBRARIES

```
  Copyright (c) 1987 Namir Clement Shammas

OPTION BASE 1

DIM LePath$(20), F$(20), Ext$(20), FindStr$(20), ReplaceStr$(20)

' Declare libraries used
$INCLUDE "DOSFILE.BAS"
$INCLUDE "TOOLBOX0.BAS"

CALL Display.Heading
OK$ = FNYesNo$("Need to invoke DOS shell")

IF OK$ = "Y" THEN
    CALL CallDos
    CALL Display.Heading
ELSE
    PRINT
END IF

NFile% = FNInteger.In.Range%("Number of files (1 to 20)",1,20)
PRINT

DO

    INPUT "Enter default pathname ";DefPath$
    PRINT
    INPUT "Enter default filename ";DefName$
    PRINT
    INPUT "Enter default file extension name ";DefExt$
    PRINT
    OK$ = FNYesNo$("Information correct")
    PRINT

LOOP UNTIL OK$ = "Y"

' Obtain filenames
FOR I% = 1 TO NFile%
    CLS
    PRINT "For file # ";I%
    PRINT
    INPUT "Enter pathname [ [Enter] = default] ";LePath$(I%)
    IF LePath$(I%) = "" THEN LePath$(I%) = DefPath$
    PRINT
    INPUT  "Enter filename [ [Enter] = default] ";F$(I%)
    IF F$(I%) = "" THEN F$(I%) = DefName$
    PRINT
    INPUT  "Enter extension filename [ [Enter] = default] ";Ext$(I%)
    IF Ext$(I%) = "" THEN Ext$(I%) = DefExt$
    PRINT
NEXT I%

CLS
' Obtain find/replace strings
NStr% = FNInteger.In.Range%("Number of find/replace strings (1 to 20)",1,20)
```

```
    FOR I% = 1 TO NStr%
        PRINT
        PRINT "For Find/Replace string # ";I%
        INPUT "Enter search string ";FindStr$(I%)
        INPUT "Enter replace string ([Enter] for find only) ";ReplaceStr$(I%)
    NEXT I%

    PRINT
    OK$ = FNYesNo$("Echo to printer")
    PRINT
    IF OK$ = "Y" THEN EchoPrint% = 1 ELSE EchoPrint% = 0

    CALL EditFiles(LePath$(),F$(),Ext$(),NFile%,
                   FindStr$(),ReplaceStr$(),NStr%,EchoPrint%)

    PRINT
    PRINT "Program terminated"


    SUB Display.Heading STATIC
    ' Subroutine to clear screen and display heading
    CLS
    CALL Center.Message("FAST MULTI-FILE EDITING PROGRAM",1)
    CALL Center.Message("-------------------------------",2)
    CALL Blank.Lines(3)

    END SUB

    END
```

Lisitng 3.63. *True BASIC source code for program TESTDOS2.TRU that performs multi-file text find/replace*

```
PROGRAM Test_DOS2

! True BASIC program that uses module DOSFILE.TRU
! to perform fast editing on a collection of files.
! Copyright (c) 1987 Namir Clement Shammas

OPTION BASE 1

DIM LePath$(20), F$(20), Ext$(20), FindStr$(20), ReplaceStr$(20)

! Declare libraries used
LIBRARY "DOSFILE.TRU","TOOLBOX0.TRU"

! Declare imported functions
DECLARE DEF YesNo$, Integer_In_Range
```

BASIC LIBRARIES

```
CALL Display_Heading
LET OK$ = YesNo$("Need t  invoke DOS shell")

IF OK$ = "Y" THEN
    CALL CallDos
    CALL Display_Heading
ELSE
    PRINT
END IF

LET NFile = Integer_In_Range("Number of files (1 to 20)",1,20)
PRINT

DO

    INPUT PROMPT "Enter default pathname ? ":DefPath$
    PRINT
    INPUT PROMPT "Enter default filename ? ":DefName$
    PRINT
    INPUT PROMPT "Enter default file extension name ? ":DefExt$
    PRINT
    LET OK$ = YesNo$("Information correct")
    PRINT

LOOP UNTIL OK$ = "Y"

' Obtain filenames
 OR I = 1 TO NFile
    CLEAR
    PRINT "For file # ";I
    PRINT
    INPUT PROMPT "Enter pathname ['.' = default] ? ":LePath$(I)
    IF LePath$(I) = "." THEN LET LePath$(I) = DefPath$
    PRINT
    INPUT PROMPT "Enter filename ['.' = default] ? ":F$(I)
    IF F$(I) = "." THEN LET F$(I) = DefName$
    PRINT
    INPUT PROMPT "Enter extension filename ['.' = default] ? ":Ext$(I)
    IF Ext$(I) = "." THEN LET Ext$(I) = DefExt$
    PRINT
NEXT I

CLEAR
! Obtain find/replace strings
LET NStr = Integer_In_Range("Number of find/replace strings (1 to 20)",1,20)

FOR I = 1 TO NStr
    PRINT
    PRINT "For Find/Replace string # ";I
    INPUT PROMPT "Enter search string ? ":FindStr$(I)
    INPUT PROMPT "Enter replace string (2 quotes for find only) ? ":ReplaceStr$(I)
NEXT I

PRINT
LET OK$ = YesNo$("Echo to printer")
PRINT
```

```
IF OK$ = "Y" THEN LET EchoPrint = 1 ELSE LET EchoPrint = 0

CALL
EditFiles(LePath$(),F$(),Ext$(),NFile,FindStr$(),ReplaceStr$(),NStr,
EchoPrint)

PRINT
PRINT "Program terminated"


SUB Display_Heading
! Subroutine to clear screen and display heading
CLEAR
CALL Center_Message("FAST MULTI-FILE EDITING PROGRAM",1)
CALL Center_Message("-----------------------------",2)
CALL Blank_Lines(3)

END SUB

END
```

Index

Alphanumeric labels, 31
ANSI BASIC, 39
Append, 68
Arrays, 38–46, 78
ASC() functions, 50
ASK <attribute> statement, 69

BASIC option, 27
BASICA, 32, 34, 71
BASTAT library: routines for
 QuickBASIC, Turbo BASIC, and
 True BASIC, 224–236
BINTREE library: routines for True
 BASIC, 343–368
Branching, 30
BUILDLIB, 85
BUILDLIB.EXE, 84

CALLable subroutines, 74
Capital$(), 58
CASE SELECT construct, 51
CASE statements, 48, 49, 50
COMMAND$ function, 20
COMPILE option, 19
Compiler options, 14, 15, 16, 17
CONST keyword, 34
Constants, 34

DATA statement pointer, 95
DATA statements, 60, 91
Data Types, 32, 33
DATAFILE. DAT, 41
DEBUG option, 21
DECLARE DEF statement, 72, 90
DEFDBL, 34
DEFINT, 34
DEFSNG, 34
DEFSTR, 34
DEFxxx, 34, 71
DIM declaration, 41
DO-LOOP, 52–54, 59, 62
DO-LOOP UNTIL, 56, 58

Doo subroutines, 79
DOSFILE library: routines for
 QuickBASIC, Turbo BASIC,
 and True BASIC, 369–414
DO-UNTIL loop, 95
DO WHILE MORE DATA loop, 58
DO WHILE-LOOP, 55, 94
Dynamic arrays, 29

ECHO off command, 24
EDIT option, 13, 19
ELSE clause, 46, 47
ERASE statement, 29, 79
ERDEV$, 62
ERL, 62
ERR, 62
Error handling, 6268
ErrorFlag%, 75, 76
EXIT DEF statement, 70
EXIT DO, 59
EXIT FOR statement, 59
EXIT HANDLER, 66
EXIT loop, 59, 61
EXIT statement, 51, 54
EXIT SUB statement, 74
EXIT WHILE, 59
Exiting Loops, 59–62
Exporting variables, 77
EXPORT list, 90
EXTERNAL keyword, 88
External function, 72
External subroutines, 24
ExtNextSpace, 72

Factorial function, 71
FILE LOAD option, 13
FILE option, 18
File attributes, 69
File handling, 68–70
First_Name$, 37
Flag#, 75
FOR loop, 60

FOR-NEXT loop, 52, 59, 63, 81
FORTRAN 77, 86

GET.FUNCTION, 32
Get.Sqrt, 76
Get_Average1, 82
Get_Average2, 82
Get_Average3, 82
Global twin, 77
GOSUB, 31, 32, 70, 81
GOTO, 31, 32

HP-BASIC, 43

I/O file, 68
IEEE floating point format, 33
IF statement, 46, 47, 50
IF-THEN-ELSE construct, 46, 47
Index table, 91
Index%, 81
Index_, 95
Indexing arrays, 91
Internal function, 72
Internal subroutines, 81
IntNextSpace, 72
Item$(), 91, 94

LBOUND(), 39, 40
LEN() function, 37
LET keyword, 28
Libraries: TOOLBOX0, 99, 100–140; TOOLBOX1, 99, 140–177; NUMANAL, 99, 177–224; BASTAT, 99, 224–236; LINREG, 99, 236–250; SORT, 99, 250–275; SETS, 99, 296–343; LISTS, 99, 275–296; BINTREE, 343–368; DOSFILE, 99, 368–414
Library development, 84–98
Line numbering, 30
LINREG library: routines for QuickBASIC, Turbo BASIC, and True BASIC 236–250
LISTS library: routines for QuickBASIC, Turbo BASIC, and True BASIC, 275–296
LOAD command, 96

LOAD option, 18
Loaded libraries, 96
Loaded modules, 96
LOCAL variables, 79
Loops, 52–59

MAIN FILE option, 18
MAT commands, 43
MAT REDIM statement, 58, 91
MAXNUM, 37
MESSAGE window, 19
Metacommands, 28, 85: $COM<size>, 29; $DYNAMIC, 29; $EVENT {ON|OFF}, 29; $IF/$ELSE/$ENDIF, 29; $INCLUDE, 29, 44; $INLINE, 30; $SEGMENT, 30; $SOUND, 30; $STACK, 30; $STATIC, 29
Microsoft Binary Format (MBF), 33
MID$(), 37
Missing.Data#, 80, 81
MS-BASIC, 32, 34, 71
Multi-line functions, 71, 74

N#, 75
Named subroutines, 74
NEW option, 18
Newton subroutine, 89
NEWTON.BAS library, 86
Nondelimited sequential files, 68
NUMANAL library: routines for QuickBASIC, Turbo BASIC, and True BASIC, 177–224

OBJ files, 84
ON ERROR GOTO, 62
Optimization options, 15
OPTION ANGLE DEGREES, 27
OPTION ANGLE RADIANS, 27
OPTION BASE statement, 27
OPTION NOLET, 28
OPTIONS, 20
OPTION TYPO, 28
Output options, 15

Pascal language, 94
PRIVATE declaration, 90

PUBLIC declaration, 90–91
PUBLIC variable, 90–91

QuickBASIC Debugger, 16
Quicksort algorithm, 250, 253

Random access I/O, 68
READ statement, 95
Recursive subroutines, 75
Recycled code, 52–59
REDIM statement, 43
Redimensioning an array, 41–45
REMaek, 28
REMed metacommands, 29
REPEAT loop, 56
RESTORE statement, 95
RESUME keyword, 62
RESUME NEXT, 62, 64
Root#, 75
RPN calculator program, 66
RUN command, 24
RUN options, 14, 19
RUN-TIME ERROR option, 21

S#, 75
SAVE option, 18
SEARCH options, 14
Search.Array, 80
SEARCH.BAS, 84
Search_Index function, 91
SELECT CASE statment, 48
Sequential input, 68
Sequential output, 68
Set_Index, 91
Set_UP subroutine, 95
SETS library: routines for QuickBASIC, Turbo BASIC, and True BASIC, 296–343
SETUP option, 20
SHARE declaration, 90
SHARED declaration, 86
SHARED variables, 75, 76, 79, 81
Shell-Metzner algorithm, 250, 252
SORT library: routines for QuickBASIC, Turbo BASIC, and True BASIC, 250–275
Sort module, 91, 95, 96

SORT.BAS, 84
Sort_, 91, 95
Sorting arrays, 91
SORTLIB.EXE, 85
Spaghetti code, 30
Square#, 75
Srch#, 81
START.LOOP, 32
STATIC declaration, 77, 78
STATIC variables, 77, 78
Static arrays, 29
Strings, 36
Swap.Flag% variable, 60

Table index, 91
Table(), 91
TABLES.BAS, 84
THEN clause, 46, 47
TOOLBOX0 library: routines for QuickBASIC and Turbo BASIC, 100–111; routines for True BASIC, 111–140
TOOLBOX1 library: routines for QuickBASIC, Turbo BASIC, and True BASIC, 140–177
TRACE option, 21
True BASIC MAT REDIM, 45
Turbo BASIC Environment, 17–21

UBOUND(), 39, 40
UNTIL construct, 56, 57, 62
USE clause, 66
User-defined functions, 70–74
USERLIB.EXE, 84

VIEW options, 14

WHEN ERROR IN, 65, 66
WHILE construct, 56, 57
WHILE-WEND loop, 52, 59
WINDOW option, 20
WRITE TO option, 18

XCopy(), 42–44

ZER() function, 43

More Software Tools from M&T Books

C Tools

C Chest and Other C Treasures
Item #40-2 $24.95 (book)
Item #49-6 $39.95 (book/disk)
This comprehensive anthology contains the popular "C Chest" columns from *Dr. Dobb's Journal of Software Tools*, along with the lively philosophical and practical discussions they inspired, in addition to other information-packed articles by C experts. The software in the book is also available on disk with full source code. MS-DOS format.

Turbo C: The Art of Advanced Program Design, Optimization, and Debugging
Item #38-0 $24.95 (book)
Item #45-3 $39.95 (book/disk)
Overflowing with example programs, this book fully describes the techniques necessary to skillfully program, optimize, and debug in Turbo C. All programs are also available on disk with full source code. MS-DOS format.

Dr. Dobb's Toolbook of C
Item #89303-615-3 $29.95
From *Dr. Dobb's* and Brady Communications, this book contains a comprehensive library of valuable C code. *Dr. Dobb's* most popular articles on C are updated and reprinted here, along with new C programming tools. Also included is a complete C compiler, an assembler, text processing programs, and more!

The Small-C Handbook
Item #81-X $17.95
The Small-C Handbook with MS/PC-DOS Addendum
Item #76-3 $22.95
Also from *DDJ* and Brady Communications, the handbook is a valuable companion to the Small-C compiler, described below. The book explains the language and the compiler, and contains entire source listings of the compiler and its library of arithmetic and logical routines.

Small-C Compiler
Item #01-1 $19.95
Like a home study course in compiler design, the *Small-C Compiler* and *The Small-C Handbook* provide all you need to learn how compilers are contructed, as well as teaching the C language at its most fundamental level. Full source code is included on disk in both CP/M and MS/PC-DOS versions.

Small Tools: Programs for Text Processing
Item #78-X $29.95
This package of text-processing programs written in Small-C is designed to perform specific, modular functions on text files. Source code only is included. Small Tools is available in both CP/M and MS/PC-DOS versions and includes complete documentation.

Small-Mac: An Assembler for Small-C
Item #77-1 $29.95
Small-Mac is a macro assembler designed to stress simplicity, portability, adaptability, and educational value. Small-Mac is available for CP/M systems only and includes source code on disk with complete documentation.

Small-Windows: A Library of Windowing Functions for the C Language
Item #35-X $29.95
Small-Windows is a complete windowing library for C. The package includes video functions, menu functions, window functions, and more. The package is available for MS-DOS systems for the following compilers: Microsoft C Version 4.0, Small-C, and Lattice C. Documentation and full C source code is included.

UNIX-Like Tools for MS-DOS

On Command: Writing a Unix-Like Shell for MS-DOS
Item #29-1 $39.95
Learn how to write shells applicable to MS-DOS, as well as to most other programming environments. This book and disk include a full description of a Unix-like shell, complete C source code, a thorough discussion of low-level DOS interfacing, and significant examples of C programming at the system level. All source code is included on disk

/util: A Unix-Like Utility package for MS-DOS
Item #12-7 $29.95
This collection of utilities is intended to be accessed through SH but can be used separately. It contains programs and subroutines that, when coupled with SH, create a fully functional Unix-like environment. The package includes a disk with full C source code and documentation in a Unix-style manual.

NR: An Implementation of the Unix NROFF -Word Processor
Item #33-X $29.95
NR is a text formatter that is written in C and compatible with Unix's NROFF. *NR* comes configured for any Diablo-compatible printer, as well as Hewlett Packard's ThinkJet and LaserJet. Both the ready-to-use program and full source code are included. For PC compatibles.

MS-DOS Tools

Program Interfacing to MS-DOS
Item #34-8 $29.95
Program Interfacing to MS-DOS will orient any experienced programmer to the MS-DOS environment. The package includes a ten-part manual with sample program files and a detailed description of how to build device drivers, along with the device driver for a memory disk and a character device driver on disk with macro assembly source code.

Taming MS-DOS
Item #24-0 $19.95 (book)
Item #59-3 $34.95 (book/disk)
Taming MS-DOS takes you beyond the basics, picking up where your DOS manual leaves off. You'll learn how to create a memory-resident clock, how to rename subdirectories and change file attributes, how to create configurable AUTOEXEC.BAT files, and how to customize CONFIG.SYS and use ANSI.SYS to change the appearance of DOS. You'll also find extensive batch file coverage with example routines that use redirection operators, filters, and pipes and ready-to-use assembly-language programs that enhance DOS. Full source code is included on disk.

Tele Operating System

Tele Operating System Toolkit
This task-scheduling algorithm drives the Tele Operating System and is composed of several components. When integrated, they form an independent operating system for any 8086-based machine. Tele has also been designed for compatibility with MS-DOS, UNIX, and the MOSI standard.

SK: THE SYSTEM KERNEL
Item #30-5 $49.95
The System Kernel contains an initialization module, general-purpose utility functions, and a real-time task management system. The kernel provides MS-DOS applications with multitasking capabilities The System Kernel is required by all other components. All source code is included on disk in MS-DOS format.

DS: WINDOW DISPLAY
Item #32-1 $39.95
This component contains BIOS level drivers for a memory-mapped display, window management support and communication coordination between the operator and tasks in a multitasking environment. All source code is included on disk in MS-DOS format.

FS: THE FILE SYSTEM
Item #65-8 $39.95
The File System supports MS-DOS disk file structures and serial communication channels. All source code is included on disk in MS-DOS format.

XS: THE INDEX SYSTEM
Item #66-6 $39.95
The Index System implements a tree-structured free-form database. All source code is included on disk in MS-DOS format.

Z80 Assembly Language

Dr. Dobb's Z80 Toolbook
Item #07-0 $25.00 (book)
Item #55-0 $40.00 (book/disk)
This book contains everything users need to write their own Z80 assembly-language programs, including a method of designing programs and coding them in assembly language and a complete, integrated toolkit of subroutines. All the software in the book is available on disk in the following formats: 8" SS/SD, Apple, Osborne, or Kaypro.

Forth

Dr. Dobb's Toolbook of Forth
Item #10-0 $22.95 (book)
Item #57-7 $39.95 (book/disk)
This comprehensive collection of useful Forth programs and tutorials contains expanded versions of *DDJ*'s best Forth articles and other material, including practical code and in-depth discussions of advanced Forth topics. The screens in the book are also available on disk as ASCII files in the following formats: MS/PC-DOS, Apple II, Macintosh, or CP/M: Osborne, 8" SS/SD.

Dr. Dobb's Toolbook of Forth, Volume II
Item #41-0 $29.95 (book)
Item #51-8 $45.95 (book/disk)
This complete anthology of Forth programming techniques and developments picks up where the Toolbook of Forth, First Edition left off. Included are the best articles on Forth from *Dr. Dobb's Journal of Software Tools*, along with the latest material from other Forth experts. The screens in the book are available on disk as ASCII files in the following formats: MS-DOS, Apple II, Macintosh, and CP/M: Osborne, or 8" SS/SD.

68000 Programming

Dr. Dobb's Toolbook of 68000 Programming
Item #13-216649-6 $29.95 (book)
Item #75-5 $49.95 (book/disk)
From *DDJ* and Brady Communications, this collection of practical programming tips and tools for the 68000 family contains the best 68000 articles reprinted from *DDJ* along with much new material. The book contains many useful applications and examples. The software in the book is also available on disk in the following formats: MS/PC-DOS, Macintosh, CP/M 8", Osborne, Amiga, and Atari 520ST.

68000 Cross Assembler
Item #71-2 $25.00
This manual and disk contain an executable version of the 68000 Cross Assembler discussed in *Dr. Dobb's Toolbook of 68000 Programming*, complete with source code and documentation. The Cross-Assembler requires CP/M 2.2 with 64K or MS-DOS with 128K. The disk is available in the following formats: MS-DOS, 8" SS/SD, and Osborne.

Turbo Pascal Tools

The Turbo Pascal Toolbook
Item #25-9 $25.95 (book)
Item #61-5 $45.95 (book/disk)
This book contains routines and sample programs to make your programming easier and more powerful. You'll find an extensive library of low-level routines; external sorting and searching tools; window management; artificial intelligence techniques; mathematical expression parsers, including two routines that convert mathematical expressions into RPN tokens; and a smart statistical regression model finder. More than 800K of source code is available on disk for MS-DOS systems.

Statistical Toolbox for Turbo Pascal
Item #22-4 $69.95
Two statistical packages in one! A library disk and reference manual that includes statistical distribution functions, random number generation, basic descriptive statistics, parametric and nonparametric statistical testing, bivariate linear regression, and multiple and polynomial regression. The demonstration disk and manual incorporate these library routines into a fully functioning statistical program. For IBM PCs and compatibles.

Turbo Advantage
Item #26-7 $49.95
A library of more than 200 routines, with source code sample programs and documentation. Routines are organized and documented under the following categories: bit manipulation, file management, MS-DOS support, string operations, arithmetic calculations, data compression, differential equations, Fourier analysis and synthesis, and much more! For MS/PC-DOS systems.

Turbo Advantage: Complex
Item #27-5 $89.95
This library provides the Turbo Pascal code for digital filters, boundary-value solutions, vector and matrix calculations with complex integers and variables, Fourier transforms, and calculations of convolution and correlation functions. Some of the *Turbo Advantage: Complex* routines are most effectively used with Turbo Advantage. Source code and documentation included.

Turbo Advantage: Display
Item #28-3 $69.95
Turbo Advantage: Display includes an easy-to-use form processor and thirty Turbo Pascal procedures and functions to facilitate linking created forms to your program. Full source code and documentation are included. Some of the *Turbo Advantage* routines are necessary to compile *Turbo Advantage: Display.*

80286, 80386 Programming

Dr. Dobb's Toolbook of 80286, 80386 Programming
Item #42-9 $24.95 (book)
Item #53-4 $39.95 (book/disk)
This toolbook is a comprehensive discussion on the powerful 80X86 family of microprocessors. The editors of *Dr. Dobb's Journal of Software Tools* have gathered their best articles, updated and expanded them, and added new material to create this valuable resource for all 80X86 programmers. All programs are available on disk with full soruce code.

The New BASICs

The New BASICs: Programming Techniques and Library Development
Item #37-2 $24.95 (book)
Item #43-7 $39.95 (book/disk)
This book will orient the advanced programmer to the syntax and programming features of The New BASICs, including Turbo BASIC 1.0, QuickBASIC 3.0, and True BASIC 2.0. You'll learn the details of implementing subroutines, functions, and libraries to permit more structured coding. Programs and subroutines are available on disk with full source code. MS-DOS format.

Public-Domain Software

Public-Domain Software: Untapped Resources for the Business User
Item #39-9 $19.95 (book)
Item #47-X $34.95 (book/disk)
Organized into a comprehensive reference, this book introduces the novice and guides the experienced user to a source of often overlooked software—public domain and Shareware. This book will tell you where it is, how to get it, what to look for, and why it's for you. The sample programs and some of the software reviewed is available on disk in MS-DOS format. Includes $15 worth of free access time on CompuServe!

Dr. Dobb's Journal Bound Volume Series

Each volume in this series contains a full year's worth of useful code and fascinating history from *Dr. Dobb's Journal of Software Tools*. Each volume contains every issue of *DDJ* for a given year, reprinted and combined into one comprehensive reference.

Volume	Year	Item	Price
Volume 1:	1976	Item #13-5	$30.75
Volume 2:	1977	Item #16-X	$30.75
Volume 3:	1978	Item #17-8	$30.75
Volume 4:	1979	Item #14-3	$30.75
Volume 5:	1980	Item #18-6	$30.75
Volume 6:	1981	Item #19-4	$30.75
Volume 7:	1982	Item #20-8	$35.75
Volume 8:	1983	Item #00-3	$35.75
Volume 9:	1984	Item #08-9	$35.75
Volume 10:	1985	Item #21-6	$35.75
Volume 11:	1986	Item #72-0	$35.75

To order any of these products send your payment, along with $2.25 per item for shipping, to M&T Books, 501 Galveston Drive, Redwood City, California 94063. California residents, please include the appropriate sales tax. Or, call toll-free 800-533-4372 (in California 800-356-2002) Monday through Friday between 8 A.M. and 5 P.M. PST. When ordering disks, please indicate format.